COBOL

A Guide to Structured, Portable, Maintainable, and Efficient Program Design

Eric Garrigue Vesely

The Analyst Workbench

PRENTICE HALL, *Englewood Cliffs, New Jersey 07632*

Library of Congress Cataloging-in-Publication Data

Vesely, Eric Garrigue.
   COBOL: a guide to structured, portable, maintainable, and efficient program design/Eric Garrigue Vesely.
      p.   cm.
   Bibliography: p.
   Includes index.
   ISBN 0-13-854050-0
   1. COBOL (Computer program language)   I. Title.
   QA76.73.C25V47 1989   88-7640
   005.13'3—dc19

TAB BOOKS Inc. offers software for
sale. For information and a catalog,
please contact TAB Software Department,
Blue Ridge Summit, PA 17294-0850.

Editorial/production supervision
  and interior design: *Mary P. Rottino*
Cover design: *20/20 Design, Inc.*
Manufacturing buyer: *Mary Ann Gloriande*

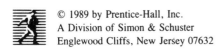
© 1989 by Prentice-Hall, Inc.
A Division of Simon & Schuster
Englewood Cliffs, New Jersey 07632

Printed in the United States of America
10 9 8 7 6 5 4 3 2

ISBN 0-13-854050-0

Prentice-Hall International (UK) Limited, *London*
Prentice-Hall of Australia Pty. Limited, *Sydney*
Prentice-Hall Canada Inc., *Toronto*
Prentice-Hall Hispanoamericana, S.A., *Mexico*
Prentice-Hall of India Private Limited, *New Delhi*
Prentice-Hall of Japan, Inc., *Tokyo*
Simon & Schuster Asia Pte. Ltd., *Singapore*
Editora Prentice-Hall do Brasil, Ltda., *Rio de Janeiro*

Contents

Foreword

In this, his second major textbook, Dr. Vesely has drawn a detailed road map for any organization to use in leading its data processing to a sane, manageable, predictable, cost-contained basis of addressing the 21st century—which is just about a decade away.

In the 20 years from 1953 to 1973, programming for business applications rose from its infancy to young maturity in an environment that is analogous to a newborn child raised by its grandparent. Postwar corporations were managed by mature, seasoned, experienced business people who rose from the ranks by hard work and organizational struggle and who just never quite understood data processing. Typically, the programmers of the 1950s and 1960s were self-taught, bright young lads or lasses who, because of their special expertise, were much in demand in a marketplace expanding in geometric proportions. Since programmers' aspirations were generally not management-oriented, they could easily pick and choose their employer on the basis of interesting work assignments in organizations that emphasized creativity and a laissez-faire management. The era of development seeded a relationship between programmers and management in which management usually felt intimidated, always on the defensive.

The recession in the data processing industry in the early 1970s had a significant and beneficial effect on this relationship. It showed corporate managers that even if they didn't understand data processing, they were still in control. This led to the structural revolution of the mid-1970s, in which most large companies started the process of acquainting their programmers with the corporate needs for methodological standards. That era also saw the proliferation of COBOL textbooks written to support that newly accepted language as an American standard.

If history regards the 1970s as the spawning of the structured programming era, the 1980s will be characterized as the beginning of complete systems analysis methodology.

    If history regards the 1970s as the spawning of the structured programming era, the 1980s will be characterized as the beginning of complete systems analysis methodology. Today, such new terms as *BSP, BICS/BIAIT, entity relationships, enterprise modeling,* and *logical data modeling* are spoken with clarity by only a few highly skilled theoretical analysts, who in most cases use this new terminology principally to browbeat both programmers and managers. It will not be until the 1990s that the fruit of the new science will be ripe and ready for harvest. However, if the fruit is to be edible, experience has taught us that it must be carefully grown in a well-controlled environment. That environment must necessarily be a business environment with a disciplined approach to how each level of data processing is done, be it planning, designing, programming, testing, or maintenance. Eric, one of the leading strategists in data modeling, is well aware of this necessity and for that reason has written an extremely complete and definitive work that simply and clearly states the basic fundamentals of how programs should be constructed, how rational data names should be established, and what attitudes management and programmers must have if there is to be any hope at all of transforming the mass of spaghetti we now call computer programs into the sensitive instruments needed to control the databases that will run the corporate factories of the 21st century.

                                                                                        Peter Harris

                                                        President, ADPAC Computing Languages Corporation

Preface

COBOL: PAST, PRESENT, FUTURE

Past

The Common Business-Oriented Language (COBOL) has been the dominant programming language in the world since it was created by the Conference on Data Systems Language (CODASYL) in 1959. It was standardized in 1968 by the American National Standards Institute (ANSI) in its publication No. X3.23-1968. ANSI updated the 1968 COBOL standard in 1974 in their publication *American National Standard Programming Language COBOL* (No. X3.23-1974) and again in 1985 in their publication *American National Standard for Information Systems: COBOL* (No. X3.23-1985).[1]

Two of the original objectives were:

- To provide a programming language that *anyone* could write
- To eliminate conversion costs when switching mainframes by having a portable language

Regardless of how COBOL fulfilled those objectives, it became popular for three reasons:

- It was promoted with enormous energy and dedication by Rear Admiral Grace Hopper of the U.S. Navy.

- The U.S. government required bidders to have a COBOL compiler for any computer procurement.
- It was simpler than assembly or machine language and was more business-oriented than FORTRAN.

COBOL was born into an unstructured world. COBOL has dataname syntax standards (name can be 1 to 30 characters long and must be composed of the letters *A–Z*, the numbers 0–9, and the hyphen [-]) but no rules or guidelines on how actually to name the data. COBOL tolerated or encouraged—depending on your view—unstructured programming. The COBOL statements ALTER and GO TO permitted unlimited branching forward and backward within a program. An anonymous source stated that "COBOL programmers are the first people in the world to learn to write before they learn to read." The meaning of this quotation is that development programmers usually write programs that cannot be understood by anyone else—including, occasionally, themselves.

The alterable GO TO statement (COBOL reserved words are written in capital letters in this text when used in their COBOL sense) is virtually impossible to decipher since it changes the GO TO procedure-name at *execution* (GO TO where?). Programmers who use the Format 3 GO TO also usually have multiple ALTER statements that can modify that GO TO.[2]

Network GO TO statements (a GO TO that branches to another paragraph or SECTION) can be followed only so far. A series of 10 or 20 or more network GO TO statements will drive any maintenance programmer to tears.

The normal rationale for using ALTER and GO TO statements is efficiency. The program runs faster with those statements rather than PERFORM statements. This may have been somewhat true when cpus had hips ratings (hundreds of instructions per second), but it is certainly not true now.

Another subtle problem created by the original DATA DIVISION is that it is GLOBAL storage. GLOBAL storage means that any statement in the program can access *and* modify any item in the DATA DIVISION. It can be very difficult to determine how a particular item was modified. The difficulty increases exponentially with the number of CORRESPONDING phrases, REDEFINES, and RENAMES in the program.

And COBOL did not forget the "tricky" programmer. It has exotic statements such as EVALUATE, INSPECT, SEARCH, STRING, and UNSTRING and originally up to three levels of indexing or subscripting, and the indexing could be direct or relative. The "sophisticated" programmer could also add qualification to make the table-handling statements "neat."

Ignorance, lack of naming and programming standards, and the flexibility of the COBOL language have led to "spaghetti" programs (Figure P.1) that are virtually unmaintainable. The problem is compounded by the fact that most of these spaghetti programs are vital—part of the payroll system, the order entry system, or the accounts receivable system.

The difficulty of maintenance has prompted many authorities to state that anywhere from 50 to 90 percent of the DP personnel budget is committed to maintenance. A significant reason that development of new programs is so slow is that there are no available programmers.

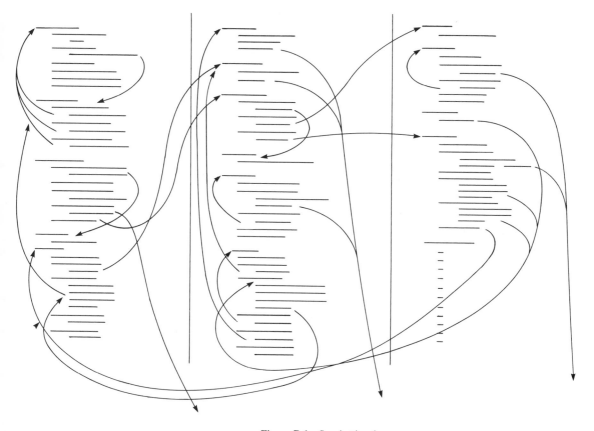

Figure P.1   Spaghetti code

Present

The cost of maintenance has prompted many organizations to adopt structured techniques (analysis, design, programming).[3] Naming and programming standards have been developed and instituted. Unfortunately, most organizations have no methods—manual or automated—for enforcing the standards. Consequently, programs may be "better," but most are still not structured. This means that maintenance will continue to be costly until adequate policing can be provided.

The policing is in development. ANSI has COBOL$_{85}$, which can be a more structured COBOL. COBOL$_{85}$ makes the ALTER statement obsolete, provides local storage, and offers many other advantages. IBM has developed its own structured language, VS COBOL II. It permits an organization to eliminate from its installed compiler any undesirable statements, options, or the like. Active data dictionaries—Cullinet's IDD is an example—can enforce naming standards and insert standardized data names in the DATA DIVISION via COPY statements. There are software products that can analyze COBOL programs and rate them as to their "structuredness." Here are just a few of these products (addresses appear in vendor list):

ADPAC:	PM/SS
Group Operations:	Scan-370
Language Technology:	Inspector
MAC Computer:	DCD II
Peat Marwick:	Profile and Path-VU

The ever-spreading knowledge of structured programming techniques, structured compilers, active data dictionaries, and analytical tools will subdue the maintenance monster in the future.[4] But what happens to the old spaghetti programs that are vital? The typical answer is to rewrite or buy an application package but in any case throw the old programs away. Throwing the old programs away sounds easy, but the real world says no![5] Users balk at the cost and time required to rewrite or substitute purchased software. The users also know that the old programs produce satisfactory results. They do not care that the programs are hard to maintain—that's DP's problem; they want their results and not excuses about why the new systems implementation slipped again. Users usually only commit to new systems if they need significant additional functions and DP states that those functions cannot be implemented in the current system. And then there is the cost. Various authorities cite that the cost of developing a *single* debugged instruction is between $10 and $100. A *small* application system of 100,000 instructions costs $5 million at the median price of $50.[6] How many organizations knowingly throw away a $5 million "part" when it is still working, even if it is working poorly?

Various companies have recognized the need for computer-assisted restructuring, among them are:[7]

The Analyst Workbench:	Extended Retrofit
Group Operations:	Superstructure
Language Technology:	Recoder
MAC Computer:	Regimenter
Peat Marwick:	Retrofit

These companies believe that restructuring working programs at a fraction of their "inventory" cost is a better way to go. The restructuring is—or should be—transparent to the user. The restructured programs are now easy to maintain and easy to modify for the new user functions.

Future

What is the future of COBOL? Many people state that it is dead (some even say that COBOL is presently in rigor mortis). Their reasons include these:

- The development of new structured languages such as Ada, C, and Pascal
- The development of fourth-generation languages (4GLs) that permit users to ask ad hoc questions themselves without programmer assistance
- The development of super micros, minis, and other machines

- The impending release of general-purpose expert languages
- The implementation of relational databases with their user-friendly query languages
- The upcoming—and mysterious—fifth-generation hardware and software

The pronouncement that COBOL is dead is premature. COBOL will live to a ripe old age for a variety of reasons:

- There exists in the world an inventory of millions of COBOL programs with billions of instructions at a cost of trillions of dollars. These programs will not die easily; their replacement will take decades.
- An overwhelming percentage of current rewrites and application packages are written in COBOL.
- Colleges, technical schools, and universities throughout the world are producing tens of thousands of graduates trained in COBOL.
- Current COBOL programmers are reluctant to learn any other languages.
- Millions of dollars have been invested in COBOL training, new COBOL compilers such as $COBOL_{85}$, COBOL analysis and restructuring tools, COBOL generators, and other devices.[8]

Further proof of the health of COBOL is the rapid proliferation of COBOL compilers for micros and minis.[9] Why would anyone spend scarce development money on a dead language?

My view of the future is as follows:

- COBOL will remain the dominant language through the end of the 20th century.
- Existing COBOL programs will be restructured using software tools.
- Restructured COBOL programs will be modified to provide additional user functions.
- Automated policing techniques will be used to enforce standardization.
- New COBOL programs will be restricted to executing business logic; screen (CRT) painting and processing will be done by software such as Cullinet's ADS/ONLINE.
- COBOL generators—such as Ken Orr's STRUCTURES®—will become prevalent.

And what of fourth-generation languages (4GLs)? 4GLs definitely have their place. The good 4GLs do permit users to ask a database ad hoc questions with no (or minimal) programmer assistance. This ability provides users with rapid turnaround and relieves the programming staff of devoting months of effort to answer the same questions.

Can't 4GLs be used for production? Yes, they can, but the real question is, should they? The most user-friendly 4GLs interface to relational databases. The first problem is that most organizations do not have *production* relational databases. The next problem is that 4GLs must define their path through a database at invocation time. This requires sophisticated programming in the 4GL and substantial input/output. The enormous drain on computer resources of 4GL use has been well documented and has led to the user information center. Information centers provide users with their own computer that is periodically downloaded from the production computer.[10]

My guess is that 4GLs will also be used as prototyping tools for developing new user systems, thereby shortcutting the current long analysis and design cycle. The successful prototype will then, for efficiency, be translated into appropriate production programs—including COBOL for business logic.

STRUCTURE OF THIS BOOK

This book is divided into three parts. Part 1 tells how to write *portable* structured COBOL code that can be read by *anybody*, Part 2 tells how to restructure existing spaghetti COBOL programs, and Part 3 tells how to develop new COBOL programs quickly. I wish you good reading and better "COBOLing."

Eric Garrigue Verely

NOTES

1. The original meeting was held in the Department of Defense's Pentagon Building on May 28 and 29, 1959. It was composed of representatives from private and government users, computer manufacturers, and other interested persons. The outcome of this meeting was the formation of the Conference on Data Systems Languages (CODASYL) committee.

   A CODASYL committee released the original COBOL specification in September 1959, or about three months after its formation. After modifications, COBOL was formally released in December 1959. COBOL had achieved the basic objective of being independent of any computer manufacturer.

   The first official publication was in April 1960 and was titled *COBOL: A Report to the Conference on Data Systems Languages, Including Initial Specifications for a Common Business Oriented Language (COBOL) for Programming Electronic Digital Computers* (Washington, D.C.: U.S. Government Printing Office). This became known as COBOL-60.

   The CODASYL executive committee established the COBOL Maintenance Committee to maintain and enhance the language. The committee was composed of both user and manufacturer representatives who met together but voted on proposals separately. The Special Task Group created COBOL-61, which was printed in mid-1961 by the U.S. Government Printing Office. The Maintenance Committee released COBOL-61 Extended in mid-1963.

   The COBOL Maintenance Committee was reorganized in January 1964 into the Language Subcommittee, the Evaluation Subcommittee, and the Publication Subcommittee. The Language Subcommittee's basic task was to continue to maintain and enhance COBOL. It was also the liaison to the other standards organizations, the United States of America Standards Institute (USASI) and the International Organization for Standardization (ISO). The Publication Subcommittee had the responsibility for producing the official COBOL publications and assisting with the content of the COBOL Information Bulletin (CIB) distributed by USASI. The Evaluation Subcommittee analyzed and evaluated compiler implementations and user surveys. It provided recommendations to the Language Subcommittee.

The Language Subcommittee was given full committee status in July 1968 and was renamed the Programming Language Committee. It produces the *COBOL Journal of Development*. The Programming Language Committee was renamed the CODASYL COBOL Committee in May 1977.

CODASYL produced 11 COBOL specifications:

COBOL-60
COBOL-61
COBOL-61 Extended
COBOL, Edition 1965
CODASYL COBOL, 1968
CODASYL COBOL, 1969
CODASYL COBOL, 1970
CODASYL COBOL, 1973
CODASYL COBOL, 1976
CODASYL COBOL, 1978
CODASYL COBOL, 1981

Meanwhile, the Computer and Business Equipment Manufacturers Association (BEMA) established the American National Standards Committee on Computers and Information Processing (X3) in 1960. A working group called Processor Specification and COBOL Standards (X3.4.4) was given the scope of "standardization of COBOL and its characteristics, establishment of an X3.4 COBOL bulletin, publication of interpretations and clarifications, and the definition of test problems." The first general meeting of X3.4.4 was held in New York on January 15 and 16, 1963. The basic recommendations were to assist CODASYL and to define the American Standard for COBOL for USASI (USASI became the American National Standards Institute— ANSI—in late 1969).

X3.4.4 released its proposed COBOL standard for comment on August 30, 1966. The standard was divided into a nucleus and eight functional modules, with each module having two or three levels. Full ANSI COBOL required the high level of each module; anything less that complied with some level of all modules was an approvable subset. This COBOL standard was approved on August 23, 1968, and became ANSI COBOL$_{68}$.

Technical Committee X3J4 evolved from X3.4.4 and was responsible for the maintenance and enhancement of ANSI COBOL. The next proposed revision was released for comment in August 1972. It was approved on May 10, 1974, and became ANSI COBOL$_{74}$.

X3J4 released a proposed ANSI COBOL-8X for comment in 1979. The user uproar was fast and furious, including threats to sue the individual members of X3J4 if COBOL-8X was adopted. The users' basic complaint was that COBOL-8X was incompatible with COBOL$_{74}$ and would require conversion of most and possibly all existing COBOL$_{74}$ programs. A single quotation should be sufficient to indicate the magnitude of the problem:

On a corporate wide basis, McAUTO has approximately 26,200 COBOL programs in production with an average program consisting of 2,000 lines of code. Revisions to the standard that affect every existing program will cost us an estimated $100 per program to cover the cost of retraining, reprogramming, machine runs, and retesting for a total of $2.6 million, assuming the use of a language conversion program (LCP). Our conversion costs will be even higher when reprogramming and retesting is required due to incompatibilities that cannot be handled by an LCP. This problem is magnified by the possible deletion of the debug module and the loss of the capabilities it provides. McAUTO is not in a unique situation. The sizeable investment that American businesses have made in COBOL programs must be protected. Upward compatibility is imperative for this and all future revisions of the COBOL standard. (Letter dated December 4, 1981, from A. J. Quackenbush, President of McAUTO, to Linda V. Willis, X3J4 chairwoman)

The net result of this user reaction was a revamping of COBOL-8X to alleviate the user complaints. After further rework and public hearings, COBOL-8X was approved in September 1985 and became COBOL$_{85}$.

More COBOL history can be found in Appendix A, "The History of COBOL," in the ANSI publication *American National Standard Programming Language COBOL* (ANSI X3.32-1985; ISO 1989-1985; New York: ANSI.)

2. COBOL accepts different syntaxes for most verbs. Each acceptable syntax is a format.

3. We at Peat Marwick's Catalyst Group concur with studies revealing that 60–90 percent of all non-operations expenditures goes to software maintenance. (Peat Marwick, *Structured Retrofit Maintenance Guidelines,* Chicago.)

Research also shows that most programmers spend 50 to 80 percent of their time on ongoing maintenance work. . . . At an average salary of $25,000 a year, program maintenance [in the United States] costs more than $10 billion per year. (Girish Parikh, "In Defense of the Maintenance Programmer," *Infosystems,* January 1985.)

The controller general of the United States estimates that "about two-thirds of the programmer and analyst labor is devoted to maintenance" and costs the federal government at least $1 billion per year. (*Federal Agencies: Maintenance of Computer Programs: Expensive and Undermanaged,* AMPD-81-25, February 26, 1981.)

The percentage of time that programmers spend on maintenance has been steadily increasing for the last several years. *Computerworld*'s annual DP budget survey (*Computerworld,* December 31, 1984/January 7, 1985) found that the percentage of an average programmer's time spent on maintenance now stands at about 55% compared with 45% last year. There are no indications that this figure will go anywhere but up. ("Keeping Maintenance Minimal," *Computerworld Softalk,* February 4, 1985.)

4. Statistics from T. Casper Jones III, "Maintenance Push Is On," *Computerworld,* April 8, 1985.

Structured programs can be updated in 25% of the time of a poorly structured program [that would save U.S. organizations $7 billion annually, according to the Parikh statistics in note 3]; the possibility of adding new bugs is reduced by 50%; poorly structured programs should be rewritten after adding 10 to 15% new code—structured programs after 50 to 60%.

5. Old computers go into computer museums, but old software goes into production. (Eric Bush, developer of Recoder, quoted in *Computerworld,* January 26, 1985.)

In our age there is something analogous to Jonathan Swift's Struldbruggs. Software systems are, if not immortal, extremely resistant to death or decommission and they become increasingly cantankerous and miserable as they age. They are the Struldbruggs of the twentieth century. (Nicholas Zvegintzov, "Immortal Software," *Datamation*, July 1984.)

UCLA Professors Bennet Lientz and Burton Swanson, questioning 487 data processing organizations on the maintenance of heavily used software, found a sizeable group of systems 12 to 20 years old. (Ibid.)

A major corporation spent $5 million on a new human resources database, programming in a fourth generation language. They never succeeded in linking it to the existing payroll software. The new development project was cancelled in a fiscal crunch; the payroll software survived. (Ibid.)

6. Hewlett-Packard advertisement, *Computerworld*, April 23, 1984.

One recent [Department of Defense] study showed that the cost of development for Air Force avionics software averaged about $75 per instruction while the cost of maintenance corrections of deployed software has ranged up to $4,000 per instruction. (Barry C. De Roze and Thomas H. Nyman, "The Software Life Cycle: A Management and Technological Challenge in the Department of Defense," *IEEE Transactions on Software Engineering*, SE-4, no. 4, July 1978.)

7. See vendor list in Appendix D for addresses.

8. An interesting thing is occurring in the world of applications development for IBM's IMS DB/DC and CICS/DL/1: COBOL is shedding its tarnished image. Rather than dying in the productivity tool revolution, it has become the foundation in the evolution of traditional IMS development.

There are many reasons for this revival, and a few are worth looking at, such as the following:

No programming language has been able to replace COBOL adequately.

Most COBOL programmers have resisted the anti-COBOL movement.

IBM has added significant improvements to its release of VS COBOL II.

IMS productivity tools have enhanced COBOL with powerful new commands and features. (Steven Pfrezinger, "Productivity Aids Revitalizing COBOL," *Computerworld*, February 11, 1985.)

In the past COBOL has been the recipient of some very bad press. The gurus of computer science heap invective on this "dinosaur of a language" even up to the point of calling it a crime perpetrated on the students of programming. The fact remains, however, that COBOL is the most widely known and used language in computing. One reason for this is that it does very well what it is supposed to do—and that is to process information in the real world, not to teach the niceties of data structure and algorithms in the classroom. Its strengths lie in areas that are the most necessary to business computing: decimal arithmetic and high-level record-oriented file operations. (Ted Mirecki, "COBOL Performs," *PC Tech Journal*, June 1985.)

9. More recently, interest in COBOL for the IBM PC family has surged; the microcomputer press is full of announcements and advertisements for new compilers from the software heavyweights. The quantum leap in the processing capacity of desktop hardware now makes it possible to implement useful, large-scale compilers that can do justice to the full

capabilities of this programming language. As mainframe jockeys begin to use the equipment they once scorned as mere toys, they are porting to it the language with which they are most familiar, COBOL. (Ibid.)

10.   4GLs are not a replacement for COBOL and when used as such can cause the loss of a competitive advantage, poor response times and unnecessary hardware additions for MIS directors. (International Data Corporation, *Fourth-Generation Languages: Information Generators to Meet Information Needs,* Framingham, Mass., 1985.)

4GLs will not replace COBOL or lead to COBOL's obsolescence. (Ibid.)

Acknowledgments

COBOL is an industry language and is not the property of any company or group of companies, or of any organization or group of organizations.

No warranty, expressed or implied, is made by any contributor or by the CODASYL COBOL Committee as to the accuracy and functioning of the programming system and language. Moreover, no responsibility is assumed by any contributor, or by the committee, in connection therewith.

The authors and copyright holders of the copyrighted materials used herein FLOW-MATIC (trademark of Sperry Rand Corporation), Programming for the UNIVAC (R) I and II, Data Automation Systems copyrighted 1958, 1959, by Sperry Rand Corporation; IBM Commercial Translater Form No. F 28-8013, copyrighted 1959 by IBM; FACT, DSI 27A5260-2760, copyrighted 1960 by Minneapolis-Honeywell have specifically authorized the use of this material in whole or in part, in the COBOL specifications. Such authorization extends to the reproduction and use of COBOL specifications in programming manuals or similar publications.

ARIGATO GOZAIMASU (Thank you)

My thanks to the Singapore Institute of Systems Science for providing an excellent environment for writing during my tenure as a visiting lecturer.

My thanks to Amy Paul, who provided valuable clerical assistance in getting this book ready for publication.

My thanks to Cynthia Salazer, who entered the COBOL programs, and especially to Jim Peterson, who corrected all my syntax errors, and to Steve Wertheimer for the computer generated artwork.

A special thank you to Peter Harris—who has been actively programming for over 30 years—for his kind foreword.

My thanks to Karl Karlstrom for authorizing this book, to Pat Henry for guiding it through the review process, and to Ed Moura for putting it into production. My thanks to Bruce Emmer, who had the difficult job of copy editing a book where virtually every word had to be scrutinized to determine if it was properly capitalized or hyphenated according to COBOL syntax. A very special thanks to Mary Rottino, who had to cope with an author wandering around Australia, Japan, and Malaysia while she was overseeing production.

And finally, a thank you to you, the reader, for reading this book. I hope that it provides you with significant information about COBOL!

Part 1 How to Write COBOL Code That Can Be Used by Anybody

1

Portability

One of the original impetuses for COBOL was that many organizations—particularly the United States government—realized that hardware-specific machine and assembly languages locked them into a particular vendor's computer or caused substantial software conversion costs to another specific language. The theory was that if each hardware manufacturer provided a compiler to translate a standard language into its specific machine code, the conversion cost would be eliminated and each organization could select the best hardware for its requirements. Nice theory, but something went wrong in the implementation. COBOL programs are somewhat portable but usually require some to much conversion effort when switching computers (even with the same vendor).[1] Computer vendors are not dumb! They are constantly striving to make it difficult for their customers to switch by offering something unique that would be hard to replicate.

The COBOL standards do not prohibit extensions to the language. Hardware vendors have added extensions for a variety of reasons:

- To provide software support for hardware features not originally contemplated
- To provide additional statements, formats, options, and other features to make COBOL more efficient
- To make COBOL easier

1

The net result is that COBOL programs cannot be moved from CPU to CPU without some manual intervention. COBOL portability has been enhanced because there are so many COBOL programmers who can translate between the various COBOL compilers. In any case, it is easier to port COBOL than machine or assembly languages.

Extensions are a serious portability problem. IBM calls its extensions "expanded language capabilities" and states that they "make possible programming applications not feasible previously." IBM uses gray shading in its COBOL manuals to indicate expanded language capabilities (i.e., capabilities not part of the ANSI COBOL standard). My conservative guess is that one-third of the standard IBM COBOL manual is gray (in fact, many pages are entirely gray).[2] Most companies do not restrict their programmers to "vanilla" (pure) ANSI COBOL, and thus each extension in each program erodes portability.

The degree of erosion in any organization can easily be tested. Each federally accepted COBOL compiler must have a "FIPS flagger." *FIPS* is the acronym for Federal Information Processing Standard, and the flagger flags any COBOL statement in the compiling program that does not conform to FIPS (which basically means that it does not conform to ANSI standards). Most of my clients are surprised (even shocked) to learn of the FIPS flagger and are even more surprised to see its results!

Is portability important? Yes. The original objective of eliminating conversion costs is still valid. Switching computers is difficult; having to do software conversion makes it more difficult.

But the most important reason for portability has nothing to do with portability. Portable ANSI COBOL programs are *simpler* because of fewer and less complex statements. Vanilla ANSI COBOL is inherently easier to understand and therefore to maintain. Restructuring is also easier.

RECOMMENDATIONS

- Provide your programmers with ANSI COBOL manuals *only*.
- Require specific approval for any ANSI exceptions.
- Police enforcement with software package.

THE VARIOUS COBOL

ANSI recognizes three standard COBOLs (ANSI X3.23-1985):

First standard COBOL, which is $COBOL_{68}$
Second standard COBOL, which is $COBOL_{74}$
Third standard COBOL, which is $COBOL_{85}$

The various CODASYL COBOLs (see Preface, note 1) were used as input to the ANSI standard but are not ANSI- or ISO-qualified.

Most existing programs are based on the $COBOL_{74}$ standard. Most programmers probably still code using a compiler based on that standard. New code should be based on the $COBOL_{85}$ standard.

This book uses subscripts to distinguish between the various COBOLs where necessary. For instance:

REMARKS$_{68}$ Means that this element was only available in COBOL$_{68}$ and is *not* available in COBOL$_{74}$ or COBOL$_{85}$.

ALTER$_{74}$ means that this element is available in COBOL$_{74}$ and obsolete in COBOL$_{85}$.[3]

CONTINUE$_{85}$ means that this element is available *only* in COBOL$_{85}$.

The subscript $_{VS}$ is used for IBM VS COBOL II and the subscript $_{OS}$ for IBM OS COBOL. COBOL$_{VS}$ or a variant will probably be approved as a COBOL$_{85}$ conforming compiler by the time you read this book.

RECOMMENDATIONS

- Write all new code (programs or enhancements) based on the COBOL$_{85}$ standard. Use comment (* in column 7 of the coding form) where applicable if your compiler does not support COBOL$_{85}$ statements such as the new END$_{85}$ explicit scope terminators. Additional details are provided in this text.
- Do not use any COBOL$_{85}$ obsolete *verbs* in new code.

HIGH-QUALITY SOFTWARE

High-quality software has the following characteristics:

- It is accurate. The program produces correct results. ROUNDED is always used; SIZE ERROR is always used; S(ign) is always used.
- It is concise. The program wastes not—it provides scope terminators, logical records, accurate comments, and COPY.
- It is consistent. The program always uses certain options: OVERFLOW is always used, FILE STATUS is always used, and INVALID KEY is always used.
- It is efficient. The program saves resources where justifiable. There are single input-output verbs for each file, single binary status elementary items, and optimized tables and/or SEARCH ALL.
- It is hierarchical. The program is displayable as a structure chart. ADPAC SS/80 would produce an error free Constantine structure chart.
- It is legible. The program is written for easy readability; verbs start in column 12, verb objects start in column 28, and blank lines separate statements and sentences.
- It is maintainable. The program can be changed easily; it uses meaningful comments, hierarchical paragraph prefixes, legible, meaningful paragraph names, and meaningful data names that conform to a consistent standard.

- It is portable. The program can be easily moved to another CPU and uses vanilla ANSI coding where possible. Unsupported ANSI is not recommended (/, REPORT WRITER[nr], COMMUNICATION SECTION[nr], etc); only extensions that do not adversely affect portability are recommended (EJECT, TITLE, OPTIMIZE, etc.).

- It is reliable. The program always produces the same results: CALL with CANCEL, initialized paragraphs, logically partitioned WORKING-STORAGE, and INITIAL[85] nested[85] programs with complete data protection.

- It is self-descriptive. The program can be understood by any programmer. Each paragraph begins with listing of input/output/control parameters and pseudo-COBOL to describe the single function, meaningful paragraph names, and meaningful data names that conform to a consistent standard.

- It is structured. The program follows structure theory. There are no sections (or paragraphless sections), no CALL ENTRY points; paragraphs perform single functions; only PERFORM or CALL are used to transfer control between physical modules. There are no PERFORM THRU to a different physical module, do while/until/forever constructs, and no ALTER[74].

- It is understandable. The program combines all of the features listed above.

NOTES

1. IBM has more than 20 manuals devoted to COBOL/COBOL conversion.

2. IBM shades only the title if the entire topic is not ANSI; however, IBM does provide *explicit* indicators, whereas many other vendors do not.

3. COBOL[85] defines an obsolete element as ''a COBOL language element in Standard COBOL that is to be deleted from the next revision of Standard COBOL'' (ANSI X3.23–1985). In other words, use at your own risk because it will not be supported in the next version of COBOL.

2

The COBOL Coding Form

Figure 2.1 is the standard COBOL coding form. It is divided into a header and a body with five areas:

- Sequence number area   columns 1–6
- Indicator area   column 7
- Area A   columns 8–11
    This area is reserved for the beginning of:
        division headers
        section headers
        paragraph headers or paragraph-names
        level indicators [FD, SD, CD, RD]
        level-numbers 01 and 77
        end program header
        pseudo-text
- Area B   columns 12–72[1]
    This area is reserved for all COBOL source statements that are not required to start in area A.
- Program identification area (not required by ANSI)   columns 73–80[2]

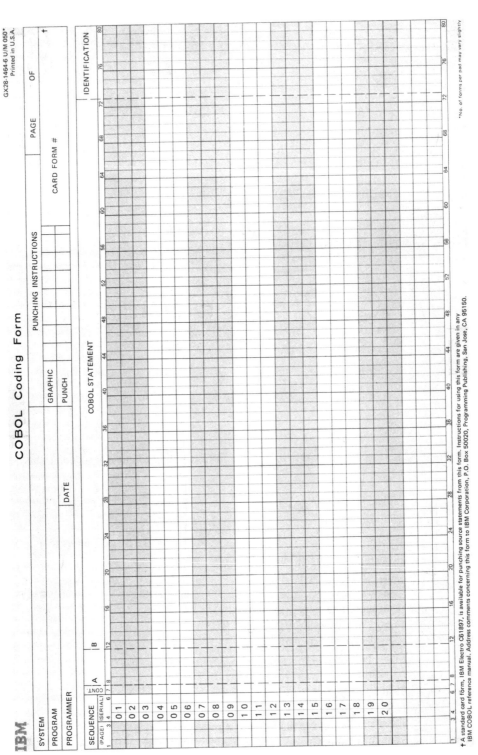

Figure 2.1 COBOL coding form. (Courtesy of International Business Machines Corporation)

SEQUENCE NUMBER AREA

The sequence number area is divided into two subareas:

- Page columns 1–3
- Serial number within page columns 4–6

The use of sequence numbers is optional.[3] Most compilers check for ascending sequence if the sequence numbers are present and print an error message for out-of-sequence lines. Many coding forms and screens have preprinted serial numbers in columns 4 and 5. The standard preprinted sequence 01–20 permits nine lines to be inserted by using 0 for the original line and 1–9 for new lines. The compiler can also resequence the numbers.

Sequence numbers should also be used in online development to prevent a new line from being inserted in the wrong place on the screen "coding form."

RECOMMENDATIONS

- Make sequence numbers mandatory.
- Have the compiler check for ascending sequence on all compiles.
- Use the preprinted serial number to reduce handwriting or typing effort.
- Always use 0 in column 6 for the original line.

INDICATOR AREA

The indicator area is used to tell the compiler

- That a literal is being continued from the previous line
- That this line is an explanatory comment
- That this is a debugging line[74]

Literal

A nonnumeric literal requires a hyphen (-) in column 7 and a quotation mark (") in column 12. A word or numeric literal requires only the hyphen in column 7.[4]

Only literals that are *absolutely* required by the statement syntax should be permitted. Most literals appear in the PROCEDURE DIVISION as "constants." These literals can be easily coded as constants in the WORKING-STORAGE SECTION with 88 levels and VALUE clauses. The rationale is based on five criteria:

- **Impact analysis.** PROCEDURE DIVISION literals make it virtually impossible to find all occurrences of an item. For instance, if ZIP code (US postal code) literals were used to determine shipment method, how would you find them to change them to ZIP + 4?

- **Date usage.** Many literals are hard-coded dates. Programs abort—or worse—causing incorrect results when dates are "exceeded." Again, dates are easy to find and change if coded in the DATA DIVISION.
- **Transaction codes.** Transaction codes are often hard-coded. How do you find all sentences (groups of COBOL statements) that refer to cash-paid-out transactions if that transaction is hard-coded as 13?
- **Security.** Literals can be used as a "back door" to bypass security measures.
- **Condition-name.** Coding constants as 88 levels (defined later) permits the use of the effective condition-name IF statements. Use of understandable condition-names makes a program easier to read and maintain.

Required literals should not be continued unless necessary. A line can contain a literal of 61 characters. If the literal is larger than 61 characters, use a hyphen.

RECOMMENDATIONS

- Use literals only if syntactically required.
- Do not continue literals unless length exceeds line length.

Quotation Mark

A few words about the quotation mark. The ANSI standard is "; the IBM standard is '. It is very frustrating to have a compiler reject literals because of the difference in quotation marks. IBM requires the JCL (job control language) PARM card to contain a QUOTE$_{os}$ keyword or QUOTE$_{vs}$ compiler option to use the ".

RECOMMENDATION (for IBM users)

- Establish a standard JCL PARM that all programmers must use for COBOL compiles that includes the QUOTE$_{os}$ keyword or the QUOTE$_{vs}$ compiler option.

NOTE$_{68}$

Placing an asterisk (*) in column 7 informs the compiler that this line is an explanatory comment. The asterisk and the comment is printed on the source listing but has no effect on the object code. ANSI also allows a slash (/), which instructs the compiler to eject to the top of the next page.

Another way to comment programs in COBOL$_{68}$ is the NOTE$_{68}$ statement. For whatever reason, the NOTE$_{68}$ statement was omitted in COBOL$_{74}$.

RECOMMENDATION

- Do not use NOTE$_{68}$.

Explanatory Comments

The objective of Part 1 is to produce readable code.[5] Readable code include comments describing the function of each paragraph. These comments should appear after the paragraph-name so that the reader can easily determine the function of the paragraph. There are also software packages—such as ADPAC's PM/SS—that print "narratives," which consist of the comment statements following each paragraph-name.

The narratives of a program that consists of meaningful comments provides any reader with significant knowledge of that program's functions.

The ANSI debugging function$_{74}$ will be discussed later.

RECOMMENDATIONS

- Use comment entry only (* in column 7); do not use NOTE$_{68}$.
- Place comment entries after *each* procedure paragraph-name that describes the function of the paragraph. (*Note:* Consistent with structured programming standards, each paragraph should only contain a single function.)
- Use a software package to print the narratives.

AREA A

Area A (columns 8–11) is reserved for

Division Headers

Division headers are the major parts of a COBOL program. The division header must be the first line of division. The divisions are as follows:

- IDENTIFICATION
- ENVIRONMENT (optional in COBOL$_{85}$)
- DATA (optional in COBOL$_{85}$)
- PROCEDURE (optional in COBOL$_{85}$)

Section Header

Sections are major subdivisions of the ENVIRONMENT, DATA, and PROCEDURE Divisions. The section header must be the first line of the SECTION. The section headers are as follows:

- CONFIGURATION SECTION.
- INPUT-OUTPUT SECTION.

- FILE SECTION.
- WORKING-STORAGE SECTION.
- LINKAGE SECTION.
- COMMUNICATION SECTION.
- REPORT SECTION.
- DECLARATIVES. and END DECLARATIVES.
- SECTION.

Paragraph Headers

The subdivisions of the IDENTIFICATION AND ENVIRONMENT divisions are paragraph headers. These are as follows:

- PROGRAM-ID.
- AUTHOR.$_{74}$
- INSTALLATION.$_{74}$
- DATE-WRITTEN.$_{74}$
- DATE-COMPILED.$_{74}$
- SECURITY.$_{74}$
- REMARKS.$_{68}$
- SOURCE-COMPUTER.
- OBJECT-COMPUTER.
- SPECIAL-NAMES.
- FILE-CONTROL.
- I-O-CONTROL.

Note: COBOL has a list of reserved words (or a combination of words concatenated with a hyphen) that have a specific meaning to the compiler and cannot be used for any other purpose. The above names are reserved. Appendix C contains reserved word listings.

Paragraph-Names

Paragraph-names can consist of 1 to 30 characters chosen from the set A–Z, 0–9, and -. Each paragraph-name should define or suggest its function. The first five characters should be as follows:

- Column 8: P (to distinguish a paragraph from a section)
- Column 9: The level of the invoked module, that is, the actual level in the organization that the module is on (see Figure 2.2)[6]. For instance, level 1 is the paragraph invoked when the program is invoked; level 2 is any paragraph invoked by the "mainline" paragraph invoked by the program; and so on.

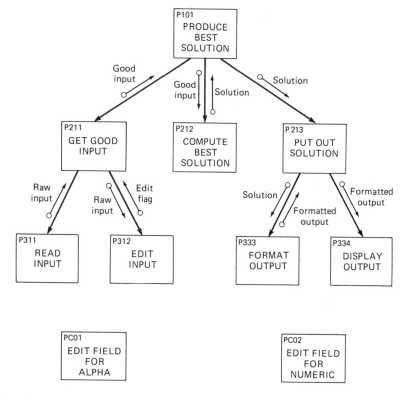

Figure 2.2 Constantine structure chart illustrating the paragraph numbering scheme. (Chris Gane/ Trish Sarson, *STRUCTURED SYSTEMS ANALYSIS: Tools & Techniques,* ©1979, p. 188. Reprinted/Adapted by permission of Prentice-Hall, Inc., Englewood Cliffs, NJ.)

- Column 10: The hierarchical sequence number of the paragraph on the previous level that invoked this paragraph. Paragraphs on each level are numbered in sequence from left to right (this is the same numbering scheme used for IBM IMS twins); a 1 means that it is the leftmost paragraph; a 3 means that it is the third paragraph from the left; and so on.
- Column 11: The hierarchical sequence number of the invoked module
- Column 12: Hyphen

For instance, the prefix P327- tells us two things:

- This paragraph is at level 3 of the program hierarchical organization.
- This paragraph is invoked by the second paragraph (reading from left to right) of level 2 (structured programming requires that paragraphs be invoked only by PERFORM statements and all noncommon paragraphs are therefore invoked by a paragraph one level higher; the invoking paragraph prefix is P2?2-).

Figure 2.2 is a Constantine structure chart illustrating this numbering scheme. Note that there are two modules (rectangles) that are unconnected. These are "common" paragraphs that are invoked by two or more different paragraphs. Common paragraphs have a special identification of PC99- where 99 equals the sequential number of the paragraph.

The numbering scheme requires a few minutes to understand and some minimal time to write. However, it makes the program easier to read. It also indirectly enforces structured programming. How do you identify a paragraph that was invoked by a "backward" GO TO or by the sequential operation of the program (fallthru)?

Level Indicators

There are four level indicators:

- FD   file description entries
- SD^{nr} sort-file description entries
- RD^{nr} report description entries
- CD^{nr} communications description entries

Note: The superscript ^{nr} is used throughout this book to indicate that this COBOL element is *not recommended*. Readers may bypass it unless interested in the reasons for not using it.

The level indicators should be coded in columns 8 and 9.

Level-Numbers

Level-numbers 01 and 77 must begin in area A and should be coded in columns 8 and 9. Level numbers 02–49, 66, and 88 can be coded in either area A or area B. Higher-level numbers should be progressively indented for readability (see Chapter 6 for specific recommendations).

Miscellaneous

End program header must start in A area. Pseudo-text can start in either area A or area B.

RECOMMENDATIONS

- Begin coding each required A entry in column 8.
- Use a meaningful paragraph prefix to aid in readability.
- Progressively indent higher level-numbers to improve readability.

AREA B

Area B is used for entries that are not required to start in area A. Typically, these are statements or sentences. The statement or sentence should start in column 12. Indentation (specific recommendations by statement type are included in later chapters) should be used to increase readability. A blank line should be left between sentences or statements for readability (some compilers require an asterisk in column 7 to ''print'' the blank line on the source output).

RECOMMENDATIONS

- Begin coding the original line of each procedure statement or sentence in column 12.
- Indent additional lines for readability.
- Separate statements or sentences with a blank line (use * in column 7 if required by compiler); do not use the SKIP$_{os/vs}$ statement.

PROGRAM IDENTIFICATION AREA

The identification area is used by some compilers to print a program identification on the left of the source line on the source listing. At least the first line of each page should have the program name from the PROGRAM-ID of the IDENTIFICATION DIVISION.

RECOMMENDATION

- Place PROGRAM-ID in the identification area on at least the first line of each page.

OTHER RECOMMENDATIONS

- If you use coding forms, select ones that have shading to separate groups of lines (usually three) from each other. This eases the eyestrain for the original development programmer.
- Use the EJECT statement or the / in column 7 as the last statement in *each* division, section, and paragraph so that each new ''topic'' begins a new page of the source listing.[7] This helps the maintenance programmer (paper is much cheaper than programming time).

SUMMARY OF RECOMMENDATIONS

- Use sequence number with compiler checking for an ascending sequence.
- Use preprinted (constants if online) serial number, and code the original line as 0 in column 6.

- Use literals only if syntactically required; do not continue literals unless necessary.
- Always use the double quotation mark (").
- Use * in column 7 for comments; do not use NOTE$_{68}$.
- Place comment entries after each procedure paragraph-name that describes the paragraph's function.
- Use a software tool to print the paragraph narratives to provide a program abstract.
- Begin coding each required A entry in column 8.
- Use meaningful paragraph prefixes and understandable paragraph-names.
- Progressively indent higher level-numbers for readability.
- Begin coding the original line of each procedure statement or sentence in column 12; indent additional lines for readability.
- Separate statements and sentences with a blank line.
- Place PROGRAM-ID on the first line of each page.
- Use coding forms with shading; reverse video or other highlighting if online.
- Use the EJECT statement or / as the last statement.

NOTES

1. The actual number of columns is implementor-specified; however, most implementors have chosen column 72 as the last column for area B (see Figure 2.1).
2. Not required by ANSI, but most implementors have specified column 80 as the last coding form column (see Figure 2.1).
3. COBOL$_{85}$ allows any character to be used.
4. A word consists of 1 to 30 characters chosen from the word character set A–Z, 0–9, and hyphen (-). A word cannot begin or end with a hyphen.
5. Structured code can isolate each function of a program in a top-down format. That is all it does. Although that is very desirable, it does not make COBOL coding more understandable. We in data processing seem to forget that program productivity—though clearly understandable, easily modifiable coding—was the major objective of the creators of COBOL. All we have to do is use COBOL as they intended. (Jerry Sitner, "Make COBOL Code Understandable," *Computerworld*, May 6, 1985.)
6. Structured programming results in a hierarchical structure. Larry Constantine is credited with inventing structure charts to portray the hierarchical program structure graphically. (For more information, see Larry Constantine and Ed Yourdon, *Structured Design*, New York: Yourdon Press, 1976.) Figure 2.2 is a Constantine structure chart for a sample program. Columns 9–11 provide specific leveling information.
7. EJECT is not ANSI; however, most compilers support it, and it is a recommended exception (most compilers do not support /).

——— 3 ———

The IDENTIFICATION DIVISION

The structure of the IDENTIFICATION DIVISION is as follows:

IDENTIFICATION DIVISION.
PROGRAM-ID.
AUTHOR.74
INSTALLATION.74
DATE-WRITTEN.74
DATE-COMPILED.74
SECURITY.74
REMARKS.68

The IDENTIFICATION DIVISION is the first division of a COBOL program. All paragraphs except PROGRAM-ID are optional.

The very first entry in a COBOL program can cause portability problems! IBM compilers permit the use of ID-DIVISION, which is not ANSI standard.

RECOMMENDATION

- Always use IDENTIFICATION DIVISION.

The formats of the paragraphs are as follows:

<u>PROGRAM ID.</u> program-name [IS <u>COMMON</u>$_{85}$/<u>INITIAL</u>$_{85}$ PROGRAM$_{85}$].

The second entry in a COBOL program does cause a portability problem. The ANSI standard for program-name is 1 to 30 characters chosen from the set *A–Z, 0–9, -*. The Hewlett-Packard (HP) 3000 compiler deletes all hyphens and uses only the first 15 characters. The IBM compiler$_{vs}$ has these four traits:

- It accepts beginning and ending quotation marks (').
- It converts the first character if numeric to a letter.
- It converts each hyphen to zero.
- It accepts only the first eight characters.

RECOMMENDATIONS

- For portability, use six alpha characters only.
- Place the real (and understandable) program-name as a comment on the next line. (See Figure 3.1 for a sample IDENTIFICATION DIVISION.)

The optional PROGRAM$_{85}$ clause allows nested$_{85}$ source programs that can be invoked by many programs (COMMON$_{85}$) and/or can also be INITIAL$_{85}$. This clause is discussed under CALL in Chapter 10.

Note: Underlined <u>CAPITALIZED</u> words are ANSI-required key words; plain CAPITALIZED words are optional; lowercase in format syntax is a programmer entry. This convention is used in this book when actual formats are used.

<u>AUTHOR.</u>$_{74}$ comment-entry$_{74}$

The term **comment-entry$_{74}$** means that the paragraph is optional.

RECOMMENDATIONS

- Place the original programmer's name here. This provides the possibility for other programmers to contact that person to answer questions.
- Place the names of any programmers who performed significant modification on subsequent lines. Include the effective date of the modification.
- Use * in column 7 to conform to COBOL$_{85}$.

<u>INSTALLATION.</u>$_{74}$ comment-entry$_{74}$

RECOMMENDATIONS

- Place the name of the installation (site) that the program is intended to run on.
- Use * in column 7 to conform to COBOL$_{85}$.

<u>DATE-WRITTEN.</u>$_{74}$ comment-entry$_{74}$

COBOL$_{74}$

IDENTIFICATION DIVISION.

PROGRAM-ID.   smlcbl.
*small-cobol-74

AUTHOR.   eric garrigue vesely
                awb - 922-6313.

INSTALLATION.   the analyst workbench.

DATE-WRITTEN.   1 may 1987.

DATE-COMPILED.
*compiler places compilation date on source listing

REMARKS.   sample of identification division.
*may require * in column 7 because remarks-68 is not supported

COBOL$_{85}$

IDENTIFICATION DIVISION.

PROGRAM-ID.   smlcbl.
*small-cobol-85

DATE-COMPILED.
*if supported; otherwise, alternative such as title if supported.

reserved words are UPPERCASE; programmer entries are lowercase.

Figure 3.1   Sample IDENTIFICATION DIVISION in COBOL$_{74}$ and COBOL$_{85}$.

RECOMMENDATIONS

- Place the date that is in the header date block here. (Alternative: Code the date that the program became operational.)
- Use * in column 7 to conform to COBOL$_{85}$.

<u>DATE-COMPILED.</u>$_{74}$ comment-entry$_{74}$ (current-date)

The compiler prints the date of the compilation on the source listing if this optional paragraph is coded. Depending on the compiler, comment entries may be destroyed. The HP compiler prints anything on the same line as the paragraph-name; the IBM compiler ignores the entire comment-entry.

I personally believe that ANSI made a mistake in obsoleting DATE-COMPILED$_{74}$ since the printed compilation date on the source listing is often the only way to determine the latest printed version of the source program.

Most compilers will probably continue to support DATE-COMPILED$_{74}$ or provide an alternative such as TITLE$_{vs}$.

RECOMMENDATION

* Always use DATE-COMPILED$_{74}$ if supported; make any **comment-entry$_{74}$** as a comment following the paragraph.

SECURITY.$^{nr}_{74}$ comment-entry$_{74}$

ANSI intended this paragraph to provide manual security information about this program. Security—if desired—should be provided by automated methods.

RECOMMENDATION

* Do not use.

REMARKS.$_{68}$ comment-entry$_{74}$

The ANSI objective was to use REMARKS$_{68}$ to define the program's function. This is an excellent concept and should be incorporated into all programs. Use * in column 7 to conform to COBOL$_{74/85}$.

RECOMMENDATION

* Define the program's function in the REMARKS$_{68}$ paragraph.

Readability

RECOMMENDATION

* Start all area A entries in column 8; start all area B entries in column 24.

SUMMARY OF RECOMMENDATIONS

* Always spell out IDENTIFICATION DIVISION.
* PROGRAM-ID. Use six alpha characters only; place real program-name as a comment following the paragraph.
* AUTHOR.$_{74}$: Use original programmer's name plus names of any other programmer who made major modification plus the modification effective date.
* INSTALLATION.$_{74}$: Enter installation name.
* DATE-WRITTEN.$_{74}$: Enter original coding date.
* DATE-COMPILED.$_{74}$: Always use; code comment-entries as comments. Use alternative if supported and DATE-COMPILED$_{74}$ is not.

- SECURITY.$_{74}$: Do not use.
- REMARKS.$_{68}$: State the program's function.
- Start A entries in column 8, B entries in column 24.
- Place * in column 7 if any paragraph is not supported by your compiler.

4

The Responsibility of Programmers

As a programmer on the Univac I and the Univac File computer, I was basically responsible for everything—loading metallic magnetic tapes on the drives, putting paper in the printer, putting cards in the card reader and punch, booting the program, running the console, and so on. There was usually an operator or two to help, but it was my final responsibility.

The program—in machine language—had to handle the minute details of positioning the magnetic tape, issuing the actual read/write commands, and handling errors, BOT (beginning of tape), BOF (beginning of file), EOF (end of file), and EOT (end of tape) markers, and all the minutiae of the other peripherals.

Since then operators have taken over the operation of the computer and operating systems have taken over the minutiae of peripherals. For instance, the OPEN statement readies the appropriate device and the READ statement reads a record from that device. The operating system generates the required machine instructions.

The moral of this tale is that the responsibility of programmers has continued to narrow as hardware and system software have become more sophisticated. That responsibility should now be restricted to programming the business logic only. The programmer should not be responsible for such entries as these:

- SEGMENT-LIMIT$_{74}$
- PROGRAM COLLATING SEQUENCE
- SPECIAL-NAMES.
- CURRENCY SIGN IS
- DECIMAL-POINT
- ASSIGN TO
- RESERVE
- FILE STATUS IS
- DECLARATIVES.

Any of these entries, if required, should be generated by system programmers and placed into the COBOL COPY library for inclusion into application programs by COPY statements. (COPY is used in this book to mean COBOL COPY and PANVALET ++INC and LIBRARIAN −INC.) Work better performed by system software should be performed by that software. Specifically, communication by communication software (ADS/ON, CICS, TSO, etc.), queries by query software (NATURAL, QBE, SQL, etc.), and reports by report writer software (CULPRIT, MARK IV & V, etc.).

The programmer should also not be responsible for data naming standards. Standard data-names should be generated by a data administrator and the appropriate DATA DIVISION entries should be in the COPY library.

RECOMMENDATION

- A programmer should be responsible only for translating the business logic to COBOL statements. Anything else should be done by some other—and usually more efficient—method.

This recommendation permeates many of the other recommendations in this book.

5

The ENVIRONMENT DIVISION

The structure of the ENVIRONMENT DIVISION is as follows:

```
ENVIRONMENT DIVISION.
  CONFIGURATION SECTION.
    SOURCE-COMPUTER.
    OBJECT-COMPUTER.
    SPECIAL-NAMES.
  INPUT-OUTPUT SECTION.
    FILE-CONTROL.
    I-O-CONTROL.
```

The ENVIRONMENT DIVISION is the optional$_{85}$ second division of a COBOL program. Its purpose is to describe the hardware environment necessary for proper program execution.

CONFIGURATION SECTION

The optional$_{85}$ CONFIGURATION SECTION optional$_{85}$ paragraph format is as follows:

SOURCE-COMPUTER.   [computer-name.][1]

The computer name and model number of the compiling CPU are inserted here by a COPY statement.

OBJECT-COMPUTER.   computer-name

The computer name and model number of the executing CPU are inserted here by a COPY statement.

The optional$_{85}$ OBJECT-COMPUTER paragraph has the following optional clauses:

MEMORY SIZE IS$_{74}$ integer WORDS/CHARACTERS/MODULES
PROGRAM COLLATING SEQUENCE IS   alphabet-name
SEGMENT-LIMIT IS$_{74}$ segment-number

The MEMORY$_{74}$ clause documents the size of the program. It is useful information in determining the SEGMENT-LIMIT$_{74}$.

The SEGMENT-LIMIT$_{74}$ provides partitioning criteria to the operating system. Both these clauses are not required on virtual memory computers. If required, they should be coded by system programmers and placed in the COPY library.

RECOMMENDATION

- COPY if required.

The SEQUENCE clause changes the collating order from the native alphabet of the OBJECT-COMPUTER to another alphabet, for example, from EBCDIC to ASCII. If required, it should be in the COPY library.

SPECIAL-NAMES is an optional paragraph that permits the program to do all of the following:

- Assign implementor-names to user-specified mnemonic names
- Process external switches
- Further clarify the collating sequence
- Change currency symbols
- Specify symbolic characters$_{85}$
- Relate class-names to character sets$_{85}$

The SPECIAL-NAMES paragraph has the following optional clauses:

implementor-name-n IS mnemonic-name-n

where **n** is an integer.

Most computers have easily identifiable names for system components such as the printer. These should not be changed by the programmer because it makes the program harder to read. If required, the paragraph should be in COPY library.

switch-n <u>ON</u> STATUS IS^{nr} condition-name-1
<u>OFF</u> STATUS IS^{nr} condition-name-2

Many early CPUs had external switches that could be set by an operator and be read by a program. For instance, a single program could be used for daily, weekly, monthly, quarterly, and annual processing with the cycle controlled by the external switch. This manual intervention—or lack thereof—could and did cause mistakes. Most current CPUs do not have external switches.[2] In any case, do not use them.

<u>ALPHABET</u>$_{85}$ alphabet-name IS
STANDARD-1/<u>STANDARD-2</u>$_{85}$/<u>NATIVE</u>/implementor-name
[literal-1 <u>THROUGH</u>/<u>THRU</u> literal-2 [[<u>ALSO</u> literal-3, ...]]

This paragraph is used to equate the alphabet name in the SEQUENCE clause to a specific alphabet known to the OBJECT-COMPUTER. STANDARD-1 is the ASCII character set, STANDARD-2$_{85}$ is the ISO character set, NATIVE is the OBJECT-COMPUTER character set (EBCDIC on IBM mainframes), and **implementor-name** and **literal** permit ''foreign'' character sets to be specified. If required, this paragraph should be in the COPY library.

<u>CURRENCY</u> SIGN IS literal. (cannot be a figurative constant$_{85}$)

This clause changes $ to another currency sign such as £ (pound sterling). If required, it should be in the COPY library.

<u>DECIMAL-POINT</u> IS <u>COMMA</u>

This clause interchanges the period and comma in PICTURE clauses. Many European countries have this requirement. For instance, $1,234,567.89 in the United States would be 1.234.567,89 francs in France. If required, it should be in the COPY library.

COBOL$_{85}$ has added two additional optional clauses:

<u>SYMBOLIC</u> CHARACTERS$_{85}$ (symbolic-character-n, ... IS/ARE integer-n, ... <u>IN</u> alphabet-name-n)

This clause permits user-defined characters to be specified for integers within the specified alphabet. This clause is used for translating foreign characters.

<u>CLASS</u>$_{85}$ class-name IS literal-n <u>THROUGH</u>/<u>THRU</u> literal-p ...

This clause assigns a specific class-name to the set of characters defined by the literals.

The class-name can be used in an IF class condition test (see the IF definition in Chapter 10).

RECOMMENDATION

- COPY should be used if ALPHABET, CURRENCY SIGN, DECIMAL-POINT, SYMBOLIC CHARACTER$_{85}$, and CLASS$_{85}$, are required.

INPUT-OUTPUT SECTION

The INPUT-OUTPUT SECTION prescribed paragraph format is as follows:

FILE-CONTROL.
SELECT   file-name
ASSIGN TO   system-name

The **file-name** is an organization name for data used by this program; the **system-name** is the organization name of the peripheral that this data is to be read from and/or written to. Both names should be in the COPY library.

SELECT has an OPTIONAL^{nr} clause (which is itself optional) that allows the specified INPUT SEQUENTIAL FILE or RELATIVE FILE$_{85}$ or INDEXED FILE$_{85}$ OPEN in I-O$_{85}$ or EXTEND$_{85}$ not to be present when the actual program is executed. This prevents an abend (*abnormal end* to a program) when the OPEN statement is invoked and the **file-name** is not present. This clause permits a programmer to specify an INPUT FILE— usually some form of error or exception—to be incorporated within a run to provide for last-minute corrections. Again, this information is static and the real world is dynamic.

RECOMMENDATION

- Do not use OPTIONAL^{nr}.

The FILE-CONTROL paragraph has the following optional clauses:

RESERVE^{nr} integer AREA/AREAS

This clause theoretically permits the programmer to control the number of buffers assigned to the selected file-name and therefore the space required and the efficiency of I-O transfer. Maybe once, but not now.

RECOMMENDATION

- Do not use RESERVE^{nr}.

ORGANIZATION IS SEQUENTIAL/RELATIVE/INDEXED.

This clause informs the operating system of the physical organizations of the selected FILE.

SEQUENTIAL means that the RECORDS in the selected FILE are physically stored in adjacent physical locations. The physical sequence is normally indicated by a data element designated as a sort key within the RECORD. Files stored on magnetic tape are generally SEQUENTIAL.

RELATIVE is a form of SEQUENTIAL. The RECORDS are physically stored in serial time sequence and can be retrieved sequentially or by the actual physical storage number.

INDEXED means that the RECORDS in the selected FILE have no physical sequence. RECORDS must be accessed using a RECORD KEY, which is a data element within the RECORD.

The ORGANIZATION clause should be standardized for use by all programmers to increase maintainability.

RECOMMENDATION

- ORGANIZATION should be in the COPY library.

ACCESS MODE IS SEQUENTIAL/RANDOM/DYNAMIC

This clause is the mirror image of the ORGANIZATION clause in that it defines the method that this program is using to retrieve the RECORDS in the selected FILE.

SEQUENTIAL means that each RECORD is accessed in pure physical sequence.

RANDOM means that RECORDS in the selected file are to be accessed by the RELATIVE physical KEY or by the RECORD data KEY.

DYNAMIC means that both forms of access (SEQUENTIAL and RANDOM) are to be used by this program. RANDOM and DYNAMIC must have a RECORD/RELATIVE KEY clause; it is optional for SEQUENTIAL. Syntax is

RECORD/RELATIVE KEY IS data-name

where **data-name** is defined in the WORKING-STORAGE SECTION.

The ACCESS clause should be standardized for use by all programmers to increase maintainability.

RECOMMENDATION

- ACCESS should be in the COPY library.

FILE STATUS IS data-name

The FILE STATUS clause informs the operating system that the status of each input/output request and certain OPEN/CLOSE statuses[85] should be placed in the specified **data-name** (defined in the WORKING-STORAGE SECTION or LINKAGE SECTION with a PIC of XX).

The left character is status 1 and defines the basic result; the right character is status 2 and provides more information if available. The possible values and meanings are presented in Table 5.1.

TABLE 5.1 Possible Values and Meanings of FILE STATUS

Status 1	Status 2	Meaning	Statements to Which Character Applies†
0		Successful completion	
	0	NO further information available	all statements
	2	Duplicate KEY	READ ind REWRITE ind START ind
	4*	RECORD LENGTH incorrect	READ all
	5*	OPTIONAL FILE NOT present	OPEN all
	7*	Magnetic TAPE clause specified for non-reel UNIT	OPEN seq CLOSE seq
1		AT END condition with unsuccesful completion	
	0	NO NEXT logical RECORD exists	READ all
	4*	RELATIVE RECORD NUMBER > RELATIVE KEY	READ rel
2		INVALID KEY condition with unsuccessful completion	
	1	SEQUENCE ERROR	READ ind REWRITE ind
	2	Duplicate KEY	REWRITE rel/ind WRITE rel/ind
	3	RECORD does NOT exist	START rel/ind READ rel/ind
	4*	Boundary violation	WRITE rel/ind
3		Permanent ERROR condition with unsuccessful completion	
	0	NO further information available	all statements
	4	Boundary violation	WRITE seq
	5*	Non-OPTIONAL FILE NOT present	OPEN all
	7*	OPEN MODE incorrect FOR FILE	OPEN all
	8*	FILE LOCK	OPEN all
	9*	Conflict between FILE attributes	OPEN all
4		Logic ERROR condition with unsuccessful completion	
	1*	FILE already OPEN	OPEN all
	2*	FILE NOT OPEN	CLOSE all
	3*	Required READ NOT successfully executed	DELETE rel/ind REWRITE all
	4*	Boundary violation	WRITE all REWRITE all
	6*	NO valid NEXT RECORD established	READ ALL
	7*	FILE NOT OPEN IN INPUT OR I-O MODE	READ all START rel/ind
	8*	FILE NOT OPEN IN OUTPUT OR EXTEND MODE	WRITE all
	9*	FILE NOT OPEN IN I-O MODE	DELETE rel/ind REWRITE all

TABLE 5.1 Possible Values and Meanings of FILE STATUS *(continued)*

Status		meaning	Statements to Which
1	2		Character Applies[†]
9		Implementor-defined condition with unsuccessful completion	
	0–9	Implementor-defined	

Note: Values not shown are not used
*This FILE STATUS available only in $COBOL_{85}$
[†]all FILE STATUS applies to listed statement in the SEQUENTIAL, RELATIVE, and INDEXED I-O modules
seq FILE STATUS applies to listed statement in the SEQUENTIAL I-O module
rel FILE STATUS applies to listed statement in the RELATIVE I-O module
ind FILE STATUS applies to listed statement in the INDEXED I-O module

$COBOL_{vs}$ has expanded this field to four characters to provide more information to an error recovery routine. This clause should *always* be present and should be in the COPY library. The error recovery routine should also be in the COPY library and be copied into the appropriate place in the PROCEDURE DIVISION.

RECOMMENDATIONS

- Always use FILE STATUS.
- There should always be a standard error recovery routine for each FILE STATUS.
- FILE STATUS and its associated standard error recovery routine should be in the COPY library for incorporation into each program.

The I-O-CONTROL paragraph is entirely optional. It has the following optional clauses.

RERUN ON$_{74}$ system-name EVERY integer RECORDS OF file-name

This clause permits backup and/or log and/or audit records to be created on the specified system-name for the specified multiple of the file-name. If required, it should be in the COPY library.

SAME SORT/SORT-MERGE/RECORD AREA^{nr} FOR filename-1, filename-2, ...

This clause is equivalent to the RESERVE clause in that it attempts to save space by sharing the same buffer area for two or more files. As with RESERVE^{nr}, do not use it.

MULTIPLE FILE TAPE CONTAINS$_{74}$ filename-1, filename-2, ...

This clause informs the operating system that the specified magnetic tape contains the specified file-names. Each file-name clause can have the following optional phrase:

$$\underline{\text{POSITION}}_{74} \text{ integer}$$

which specifies the actual starting physical location for the specified file-name. POSI-TION$_{74}$, if required, should be in the COPY library.

SUMMARY OF RECOMMENDATIONS

- The entire ENVIRONMENT DIVISION should be copied into the program via the COPY statement.
- The FILE STATUS clause should always be coded. (Both it and its standard error recovery routine should be in the COPY library.)
- The following clauses should *not* be coded:
  - SWITCH $\underline{\text{ON}}$ STATUS^{nr}
  - $\underline{\text{RESERVE}}$ AREA^{nr}
  - $\underline{\text{SAME}}$ $\underline{\text{SORT}}$/$\underline{\text{SORT-MERGE}}$/$\underline{\text{RECORD}}$ AREA FOR^{nr}

NOTES

1. DEBUGGING$_{74}$ MODE is discussed in Chapter 10. Exact ANSI syntax is not given because there are numerous implementor options and it is recommended later that the entire ENVIRONMENT DIVISION be COPied if required.

2. Many current CPUs emulate external switches through software such as IBM's JCL.

— 6 —

The DATA DIVISION

The DATA DIVISION is the optional[85] third division of a COBOL program. Its primary purpose is to define the data being processed by the PROCEDURE DIVISION. This chapter describes how COBOL defines the overall structure of FILE and RECORD, and the next chapter describes how COBOL defines the detail structure of those RECORDS. COBOL has the following data hierarchy:

- FILE   a collection of logically related RECORDS
- RECORD   a collection of logically related data items

Data items are further subdivided:

- GROUP ITEM   A group item is really a structure composed of other group items and/or elementary items; specifically, a data item without a PICTURE (PIC) clause.
- ELEMENTARY ITEM   An elementary item has no subordinate substructure; specifically, it has a PIC clause.

The DATA DIVISION has five optional sections:

- FILE SECTION.
- WORKING-STORAGE SECTION.
- LINKAGE SECTION.
- COMMUNICATION SECTION[nr].
- REPORT SECTION[nr].

FILE SECTION

The FILE SECTION defines the FILE, RECORD, and data items to the program. There is only one mandatory paragraph required if the FILE SECTION is present:

FD file-name

where **file-name** is one of the **file-names** in the SELECT clause of the FILE-CONTROL paragraph of the ENVIRONMENT DIVISION.

The only mandatory clause in COBOL$_{74}$ is

LABEL RECORD/S IS/ARE STANDARD/OMITTED

This clause is required because operating systems must initiate and terminate various peripherals (magnetic tape, disk, printer, card reader, etc.). Also, good operational procedures require that mountable devices (tape, disks, cassettes, etc.) have a label that the operating system can verify as being the correct medium for the execution of this program. The appropriate option for mountable devices is STANDARD. This informs the operating systems that ANSI STANDARD labels are to be read, verified, and *written* on the mountable devices. The OMITTED option is used for peripherals such as printers.

Most hardware vendors have developed their own labels. In this case, the syntax is usually

LABEL RECORD/S IS/ARE data-name-1, ...

where **data-name = hardware-vendor-label**.

In any case, the programmer should not be responsible for the LABEL clause. It should be in the COPY library.

COBOL$_{85}$ allows the LABEL clause to be omitted, and if it is, LABEL RECORDS ARE STANDARD is assumed. Nothing should ever be assumed.

RECOMMENDATION

- The LABEL clause should always be present and should be copied

The other optional clauses are

BLOCK CONTAINS integer-1 TO integer-2 RECORDS/CHARACTERS

This clause provides the operating system with the criteria to unblock a large physical RECORD into smaller logical RECORDS. The rationale for the large physical RECORD was the interrecord gap on magnetic tape. A magnetic tape drive must rev up to speed to READ the bits magnetically encoded on the tape and then brake to a halt at the completion of the READ. The magnetic tape drive therefore required braking space and start-up space. This space was the interrecord gap. Interrecord gaps of inches were common. The normal objective of a physical designer was to have physical RECORDS larger than the interrecord gap to reduce wasted space, thereby saving reels of magnetic tape and increasing efficiency. The resultant physical RECORD was usually far larger than the logical RECORD that a program required. Therefore, $\underline{n}$ logical RECORDS would be blocked into a large physical RECORD requiring unblocking. This clause provides the information that the operating system needs in performing the unblocking.

The syntax for fixed-length RECORDS is

<u>BLOCK</u> CONTAINS integer <u>RECORDS</u>

The option CHARACTERS could be substituted so that a BLOCK of ten logical RECORDS each containing 100 CHARACTERS could be specified:

<u>BLOCK</u> CONTAINS 1000 CHARACTERS

The option **integer-1 TO integer-2^{nr}** means that the BLOCK size is of variable length containing a variable number of RECORDS and CHARACTERS. This requires the operating system to establish a physical buffer for the maximum possible size and complicates the unblocking algorithm.

The intent of variable length RECORDS is to save space on the storage media. The cost of variable length records is processing complexity and reduced efficiency. The induced programming complexity is not worth the savings of variable length records. This is particularly true today because of the availability of expansion/compaction algorithms. Expansion/compaction algorithms are performed by system software (operating system, database management system, etc.) and are "transparent" (programmer does not know or care that expansion and/or contraction is happening). The system software analyzes data items and compresses leading zeros, trailing blanks, and sometimes repeating characters by reducing them to a control data item. This control data item is then used by the expansion routine to reconstitute the data element to its original value. Advocates of expansion/contraction often claim larger space savings than using variable length RECORDS. What is clear is that transparent expansion/compaction does not induce programming complexity into COBOL programs.

RECOMMENDATION

- Do not use variable length RECORDS; use transparent expansion/contraction algorithms for space savings.

The BLOCK clause is optional if the physical RECORD contains only one logical RECORD or if specified by the operating environment[85]; otherwise, it is mandatory.

RECOMMENDATION

- For consistency, always code the BLOCK clause, even if the physical RECORD equals the logical RECORD or if specified by the operating environment[85].

The next clause describes the logical RECORDS and is similar to BLOCK:

<u>RECORD</u> CONTAINS integer-1 <u>TO</u> integer-2 CHARACTERS

This clause is purely documentary because the RECORD length is derived from the JCL and/or the detailed data description of the FD.

COBOL[85] has an additional clause to specify variable length RECORDS:

<u>RECORD</u> IS <u>VARYING</u>[85] IN SIZE FROM integer-1 <u>TO</u> integer-2 <u>DEPENDING</u> ON data-name

RECOMMENDATIONS

- Do not use variable length RECORDS.
- Use the RECORD clause to inform the program reader of the approximate length of the logical RECORD.

<u>DATA</u> <u>RECORD</u>/S[74] IS/ARE data-name-1, data-name-2

The DATA RECORD[74] clause specifies two things:

- The file buffer area name used within the program for the FD.
- The existence of more than one data record in the specified file.

This is an optional clause in that this information is retrieved from either the JCL or the data description. However, it provides information to the maintenance programmer and therefore should be used for documentation.

RECOMMENDATION

- Use DATA RECORD[74] if supported to supply maintenance data.

<u>VALUE OF</u>[nr][74]   implementor-name-1 IS data-name-1/literal-1,
                          [implementor-name-2 IS data-name-2/literal-2],...

This clause was intended to provide security for media read by the program. It has two defects:

- It is static information in a dynamic world.
- Better ways of automated security are available.

RECOMMENDATION

• Do not use $\underline{\text{VALUE OF}}^{nr}_{74}$.

CODE-SET IS alphabet-name

The CODE-SET clause specifies the character set actually used by the external storage device for the specified file name. It is similar to the PROGRAM COLLATING SEQUENCE clause and the alphabet-name clause in that it permits different bit configurations to be processed (usually used for ASCII-to-EBCDIC conversions).

RECOMMENDATION

• $\underline{\text{CODE-SET}}$ should be copied if required.

$\underline{\text{LINAGE}}$ IS^{nr} data-name-1/integer-1 LINES
WITH $\underline{\text{FOOTING}}$ AT data-name-2/integer-2
LINES AT $\underline{\text{TOP}}$ data-name-3/integer-3
LINES AT $\underline{\text{BOTTOM}}$ data-name-4/integer-4

The LINAGE^{nr} clause was inserted into COBOL$_{74}$ to simplify the printing of pages in multipage reports. It specifies the physical PAGE size and then subdivides the physical PAGE into a logical PAGE containing a TOP^{nr}, body, FOOTING^{nr}, and BOTTOM^{nr}.

This ANSI clause is not supported by many compilers and would impair portability if used. Also, as stated before, COBOL should not be used to generate reports.

RECOMMENDATION

• Do not use LINAGE IS^{nr}.

The level indicator can also be SD^{nr} for sort, RD^{nr} for report, and CD^{nr} for communication. SD^{nr} indicates that the specified file-name is to be used as input to a COBOL SORT^{nr}. There are better ways to sort.

RECOMMENDATION

• Do not use SORT^{nr}.

RD^{nr} means that the specified file-name is to be used as input to the COBOL REPORT^{nr} writer. As recommended earlier, there are better methods to generate reports (also, COBOL$_{85}$ makes the REPORT writer^{nr} optional).

RECOMMENDATION

• Do not use REPORT^{nr}.

CD^{nr} is used in the optional COMMUNICATION SECTION^{nr} to specify parameters for the Message Control System to process input-output from remote terminals. Again, there are better ways to implement remote terminal communication, and also, many compilers do not support this.

RECOMMENDATION

- Do not communicate with COBOL.

SUMMARY OF RECOMMENDATIONS

- The entire FD portion of the DATA DIVISION should be copied.
- Always use ANSI standard labels where possible.
- Do not use variable length records; use expansion/contraction algorithms where effective.
- Always use the BLOCK CONTAINS, RECORD CONTAINS, and (if supported) DATA RECORD$_{74}$ clauses for consistency and maintenance documentation.
- The following clauses should <u>not</u> be coded:
  - VALUE OF[nr]
  - LINAGE[nr] IS ...
  - SD[nr] level (SORT/MERGE module)
  - RD[nr] level (REPORT writer module)
  - CD[nr] level (COMMUNICATION module)

7

Data Description in the DATA DIVISION

Technically, the data description portion of the DATA DIVISION is the second paragraph in the FILE SECTION. However, most authors treat it as a separate component because of its wordiness, and this text continues the tradition. COBOL has been described as a wordy language, meaning that it requires a significant number of words to produce a workable program. Most of that wordiness is in the data description.

4GLs

Many 4GL advertising pieces show a comparison between COBOL and their product, indicating that it takes minimal 4GL words to accomplish what it would take many pages of COBOL to achieve. Not only are the examples biased (naturally), but most of the COBOL wordiness is in the data description.

The data description does require the programmer to describe the data being used by the program in excruciating detail. This detail causes the wordiness and therefore the lopsided comparisons.

What the 4GL advertisements do not tell the reader is that the same amount of excruciating detail about the data must have been coded by somebody somewhere. The somewhere is usually in a data dictionary, which is accessible by the 4GL for its data descriptions.

The COBOL programmer has the same option via the COPY statement. COBOL provides a facility where common things can be placed into a library via the COPY statement. As you may have realized by now, I recommend COPY statements for virtually all the required entries defined to this point. One reason is that I am lazy and feel that it is better to have the system do whatever it can than for me to "reinvent the wheel." A second and more important reason is consistency: If all programmers use the same things, then maintenance, productivity, and readability are *exponentially* improved.

Those 4GL advertisements would not appear all that enticing if the COBOL programs displayed used COPY statements. If 4GLs are forced into truth in advertising, they will probably resort to pretty ladies in bikinis for distraction.

I am in favor of 4GLs. They do provide users with an easier method of accessing a database (the user does not need to know the name of the COPYLIB member), and they do provide dp with the possibility of prototyping. 4GLs are useful in their own right and do not need deceptive advertising!

The data description requires two entries:

- Level-number
- Data-name

LEVEL-NUMBER

Level-numbers can range from 01 to 49; level-numbers 66, 77, and 88 are reserved for special uses.

Leading 0

RECOMMENDATION

- Always use leading 0 for portability and maintainability.

The 01 level is reserved for the initial data description of a file-name specified in the SELECT clause. The 01 level must start in area A. The other level-numbers represent a hierarchical decomposition of the specified file-name; that is, a higher level-number is "owned" by the preceding lower-level number. For example:

```
01 owner of 02 and all subsequent higher level-numbers
   02 owned by 01 and owner of all higher level-numbers (i.e., the
      next 02 starts a new hierarchy)
      03 owned by "parent" (owner) level of 02 and thereafter
         by the "grandparent" level of 01
         04 etc.
```

RECOMMENDATION

- Place 01 in columns 8 and 9.

Indentation

All authors recommend the use of indentation to indicate hierarchy.

RECOMMENDATION

- Separate each level by four columns, which is the indicated breakpoint on the standard COBOL coding form (see Figure 2.1 in Chapter 2).

Level Spacing

Most authors recommend spacing of 5 between level-numbers:

```
01
    05
        10
            15
                20
                    25
                        etc.
```

The usual reason given is that this spacing provides for insertion of new levels, like this:

```
01
    03
        05
            07
                10
                    13
                        etc.
```

All documentation should be as meaningful to the reader as possible.

RECOMMENDATION

- Use a level spacing of 1 so that the reader instantly knows the level of the data hierarchy of each data element. Inserts can be easily handled by the various editing software available to development programmers.

NAMING DATA

The data-name is the specific name that the program can use to reference any group or elementary item. The syntax is 1 to 30 characters chosen from the set of

- 0 through 9
- A through Z (lowercase a through z are equivalent to uppercase)
- - (hyphen)

The data-name cannot start or end with a hyphen and must contain at least one alpha character (*A–Z*). Hyphens must be used to separate ''syllables'' since a space (blank) is used as a word separator.

The syntax is easy, but the construction of the data-name is difficult. One of the major readability (maintenance) problems in existing COBOL programs is the multiplicity of homonyms, aliases, and synonyms. Although there is some discrepancy in the formal definitions, the basic meanings are as follows:

Homonym   Two or more different items with the same data-name.
Alias   Multiple data-names for the same item.
Synonym   Multiple PIC clauses for the same item.

My client studies have consistently shown a ratio of 20 bad names for each required item. One article states that ratios of 200:1 have occurred![1] Maintaining programs— which are usually spaghetti-coded—that also have 20 or more data-names for the same item is at best difficult and usually impossible.

Each organization should have data-naming standards that are enforced by using COBOL COPY for data descriptions.

Data Element (Attribute) Naming Standards[2]

One of the largest DP quagmires is data element naming standards. There are absolutely no generally accepted standards, and not even IBM could make its OF language an accept- able standard. This section explores the quagmire with recommendations by the author (only fools rush in where angels fear to tread).

OF language (global naming).   The IBM OF language is a technique for cre- ating unique readable object names. The object name is formed with a single classword followed by a prime word followed by one or more modifiers, with each word separated by a predefined connector.

The syntax is as follows:

```
CLASSWORD/CONNECTOR/PRIME-WORD/CONNECTOR/FIRST-MODIFIER-WORD/
CONNECTOR/SECOND-MODIFIER-WORD/CONNECTOR/.../LAST-MODIFIER-WORD
```

The classword is a single alphabetic character with a specific meaning. These are the most commonly used letters and meanings:

A	amount (currency)	D	date
C	code	F	flag
G	group	P	percent
I	indicator	Q	quantity (count)
K	constant	T	text
M	name (identifier)	U	unidentified
N	number (identifier)	X	control

The connector is a single special symbol. Here are the most commonly used symbols and meanings:

	of		of
*	which is/are	/	which is/are
¦	or : or	$	or
&	and	#	and
/	by, per, within	a	by, per, within
-	compound-word	-	initiator

A cursory review of the symbols indicates that there is significant disagreement over the special symbols and their meaning. Most of these differences arise from available print "trains" (fonts) and/or the dominant programming language in an organization. The left-most column is the set specified in Appendix A of Guide Publication GPP-41, *DB/DC Data Dictionary Usage Manual* (Guide is an IBM user group—see the list of vendors in Appendix E for the address).

The prime word and the modifier words are usually taken from a list of predefined keywords. The modifier words are inserted in sequence from most general to most specific. The keywords are usually nouns and are usually limited to four, five, or six characters. At Logic University, the unabbreviated keyword list could contain these words:

student	instructor	alumni
course	major	minor
equipment	classroom	semester
history	dayofweek	degree (academic)

There is no generally accepted standard for forming abbreviations. A relatively easy technique is to force all names to the same length, eliminating all vowels (including *y*) except as the first letter of a word. If the name is still too long, eliminate consonants, beginning with the last consonant and working forward toward the beginning of the word. If the name is too short, add vowels from the beginning of the name or zeros up to the fixed length. Reserve the last character (byte) of the name for a tie-breaker digit. Here is the keyword list for Logic University with the last character reserved for the tie-breaker digit:

std0	stdn0	stdnt0
ins0	inst0	instr0
alm0	almn0	alumn0
crs0	cors0	cours0
mjr0	majr0	major0
mnr0	minr0	minor0
eqp0	eqpm0	eqpmn0
cls0	clss0	clssr0
sms0	smst0	smstr0
hst0	hstr0	histr0
dfw0	dfwk0	dafwk0
dgr0	degr0	degre0

The rules may be easy, but is the name created understandable? Here is the course table with the attribute names created using the classword table, the Guide connectors, and a four-character keyword list:

    N crs0   T crs0*tt10   M crs0 crr0-sch0*name0
    Q crs0*hrs0&crd0&mnm0   Q crs0*hrs0&crd0&mxm0
    Q crs0*cls0&mnm0   Q crs0*cls0&mxm0
    Q crs0*hrs0&drt0

Now here is the original course table:

    course-number
    course-title
    course.schoolname-curriculum
    course-hours-credit-minimum
    course-hours-credit-maximum
    course-classsize-minimum
    course-classsize-maximum
    course-hours-duration

To me, these OF names are gibberish! They may be useful to data administration personnel, but of what use are they to users, analysts, programmers, and everyone else? If these are the only names provided, the other users of the data dictionary have a right to believe that they have stumbled into the Black Hole of Calcutta or possibly the Twilight Zone. Longer keywords would certainly help (using six letters without a tie-breaker digit):

    N course   T course*title   M course crrclm-school*name
    Q course*hours&credit&minimm   Q course*hours&credit&maximm
    Q course*classz&minimm   Q course*classz&maximm
    Q course*hours&duratn

This is indeed better, but still confusing. (*Note:* I apologize for any incorrectly constructed names and/or wrong connectors. I do not believe the OF language is a solution.)

Prime word and class word.   A variation of the OF language suggested by Duncan Connell in the *Data Base Newsletter* (see Appendix E for address) is to place the prime word first followed by classword modifiers from general to specific. Using the identified entity types as prime words and the OF classwords (not the single alphabetic character) and the Guide connector symbols yields the following for the course table:

    course-number   course-title
    course*name school&curriculum   course-hours*credit&minimum
    course-hours*credit&maximum   course-classize*minimum
    course-classize*maximum   course-hours*duration

Definitely more understandable! Using the period as the OF symbol to confirm that a set of words is a single name helps:

course*name.school*curriculum

instead of

course*name school&curriculum

Modified English genitive structure.   The syntax of this structure is

ENTITY-TYPE/ADJECTIVE-MODIFYING-TYPE/
ADJECTIVE-MODIFYING-ATTRIBUTE/ATTRIBUTE-NAME/ATTRIBUTE-TYPE

Here is an example for Logic University:

ENTITY TYPE	student
ADJECTIVE MODIFYING ENTITY TYPE	undergraduate
ADJECTIVE MODIFYING ATTRIBUTE	current
ATTRIBUTE NAME	home address
ATTRIBUTE TYPE [similar to OF classword]	T (text)

Now the full attribute name of the preceding:

student-undergraduate-current-home-address-T

Here are suggested attribute type suffixes for this syntax:

A	amount (currency)	I	identifier (numeric or alpha)
C	code	P	percent
D	date	Q	quantity (count)

This list is shorter than the OF classword list, but the idea is the same.
The course table in this syntax looks like this:

course..number-I	course..title
course.curriculum-schoolname-I	
course.credit&minimum-hours-Q	course.credit&maximum-hours-Q
course.minimum-classize-Q	course.maximum-classize-Q
course.duration-hours-Q	

. = no entry

& = and

Thus **course..number-I** means that there is no adjective modifying course AND no adjective modifying number, and **credit&minimum** means that BOTH adjectives are applied to **hours.**

Vesely's syntax.   I have invented my own attribute syntax. For an attribute of a single entity type, I use this format:

ENTITY-TYPE/ATTRIBUTE-NAME/ATTRIBUTE-MODIFIER-1/ATTRIBUTE-
MODIFIER-2 .../ATTRIBUTE-MODIFIER-LAST

where the hyphen (-) is used to separate the components. For an attribute that is an intersection (junction of two or more entity types), I use this form:

ENTITY-TYPE-1/ENTITY-TYPE-2/.../ENTITY-TYPE-LAST/ATTRIBUTE-NAME/

where

A period (.) separates entity types.

A colon (:) separates the subtypes of a supertype entity type.

Brackets ([ ]) enclose a statement of the specific role that the attribute is playing in the definition.

A slash (/) identifies an OR attribute modifier.

The hyphen (-) separates the attribute name from the entity type and attribute modifiers from the attribute name.

Compound names, such as **day of week,** are compressed to **dayofweek.**

Entity type requires storage of independent data.

The attribute name should be a generic noun; the attribute modifiers should be specified from general to specific.

A process of generalization identifies supertype entity type and the subtypes (entity occurrences) associated with the supertype. The original entity type analysis at Logic University identified **student, alumni,** and **instructor** as separate entity types. All three, however, are in fact subtypes of a more generic supertype, **person-involved-with-courses.** It is advisable to show each subtype where possible separated by colons (:). Therefore, anything in the supertype **students, instructors,** or **alumni** should have a prefix of

student:instructor:alumni

Occasionally an attribute modifier, such as

current   taken   tally

is not an "adjective" but a description of the role that the attribute is playing at the instant of the table definition. The **student:instructor:alumni** table could contain two instances of

> student:instructor:alumni-number

The first occurrence is the identifier number (primary key) of a specific **student:instructor:alumni**; the second occurrence is the identifier number (foreign key) of a specific instructor who is playing the role of adviser to that specific student. The addition of the role brackets [ ] clarifies the situation.

> student:instructor:alumni-number   primary key
> student:instructor:alumni-number[adviser]   role (foreign key)

Another occurrence is the **course-prerequisite** table. How would you interpret the following?

> course-prerequisite(*course-number, course-number*)

Why is **course-number** repeated? Why are both keys? The confusion can be eliminated by adding the role:

> course-prerequisite(*course-number,course-number[prerequisite]*)

Because multiple subtypes and/or roles can occur, it is sometimes necessary to include a multiple OR attribute modifier. **Student** and **alumni** roles take a course; **instructor** teaches a course. The attribute modifier is **taken** or **taught.**

The now familiar course table looks like this:

> course-number   course-title
> course.schoolname-curriculum   course-hours-credit-minimum
> course-hours-credit-maximum   course-classize-minimum
> course-classize-maximum   course-hours-duration

This is very similar to the prime word and classword syntax. The difference becomes more apparent when trying to name subtypes:

What one prime word describes **student:instructor:alumni**

Or what class word describes a role

Or what combination of prime word and classword describes an intersection attribute such as portrayed in the **student:instructor.course-history** table?

> student:instructor:alumni-number
> student:instructor:alumni.course-number-taken/taught
> student:instructor:alumni.course-hours-credit-taken
> student:instructor:alumni.course-hours-credit-earned
> student:instructor:alumni.course-grade-earned

The data naming standard is understandable for these reasons:

- No abbreviations are used.
- The sequential syntax approximates normal English syntax.
- The special symbols -.:/[ ] describe classes rather than adjectival phrases (*of, which is/are, or, and,* etc.).

There are three major complaints:

- The name is too long (most data dictionaries have a restriction of 32 characters or less; the COBOL restriction is 30 characters).
- The special symbols are not implementable in programming languages such as COBOL.
- There are no classwords.

Abbreviations are difficult because there is no foolproof method for deriving standard abbreviations or determining which words to abbreviate. Mnemonics are easy. Mnemonisizing the prefix creates a short list of words that should be printed on all data dictionary reports. At Logic University:

C course	H school-name	M major:minor	R classroom
S student:instructor:alumni		T semester	

A better alternative is to have an expansion routine that converts each mnemonic to its full name.

RECOMMENDATION

- Use mnemonic prefixes; mnemonics should be the same length.

The mnemonisizing should reduce names to an acceptable length for most data dictionaries and programming languages. If the names are still too long, you must abbreviate.

The use of special symbols is a problem. Cobol restricts names to *A–Z, 0–9,* and - (hyphen). There is a solution, however. Since all data names are constructed from alpha characters, substitute numbers for the special symbols:

0 for .	1 for :	2 for /
6 or [	9 for]	

Thus the COBOL name for

> student:instructor:alumni.course-number-taken/taught

is

> s0c-number-taken2taught

instead of

s-c-number-taken-taught

Mnemonics and number substitution solve the length and special symbol complaints. What about the lack of classwords? Is anybody besides data administration personnel interested in them? Probably not. In any case, the OF classword mnemonic can be added as the final suffix and placed in the data dictionary as an approved data administration alias. If the classword is desirable, make it the final suffix of the primary name.

Automated Tools

I know of no tools that automatically construct standard data names. The various data dictionaries can enforce naming standards (usually via user exits). A few tools can expand short data-names into the real data-names.

Group Items

Group items are completely defined by the level number and the data-name. Elementary items require at least the PICTURE IS clause in addition to the level-number and the data-name.

COBOL$_{85}$ also supports an optional EXTERNAL$_{85}$/GLOBAL$_{85}$ clause (see Chapters 6 and 10 for more information).

PICTURE IS

PICTURE IS (the ANSI abbreviation of PIC has become standard and is recommended) defines the data type of the elementary item. Specifically, COBOL supports the following five data types:

1. ALPHABETIC	*A* through *Z* or *a* through *z*$_{85}$ and space
2. ALPHANUMERIC$_{85}$	Any allowable character in the specific computer's character set
3. NUMERIC[3]	0 through 9, operational sign (S), assumed decimal point (V), and assumed decimal scaling position (P)
4. ALPHANUMERIC-EDITED$_{85}$	Any allowable characters and certain editing symbols
5. NUMERIC-EDITED$_{85}$	Numeric plus certain editing symbols

Consistent with previous recommendations that COBOL not be used for remote terminal communication and/or printed reports, data types 4 and 5 should be avoided.

RECOMMENDATION

- Do not use edited options.

Eliminating the edited PIC clauses reduces the placeholder symbol list to A (alphabetic), X (alphanumeric), and 9 (numeric). Each of these symbols is a placeholder; it reserves one "space" for a character of the correct type.[4] For instance:

- AAA   Space is reserved for three alphabetic characters.
- XX   Space is reserved for two alphanumeric characters.
- 9   Space is reserved for one numeric character.

COBOL permits a replication factor to be used to reduce keystrokes. Instead of writing

AAAAAAAAAAAAAAAAAAAA

the programmer can write A(20), with the integer in the parenthesis representing the number of placeholder symbols.

RECOMMENDATION

- Use the replication factor.

It is relatively standard practice for programmers to code all alpha items as X. This invalidates the use of the class test (item is ALPHABETIC/NUMERIC) for alphabetic items.

RECOMMENDATIONS

- Use A when the character domain is $A-Z$ or a-z[85] and space.

Numeric items can have three nonplaceholder symbols (space is not reserved, but the symbol provides specific information to the compiler about the domain value):

S Operationsl sign (number can be positive or negative)
V Assumed decimal point of the number
P Assumed decimal point of the number when that decimal point is not within the range of the number actually stored by the PIC clause

The S can only be used once per PIC and must be the leftmost symbol. Failure to include the S means that all values placed into this numeric item are positive even if the original value was negative. This seemingly trivial oversight can cause significant problems in user reports and maintenance.

RECOMMENDATIONS

- Always use S in numeric PIC clauses.

- Use the sign condition to test for positive and negative (item/arithmetic-expression IS POSITIVE/NEGATIVE/ZERO).

Computers normally perform arithmetic operations with binary integers. Therefore, the decimal point cannot be used within the actual arithmetic operation. However, the program needs to know, and that is why the V is used. If the number is an integer, V is not required. "Negative" information can cause readability problems; that is, the lack of something implies its opposite. In this case, the lack of V means that the value must be an integer.

RECOMMENDATION

- Use V as the rightmost symbol for all integer PIC clauses.

P^{nr} was introduced into COBOL to provide limited floating-point capability without using the standard floating-point notation of mantissa and exponent. Each P represents an implied power of 10 that is not actually stored. When used, it usually represents small values. For instance, a PIC clause of

PIC SV999999999999999999 or SV9(18)

could be represented as

PIC SVPPPPPPPPPPPPPPP999 or SVP(15)999

if only the 16th, 17th, and 18th digits were actually to be stored.

P^{nr} can also be used on the left side of the decimal point for large values.

PIC S999999999999999999 or S9(18)V

could be represented as

PIC SPPPPPPPPPPPPPPP999V or SP(15)999V

again if only the 16th, 17th, and 18th digits were actually to be stored.

Most business COBOL programs require only dollars and cents and therefore P^{nr} is unnecessary. Where P^{nr} could be used, it is analogous to fixed length versus variable length.

RECOMMENDATION

- Never use P^{nr}; always use 9.

Finally, for readability:

RECOMMENDATION

- Always start the PIC clause in column 44.

USAGE IS

A numeric PIC clause can have a USAGE IS clause to specify the internal storage format. The USAGE IS clause is optional and defaults to DISPLAY. Again, COBOL should only use numeric items for computation.

RECOMMENDATION

- Use USAGE COMP (standard ANSI abbreviation) or $BINARY_{85}$ for numeric elementary items.

$COBOL_{74}$ allows only COMP, whose radix (base of a numbering system) and format are specified by the implementor. $COBOL_{85}$ allows $BINARY_{85}$, whose radix is 2, and $PACKED\text{-}DECIMAL_{85}$, whose radix is 10 and whose format should use minimum bits (usually four) to represent a single decimal digit.

Many compilers support other variations. For instance, various IBM compilers support these:

```
COMP-1  Short-precision internal floating point
COMP-2  Long-precision floating point
COMP-3  Packed decimal (probably equivalent to PACKED-DECIMAL₈₅)
COMP-4  System-independent binary (probably equivalent to BINARY₈₅)
```

Again, each organization should review and specify acceptable formats.

Let's look at the other optional clauses that pertain to a specific elementary item PIC clause.

<u>SIGN</u> IS <u>LEADING</u>/<u>TRAILING</u> [<u>SEPARATE</u> CHARACTER^{nr}]

The SIGN IS clause applies only to DISPLAY numeric elementary items for editing.

RECOMMENDATION

- Do not use SIGN IS (numeric items should be COMP or $BINARY_{85}$).

<u>BLANK</u> WHEN <u>ZERO</u>^{nr}

RECOMMENDATION

- Do not use BLANK WHEN ZERO (editing function).

<u>SYNCHRONIZED</u> <u>LEFT</u>/<u>RIGHT</u>

The SYNCHRONIZED clause permits a programmer to specify that the elementary numeric item begins on a computer internal boundary for more efficient computational processing. The application programmer should not need to know this information and it should be copied if required.

RECOMMENDATION

- Use COPY if SYNCHRONIZED LEFT/RIGHT is required.

<u>JUSTIFIED</u> RIGHT

The JUSTIFIED clause specifies nonstandard positions of data within a receiving data item.

RECOMMENDATION

- Use COPY if JUSTIFIED is required.

REDEFINES[nr] permits a previously defined storage to be redefined, and OCCURS allows variable occurrences of items and/or tables. The REDEFINES[nr] clause permits the storage of many different items in the same physical storage location. REDEFINES[nr] does not redefine items; it REDEFINES[nr] physical storage. For example:

```
02  item-tobe-redefined.
    03  elementary-item-1      PIC AAA.
    03  elementary-item-2      PIC A.
    03  elementary-item-3      PIC S99V.
02  redefining-item REDEFINES[nr]  item-tobe-redefined.
                                   PIC X(6).
```

Both **item-tobe-redefined** and **redefining-item** share the same physical storage location. The program can refer to **item-tobe-redefined** (or any of its subordinate elementary-items) or **redefining-item**. The **redefining-item** can also have subordinate elementary items.

```
02  redefining-item REDEFINES[nr] item-tobe-redefined.
    03  redefined-elementary-item-1 PIC S99V.
    03  redefined-elementary-item-2 PIC AA.
    03  redefined-elementary-item-3 PIC S9V.
    03  redefined-elementary-item-4 PIC S9V.
```

There are numerous restrictions on the use of REDEFINES[nr]. The major restriction is that the redefining-item must have the same physical size[74] as the item-tobe-redefined.[5] Note from the above *trivial* example that there can be more elementary-items in the **redefined** clause than the **item-tobe-redefined** clause (could also be less or the same) and that the length and type within the PIC clause can be different (or the same). This is one of the most complex clauses in COBOL and causes user report errors and maintenance problems. The reason for its use is to save physical memory storage, which is ludicrous in today's terms of megabyte storage.

RECOMMENDATION

- Do not use REDEFINES[nr]; if required for compatibility with existing systems, use a group MOVE (see MOVE description) to a WORKING-STORAGE redefinition of the item-tobe-redefined (also see the logical record discussion later in this chapter).

The OCCURS clause has two different functions:

- Processing of variable occurrences of an item
- Defining tables

The basic syntax for variable occurrences of items is

OCCURS integer-1 TO integer-2 TIMES DEPENDING[nr] ON data-name-1

The DEPENDING[nr] ON clause means that the specified item can occur a variable number of TIMES. The minimum number of TIMES is specified by **integer-1** (can be zero[85]), and the maximum number of TIMES is specified by **integer-2** (must be greater than **integer-1**). Note that the variable specified is the number of occurrences (TIMES), not the actual length of the item. Each item is always the same length in each occurrence.

The DEPENDING[nr] ON clause was placed into COBOL to handle variable-length trailer records. The master record contained one-to-one data on the master. For instance, the student master could contain

```
student-name
student-address-home
student-address-local
student-social-security-number
student-status (graduate/undergraduate, full/part-time, etc.)
...
```

where there was one occurrence of each elementary item per each occurrence of the student master.

The student trailers would contain one-to-many data. For instance, the **student-course-history** trailer could contain

```
course-number
course-title
course-grade
course-credit-earned-hours
course-credit-taken-hours
course-grade
instructor-name
...
```

and would occur from zero (entering freshman) to n (maximum number of courses that could be accumulated at the university). Each **student-course-history** is of the same physical size; only the number of occurrences is variable.

RECOMMENDATION

- Do not use the DEPENDING^{nr} ON clause for variable occurrences of an item. Use logical RECORDS (described later in this chapter).

The basic syntax for table definition is

<u>OCCURS</u> integer TIMES

where **integer** defines the number of fixed occurrences. An example:

```
02  table-1.
      03  table-entry      PIC A
                           OCCURS 12 TIMES.
```

This informs the compiler that there is an item (**table-1**) that requires 12 spaces (1×12) with each entry *individually addressable*. The table

```
02  table-2.
      03  table-entry      PIC S9(10)V
                           OCCURS 1000 TIMES.
```

informs the compiler that **table-2** requires 10,000 spaces (10×1000) and that each of the 1000 entries is individually addressable.

Defining **table-1** with individual PIC clauses would not be onerous but is bad programming.

```
02  table-1.
      03  table-entry-1     PIC A.
      03  table-entry-2     PIC A.
      03  table-entry-3     PIC A.
      03  table-entry-4     PIC A.
      03  table-entry-5     PIC A.
      03  table-entry-6     PIC A.
      03  table-entry-7     PIC A.
      03  table-entry-8     PIC A.
      03  table-entry-9     PIC A.
      03  table-entry-10    PIC A.
      03  table-entry-11    PIC A.
      03  table-entry-12    PIC A.
```

But defining **table-2** with individual PIC clauses would be onerous. Also, using individual PIC clauses prohibits the use of the powerful COBOL table-handling commands.

COBOL provides two methods for accessing individual table-entries: the subscript and the index. A subscript is defined as a numeric elementary item in WORKING-STORAGE; an index is defined by the INDEXED BY clause of the OCCURS statement. The index is a feature provided by the compiler and must not be defined anywhere else in the DATA DIVISION. There are four major differences:

- Method of accessing individual table-entries
- "Binding"
- Relative addressing
- PROCEDURE DIVISION statements

The index has flexibility over the subscript in $COBOL_{74}$ because relative addressing can be used. The basic syntax is

$$\text{data-name (index-name}_{74} \text{ or subscript}_{85} \text{ +/- integer)}^{nr}$$

where integer is a literal. Considering the earlier recommendation that literals not be used, relative addressing likewise should not be used. Placing a static offset into a dynamic world causes problems. The SET statement, discussed later, can provide dynamic offsets.

RECOMMENDATION

- Do not use relative addressing; use SET if dynamic offsetting is required.

COBOL provides PROCEDURE DIVISION statements/formats specifically for indices:

SET	Place value in index.
PERFORM VARYING	Loop through an indexed table.
SEARCH (ALL)	SEARCH an indexed table for specific condition(s).

These three instructions are discussed later; however, the PERFORM VARYING and SEARCH statements simplify table handling.

RECOMMENDATIONS

- Use indices whenever possible.
- Do not intermix subscripts and indices in the same data reference[85].

$COBOL_{74}$ permits three OCCURS clauses per table ($COBOL_{85}$ permits seven), thereby permitting one-dimensional tables (often called lists), two-dimensional tables, three-dimensional tables, and larger multidimensional[85] tables to be processed. For instance, if a university has ten colleges, a table providing the standard college names could be defined as follows:

```
01  college-name-table.
    02  college-name-standard   PIC A(16)
                                OCCURS 10 TIMES
                                INDEXED BY college-name-index.
```

If each college has 20 curricula, the table providing the ten standard college name and 20 standard curriculum names could be defined as follows:

```
01  college-name-table.
    02  college-name-standard   PIC A(16)
                                OCCURS 10 TIMES
                                INDEXED BY college-name-index.
        03  curriculum-name     PIC A(20)
                                OCCURS 20 TIMES
                                INDEXED BY curriculum-name-index.
```

Direct accessing using either subscripts or indices appears to be the same. The value corresponding to the sequential physical occurrence of the table-entry is placed into the subscript or index. For instance, the first table-entry in either table is accessed by placing a 1 in the subscript or index, table-entry-10 in either table by placing a 10 in the subscript or index, and table-entry-999 in the second table by placing a 999 in the subscript or index (any value greater than 12 would be invalid for the first table; any value greater than 1000 would be invalid for the second table).

The difference is in the actual execution of the subscript and index when the program is actually running. Some part of the operating system knows the starting absolute address of the table in the computer's memory. To address a particular table-entry requires that the offset (number of spaces from the beginning of the table to the starting space of the specified table-entry) be available (the actual physical address of the table entry is **absolute-starting-address + offset**). For instance, if each table-entry in a table occupies one basic unit of space and that table is physically stored at memory location space 1001, **table-entry-1** is in physical memory location 1001, **table-entry-2** in 1002, **table-entry-12** in 1012, and so on.

The difference between the subscript and the index at execution is that the subscript offset must be calculated, whereas the index contains the actual offset, thereby saving the calculation. The index thus enjoys a slight efficiency factor over subscripting.

The difference in deriving the offset causes a significant difference in binding the subscript or index to tables. A subscript can be bound to (used to access) any table in the DATA DIVISION, whereas the index can be bound only to the table that contains the OCCURS statement. A subscript therefore can be used for many tables and an index for a single specific table. The additional flexibility of subscripting is not an advantage. The possibility of having an incorrect value in the subscript when that subscript is being used for multiple tables—thereby causing user report errors and maintenance problems—is not worth any space or efficiency savings that are theoretically possible.

RECOMMENDATION

• If subscripts are used, limit each subscript to a single specified table; that is, treat the subscript as an index.

If each curriculum could be either major or minor and if each required a different number of credit-hours for graduation, the final table could be defined as follows:

```
01  college-curriculum-hours-table.
    02  college-name-standard          PIC A(16)
                                        OCCURS 10 TIMES
                                        INDEXED BY college-name-index.
        03  curriculum-name-standard   PIC A(20)
                                        OCCURS 20 TIMES
                                        INDEXED BY curriculum-name-index.
            04  major-minor-hours       PIC S99V
                                        OCCURS 2 TIMES INDEXED BY hours-index.
```

The space required is computed by multiplying the OCCURS; thus the **college-curriculum-hours-table** would require 4960 spaces.[6] The first index (**college-name-index**) is the *major* index; the second index (**curriculum-name-index**) is the *intermediate* index; the third index (**hours-index**) is the *minor* index. To find the specific hours required to graduate for a specific curriculum type in a specific college requires that all three indices be SET to the correct value. For instance, if Computer Science is the third college, COBOL is the fifth curriculum, and major comes before minor, the indices and their values are as follows:

```
        college-name-index      3
        curriculum-name-index   5
        hours-index             1
```

In effect, each dimension of the table is treated as a list, and the index for that list must be SET to the sequential physical occurrence of the entry in that list.

To loop through a table requires that each index be SET to 1, with the minor index being incremented until exhausted, then the intermediate index incremented until exhausted with the minor index reset to 1 each time, and then the major index incremented until exhausted with the minor and intermediate indices reset to 1 each time.

Table 7.1 shows the index values for looping through the following example table:

```
        01  example-table.
            02  major-entry     PIC A
                                OCCURS 2 TIMES
                                INDEXED BY major-index.
```

```
03  intermediate-entry   PIC A
                         OCCURS 3 TIMES
                         INDEXED BY inter-index.
     04  minor-entry      PIC A
                         OCCURS 4 TIMES
                         INDEXED BY minor-index.
```

TABLE 7.1 Index values for looping through a three-dimensional table

Major Index	Intermediate Index	Minor Index	
1	1	1	SET all indices to 1.
		2	
		3	
		4	minor-index exhausted. increment inter-index.
	2	1	reset minor-index to 1.
		2	
		3	
		4	minor-index exhausted. increment inter-index.
	3	1	reset minor-index to 1.
		2	
		3	
		4	minor-index exhausted. inter-index exhausted. increment major-index.
2	1	1	reset minor-index and inter-index to 1.
		2	
		3	
		4	minor-index exhausted. increment inter-index.
	2	1	reset minor-index to 1.
		2	
		3	
		4	minor-index exhausted. increment inter-index.
	3	1	reset minor-index to 1.
		2	
		3	
		4	minor-index exhausted. inter-index exhausted. major-index exhausted. end-of-loop (table).

Fortunately, the programmer does not have to perform this arithmetic; PERFORM VARY-ING or SEARCH maintains the indices. However, many studies have indicated that table handling is prone to programmer error and should be carefully coded and reviewed by senior programmers or programming quality control.

COBOL$_{85}$ permits seven levels of indexing, and the looping mechanism is the same except for the fact that seven indices are being incremented, exhausted, reset, tested, and so on. These multidimensional tables should be reviewed minutely.

RECOMMENDATIONS

- Assign one-dimensional table-handling programs to good programmers; assign two- or three-dimensional table-handling programs to better programmers; assign multidimensional table-handling programs to the best programmers.
- Conduct code inspections (structured walkthroughs) on table-handling portions of programs.

The ANSI OCCURS allows only numeric integer literals to specify the TIMES. Literals are also a source of bugs and cause maintainability problems. Most compilers support the non-ANSI format

OCCURS integer TIMES DEPENDING ON data-name$_{vs}$

which was intended to support a variable number of occurrences. However, nothing in the format prohibits it from being used to define a fixed-occurrence table. The technique is to equate **integer** to **data-name**, thereby making the table occurrences available to analysis software.

RECOMMENDATION (non-ANSI)

- Use the DEPENDING ON clause to define the *fixed* number of occurrences for all tables if supported.

Finally, OCCURS has an ASCENDING/DESCENDING optional clause that is used in conjuction with the SEARCH ALL statement. It defines whether the data values in the table are arranged in ASCENDING or DESCENDING sequence. This is described further in the discussion of SEARCH ALL.

Two topics referring to data names remain: FILLER and dataname qualification.

FILLER is a reserved word meaning that memory spaces must be reserved (defined by a PIC clause) but bits are not explicitly accessible to the program. This is an ANSI attempt at data security. The data must be safe since the program cannot explicitly access the dataname. The operative adjective is *explicitly*; there is no prohibition on a group move, and the receiving area could be defined. For instance:

```
01  student-record.
    02  student-name     PIC A(20).
    02  FILLER           PIC S9V99.      (or XXX for more security.)
```

where FILLER is really the student-grade-point-average, which could be MOVE to

```
01 student-record-ws.
   02 student-name-ws            PIC A(20).
   02 student-grade-point-average  PIC S9V99.
```

making the student-grade-point-average now accessible. Table-handling statements can also access or modify FILLER fields.

FILLER is definitely better than the common technique of defining all record fields regardless of whether the program accesses the field.

COBOL$_{85}$ permits FILLER to be omitted and it is assumed. Never assume.

RECOMMENDATION

• Use FILLER where required for maintainability and portability.

88s can be used with FILLER to provide condition-names while logically protecting the field from modifications.

The best way to prevent access is to use logical records. A logical record is composed of only the fields that are actually referenced by the program. For instance, the entire RECORD could be

```
01 student-record.
   02 student-name                            PIC A(20).
   02 student-telephone-number (or FILLER)   PIC S9(10)V.
   02 student-address-home                    PIC X(60).
   02 FILLER                                  PIC X(40).
   02 student-address-local                   PIC X(60).
   02 FILLER                                  PIC X(40).
   02 student-address-employer                PIC X(60).
```

The logical record for a program only requiring name, local address, and phone could be

```
01 student-local-logical-record.
   02 student-name                PIC A(20).
   02 student-address-local       PIC X(60).
   02 student-telephone-number    PIC S9(10)V.
```

The fields do not have to be in the same sequence as the original RECORD and can be in any sequence required by the program.

The significant advantage to logical records is *data independence*, which relates to the freedom that data has from the programs and the freedom that programs have from the data:

• Data not read into a program cannot be accessed or modified.

• Changes to PIC clauses do not affect any program that does not specifically reference that data. (If the PIC clause of a FILLER item changes, all programs that use the record containing the FILLER item must be recompiled and probably retested.)

Logical records were not developed for data independence; they were developed to eliminate "programmer navigation." Most current business applications interface to a database management system (DBMS) to access the data. Many DBMSs require significant knowledge of the physical structure of the database to perform any operation (programmer navigation). Many programmers do not have this knowledge, and their programs are either very inefficient or cause corruption (database contains erroneous data and/or fails). Some DBMS vendors have recognized this problem and provided a logical record facility (LRF). In a logical record environment, the programmer need only specify the fields that the program requires, and some system software provides those fields. Consistent with previous recommendations that COBOL programmers should program only business logic, each organization should use or develop a logical record facility to be employed by all programmers in all programs.

RECOMMENDATION

- Use a logical record facility for all data access. If LRF is not available, use FILLER to mask all fields not referenced by a program.[7]

Qualification distinguishs between identical datanames in different structures. Some datanaming standards require that datanames be generic; that is, the dataname of **address-home** would be used for students, instructors, alumni, deans, janitors, guards, and others without any differentiating prefix or suffix. A RECORD might look like this:

```
01 address-record.
   02 student.
      03 address-home   PIC X(60).
   02 instructor.
      03 address-home   PIC X(60).
   02 alumni.
      03 address-home   PIC X(60).
   02 dean.
      03 address-home   PIC X(60).
```

A statement in the PROCEDURE DIVISION referencing **address-home** would be unresolvable because the compiler would not know which of the **address-home** data names was being referenced. Qualification is used to distinguish between the identical data names. The syntax is

data-name OF/IN data-name-1 [OF/IN data-name-2]...

ANSI does not restrict the number of OF/IN clauses[8] and permits qualified datanames to be subscripted and/or indexed (subscript and/or index-name follows the final

OF/IN clause data-name). For instance, the student **address-home** could be accessed as

address-home OF student OF address-record

The OF address-record clause is not required because the OF student clause uniquely identifies (qualifies) a specific **address-home**. However, if there was a similar record in WORKING-STORAGE:

```
01  address-record-ws.
    02  student.
        03  address-home   PIC X(60).
    02  instructor.
        03  address-home   PIC X(60).
    02  alumni.
        03  address-home   PIC X(60).
    02  dean.
        03  address-home   PIC X(60).
```

full qualification is required:

address-home OF student OF address-record/address-record-ws.

I believe in the underlying theory of qualification—that data-names should be generic and should be the same across all entity types in an organization.[9] My naming standard uses an entity type prefix to differentiate between generic attributes (data-names) of different entity types:

student.address-home
instructor.address-home
alumni.address-home
dean.address-home

The OF language uses classwords and connectors to separate:

T.address-home*student
T.address-home*instructor
T.address-home*alumni
T.address-home*dean.

Using any of the data naming standards previously discussed would eliminate the need for qualification. However, if a pure generic data-name is used, some form of qualification is required.

COBOL qualification is wordy and confusing. A better way is to use the REPLACING option of the COPY statement or the REPLACE[85] statement. Assuming that entity type prefixing is to be used, the generic data-names could be stored in the COBOL COPY library as follows:

prefix-generic-data-name-1
prefix-generic-data-name-2
prefix-generic-data-name-3

...

prefix-generic-data-name-n

The prefix characters are then replaced by the appropriate entity type identifier as required in each program by the appropriate COPY REPLACING or REPLACE$_{85}$ statement.

RECOMMENDATION

- Use a data naming standard that does not require qualification; if qualification is required, use the COPY REPLACING or REPLACE$_{85}$ statement to effect.

SUMMARY OF RECOMMENDATIONS

- Code level 01 in columns 8 and 9 of area A.
  Always use leading 0 for portability.
  Increase each higher level number by 1.
  Indent each higher level by four columns.
- Establish a data naming standard.
  Use COPY REPLACING or REPLACE$_{85}$ if qualification is required.
- Use PIC instead of PICTURE IS and code in columns 44 through 46.
  Use nonedited formats only.
    Use alphabetic A where character domain permits.
    Use alphanumeric X for any legitimate character.
    Use numeric 9 only for computations (USAGE COMP or BINARY$_{85}$).
      Always use S.
        Use sign condition to test for positive and negative values.
      Always use V (even for integers).
      Never use P^{nr}.
    Use replication factor to minimize keystrokes.
- Use COPY for the following clauses if required:
  SYNCHRONIZED LEFT/RIGHT.
  JUSTIFIED RIGHT (highlight to warn maintenance programmers).
- Do not use the following clauses:
  SIGN^{nr} IS LEADING/TRAILING SEPARATE CHARACTER.
  BLANK^{nr} WHEN ZERO.
  REDEFINES^{nr} (use group MOVE to WORKING-STORAGE if function is required for compatibility).
- For the OCCURS CLAUSE:
  Do not use TIMES DEPENDING ON to define a variable number of occurrences.
  Do use TIMES DEPENDING ON$_{vs}$ to define a fixed number of occurrences if supported (non-ANSI).
  Use indices only.

If subscript must be used, limit subscript to a single table.

Do not intermix subscripts and indices in the same data reference[nr].

Do not use relative[nr] addressing; use SET for dynamic offsetting.

Use experienced programmers to write OCCURS.

Conduct code inspections.

- For **RECORDS**:

    Do not use variable-length records (use compaction/expansion system software where feasible).

    Use logical records to access only the data fields required by a program (requires a logical record facility).

    Use FILLER if logical record facility unavailable to mask data fields not required by a program.

NOTES

1. "Improving Data Consistency, Reliability and Accuracy" - 22-05-08, Data Base Management, Auerbach Publishers, Inc.

2. The following details on datanaming standards are based on E. Vesely, *The Practitioner's Blueprint for Logical and Physical Database Design* (Englewood Cliffs, N.J.: Prentice-Hall, 1986).

3. $COBOL_{74}$ allows only fixed-point numbers to be stored in either DISPLAY format or numeric format suitable for arithmetic operations (COMPUTATIONAL). Many compilers allow floating-point and various forms of numeric storage. $COBOL_{85}$ permits $BINARY_{85}$ and $PACKED\text{-}DECIMAL_{85}$. Each installation should review carefully and prescribe the acceptable formats.

4. Space is the number of bits required to store the specified character. It differs from computer to computer and is also dependent on the USAGE clause for numeric items.

5. Determining the actual physical size required becomes difficult when COMP and SYNC clauses are used. The difficulty increases if the computer/compiler allows slack bytes and /or permits the redefining-item to be smaller than the item-to-be-redefined. Slack bytes (which contain no meaningful data) are inserted by the compiler and/or programmer between items to ensure correct alignment of numeric items on internal boundaries for efficient computation.

6. $(16 \text{ PIC} \times 10 \text{ OCCURS}) + [20 \text{ PIC} \times 200 (10 \text{ OCCURS} \times 20 \text{ OCCURS})] + [2 \text{ PIC} \times 400 (10 \text{ OCCURS} \times 20 \text{ OCCURS} \times 2 \text{ OCCURS})] = 160 + 4000 + 800 = 4960$

7. For more information, see E. Vesely, *The Practitioner's Blueprint for Logical and Physical Database Design* (Englewood Cliffs, N.J.: Prentice-Hall, 1986).

8. $COBOL_{74}$ requires that at least five levels of qualification be provided; $COBOL_{85}$ requires at least 50 levels!

9. An entity type is something that an organization needs to maintain independent information about.

8

Special Level-Numbers in the DATA DIVISION

There are three special (reserved) level-numbers:

66^{nr} RENAMES

77^{nr} Noncontiguous independent elementary items in WORKING-STORAGE and LINKAGE sections

88   Condition-names

66 RENAMES

The 66 RENAMES^{nr} level permits alternate data-names (aliases) or alternate structures. The following example RECORD is used for illustration:

```
01  example-record.
    02  group-item-1.
        03  elementary-item-1a    PIC A.
        03  elementary-item-1b    PIC AA.
    02  group-item-2.
        03  elementary-item-2a    PIC AAA.
        03  elementary-item-2b    PIC AAAA.
        03  elementary-item-2c    PIC A(5).
```

```
                02 group-item-3.
                   03 elementary-item-3a     PIC A(6).
                   03 elementary-item-3b     PIC A(7).
                   03 elementary-item-3c     PIC A(8).
                   03 elementary-item-3d     PIC A(9).
```

The simplest syntax of the 66^{nr} is:

```
        66ⁿʳ  data-name-1          RENAMES  data-name-2.
```

Two examples are:

```
        66ⁿʳ  group-item-a         RENAMES  group-item-1.
        66ⁿʳ  elementary-item-x    RENAMES  elementary-item-1a.
```

This syntax permits a programmer to create aliases that are a major contribution to maintenance problems.

RECOMMENDATION

- Do not use the single 66^{nr} data-name syntax.

The alternate structure syntax of the 66^{nr} is:

```
        66ⁿʳ  data-name-1          RENAMES  data-name-2
                                   THRU     data-name-3.
```

Two examples are:

```
        66ⁿʳ  alternate-structure-1  RENAMES  group-item-1
                                     THRU     elementary-item-2b.
        66ⁿʳ  alternate-structure-2  RENAMES  elementary-item-2b
                                     THRU     elementary-item-3c.
```

PROCEDURE DIVISION statements could access the example-record either via the data-names in the original record or via the alternate-structure names in the 66^{nr} levels. For instance, the statements

```
        MOVE group-item-1                    TO ...
        MOVE elementary-item-2a              TO ...
        MOVE elementary-item-2b              TO ...
```

can be replaced by

```
        MOVE alternate-structure-1           TO ...
```

Similarly, the statements

                MOVE elementary-item-2b   TO ...
                MOVE elementary-item-2c   TO ...
                MOVE elementary-item-3a   TO ...
                MOVE elementary-item-3b   TO ...
                MOVE elementary-item-3c   TO ...

can be replaced by

                MOVE alternate-structure-2   TO ...

The foregoing examples indicate the shorthand capability of 66^{nr}, which permits a reduction in wordiness. Programmers can also create lists (one-dimensional tables) by using 66^{nr}. For example, if the PIC clauses of the example-record were all PIC A, the following 66^{nr} levels could establish lists:[1]

```
66ⁿʳ   tally-group-item-1-and-group-item-2
                  RENAMES   group-item-1
                  THRU      group-item-2.
66ⁿʳ   tally-group-item-1-and-group-item-2-and-group-item-3
                  RENAMES   group-item-1
                  THRU      group-item-3.
66ⁿʳ   tally-group-item-2-and-group-item-3
                  RENAMES   group-item-2
                  THRU      group-item-3.
```

and the INSPECT verb with the TALLYING clause (verbs are described later) could be used to tally (count) the occurrences of specific alpha characters (letters) in the alternate structures.

The alternate structure 66^{nr} RENAMES does offer some benefits. They are out-weighed, however, by the following disadvantages:

- There are many compiler restrictions on its use.
- Confusion and maintenance problems occur when it it combined with REDEFINES.
- The alternate structure data-name can mask the actual data-name.
- Many programmers do not understand 66^{nr}.
- 66^{nr} is static information in a dynamic environment; for example, if **elementary-item-2d** is inserted at the end of **group-item-2,** then **alternate-structure-2** is probably wrong.

RECOMMENDATION

- Do not use 66^{nr} RENAMES.

77 LEVEL

The 77^{nr} level is basically used for storage of switches (flags) and counters. It could be used for literal definition. Here are some typical COBOL switches:

77^{nr}	end-of-file (yes/no)	PIC A.
77^{nr}	more-records (yes/no)	PIC A.
77^{nr}	execution-ok (yes/no)	PIC A.

These are typical counters:

77^{nr}	number-of-master-records	PIC S9(6)V.
77^{nr}	number-of-transaction-records	PIC S9(6)V.
77^{nr}	number-of-additions	PIC S9(6)V.
77^{nr}	number-of-deletes	PIC S9(6)V.
77^{nr}	number-of-updates	PIC S9(6)V.

Unfortunately, 77^{nr} is not normally used for literal definition since most programmers simply code the literals as constants in the PROCEDURE DIVISION. ANSI could have saved DP billions of maintenance dollars if it had insisted that literals be defined only in WORKING-STORAGE because impact analysis could then be done with software.

77^{nr} items are elementary and must contain a PIC clause. This restriction limits the usefulness of 77^{nr}. The following constructions are easier to understand and therefore to maintain.

```
01 program-switches.
   02 end-of-file                        PIC A.
   02 more-records                       PIC A.
   02 execution-ok                       PIC A.
01 program-counters.
   02 number-of-master-records           PIC S9(6)V.
   02 number-of-transaction-records      PIC S9(6)V.
   02 number-of-additions                PIC S9(6)V.
   02 number-of-deletes                  PIC S9(6)V.
   02 number-of-updates                  PIC S9(6)V.
```

RECOMMENDATION

- Do not use 77^{nr} levels.

88 LEVEL

The 88 level is used to define specific condition-names for specific VALUES of a data-name. The condition-name can then be used effectively in IF statements. For instance, if the status of a student can be

student-status	VALUE
undergraduate	1
graduate	2
full-time	4
part-time	8
day-student	16
night-student	32

then the PROCEDURE DIVISION coding could be

```
IF student-status =  1      THEN85 PERFORM . . .
IF student-status =  2      THEN85 PERFORM . . .
IF student-status =  4      THEN85 PERFORM . . .
IF student-status =  8      THEN85 PERFORM . . .
IF student-status = 16      THEN85 PERFORM . . .
IF student-status = 32      THEN85 PERFORM . . .
```

The meaning of the IF statements is clear: Specific routines are invoked because of a specific value in **student-status**. Unfortunately, what that value defines cannot be ascertained from the code. The maintenance programmer must read external documentation to determine the actual meanings of such values. The first problem is that the documentation probably does not exist; if the documentation does exist, it was probably produced manually and is probably out of date. As numerous studies have indicated, maintenance programmers rarely read and almost never rely on manually produced documentation because it does not reflect the current status of the program.

The superior method is to use 88s:

```
01 student-record.
   02 student-status        PIC S99V.
      88 undergraduate      VALUE    1.
      88 graduate           VALUE    2.
      88 full-time          VALUE    4.
      88 part-time          VALUE    8.
      88 day-student        VALUE   16.
      88 night-student      VALUE   32.
```

The PROCEDURE DIVISION coding is now as follows:

```
IF undergraduate      THEN85 PERFORM . . .
IF graduate           THEN85 PERFORM . . .
IF full-time          THEN85 PERFORM . . .
IF part-time          THEN85 PERFORM . . .
IF day-student        THEN85 PERFORM . . .
IF night-student      THEN85 PERFORM . . .
```

The maintenance programmer now knows that specific routines are invoked and can tell what condition invoked that specific routine merely by reading the code. The code is the current status, and the maintenance programmer is reading correct documentation.

Other benefits of the 88 technique include eliminating literals from the PROCE-DURE DIVISION and impact analysis.

Impact Analysis

Impact analysis is the term generally used to describe the procedure for evaluating the effect on programs of modifying a data element's metadata. For instance, if the **student-status** values must be revised to

student-status	VALUE
undergraduate	UN
graduate	GR
full-time	FT
part-time	PT
day-student	DS
night-student	NS

a maintenance programmer must locate every program that actually used **student-status** and painstakingly change 1 to UN, 2 to GR, 4 to FT, 8 to PT, 16 to DS, and 32 to NS. Combining 88s with COPYLIB requires that only the single COPYLIB member be changed and only programs that have **student-status** in the DATA DIVISION be recompiled. No change is required to the PROCEDURE DIVISION.

RECOMMENDATION

- Always use 88 levels.

Binary Progression

You may have noticed an unusual progression in the numeric VALUES OF **student-status** (1, 2, 4, 8, 16, 32) instead of the "normal" progression (1, 2, 3, 4, 5, 6). The unusual progression is binary (related to powers of 2):

$$2^0 = 1 \qquad 2^1 = 2 \qquad 2^2 = 4 \qquad 2^3 = 8 \qquad 2^4 = 16 \qquad 2^5 = 32$$

The binary progression permits unique VALUES to be established for all valid combinations:

- A student is either an undergraduate or a graduate.
- A student is either full-time or part-time.
- A student is either a day-student or a night-student.

A student must be a valid combination of these three conditions.

The 88 coding is as follows:

```
01  student-record.
    02  student-status                                    PIC S99V.
        88  undergraduate                                 VALUE    1.
        88  graduate                                      VALUE    2.
        88  full-time                                     VALUE    4.
        88  full-time-undergraduate                       VALUE    5.
        88  full-time-graduate                            VALUE    6.
        88  part-time                                     VALUE    8.
        88  part-time-undergraduate                       VALUE    9.
        88  part-time-graduate                            VALUE    10.
        88  day-student                                   VALUE    16.
        88  day-student-undergraduate                     VALUE    17.
        88  day-student-graduate                          VALUE    18.
        88  day-student-full-time                         VALUE    20.
        88  day-student-full-time-undergraduate           VALUE    21.
        88  day-student-full-time-graduate                VALUE    22.
        88  night-student                                 VALUE    32.
        88  night-student-undergraduate                   VALUE    33.
        88  night-student-graduate                        VALUE    34.
        88  night-student-full-time-undergraduate         VALUE    37.
        88  night-student-full-time-graduate              VALUE    38.
```

The 88s in this listing represent all the valid permutations of **student-status.** Many programmers would say it is too wordy. It is not if it is coded once, placed in the COPYLIB, and copied into any program that needs **student-status.** In fact, the 88/COPYLIB technique compares favorably with 4GLs in the sparseness in processing any valid permutations of status data elements.

The **student-status** is made complete by adding one more 88:

```
88  invalid-student-status        VALUES 3, 7, 11, 12, 13, 14, 15, 19,
                                          23, 24, 25, 26, 27, 28, 29,
                                          30, 31, 35, 36, 39, 40, 41,
                                          ..., 99
```

The THRU phrase can be used to reduce the number of numeric entries.

```
88  invalid-student-status        VALUES 3, 7, 11 THRU 15, 19, 23 THRU
                                          31, 35, 36, 39 THRU 99.
```

An arithmetic progression does not work:

```
        88  undergraduate     VALUE    1.
        88  graduate          VALUE    2.
        88  full-time         VALUE    3.
        88  part-time         VALUE    4.
        88  day-student       VALUE    5.
        88  night-student     VALUE    6.
```

For example, the value of 4 could be **part-time** or **full-time-undergraduate;** the value of 5 could be **day-student** or **part-time-undergraduate** or **full-time-graduate.**

Status Items

Many programmers would use separate elementary items for each status:

```
01 student-record.
   02 student-status.
      03 undergraduate-graduate    PIC A.
         88 undergraduate          VALUE    "U".
         88 graduate               VALUE    "G".
      03 fullpart-time             PIC A.
         88 full-time              VALUE    "F".
         88 part-time              VALUE    "P".
      03 daynight-student          PIC A.
         88 day-student            VALUE    "D".
         88 night-student          VALUE    "N".
```

The first problem with this technique is that it wastes storage media space. If each PIC A requires one byte (eight bits), then the above student-record wastes two bytes per student. If **insured** were substituted for **student** and this record were part of the U.S. Social Security System, the wasted space would exceed 400 million bytes on external storage! External storage is inexpensive and declining, but saving space with a technique that simplifies maintenance is desirable. For instance, a programmer interested in all full-time undergraduate students who attend days needs only to code

```
                    IF day-student-full-time-undergraduate
```

with the single elementary item, whereas the coding with the multiple elementary items is

```
             IF      undergraduate
             AND full-time
             AND day-student
```

If the programmer does not know how to use AND or the programming standards do not permit AND, then

```
             IF      undergraduate
               IF    full-time
                 IF    day-student
```

or other inelegant coding results.

Changing the example to reflect real programs where the status elementary item could have 10, 15, 20, or more valid values causes the complexity of multiple status data elements to increase exponentially. Add the requirement of testing different legitimate status elementary items such as the query

```
   How many students are undergraduate AND full-time AND attend days AND
   have a major of computer science AND a minor of mathematics OR physics?
```

and the coding required by multiple unnecessary status data elements becomes a nightmare even if structured programming techniques are used.

RECOMMENDATIONS

- Combine all valid status values into a single elementary item.
- Define the entire domain of the status data element with 88s.
- Use a binary progression to ensure unique values for legitimate permutations.

VALUE IS

The specific format

<u>VALUE</u> IS/<u>VALUES</u> ARE   literal-1[<u>THROUGH</u>/<u>THRU</u> literal-2]...

can be used in the WORKING-STORAGE SECTION to initialize VALUES for any elementary item. This is usually used to set specific data items to ZERO or SPACE. ZERO (ZEROS), SPACE (SPACES), QUOTE (QUOTES), HIGH-VALUE^{nr} (HIGH-VALUES)^{nr}, and LOW-VALUE^{nr} (LOW-VALUES)^{nr} are figurative constants that can be used in place of literals in any format that accepts literals. QUOTE is rarely used; HIGH-VALUE^{nr} and LOW-VALUE^{nr} are normally used as ''flags'' that control file processing; for example, LOW-VALUE^{nr} indicates that the file is OPEN but no records have been read, and HIGH-VALUE^{nr} indicates that the last record has been read and processed. As will be explained later, there are better ways to code BOF and EOF conditions.

ALL   The COBOL high-nucleus module allows the use of ALL in the VALUE clause to repeat a non-numeric literal:

```
01  all-example.
    02  data-item-with-repeated-value    PIC X(100)
                                          VALUE ALL "*".
```

would initialize **data-item-with-repeated-value** to all *. This is certainly easier than writing

```
VALUE "*********************************..."
```

ALL can be used with figurative constants, but it is redundant.

```
    02  data-item-to-be-initialized      PIC 10(A)
                                          VALUE SPACES.
                                   or
                                          VALUE ALL SPACES.
```

is equivalent.

RECOMMENDATIONS

- Avoid figurative constants in the PROCEDURE DIVISION.
- Never use HIGH-VALUE[nr] and LOW-VALUE[nr].
- Standardize on a single spelling (personal preference is ZERO, SPACE, and QUOTE because the other spellings are not supported in the nucleus low level[74]).
- Use ALL where appropriate to reduce keystrokes.

Some books recommend the combinative use of VALUE and REDEFINE[nr] to "trick" COBOL[74] into initializing tables. The normal example is the two-alpha-character U.S. state postal code:

```
01 state-codes.
    02 FILLER  PIC A(20)   VALUE  "AKALARAZCACOCTEDFLGA".
    02 FILLER  PIC A(20)   VALUE  "HIIAIDILINKSKYLAMAMD".
    02 FILLER  PIC A(20)   VALUE  "MEMIMNMOMSMTNCNDNENH".
    02 FILLER  PIC A(20)   VALUE  "NINMNVNYOHOKORPARISC".
    02 FILLER  PIC A(20)   VALUE  "SDTNTXUTVAVTWAWIWVWY".
   *FILLER is used since each statecode is addressed via an index
01 state-code-table  REDEFINES state-codes
             PIC AA       OCCURS 50 TIMES.
```

The state-code-table is not directly initializable because COBOL[74] does not permit the VALUE clause and the OCCURS clause to be used in combination. I have no objection per se to this trick, but I still prefer the state-code-table to be defined separately, with the state codes moved into the state-code-table in the initialization paragraph:

```
    02 state-codes      PIC A(100)  VALUE  "AKAL . . ."
    02 state-code-table  PIC AA     OCCURS 50 TIMES.
```

The advantage of this coding is that it eliminates the need for REDEFINES[nr], which can be used inappropriately.

COBOL[85] permits the VALUE clause to be specified within the OCCURS clause and therefore the VALUE/REDEFINES[nr] trick is no longer necessary.

RECOMMENDATION

- Do not use VALUE/REDEFINE[nr] to initialize tables.

SUMMARY OF RECOMMENDATIONS

- Do not use 66[nr] or 77[nr] levels.
- Use 88 levels to define completely the domain of any status item.
  Combine all status items into a single elementary item.
  Use binary coding to establish unique permutations.

- Regarding figurative constants:
  Avoid in the PROCEDURE DIVISION.
  Never use HIGH-VALUE[nr] or LOW-VALUE[nr].
  Standardize on a single spelling.
  Use ALL.
- Do not use VALUE/REDEFINES[nr] to initialize tables.

NOTE

1. Data-names exceed the COBOL limitation of 30 characters; they are used for clarity.

9

Other Sections in the DATA DIVISION

The DATA DIVISION can have the following other sections:

- WORKING-STORAGE SECTION.
- LINKAGE SECTION.
- REPORT SECTION[nr] (optional in COBOL$_{85}$)
- COMMUNICATION SECTION[nr]

NONRECOMMENDED SECTIONS

The REPORT SECTION[nr] permits COBOL to generate printed reports. Specific report generation software such as Mark IV/V and Culprit is easier to use. COBOL should be restricted to implementing business logic.

RECOMMENDATION

- Do not use the REPORT SECTION[nr].

The COMMUNICATION SECTION[nr] permits COBOL to communicate with remote terminals (CRTs, local printers, etc.). Specific system software such as CICS, CMS, and TSO, is significantly easier to use.

RECOMMENDATION

- Do not use the COMMUNICATION SECTION[nr].

WORKING-STORAGE SECTION

The WORKING-STORAGE SECTION is the data "Workhorse" of COBOL. Data is READ into and written from the FILE SECTION of the DATA DIVISION. Data is normally processed in the WORKING-STORAGE SECTION by PROCEDURE DIVISION statements.

ANSI specifies a basic organization:

```
WORKING-STORAGE SECTION
77[nr]        level elementary items.
01            hierarchical records.
```

Since 77[nr] levels should not be used, WORKING-STORAGE should be composed of groups of 01 levels. Most programs are in fact written this way. However, many development programmers assume that their programs are perfect and never need debugging. Unfortunately, most programs do need debugging, and some may require memory dumps.[1]

The following organization is recommended for

- Readability
- Logical data element isolation
- Providing memory dump tracers[2]

```
WORKING-STORAGE SECTION.
  01 program-unique-data.
    02 FILLER                          PIC A(8)       VALUE "COUNTERS".
    02 program-record-counters.
      03 @@@@@@-record-counter         PIC S9(?)V     USAGE COMP
                                                       VALUE ZERO.
*@@@@@@ is replaced by appropriate prefix
*comment on how @@@@@@-record-counter is incremented
      03 @@@@@@-record-counter         PIC S9(?)V     USAGE COMP
                                                       VALUE ZERO.
*comment on how @@@@@@-record-counter is incremented
      03 ...
    02 FILLER                          PIC A(8)       VALUE "KEYFIELD".
    02 program-key-fields.
      03 @@@@@@-key-field-1            PIC ?.
```

```
*comment on how @@@@@@-key-field-1 is used
        03  @@@@@@-key-field-2          PIC ?.
*comment on how @@@@@@-key-field-2 is used
        03  ...
    02  FILLER                          PIC A(8)      VALUE "CONSTANT".
    02  program-constants.
        03  constant-1                  PIC ?         VALUE ?.
*comment on how constant-1 is used
        03  constant-2                  PIC ?         VALUE ?.
*comment on how constant-2 is used
        03  ...
    02  FILLER                          PIC A(8)      VALUE "TABLES   ".
    02  program-tables.
        03  @@@@@@-table                PIC ?         OCCURS ?.
*comment on how @@@@@@-table is used
        03  @@@@@@-table                PIC ?         OCCURS ?.
*comment on how @@@@@@-table is used
        03  ...
01  paragraph-unique-parameters.
    02  FILLER                          PIC A(8)      VALUE "PARMS   ".
    02  P???-input-parameters           PIC ?.
*??? is paragraph prefix number (see chapter 2)
    02  P???-output-parameters          PIC ?.
    02  P???-control-parameters         PIC ?.
    02  ...
01  @@@@@@-read-into.
    02  FILLER                          PIC A(8)      VALUE "@@@@@@@@".
*@@@@@@ is replaced by record name
01  @@@@@@-read-into-area               PIC ?.
01  @@@@@@-write-from                   PIC ?.
    02  FILLER                          PIC A(8)      VALUE "@@@@@@@@".
01  @@@@@@-write-from-area              PIC ?.
01  working-storage-end.
    02  FILLER                          PIC A(8)      VALUE "WSEND   ".
```

FILLER provides a known "eyecatcher" for maintenance programmers scanning a memory dump trying to isolate a programming bug. In a formatted dump (a software-driven printout of the character equivalent of the bits), words like **counters** and **keyfields** are appropriate and should be standardized. If only unformatted hex (base 16) or octal (base 8) dumps are available, appropriate hex and octal tracers should be used, for example:

$$COFFFEFF_{16} \qquad \text{for counters}$$
$$FEFFFEFD_{16} \qquad \text{for keyfields}$$
$$COFFFAFF_{16} \qquad \text{for constant}$$
$$FFAFFEFF_{16} \qquad \text{for tables}$$

The tracers permit quick partitioning of the memory dump. ANSI does not require memory dumps, but most vendors do supply them (see Chapter 10). Users of small computers may feel that memory dumps are passé and no longer useful; mainframe users might disagree. The reason is that small computers tend to have small programs and few simultaneous users, whereas large mainframes tend to have large programs and many simultaneous users. An abend on a small computer is usually isolated to a specific program area and a specific user transaction with a reasonably defined error code; an abend on a mainframe usually has an ill-defined error code with no indication as to the user transaction that caused the abend. In this case, the memory dump provides a snapshot of what data was actually being processed at the moment of the abend. Sometimes this is the only clue!

In any case, memory tracers such as COUNTERS, KEYFIELDS, and CONSTANT require minimal coding time and will pay rich rewards when a memory dump must be analyzed.

RECOMMENDATIONS

- Use standardized tracers to provide quick visual partitioning of memory dumps.
- Use formatted memory dumps when possible.

The grouping of related data elements (counters, keyfields, constants, etc.) under a single group item again simplifies finding them in a memory dump. Each organization should establish a standard sequence.

RECOMMENDATION

- Group related WORKING-STORAGE data elements under their own group item in an organizational defined sequence.

As mentioned in the preface, COBOL$_{74}$ provides only GLOBAL storage in the DATA DIVISION proper and in WORKING-STORAGE. GLOBAL storage means that any arithmetic and data manipulation statement in the PROCEDURE DIVISION can access and modify any named item. It can be extremely difficult to determine how an elementary item was modified in a spaghetti-coded program that features REDEFINES[nr], RENAMES[nr], and CORRESPONDING[nr]. A second problem is that GLOBAL storage permits lazy development programmers to omit documentation on what parameters are passed between each paragraph and/or SECTION thereby requiring investigation by the maintenance programmer to determine the data transformations performed by each paragraph or SECTION.

Logical isolation by establishing separate paragraph-unique-parameters divided into input, output, and control provides the maintenance programmer with a clear understanding of the parameters used in each paragraph and forces the development programmer to document and think about those parameters. This, coupled with a recommendation in Chapter 10 that each paragraph contain comments about the parameters, provides an effective static means of isolating and defining parameters.

Static Documentation

Static documentation is a snapshot of something (in this case it is the parameters) in a program at a particular moment of time (such as the original coding by a development programmer). Any changes by any programmer that are not redocumented cause the static documentation to be out of date. Maintenance programmers do not normally refer to out-of-date static documentation because it usually causes more confusion than assistance. Dynamic documentation is always up to date, since it is derived from the current status of the program.

RECOMMENDATIONS

- Use a separate group item to logically isolate the parameters for each paragraph.
- Use dynamic documentation when possible; keep static documentation updated.[3]

READ INTO and WRITE FROM

"Efficient" programmers would complain about the inefficiency of the group MOVE generated by COBOL to perform a READ INTO or a WRITE FROM. These programmers forget that current mainframes run at many million executed instructions per second (mips), and CPUs that operate at 1 billion instructions per second (bips) or more are envisioned. A current mainframe can perform thousands of READ INTO in a single second. The benefit is documentation when there is an abend. The maintenance programmer can see what the original input was in the FD and what changes were made in WORKING-STORAGE (READ INTO); what was supposed to be written out and what actually was written out (WRITE FROM). This sometimes provides the only clues to the program's malfunctions. To accentuate INTO/FROM use, only 01 group items with no subordinate breakdowns should be used in the DATA DIVISION.

RECOMMENDATIONS

- Always use READ INTO and WRITE FROM.
- Always use 01 group items with no elementary items in the DATA DIVISION (COBOL$_{85}$ partially enforces this recommendation).

GENERAL RECOMMENDATION

- Use COPY wherever possible.

SUMMARY OF RECOMMENDATIONS FOR THE WORKING-STORAGE SECTION

- Use a standardized format with defined FILLER tracers.
- Use formatted memory dumps.
- Group related elementary items under their own group item.

- Never use 77^{nr} levels.
- Logically isolate each paragraph's parameters.
- Always use READ INTO and WRITE FROM.
  Always define DATA DIVISION FD with only the 01
  level with no subordinate elementary items.
- Use COPY.

LINKAGE SECTION

The only other recommended optional section in this text is the LINKAGE SECTION. The LINKAGE SECTION is used to allow a *called* program (a subprogram invoked by a CALL statement in another program, the *calling* program) to share data residing in the calling program. The $CALL_{74}$ statement basically passes the address where the data is stored in the calling program. Therefore, the LINKAGE SECTION does not require any memory space in the called program. The LINKAGE SECTION provides restricted storage (as opposed to the GLOBAL storage of the DATA DIVISION and the WORKING-STORAGE SECTION) in that the called program can only directly modify the contents of the items passed in the LINKAGE SECTION.[4]

COBOL$_{85}$ can also pass only the value (BY CONTENT$_{85}$) of the defined items that cannot be modified in the calling program by the called program.

RECOMMENDATIONS for the LINKAGE SECTION

- Never use 77^{nr} levels.
- Place all parameters (elementary items) into a single group item (further discussion in the description of the CALL statement in Chapter 10).

SUMMARY OF RECOMMENDATIONS FOR DATA DIVISION SECTIONS

- Do not use REPORT SECTION^{nr} or COMMUNICATION SECTION^{nr} because there are better ways to perform both functions.
- WORKING-STORAGE SECTION
  Do not use 77^{nr} levels.
  All entries should be groups of 01 levels.
    The 01 levels should be separated by standardized memory tracer keywords.
    The 01 levels should provide logical data element isolation.
- LINKAGE SECTION
  Do not use 77^{nr} levels.
  All parameter elementary items should be placed into a single 01 group item.
- Use formatted memory dumps when required.
- Use dynamic documentation wherever possible.
  Keep static documentation updated.

- Always use READ INTO and WRITE FROM.
  Each DATA DIVISION entry should contain only the 01 level with no subordinate levels.
- Use COPY as much as possible.

NOTES

1. Debugging is the *art* of detecting, tracing, and deleting errors from computer programs. A memory dump involves printing the contents of a specified portion of memory to assist in debugging. The memory dump can be specifically requested or automatically generated by an abend (abnormal termination). Memory dumps are often the last resort since many other debugging tools are currently available. However, some old spaghetti mainframe COBOL programs are so intertwined that only memory dumps can provide debugging clues.

2. A memory dump tracer is a specific word or bit configuration used to partition memory dumps into easy-to-locate segments. Words often used are **counters, keyfield,** and **constant;** bit configurations often used are **cofffeff**$_{16}$ and **fefffefd**$_{16}$.

3. For instance, to maintain the static parameter documentation, a cross-reference (xref) report should be printed after each compilation and parameter metadata updated if required. (An xref report lists all PROCEDURE DIVISION statements that reference a data item.)

4. Many compilers produce executable code that can erroneously destroy some or all of the calling program memory by permitting an index or subscript to exceed its legal range. Preventive measures are presented in the discussion of the CALL statement in Chapter 10.

——— *10* ———

The PROCEDURE DIVISION

The PROCEDURE DIVISION is the optional$_{85}$ fourth division of a COBOL program. It is the only division header that has an optional clause:

<u>PROCEDURE</u> <u>DIVISION</u> [<u>USING</u> identifier-1, identifier-2,...]

The presence of the optional USING clause defines this program as a *called* subprogram. The identifiers identify parameters (items) that are shared with the calling program. These parameters must be explicitly defined in the called program LINKAGE SECTION.[1] Further details are available in the description of the CALL statement later in this chapter.

The PROCEDURE DIVISION has the following hierarchical structure:

- SECTION
  A logical subdivision that can contain from zero to many paragraphs
- PARAGRAPH
  A set of related sentences that effect a function
- SENTENCE
  One or more statements that terminate with a period and a space (.)
- STATEMENT
  A set of syntactically valid combinations of words and symbols that begins with a VERB. A statement usually

instructs the compiler to generate executable code to effect a specific transaction (such as MOVE *a* TO *b*).

SECTION

The SECTION name must begin in area A (column 8) and must be unique within the program. The prefixing technique described in Chapter 2 should also be used for each SECTION:

Column 8   S (to distinguish SECTION from paragraph)
Column 9   Level of the invoked SECTION
Column 10 Hierarchical sequence number of the SECTION that invoked
           this SECTION
Column 11 Hierarchical sequence number of the invoked SECTION
Column 12 (-) hyphen

The actual SECTION name should be readable and should briefly describe the function of the SECTION.

Sections are optional unless the program meets one of these criteria:

- It uses the REPORT WRITER[nr] (optional in $COBOL_{85}$).
- It uses the SORT[nr] verb.
- It requires segmentation[74] (overlay).
- It requires DECLARATIVES[nr].

The REPORT WRITER[nr] and the SORT[nr] verb are not recommended; thus no sections are required for these purposes.

Segmentation is required whenever the program executable code does not fit into available memory. However, most mainframes have virtual storage (VS),[2] thereby eliminating the need for segmentation[74].[3] Hewlett-Packard and Burroughs use stack architecture for some of their computers,[4] and segmentation can be required. In this case, SECTION with following optional clause must be used.

prefix-section-name SECTION   segment-number[74].

The **segment-number[74]** divides the program into segments with each SECTION having the same **segment-number[74]** belonging to the same SEGMENT. The **segment-number[74]** has a domain of 00 to 99 with the actual value determining whether the SEGMENT[74] is

- permanent fixed[74]
- overlayable fixed[74]
- independent[74]

A fixed SEGMENT$_{74}$ is logically considered always to be in memory (the operating system may swap the fixed SEGMENTs$_{74}$ but such swapping is transparent to the programmer and program).[5] A permanent fixed SEGMENT$_{74}$ cannot be overlaid. An overlayable fixed SEGMENT$_{74}$ can be overlaid but is always restored to the state it was in before swapping (it is not reinitialized). An independent SEGMENT$_{74}$ can be overlaid and is always restored in its initial state. Table 10.1 is a recap.

TABLE 10.1 SEGMENT$_{74}$ Characteristics

SEGMENT$_{74}$ Type	Overlayable	Reinitialized
Permanent fixed	no	no
Overlayable fixed	yes	no
Independent	yes	yes

Any SEGMENT$_{74}$ with a **segment-number$_{74}$** of 50 to 99 is independent. Any SEGMENT$_{74}$ with a **segment-number$_{74}$** of 00 to 49 is permanent fixed unless a SEGMENT-LIMIT$_{74}$ is used:

$$\underline{\text{SEGMENT-LIMIT}_{74} \text{ is segment-number}_{74}}$$

where **segment-number$_{74}$** has a range of 00 to 49. Any SEGMENT having a **segment-number$_{74}$** below the specified SEGMENT-LIMIT$_{74}$ **segment-number$_{74}$** is permanent fixed; otherwise, it is overlayable fixed.

Segmentation$_{74}$, if required, is difficult. Segmentation$_{74}$ should be done by a system programmer in conjuction with the development programmer.

RECOMMENDATIONS

- Do not use segmentation$_{74}$ unless required.
- Have a system programmer assign **segment-numbers$_{74}$**.

DECLARATIVES provide asynchronous processing of two kinds of procedures:

- Input-output error-checking procedures
- REPORT WRITER[nr] exception procedures

DECLARATIVES, if required, should be copied into the program.

Most programs do not require sections. The question then is should sections be used even if not required? The answer is derived from structured programming theory. Most structured programming authorities state that each program module should be a "black box."[6] A black box has a single entrance at the top, performs a single function, and has a single exit at the bottom.

A module in a COBOL program can be either a SECTION or a paragraph because both can be specifically invoked by name. A SECTION usually has many subordinate paragraphs and therefore many potential entrances. The existence of many entrances violates structured programming theory, and therefore a SECTION with subordinate paragraphs should not be used because a maintenance programmer cannot determine from reading the code how a SECTION is invoked.

RECOMMENDATIONS

- Do not use SECTION unless specifically required.
  If SECTION is required, use SECTION without subordinate paragraphs unless the paragraphs are specifically required.
- Each SECTION should have an identifying prefix and a meaningful name.
- Each paragraphless SECTION should be formatted like paragraphs (see discussion that follows).

Caution: ANSI standards require that each paragraph be part of a SECTION if any SECTION has a subordinate paragraph.

PARAGRAPHS

Paragraphs are the basic building blocks. The recommended format is

```
     prefix-paragraph-name.
     *************************************************************
     *narrative describing the paragraph function
     *narrative describing the paragraph function
     *narrative describing the paragraph function
     *etc.
     *
     *@IN parameters used by this paragraph
     *@IN parameters used by this paragraph
     *@IN parameters used by this paragraph
     *etc.
     *@OUT parameters derived by this paragraph for later use
     *@OUT parameters derived by this paragraph for later use
     *@OUT parameters derived by this paragraph for later use
     *etc.
     *@OUT CONTROL control information being returned to invoking module
     *************************************************************


     *
          COBOL statement


          COBOL statement
     *   Comments describing any unusual statements

          COBOL statement
```

```
           ...
     *
          prefix-X. EXIT.

          EJECT (or / in column 7 if supported)
```

The prefix is the paragraph numbering technique recommended in Chapter 2 and described briefly under SECTION in this chapter. If the paragraph is part of a SECTION, the recommended prefix is

Column 8	P
Column 9	Hierarchical sequence number of this paragraph within the SECTION
Column 10	S
Columns 11–13	SECTION prefix number
Column 14	- (hyphen)

A paragraph name must be unique within the program or within a SECTION if a SECTION is used. If the identical paragraph-name is used in two or more sections, it must be qualified:

```
          PERFORM      paragraph-name IN/OFⁿʳ      section-name.
```

RECOMMENDATION

- Paragraph qualification should never be used; all paragraph-names should be unique.

The paragraph-name should be meaningful and should briefly describe the function of the paragraph.

The row of asterisks is an eye-catcher separator.

The narrative is comment lines that describe the paragraph function in structured English, pseudocode, or any other acceptable documentation technique. Note that more than one comment line is usually required.

*@IN defines the parameters that the paragraph uses to perform its function. Usually more than one *@IN is required.

Note: If the paragraph does not need any input, *@IN *NONE* should be used.

*@OUT defines the parameters that the paragraph created for subsequent use by other modules. Usually more than one *@OUT is required, and if there is no output, *@OUT *NONE* should be used.

*@OUT CONTROL defines any control information (such as ''no more transactions'') being returned to the invoking module.

The syntax of the model paragraph has been written so that it can be documented automatically by the ADPAC PM/SS software documentation package. PM/SS prints narratives for all paragraphs consisting of all comment lines immediately following the paragraph-name. *@ in columns 7 and 8 is a flag for PM/SS to collect the parameters for separate analysis and documentation. Other software documentation packages require different syntax, but the intent is the same—source-driven automatic documentation. The syntax of the available documentation package should be used.

The row of asterisks is again an eye-catcher separator.

The last statement should be followed by a blank line (or ∗) and an EXIT paragraph. The recommended format for the EXIT paragraph is the paragraph prefix (for instance, P327-) followed by the letter X. The EXIT statement is placed in area B on the same line. This convention absolutely defines the end of the paragraph and is useful for other purposes, described later in this chapter.

The EJECT (non-ANSI but usually supported) or the / in column 7 (ANSI but usually *not* supported) is used to skip to the top of the next page in the source listing, thereby mechanically isolating each paragraph and making the source listing easier to read.

RECOMMENDATIONS

- Use paragraphs instead of sections whenever possible.
- The paragraph-name should consist of an identifying prefix and a meaningful name.
- Each paragraph should contain sufficient comments about its function and parameters.
- A software documentation package should be used to print narratives, parameter usage, item cross-references, and the like.
- Each paragraph should terminate with EXIT and EJECT.

SENTENCE

A sentence consists of one or more statements terminated by a period and space (.). Most programs consist of single-statement sentences since many programmers believe that each statement must be terminated by a period and space. Basically, the compiler searches for the verb that is the beginning of a new statement rather than the period and space. The compiler translates each statement into the appropriate executable code. Therefore, the following code is equivalent:

```
MOVE a TO b        MOVE a TO b.
MOVE c TO d        MOVE c TO d.
MOVE e TO f        MOVE e TO f.
MOVE g TO h        MOVE g TO h.
```

MOVE is an imperative statement that specifies an unconditional action. Imperative statements in any sequence do not need to be terminated by a period and space; a semicolon (;) or comma (,) may also be used interchangeably as a statement separator for readability.

RECOMMENDATION

- Do not separate imperative statements with a period and space; use proper formatting (discussed later) for readability.

The compiler does need to know about sentences when interpreting conditional statements (statements that can interrupt sequential processing by transferring control to another program module). For instance, a valid IF syntax is

IF condition NEXT SENTENCE

which informs the compiler to transfer control to the NEXT SENTENCE if the condition is true. Obviously, the compiler needs the period and space to locate the NEXT SENTENCE.

$COBOL_{85}$ has incorporated the explicit scope terminators$_{85}$ shown in Table 10.2.

TABLE 10.2 $COBOL_{85}$ explicit scope terminators$_{85}$

END-ADD$_{85}$	END-CALL$_{85}$	END-COMPUTE$_{85}$	END-DELETE$_{85}$
END-DIVIDE$_{85}$	END-EVALUATE$_{85}$	END-IF$_{85}$	END-MULTIPLY$_{85}$
END-PERFORM$_{85}$	END-READ$_{85}$	END-RECEIVE$_{85}$	END-RETURN$_{85}$
END-REWRITE$_{85}$	END-SEARCH$_{85}$	END-START$_{85}$	END-STRING$_{85}$
END-SUBTRACT$_{85}$	END-UNSTRING$_{85}$	END-WRITE$_{85}$	

A scope terminator$_{85}$ can be used instead of the period and space to terminate statements. The explicit scope terminators$_{85}$ are the superior method for two main reasons:

- They eliminate spurious periods, which can cause maintenance problems.
- They provide explicit, easy-to-see statement boundaries.

RECOMMENDATION

- Replace periods with scope terminators$_{85}$. If your compiler does not support them, include them as comment lines (*). This still provides the easy-to-see statement boundaries and also forces the programmer to determine the actual statement scope.

STATEMENTS

$COBOL_{74}$ divides statements into three categories, and $COBOL_{85}$ added delimiter scope$_{85}$ statements:

- imperative   Specifies an unconditional action to be taken or is a conditional statement delimited by its explicit scope terminator[85]

- conditional   Specifies a condition to be tested and the action to be taken depending on the condition status

- compiler directing   Specifies an action to be taken by the compiler during compilation

- delimited scope[85]   Consists of any statement that includes its explicit scope terminator[85]

Statement Category

Each statement category is divided into subcategories. The ANSI list appears in Figure 10.1. ANSI specifies four types of statements: imperative, conditional, compiler directing, and delimited scope. Imperative and conditional statements are further divided into subtypes.

imperative	arithmetic	ADD, COMPUTE[nr], DIVIDE, INSPECT (TALLYING), MULTIPLY, SUBTRACT
	data movement	ACCEPT (DATE, DAY, DAY-OF-WEEK[85], TIME, MESSAGE COUNT[nr]), INITIALIZE[nr][85], INSPECT (REPLACING), MOVE, STRING[nr], UNSTRING[nr]
	ending	STOP, EXIT PROGRAM
	input-output	ACCEPT (IDENTIFIER[nr]), CLOSE, DELETE, DISABLE[nr], DISPLAY[nr], ENABLE[nr], OPEN, PURGE[nr][85], READ, RECEIVE[nr], REWRITE, SEND[nr], START[nr], STOP (literal[nr][74]), WRITE
	inter-program	CALL, CANCEL
	ordering[nr]	MERGE[nr], RELEASE[nr], RETURN[nr], SORT[nr]
	procedure branching	ALTER[nr], CALL, CONTINUE[85], EXIT, GO TO, PERFORM
	report writing[nr]	GENERATE[nr], INITIATE[nr], SUPPRESS[nr], TERMINATE[nr]
	table handling	SET
conditional	arithmetic	ADD (SIZE ERROR), COMPUTE[nr] (SIZE ERROR), DIVIDE (SIZE ERROR), MULTIPLY (SIZE ERROR), SUBTRACT (SIZE ERROR)

continued

	data movement	STRING^{nr} (OVERFLOW), UNSTRING^{nr} (OVERFLOW)
	input-output	DELETE (INVALID KEY), READ (END or INVALID KEY), RECEIVE^{nr} (DATA), REWRITE (INVALID KEY), START^{nr} (INVALID KEY), WRITE (INVALID KEY OR END-OF-PAGE^{nr})
	inter-program	CALL (OVERFLOW or EXCEPTION$_{85}$)
	ordering^{nr}	RETURN^{nr}
	table-handling	SEARCH (ALL)
	testing	EVALUATE$^{nr}_{85}$, IF
compiler directing		COPY, ENTER$^{nr}_{74}$, REPLACE$_{85}$, USE, /
delimited scope		END-ADD$_{85}$, END-CALL$_{85}$ END-COMPUTE$_{85}$, END-DELETE$_{85}$, END-DIVIDE$_{85}$, END-EVALUATE$_{85}$, END-IF$_{85}$, END-MULTIPLY$_{85}$, END-PERFORM$_{85}$, END-READ$_{85}$, END-RECEIVE$_{85}$, END-RETURN$_{85}$, END-REWRITE$_{85}$, END-SEARCH$_{85}$, END-START$_{85}$, END-STRING$_{85}$, END-SUBTRACT$_{85}$, END-UNSTRING$_{85}$, END-WRITE$_{85}$

Figure 10.1   ANSI statement subcategories.

Words in parentheses are optional generic clauses for a statement and can change whether the statement is imperative or conditional. For instance, the use of the SIZE ERROR clause in any appropriate arithmetic statement makes that statement conditional.

Most compilers, if not all, add verbs, clauses, and other terms to extend COBOL's capabilities. Extensions are discussed where appropriate.

Procedure Branching

GO TO   The GO TO statement is probably the most infamous verb in programming history. Its infamy began in an article by Edsger Dijkstra published in 1968 titled ''GOTO Statement Considered Harmful.''[7] Professor Dijkstra had examined numerous programs and determined that bad (spaghetti) programs had more GO tos than good (structured) programs. The obvious conclusion was that fewer GO tos are better. The least less is zero and so go to less programming was created. Proponents of go to less programming forgot that the objective of structured programming is code that is easy to read and understand. Elimination of every GO TO usually requires multinested IF statements to effect the correct transfer of control. The multinested IF and other artificial constructs are more difficult to understand than a simple GO TO.

Dave Higgins in his 1981 article "Structured Maintenance,"[8] wrote a simple report program consisting of 30 statements including five GO tos. He redid the program (using a Warnier-Orr diagram) to eliminate the five GO TO statements. His conclusions:

- The new program had 33 percent more lines of code.
- A new end-of-file switch was required to control the loops.
- The program had become badly fragmented, requiring constant flipping back and forth between pages of the source listing.

His final conclusion was that the new go to less program would be "harder for someone to pick up and read than the original." Imagine the exponential increase in difficulty in understanding if the program contained 3000 statements instead of 30.

The GO TO confusion is basically caused by the fact that most people do not distinguish between the "villainous" network GO TO and the "innocent" local GO TO.

Network. The network[nr] GO TO transfers control outside of the paragraph or SECTION in which it was executed; for example:

```
paragraph-a.

    ...

    GO TO paragraph-c.

paragraph-b.

    ...

    GO TO paragraph-d.

paragraph-c.

    ...

    GO TO paragraph-b.

paragraph-d.

    ...

    GO TO paragraph-e.
```

Each GO TO in this program is a network[nr] GO TO in that it transfers control to a different paragraph. Two GO tos are "backward" in that they transfer control to a paragraph higher in the program hierarchy. The GO TO logic must sooner or later return to the main processing path. This usually requires the testing of switches since a GO TO does not have an automatic return. The switches are often "buried" in multinested IF statements using meaningless literals, thereby creating the unreadable spaghetti programs.

RECOMMENDATION

- Network[nr] GO TO should be abolished.

Local. A local GO TO transfers control within the same paragraph. Only two local GO TO statements are possible:

- A backward GO TO to the top of the paragraph

```
                    paragraph-local.

                    ...

                    GO TO paragraph-local.

                    ...
```

- A terminating GO TO to the paragraph EXIT[9]

```
                    paragraph-local.

                    ...

                    GO TO paragraph-local-exit.

                    ...

                    GO TO paragraph-local-exit.

                    ...

                    paragraph-local-exit.    EXIT.
```

Structured programming theory allows three types of iteration structures (loops):

$$\text{dountil} \qquad \text{dowhile} \qquad \text{doinfinite}$$

The iteration structure consists of a block of statements to be executed and a condition to be tested to determine if the iteration continues. In Figure 10.2, the rectangle is the block of statements, the diamond is the condition, and the circle is a collector. The **dountil** (part a) executes the block once and then tests the condition. If the condition is false, the block is reexecuted. The **dowhile** (part b) tests the condition first, and if the condition is true, the block is executed. (If the condition is false on the first test, the block is never executed.) The **doinfinite** (part c) places the condition within the block. If the condition is true, the iteration is terminated; otherwise, the rest of the block is executed and control returns to the top of the block.

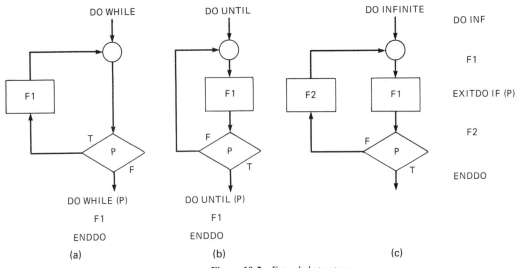

Figure 10.2 Extended structures.

COBOL$_{74}$ implemented only one of the three iteration structures (PERFORM UNTIL, discussed later in the chapter, is a version of **dowhile**). Implementing the other iteration structures in COBOL$_{74}$ requires local GO TO constructs.

Two local GO TO statements are required to implement a **dountil:**

```
paragraph-dountil.

    block F1

    IF dountil-condition true
            GO TO paragraph-dountil-exit
    ELSE dountil-condition false
            GO TO paragraph-dountil.
    END-IF

paragraph-dountil-exit.     EXIT.
```

An alternate COBOL **dountil** construct is

```
paragraph-dountil-control.

    PERFORM paragraph-dountil
    END-PERFORM

    PERFORM paragraph-dountil
        UNTIL dountil-condition true.
```

END-PERFORM

paragraph-dountil-control-exit. EXIT.

The first imperative PERFORM executes F1 as required by the **dountil**; the second conditional PERFORM UNTIL tests P as required by the **dountil**. This alternative construct requires two paragraphs and is therefore more complicated than the single paragraph using a local GO TO.

RECOMMENDATION

• Use local GO TO constructs to simulate **dountil**.

Two local GO TO statements are also required to implement a **doinfinite**:

paragraph-doinfinite.

    block F1

    IF doinfinite-condition true
      GO TO paragraph-doinifinite-exit
    ELSE doinfinite-condition false
      NEXT SENTENCE.

    block F2

    GO TO paragraph-doinfinite.

paragraph-doinfinite-exit. EXIT.

RECOMMENDATION

• Use local GO TO constructs to simulate **doinfinite**.

$COBOL_{85}$ has added support for the **dountil** iteration structure. A full discussion is provided under PERFORM in this chapter.

Another excellent and recommended use of the terminating local GO TO is to transfer control to the EXIT paragraph whenever any of a multiple set of terminating conditions is detected.

The actual formats for the GO TO statement are as follows:

Format 1   <u>GO</u> TO procedure-name-1

Format 2^{nr} <u>GO</u> TO procedure-name-1, procedure-name-2, ...
            <u>DEPENDING</u> on identifier

Format 3^{nr} <u>GO</u> TO.

RECOMMENDATION

- Always use GO TO for portability.

Notes: Commas (,) or semicolons[85] (;) are not required as separators (see Format 2) but can be used to increase readability. Normally, any number of spaces can also be used to increase readability. Format 3 is really a sentence because the period is required.

Format 1 is the simple GO TO, and **procedure-name-1** is the name of a SECTION or paragraph. It is alterable (see ALTER[74] syntax in this chapter).

Format 3 must be altered[74] before execution.

Format 2 is the ANSI implementation of the numeric case structure. In structured programming theory, the case structure requires that each value in the domain of a numeric identifier be unique and require specific processing (see Figure 10.3).

The Format 2[nr] identifier is a numeric integer with a one-to-one correspondence with the procedure-names:

value 1	invokes procedure-name-1
value 2	invokes procedure-name-2
value "n"	invokes procedure-name-n

GO TO DEPENDING ON   GO TO DEPENDING[nr] ON is a shorthand method of writing many IF statements:

```
IF      value = 1
        GO TO procedure-name-1
IF      value = 2
        GO TO procedure-name-2
IF      value = n
```

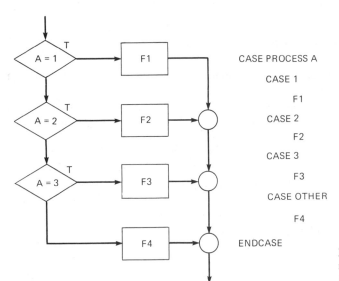

```
CASE PROCESS A

   CASE 1

       F1

   CASE 2

       F2

   CASE 3

       F3

   CASE OTHER

       F4

ENDCASE
```

Figure 10.3 The extended structures for numeric case provides superior readability and superior performance.

```
                                    GO TO procedure-name-n
                    END-IF
```

Since many compilers allow more than 2000 procedure-names, the theoretical savings in writing time can be significant. Unfortunately, most COBOL shorthand techniques short-change the maintenance programmer. The maintenance programmer knows from reading the code that a specific value invokes a specific procedure. Unless the procedure-names are meaningful (and they usually are not), the maintenance programmer does not know the specific condition that invoked the procedure.

A better technique is to use IF statements combined with meaningful 88s. This case structure implementation has two main benefits:

- Numeric values do not have to start at 1 and do not have to be sequential.
- Alpha identifiers can be used.

RECOMMENDATION

- Never use GO TO DEPENDING^{nr} ON; always implement the case structure with IF statements and 88s.

DEFENSIVE PROGRAMMING

If you insist on using GO TO DEPENDING^{nr} ON, be sure that you have implemented defensive programming. If the identifier value is invalid, the GO TO is ignored and processing continues with the next statement. This is obviously wrong, and Murphy's law guarantees that something bad will happen. Defensive programming requires that you place a ''safety'' IF preceding the GO TO:

```
                    IF          identifier < one
                    OR          identifier > n
                                GO TO abort-procedure
                    END-IF
```

one is not a literal but is defined in WORKING-STORAGE; **n** is the maximum number of procedure-names and is also defined in WORKING-STORAGE.

ALTER$^{nr}_{74}$ The ALTER$^{nr}_{74}$ statement is always a villain. ALTER$^{nr}_{74}$ changes the procedure-name of a Format 1 or 3 GO TO during execution of the program. There is absolutely no way to determine the execution sequence of a program from reading the source code listing. Attempting to analyze a memory dump to determine execution sequence is difficult. It is basically impossible if there are multiple ALTER$^{nr}_{74}$ statements and multiple alterable$^{nr}_{74}$ GO TO statements.

RECOMMENDATION

- Absolutely abolish ALTER$^{nr}_{74}$.

Fallthru (lexical inclusion)

Fallthru is not a statement. It describes the phenomenon of a procedure being invoked by the sequential operation of the compiler. Some books advocate that the ''mainline'' format be as follows:

```
PROCEDURE DIVISION.

P001-initialization.

    initialization block.

P002-processing.

    processing block.

P003-termination.

    termination block.

STOP RUN.
```

P001 is invoked when the program is invoked by the operating system. P002 is invoked by the simple process of fallthru because P001 was not invoked by a PERFORM and the occurrence of P002 did not trigger a return (see PERFORM for further details). Similarly, P003 was invoked by fallthru (some writers use the term *lexical inclusion* instead of *fallthru*). Here is a different format:

```
PROCEDURE DIVISION.

P001-mainline.

    PERFORM P111-initialization

    PERFORM P112-processing

    PERFORM P113-termination

STOP RUN.
```

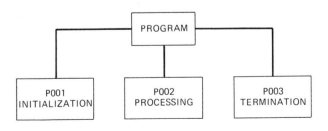

Figure 10.4 Fallthru format.

The difference between the two formats is the structure that is created. The fallthru format places initialization, processing, and termination on the same level as illustrated in Figure 10.4.

The PERFORM format places a "dummy" level (mainline) under the program, as illustrated in Figure 10.5.

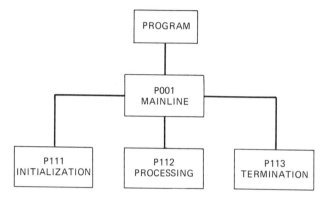

Figure 10.5 PERFORM format.

Some people object to the dummy level and use fallthru; others object to using fallthru. Here is a compromise used by Cris Miller:[10]

```
PROCEDURE DIVISION.

    P001-initialization.

        initialization block

        GO TO P002-processing. (dummy GO TO)

    P002-processing.

        processing block

        GO TO P003-termination.

    P003-termination.

        termination block

    STOP RUN.
```

The sequential execution of the program is the same with the fallthru or the dummy GO TO. The use of the dummy GO TO eliminates the dummy level in the PERFORM variation and the fallthru.

CONTINUE $COBOL_{85}$ has formalized the dummy GO TO by incorporating a $CONTINUE_{85}$ statement that has the same effect.

RECOMMENDATIONS

- Never use fallthru except in the mainline procedure.
- Use a dummy GO TO or $CONTINUE_{85}$ to document the fallthru (please, no comments about how much time the dummy GO TO or $CONTINUE_{85}$ requires).

PERFORM   The PERFORM statement is the only recommended method of transferring control between physically and logically different procedures. PERFORM explicitly transfers control to the first statement of the named procedure. Based on the PERFORM format, the successful PERFORM implicitly returns control to the first executable statement following the invoking PERFORM. The difference is whether the PERFORM is a simple imperative statement or part of a conditional sentence:

```
PERFORM...

next statement (control returns here after successful execution)

.............................

IF          condition true
            PERFORM...
ELSE        condition false
            else statements
END-IF

next statement (control returns here after successful execution)
```

The first PERFORM is a simple imperative PERFORM, and control returns to the next statement. The second PERFORM is part of an IF and returns control to the first statement following the period and space (.) or $END-IF_{85}$. ELSE is the next physical source statement, but it is not executed when the condition is true.

PERFORM has four formats:

1. PERFORM
2. PERFORM n $TIMES^{nr}$
3. PERFORM UNTIL
4. PERFORM VARYING

Each PERFORM can have a THRU/THROUGH clause.

Format 1 is the simple PERFORM that transfers control to the first statement of the procedure returning control to the next executable statement following the PERFORM after the last statement in the invoked procedure has been executed. The ''legalese'' of the preceding sentence is important since many books and compiler reference manuals state that "the procedures referred to are executed once." If the invoked procedure contains only imperative statements, the quotation is correct. If the invoked procedure contains conditional statements (as in **dountil** and **doinfinite** constructs), however, it is unknown what statements are to be executed and how many times. A comment (*) should precede the "unsimple" PERFORM to document all the PERFORM terminating conditions.

Format 2^{nr} invokes the procedure the number of times specified by an integer (literal) or an identifier. Based on previous recommendations, the integer should not be used. The identifier must be a numeric integer > 0 for the PERFORM to be executed. The identifier often represents an artificial construct—some condition must be translated to a numeric integer. In this case, the identifier masks the true terminating condition and inhibits readability. In any case, PERFORM UNTIL can always be used instead of PERFORM n TIMES^{nr}.

RECOMMENDATION

- Do not use PERFORM n TIMES^{nr}; substitute PERFORM UNTIL.

COBOL$_{74}$ Format 3 syntax is as follows:

PERFORM	procedure-name-1
[THRU	procedure-name-2]
UNTIL	condition-1

This PERFORM is "out of line" because it transfers control to a statement that is not the next physical source statement in the program.

COBOL$_{85}$ partial Format 3 syntax is

PERFORM	[procedure-name-1]$_{85}$
[THRU	procedure-name-2]
[WITH TEST$_{85}$	BEFORE$_{85}$/AFTER$_{85}$]
UNTIL	condition-1
[END-PERFORM]	

The first pair of brackets means that **procedure-name-1** is optional in COBOL$_{85}$. If **procedure-name-1** is omitted, transfer of control is to the next physical source statement. This is an "in-line" PERFORM.

PERFORM$_{74}$ is only a **dowhile**; PERFORM$_{85}$ can be a **dowhile** or a **dountil**, depending on the optional TEST$_{85}$ clause and defaults to **dowhile** if the TEST$_{85}$ clause is omitted.

Figure 10.6a shows the COBOL **dowhile** construct (implied or explicit TEST$_{85}$ BEFORE$_{85}$). The COBOL **dowhile** construct differs from the structured programming construct (see Figure 10.2b) in that the procedure (F1) is executed if the condition is false, whereas structured programming executes the procedure if the condition is true. Figure 10.6b shows the COBOL **dountil$_{85}$** construct (explicit TEST$_{85}$ AFTER$_{85}$), on which COBOL$_{85}$ and structured programming agree.

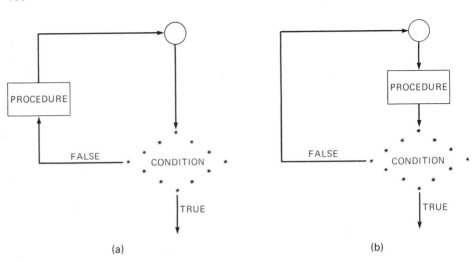

Figure 10.6   COBOL **dowhile** (a) and **dountil**₈₅ (b) constructs.

COBOL **dowhile** does not permit any procedure statement to be executed if the condition is true the first time; COBOL **dountil**₈₅ permits all procedure statements to be executed once even if the condition is true the first time. Neither **dowhile** nor **dountil**₈₅ permits some statements to be executed before the condition is tested **(doinfinite).**

RECOMMENDATIONS

- Use TEST₈₅ AFTER₈₅ where appropriate.
  Always code the TEST₈₅ BEFORE₈₅/AFTER₈₅ clause, even if the TEST₈₅ is the default BEFORE₈₅ (never assume).
  Use the **doutil** construct previously described in this chapter if TEST₈₅ AFTER₈₅ is not supported by your compiler.
- Use the **doinfinite** construct previously described where appropriate.

Structured programming theory requires that each module (paragraph) perform a single logical function. If the editing tests for an elementary item were numeric and positive and each was a separate function, the coding could be as follows:

```
P001-edit-elementary-item.
    PERFORM   P001-numeric-test
              THRU P001-X
    PERFORM   P002-positive-test
              THRU P002-X
    next statement
            P001-numeric-test.
                IF        elementary-item   ALPHABETIC
                          PERFORM P003-not-numeric
                          THRU P003-X.
```

```
                    END-IF
                    P001-X.  EXIT.
                       EJECT
                    P002-positive-test.
                       IF      elementary-item   NOT POSITIVE
                               PERFORM P004-not-positive
                               THRU P004-X.
                       END-IF
                    P002-X.  EXIT.
                       EJECT
```

(*Note:* P001 and P002 are indented to illustrate that they are not in the normal program sequence.)

The object of structured programming is readability. Separating small functions into separate paragraphs inhibits readability.

Most structured programming authors suggest that in-line functions of approximately ten statements should be lexically included. The in-line$_{85}$ PERFORM permits structured programming theorists to "have their cake and eat it too." The PERFORM defines a separate logical function, and that function is coded in-line$_{85}$ for readability. Again, currently available software could isolate in-line$_{85}$ PERFORM blocks to assist in porting when necessary.

The UNTIL condition can be any COBOL condition type:

- Relation condition
- Class condition
- Condition-name condition
- **switch-status^{nr}** condition
- Sign condition
- NOT condition

Any number of condition types can be combined with AND/OR connectors. This flexibility provides the tricky programmer with a glorious opportunity to obfuscate the program.

RECOMMENDATIONS

- Use only a single condition; that is, do not use AND/OR connectors.
- Do not use **switch-status^{nr}** condition type.
- Avoid NOT (people normally have trouble understanding negative logic).

Format 4 is the table-handling PERFORM. The syntax for a one-dimensional table (list) is as follows:

```
        PERFORM     [procedure-name-1]₈₅
        [THRU       procedure-name-2]
```

```
[WITH TEST₈₅  BEFORE₈₅/AFTER₈₅]
VARYING      index-name-1/identifier-1
FROM         index-name-2/literal-1/identifier-2
BY           literal-2/identifier-3
UNTIL        condition-1
[END-PERFORM]₈₅
```

A two-dimensional PERFORM uses the following additional syntax:

```
AFTER       index-name-3/identifier-4
FROM        index-name-4/literal-3/identifier-5
BY          literal-4/identifier-6
UNTIL       condition-2
```

The AFTER clause is then repeated for each additional level. $PERFORM_{74}$ permits three levels; $PERFORM_{85}$ permits seven levels.

The $TEST_{85}$ clause applies to all conditions, and $BEFORE_{85}$ and $AFTER_{85}$ cannot be intermixed.

$TEST_{85}$ $BEFORE_{85}$/$AFTER_{85}$ recommendations are the same as previously stated in PERFORM UNTIL.

PERFORM VARYING is used in conjunction with a table defined in the DATA DIVISION. The VARYING/AFTER index-name is the index defined by the INDEXED BY phrase of the associated OCCURS clause; the VARYING/AFTER identifier is a subscript associated with the table.

The FROM phrase sets the VARYING/AFTER index/subscript to its initial value. As recommended many times before, literal should not be used. Even if the VARYING/AFTER index/subscript is always SET to the same initial value, such as 1, an identifier should be used to define the constant. The FROM index-name/identifier can be used to establish a position within the table rather than the beginning of the table.

The BY phrase augments the VARYING/AFTER index/subscript. Again, a literal should not be used.

The three-dimensional example-table used in the OCCURS description in Chapter 7 would require the following PERFORM VARYING:

```
PERFORM   iterate-thru-example-table
VARYING   major-index
FROM      one
BY        one
UNTIL     major-index > two
AFTER     inter-index
FROM      one
BY        one
UNTIL     inter-index > three
AFTER     minor-index
FROM      one
BY        one
```

```
UNIL          minor-index > four
END-PERFORM
```

one, two, three, and **four** are not literals but numeric elementary items defined in WORKING-STORAGE with appropriate VALUES. Using literals inhibits analysis and is lazy coding.

RECOMMENDATIONS

- Do not use literals.
- Use simple single conditions; avoid NOT.

IBM introduced an intensified structure walkthrough known as code inspection.[11] The participants include the development programmer and peers. The peers "play" computer and attempt to uncover both logic problems and violations of structured programming theory. IBM has many programmers and many programs and has been able to create a database of problem statements. This is a problem statement and should be reviewed carefully. A common problem is that the = is used instead of > (e.g., **UNTIL minor-index = four** rather than **> four**). The = condition would terminate the loop after three iterations because the value **four** makes the condition true, thereby terminating the loop.

RECOMMENDATION

- Use code inspections.

Figures 10.7 to 10.9 are flowcharts illustrating the PERFORM VARYING logic.
   The explicit procedure-name in all formats is either a SECTION or a paragraph. Return of control happens when the last statement of the out-of-line SECTION or the last statement of the out-of-line paragraph is executed. The compiler "knows" when it has executed the last out-of-line statement because it has detected a new SECTION or a new paragraph or the physical end of the program; the END-PERFORM$_{85}$ terminates the in-line PERFORM. The reason that a SECTION with subordinate paragraphs is not recommended is that either the entire SECTION or any paragraph within the SECTION can be invoked in violation of the structure theory that each module have only one entrance at the top.
   The THRU clause provides the programmer with yet another way to violate structured programming. The basic syntax is

```
PERFORM      procedure-name-1
   THRU      procedure-name-2
```

There is no COBOL limitation as to how many sections or paragraphs can be spanned by the THRU clause. Consider the following:

P001-paragraph.
P001-block
P002-paragraph.
P002-block
P003-paragraph.
P003-block
P004-paragraph.
P004-block
P005-paragraph.
P005-block

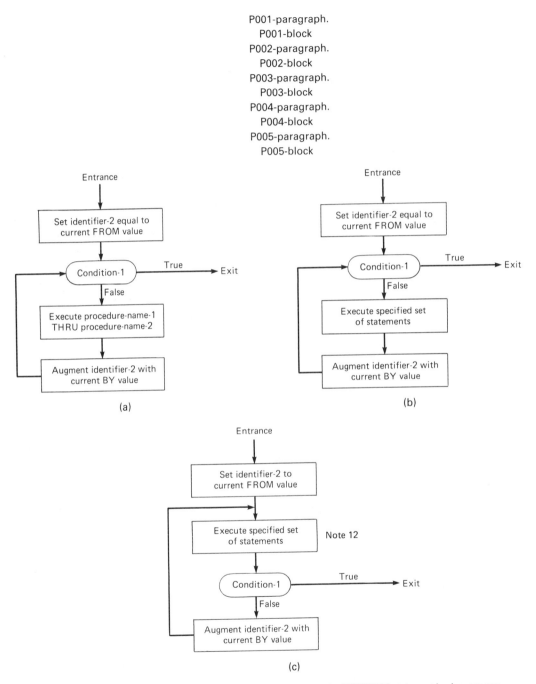

Figure 10.7 (a) Flowchart for the VARYING phrase of a PERFORM statement having one condition (COBOL$_{74}$). (b) VARYING option of a PERFORM statement with the TEST BEFORE phrase having one condition (COBOL$_{85}$). (c) VARYING option of a PERFORM statement with the TEST AFTER phrase having one condition (COBOL$_{85}$). (Courtesy ANSI)

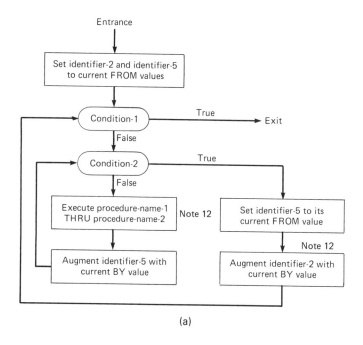

(a)

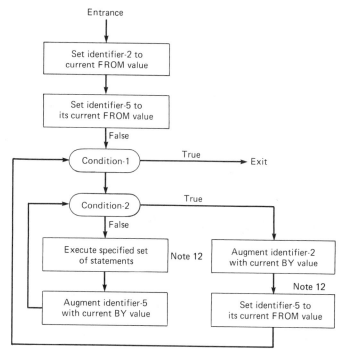

(b)

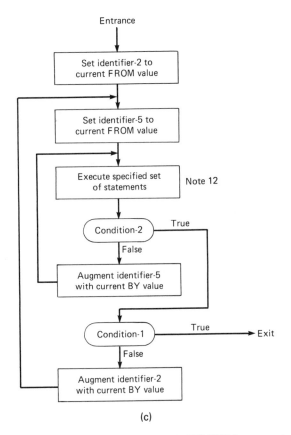

(c)

Figure 10.8   (a) Flowchart for the VARYING phrase of a PERFORM statement having two conditions (COBOL$_{74}$). (b) VARYING option of a PERFORM statement with the TEST BEFORE phrase having two conditions (COBOL$_{85}$). (c) VARYING option of a PERFORM statement with the TEST AFTER phrase having two conditions (COBOL$_{85}$).[12] (Courtesy ANSI)

The following PERFORM statements are possible:

```
PERFORM P001 or      P002 or      P003 or      P004 or      P005
PERFORM P001 THRU P002 or      P003 or      P004 or      P005
PERFORM                P002 THRU P003 or      P004 or      P005
PERFORM                             P003 THRU P004 or      P005
PERFORM                                          P004 THRU P005
```

The use of the THRU clause to concatenate different physical and logical paragraphs violates structured programming theory of one entrance.

RECOMMENDATION

• Do not use THRU to concatenate physical and logical paragraphs.

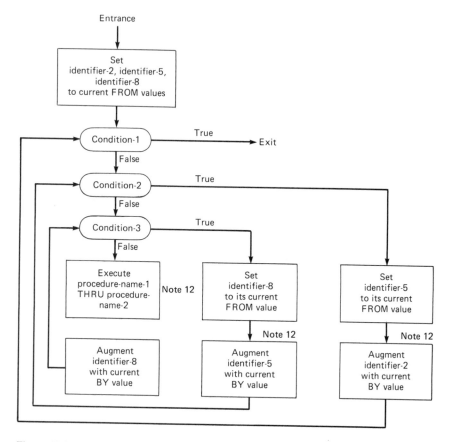

Figure 10.9   Flowchart for the VARYING phrase of a PERFORM statement having three conditions. (Courtesy ANSI)

The key phrase in the recommendation is "physical and logical." A previous recommendation in this chapter was to place an EXIT paragraph to terminate each performable paragraph.

```
P001-performable-paragraph.
   P001-narrative
   P001-parameters
   P001-statements.
P001-X.   EXIT.
```

The EXIT paragraph is a null paragraph that does not produce any executable code. It is there to provide a common EXIT for multiple paths and a visual paragraph end. Unfortunately, COBOL does treat it as a new physical paragraph and would return control after the last P001 statement because it detected a new paragraph. Any local GO TO statements to the EXIT paragraph would not return control (most compilers produce executable code that would continue processing of the next statement after the EXIT paragraph). The only COBOL solution is to use the THRU clause:

```
PERFORM        P001-performable-paragraph
   THRU        P001-X.
```

RECOMMENDATIONS

- Always terminate performable paragraphs with an EXIT paragraph; use THRU to trigger EXIT.
- Use an identifying prefix in the paragraph-name; use the same identifying prefix with the letter X as the EXIT paragraph-name.
- Use software to verify that the THRU clause is not being misused.

Many programmers believe that control is returned upon detection of a new procedure or the EXIT paragraph. This is true only if the return trigger has been set by the appropriate PERFORM. If the trigger is not set, most compilers produce code to continue sequential execution with the next statement. This is wrong and causes untold problems. A method to prevent "runaways" is to insert an **abort** paragraph after each EXIT paragraph.

```
P001-X. EXIT.
PABT-abort-paragraph.
   MOVE       abort-runaway-code
   TO         abort-code
   GO TO      abort-routine.
PABT-X. EXIT.
   EJECT
```

The MOVE places a specific value in a known field that defines the "impossible" condition that caused the program-detected abend (as opposed to an operating system abend). The GO TO is more honest than a PERFORM because the program is terminating.

I have heard the screams of development programmers about all the extra coding to protect against an improbable situation. The defensive paragraphs can be inserted by COPY statements. In a program with 200 paragraphs (approximately 5000 to 10,000 lines of code if structured programming was used), how much time would be required to code 200 COPY statements? (Usually less time than it takes to argue about it.) The gain is to stop an improbable condition from causing severe damage.

Most programmers believe that the worst thing that can happen to them is an abend. The actual worst thing is a program that malfunctions but runs to normal end-of-job (EOJ). The mistake is not normally caught unless there is an obvious error in a financial document (e.g., the bank credited an account $1 million for an actual deposit of $100 or a check was issued for $500,000 instead of $500). The error is usually detected many days or weeks later by a senior user who notices that something has gone awry. The hours required to recast reports or to correct a corrupted database can be enormous. The "insurance premium" of defensive programming is small compared with the hours saved when an improbable condition is trapped immediately.

RECOMMENDATION

- Use defensive programming even if each line of code must be individually written (i.e., if COPY or software editor is unavailable).

SUMMARY OF RECOMMENDATIONS FOR PERFORM

- Do not use THRU to concatenate physical and logical paragraphs.
- Always terminate with EXIT; use THRU to trigger EXIT.
- Use software to verify THRU usage.
- The EXIT paragraph should use the parent paragraph prefix plus **-X.** (**P327-X.**)
- Insert an **abort** paragraph or a **GO TO abort** after every EXIT paragraph.
- For Format 2: Do not PERFORM n TIMES^{nr}; substitute PERFORM UNTIL.
- For Formats 2, 3, and 4: Do not use literals.
- For Formats 3 and 4:
  Always code TEST$_{85}$.
  Use TEST$_{85}$ AFTER$_{85}$ or the suggested **dountil GO TO** construct if all statements should be executed upon invocation, even if the condition is true upon invocation.
  Use the single condition only.
  Do not use the **switch^{nr}**condition.
  Avoid NOT.
- For Format 4: Use code inspections.
- Use the suggested **doinfinite GO TO** construct when some statements should be executed upon invocation, regardless of whether the condition is true upon invocation.
- Use **in-line$_{85}$ PERFORM** where the number of statements in the invoked function is approximately ten.

EXIT   The EXIT statement allows a user to assign a common termination procedure-name to a specific place in a procedure.

RECOMMENDATION

- Always use the EXIT statement as the last statement with a performable paragraph or SECTION followed by an EJECT or /.

Imperative Date Movement

INSPECT   The COBOL$_{68}$ EXAMINE$_{68}$ verb was replaced by the INSPECT verb in COBOL$_{74}$ and retained in COBOL$_{85}$.

The INSPECT statement is a schizophrenic statement in that ANSI classifies it as an arithmetic statement if the TALLYING clause is used and as a data movement statement if the REPLACING clause is used. It is truly schizophrenic if both TALLYING and REPLACING are used.

The INSPECT statement allows the TALLYING (counting) and/or REPLACING of individual or groups of specified characters in a USAGE IS DISPLAY data item. It is usually used to perform editing and therefore would rarely occur in a business logic program.

COBOL$_{85}$ has added a new format (4):

> INSPECT   identifier-1
> CONVERTING$_{85}$ identifier-2/literal-1
> TO   identifier-3/literal-2

The CONVERTING$_{85}$ format is a replacement for the non-ANSI TRANSFORM$_{os}$ format supported by many compilers. The CONVERTING$_{85}$ or TRANSFORM$_{os}$ is basically used to translate between EBCDIC (IBM) and ASCII (non-IBM). This translation should occur only twice: for "foreign" data being entered and for foreign data needed for output. A special utility program should be used that performs only the translation (i.e., the program does a READ, a CONVERT$_{85}$ or TRANSFORM$_{os/vs,}$ and a WRITE).

RECOMMENDATIONS

- Do not use literals.
- Subject all non-CONVERTING$_{85}$ INSPECT statements to code inspection.
- Use CONVERTING$_{85}$ to translate between foreign alphabets.
  Use TRANSFORM$_{os}$ if supported and CONVERTING$_{85}$ is not supported.

MOVE   The MOVE statement is the most used statement in COBOL. It appears to be simple—**MOVE a TO b**—but is in fact a complex statement. Its complexity is evidenced by Figure 10.10. The complexity is hidden, and therefore many programmers misunderstand MOVE, thereby causing both maintenance problems and errors.

The MOVE statement has two formats:

> 1. MOVE   identifier-1/literal
>   TO   identifier-2, [identifier-3], ...
> 2. MOVE CORRESPONDING^{nr} identifier-1
>   TO   identifier-2

The actual results of an elementary MOVE are controlled by the PIC clause and the optional JUSTIFIED and USAGE IS clauses and implicit de-editing$_{85}$.[13] The problem areas include

- Different PIC types
- Different field sizes
- Loss of operational SIGN
- Overlapping fields

COBOL is both a flexible and a forgiving language. As the Y's in Figure 10.10 indicate, almost any field type can MOVE to any other field type (70 of the 91 possible

Source Field \ Receiving Field	GR	AL	AN	ED	BI	NE	ANE	ID	EF	IF	SN	SR
Group (GR)	Y	Y	Y	Y	Y^1	Y^1	Y^1	Y^1	Y^1	Y^1	Y^1	Y^1
Alphabetic (AL)	Y	Y	Y	N	N	N	Y	N	N	N	N	N
Alphanumeric (AN)	Y	Y	Y	Y^4	Y^4	Y^4	Y	Y^4	Y^4	Y^4	Y^4	Y^4
External Decimal (ED)	Y^1	N	Y^2	Y	Y	Y	Y^2	Y	Y	Y	Y	Y
Binary (BI)	Y^1	N	Y^2	Y	Y	Y	Y^2	Y	Y	Y	Y	Y
Numeric Edited (NE)	Y	N	Y	N	N	N	Y	N	N	N	N	N
Alphanumeric Edited (ANE)	Y	Y	Y	N	N	N	Y	N	N	N	N	N
ZEROS (numeric or alphanumeric)	Y	N	Y	Y^3	Y^3	Y^3	Y	Y^3	Y^3	Y^3	Y^3	Y^3
SPACES (AL)	Y	Y	Y	N	N	N	Y	N	N	N	N	N
HIGH-VALUE, LOW-VALUE, QUOTES	Y	N	Y	N	N	N	Y	N	N	N	N	N
ALL literal	Y	Y	Y	Y^5	Y^5	Y^5	Y	Y^5	N	N	N	N
Numeric Literal	Y^1	N	Y^2	Y	Y	Y	Y^2	Y	Y	Y	Y	Y
Nonnumeric Literal	Y	Y	Y	Y^5	Y^5	Y^5	Y	Y^5	N	N	N	N
Internal Decimal (ID)	Y^1	N	Y^2	Y	Y	Y	Y^2	Y	Y	Y	Y	Y
External Floating-point (EF)	Y^1	N	N	Y	Y	Y	N	Y	Y	Y	Y	Y
Internal Floating-point (IF)	Y^1	N	N	Y	Y	Y	N	Y	Y	Y	Y	Y
Sterling Nonreport (SN)	Y^1	N	Y	Y	Y	Y	N	Y	Y	Y	Y	Y
Sterling Report (SR)	Y	N	Y	N	N	N	Y	N	N	N	N	N
Floating-point Literal	Y^1	N	N	Y	Y	Y	N	Y	Y	Y	Y	Y

[1] Move without conversion (like AN to AN)

[2] Only if the decimal point is at the right of the least significant digit

[3] Numeric move

[4] The alphanumeric field is treated as an unsigned ED (integer) field

[5] The literal must consist only of numeric characters and is treated as an ED integer field

Figure 10.10 IBM OS Full American National Standard COBOL (GC28-6396-6). (Courtesy of International Business Machines Corporation)

ANSI MOVE permutations are permitted). Permissible does not mean correct, however. At the very least, the compiler must generate executable code that converts the sending PIC format to the receiving PIC format (people who complain about other coding ineffi-

ciencies rarely complain about the inefficiency of moving unlike PIC elementary items).
At worst, the results are unpredictable. In a business logic program (without editing),
there should be little need for using a different PIC MOVE.

RECOMMENDATION

- MOVE statements should be between elementary items with identical PIC
  types.

Sending fields that are larger than the receiving fields are always truncated without warning at execution. Loss of bits causes problems.

RECOMMENDATION

- Receiving field size must be as large as or greater than sending field size.

Losing an operational SIGN is easy:

- MOVE a numeric PIC with an operational SIGN to an alpha PIC.
- MOVE a numeric PIC with an operational SIGN to a numeric PIC without an
  operational SIGN.

The net result is that negative values suddenly become positive.

RECOMMENDATION

- All numeric fields must have an operational SIGN.

Results of overlapping field MOVE statements are unpredictable. Overlapping
fields can be created by REDEFINES[nr], by RENAMES[nr], or by using GROUP items.
REDEFINES[nr] and RENAMES[nr] have previously been not recommended. Here is a
simple example of an overlapping MOVE using a GROUP item:

```
            MOVE elementary-item-2     TO GROUP-item-1
```

where

```
        02 GROUP-item-1.
           03 elementary-item-1   PIC A.
           03 elementary-item-2   PIC A(13).
```

Another problem of moving GROUP items in Format 1 is that conversion between
different PIC types is not performed. This means that data with the wrong format (e.g.,
alpha in a numeric elementary item) can happen.

An exception to a GROUP MOVE is to emulate REDEFINES[nr] as discussed
previously.

RECOMMENDATION

- Do not use GROUP items in Format 1 MOVE statements except to emulate REDEFINES[nr].

Format 2 is another COBOL shorthand statement. It transfers data between fields with the same exact name in different groups by specifying the GROUP names in **identifier-1** and **identifier-2**.

```
MOVE CORR[nr]      address
TO                 address-ws
```

where

```
02    address.
      03  address-id       PIC AA.
      03  address-street   PIC X(20).
      03  address-city     PIC A(20).
      03  address-state    PIC A(10).
      03  address-zip      PIC S9(5)V.
```

and

```
02    address-ws.
      03  address-code     PIC AA.
      03  address-street   PIC X(20).
      03  address-city     PIC A(20).
      03  address-state    PIC A(10).
      03  address-zip      PIC S9(5)V.
      03  address-country  PIC A(20).
```

is equivalent to

```
MOVE      address-street   OF address
TO        address-street   OF address-ws

MOVE      address-city     OF address
TO        address-city     OF address-ws

MOVE      address-state    OF address
TO        address-state    OF address-ws

MOVE      address-zip      OF address
TO        address-zip      OF address
```

address-id OF address is not moved because there is no CORRESPONDING[nr] elementary item in **address-ws**. **address-code** and **address-country OF address-ws** are unaffected by the MOVE because again there are no CORRESPONDING^{nr} elementary items in address.

The CORRESPONDING^{nr} phrase is not recommended, for these reasons:

- It requires qualification of elementary items in statements that do not have the CORRESPONDING^{nr} phrase.
- It inhibits readability (what is actually being moved?).
- It is easy to misuse (in the preceding example, **address-id OF address** and **address-code OF address-ws** are probably the same elementary item, and the value in **address-id** should be transferred, but it is not).

SUMMARY OF RECOMMENDATIONS FOR MOVE

- Do not use literals.
- MOVE elementary items with identical PIC types.
- Receiving elementary item size must be equal to or greater than sending elementary item size.
- All elementary numeric items must have an operational SIGN.
- GROUP items should not be used in Format 1 MOVE statements except to emulate REDEFINES^{nr}.
- The CORRESPONDING^{nr} phrase (Format 2) should not be used.

STRING^{nr} and UNSTRING^{nr} statements are discussed as conditionals because the OVERFLOW phrase is always recommended if these verbs are used.

INITIALIZE$^{nr}_{85}$ INITIALIZE$^{nr}_{85}$ is a special MOVE statement for initialization whose syntax is

INITIALIZE$^{nr}_{85}$	identifier-1, [identifier-2], ...
[REPLACING^{nr}	ALPHABETIC/ALPHANUMERIC/NUMERIC/
	ALPHANUMERIC-EDITED/NUMERIC-EDITED
DATA <u>BY</u>	identifier-n/literal-1], ...

The basic INITIALIZE$^{nr}_{85}$ statement without the REPLACING^{nr} phrase is an implicit MOVE of either the figurative constant SPACE or ZERO to **identifier-1** depending on its PIC (SPACE to ALPHABETIC/ALPHANUMERIC/ALPHANUMERIC-EDITED and ZERO to NUMERIC/NUMERIC-EDITED).

There is no need for a new MOVE statement, particularly when

MOVE SPACE/ZERO to identifier-1, [identifier-2], ...

contains the maintenance metadata of the actual figurative constant used.

The REPLACING^{nr} BY phrase is a complex MOVE CORRESPONDING^{nr} in disguise.

RECOMMENDATION

- Do not use INITIALIZE$^{nr}_{85}$ for reasons of maintainability and portability.

Arithmetic

ADD, COMPUTE^{nr}, DIVIDE, MULTIPLY, and SUBTRACT are discussed as conditionals because the SIZE ERROR phrase is always recommended. INSPECT (TALLYING) was discussed previously under INSPECT (REPLACING).

Ending Statements

EXIT PROGRAM
The EXIT PROGRAM statement should be used only in a subprogram (a program that has been called by another program) to return control to the invoking (calling) program. An EXIT PROGRAM in a main program is nonoperational, and execution continues with the next statement (an untriggered EXIT PROGRAM in a subprogram is also nonoperational).

COBOL$_{85}$ executes an implicit EXIT PROGRAM if there is no next executable statement (physical program end).

Some compliers support a non-ANSI GOBACK$_{os/vs}$ statement that has the same effect as the EXIT PROGRAM. Do not use it.

STOP
The STOP RUN statement can be used in either a main program or a subprogram. Its actual effect is dependent on the operating system, but it normally terminates the main program even when invoked from a subprogram. In IBM jargon, it causes the end of a job step.

STOP RUN should always be used in a main program and avoided in subprograms. Subprograms should attempt to return in an orderly fashion with a status code indicating type of abort.[14] This allows the calling program to take any appropriate action.

The STOP statement also has a literal syntax:

$$\text{STOP literal}^{nr}_{74}$$

The execution of the program is suspended at the STOP statement and the literal is transmitted to the operator's console. The operator must either terminate the job step or resume the execution of the stopped program at the next executable statement. Do not use this statement.

SUMMARY OF RECOMMENDATIONS FOR ENDING STATEMENTS

- Use STOP RUN in main programs.
- Use EXIT PROGRAM in subprograms whenever possible.
  Return status code to calling program.
  Place a defensive programming paragraph or statement after the EXIT PROGRAM to prevent runaway.

Avoid STOP RUN in subprograms.
Do not use GOBACK$^{nr}_{os/vs}$ (non-ANSI).
Do not use STOP literal$^{nr}_{74}$.

Input-Output Statements

ACCEPT   The ACCEPT statement has three formats:

1.^{nr}	<u>ACCEPT</u>	identifier
	[<u>FROM</u>	mnemonic-name^{nr}]
2.	<u>ACCEPT</u>	identifier
	<u>FROM</u>	<u>DATE</u>/<u>DAY</u>/<u>DAY-OF-WEEK</u>$_{85}$/<u>TIME</u>
3.^{nr}	<u>ACCEPT</u>	cd-name MESSAGE <u>COUNT</u>^{nr}

Format 1^{nr} permits data to be entered from the specified device (**mnemonic-name^{nr}**) directly into the program. There are better ways, so do not use this format.

Format 2 permits the program to obtain calendar and time data from the system clock of the computer. Many organizations have standards requiring time stamping of program execution, reports, and other productions.

Format 3^{nr} returns the number of messages in the queue specified by **cd-name.** There are better ways, so do not use this format.

RECOMMENDATION

• Use only Format 2 ACCEPT for time-stamping data.

OPEN and CLOSE   The OPEN statement provides information to the operating system to initiate file processing, including standard label checking and positioning. The CLOSE statement informs the operating system to terminate file processing. Both statements have many optional clauses.

RECOMMENDATION

• OPEN and CLOSE statements should be copied.

Nonrecommended statements   DISPLAY^{nr} permits messages to be transmitted to "human" consoles. There are better ways.

RECOMMENDATION

• Do not use DISPLAY^{nr}.

DISABLE^{nr}, ENABLE^{nr}, RECEIVE^{nr}, and SEND^{nr} are not recommended because they are part of the Communications Module. There are better ways to communicate.

RECOMMENDATION

• Do not use Communications Module statements (DISABLE^{nr}, ENABLE^{nr}, RECEIVE^{nr}, and SEND^{nr}).

READ, REWRITE, START, and STOP are discussed as conditionals because error statuses are always recommended.

Inter-program Statements

CALL and CANCEL are discussed as conditionals.

ordering[nr]

There are better ways to sort or merge.

RECOMMENDATION

* Do not use Sort-Merge Module verbs (MERGE[nr], RELEASE[nr], RETURN[nr], or SORT[nr]).

report writer[nr] (optional in COBOL$_{85}$)

There are better ways to prepare reports.

RECOMMENDATION

* Do not use Report Writer verbs (GENERATE[nr], INITIATE[nr], SUPPRESS[nr], or TERMINATE[nr]).

Table Handling

SET   The SET statement places a value into either an index or a subscript. There are two original formats:

```
1. SET      index-name-1/identifier-1,
            [index-name-2/identifier-2], ...
   TO       index-name-3/identifier-3/literal-1
2. SET                    index-name-1, [index-name-2], ...
   UP BY/DOWN BY          identifier-1/literal-1
```

These formats are normally used to retrieve a specific value from a table or to initialize an index or subscript before searching. The other way to SET indices is with PERFORM VARYING. As always, do not use literals.

COBOL$_{85}$ has added two new formats:

```
3.[nr] SET   mnemonic-name-1₈₅, [mnemonic-name-2₈₅], ...
       TO    ON/OFF[nr]
```

mnemonic-name$_{85}$ references external switches, which should not be used.

```
4.[nr] SET   condition-name-1₈₅, [condition-name-2₈₅], ...
       TO    TRUE[nr]₈₅
```

condition-name refers to an 88-level defined set of VALUES. This SET format assigns a TRUE^{nr} to the condition-name and its VALUE to the associated data-name. For example:

03	marital-status	PIC S99V.
88	married	VALUE IS 1.
88	single	VALUE IS 2.
88	divorced	VALUE IS 4.
88	widowed	VALUE IS 8.
88	unknown	VALUE IS 16.
88	invalid-status	VALUES ARE 3, 5 THRU 7, 9 THRU 15, 17 THRU 99.

SET married TO TRUE$^{nr}_{85}$ would SET **marital-status** to **married** and its VALUE to 1; **SET single TO TRUE$^{nr}_{85}$** would SET **marital-status** to **single** and its VALUE to 2; **SET invalid-status to TRUE$^{nr}_{85}$** would SET **invalid-status** to **invalid** and would assign it the first invalid VALUE of 3.

This format is static information in a dynamic world. Do not use it.

RECOMMENDATIONS

- Do not use literals in Formats 1 and 2.
- Do not use Format 3$^{nr}_{85}$ or Format 4$^{nr}_{85}$.

Defensive Programming

A good way to destroy data, a program, or all of memory on some computers is to have a runaway index or subscript. For instance, MOVE HIGH-VALUE^{nr} to the PERFORM VARYING condition coupled with a MOVE data statement would cycle through memory until the operating system issued a "boundary fault," thereby abending the program. Here is an example:

```
MOVE         HIGH-VALUE
TO           until-condition

PERFORM      P???-initialize-table
THRU         P???-X
VARYING      initialize-table-index
FROM         one
BY           one
UNTIL        until-condition
END-PERFORM
```

where

```
P???-initialize-table.
```

```
MOVE         SPACE
TO           initialize-table(initialize-table-index).

P???-X.   EXIT.
```

Defensive programming requires that each index or subscript be verified as in-range before use (some compilers generate range-checking executable code on request; see "Compiler Directing Statements").

RECOMMENDATIONS

- Do not use literals.
- Make sure index or subscript is in-range before use.

Testing

IF   The IF statement looks simple. The basic syntax is

```
IF          condition
THEN₈₅      statement-1/ ... /NEXT SENTENCE
ELSE        statement-2/ ... /NEXT SENTENCE
[END-IF₈₅]
```

Condition is a generic term for one of the following condition types:

- relation
- class
- condition-name
- switch-status^{nr}
- sign

The relation condition compares two operands. The basic syntax is

```
IF   identifier-1/literal-1/arithmetic-expression-1/index-name-1₈₅
     relational-operator
     identifier-2/literal-2/arithmetic-expression-2/index-name-2₈₅
```

The relational operator can be any of the following:

- IS [NOT] GREATER THAN   or   IS [NOT] $\geq$
- IS [NOT] LESS THAN   or   IS [NOT] $\leq$
- IS [NOT] EQUAL THAN   or   IS [NOT] $=$
- IS GREATER THAN OR EQUAL TO or   IS $>=$₈₅ and is equivalent to IS NOT LESS THAN
- IS LESS THAN OR EQUAL TO   or   IS $<=$₈₅ and is equivalent to IS NOT GREATER THAN

I prefer the algebraic symbols $<$, $=$, and $>$ and use them in the text. Naturally, literals should not be used. Identifiers are basically divided into numeric and nonnumeric (**index-names**[85] are basically treated as numeric).

Two numeric identifiers (PIC 9) are algebraically compared regardless of the identifier size and any USAGE clause.

Two nonnumeric identifiers (PIC A and X) are compared based on the collating sequence of the computer. Normally, bit configuration 00000000 is low and 11111111 is high. If the identifier size is equal, comparison proceeds from left to right until an unequal match is detected. If the identifiers are unequal in size, the shorter identifier is "padded" with spaces on the right until both operands are the same length (the padding is done in the computer's working memory, thereby preserving the actual identifier).

A numeric *integer* can be compared with a nonnumeric value with the same USAGE clause. The ANSI rule basically is that the numeric identifier is in effect moved to an alphanumeric field (PIC X) and the comparison is nonnumeric (i.e., based on collating sequence).

An arithmetic expression can be any of the following:

- An elementary numeric item (PIC 9)
- A numeric literal[nr] or the ZERO (ZEROS, ZEROES) figurative constant[85]
- Two or more elementary numeric items or literals[nr] separated by arithmetic operators

These are the arithmetic operators:

$+$	for addition
$-$	for subtraction
$*$	for multiplication
$/$	for division
$**$	for exponentiation

The unary[nr] operators $+$ and $-$ are also allowed ($+$ multiplies the operand by $+1$ and $-$ multiplies the operand by -1). Any number of paired parentheses ( ) are allowed to specify the evaluation sequence.

Arithmetic expressions can be as complicated as the programmer desires. However, readability is still the goal, and any arithmetic expression should be simple (limited to one or two elementary items). More complicated arithmetic expressions should be decomposed into simple formulas for readability and maintainability.

RECOMMENDATIONS

- Do not use literals.
- Do not compare numeric identifiers with nonnumeric identifiers.
- Avoid comparing nonnumeric identifiers of unequal length.

- Do not use unary[nr] operators; they are too easy to confuse with the "real" + and $-$.

- Use simple arithmetic expressions.

The **class** condition tests that an identifier is within a specific character set. The basic syntax is

IF   identifier   IS [NOT]   NUMERIC/ALPHABETIC/
                                    ALPHABETIC-LOWER$_{85}$/
                                    ALPHABETIC-UPPER$_{85}$
                                    class-name-n$_{85}$

The NUMERIC character set is 0 through 9, with or without operational sign; ALPHABETIC is any combination of *A* through *Z* or *a* through *z* and space; ALPHABETIC-LOWER$_{85}$ is *a* through *z* and space; ALPHABETIC-UPPER$_{85}$ is *A* through *Z* and space; **class-name-n$_{85}$** is a specific set of characters defined in the SPECIAL-NAMES paragraph.

The **class** condition is useful in defensive programming. All PIC 9 items should be tested for NUMERIC after a value has been MOVE to it;[15] all PIC A items should be tested for ALPHABETIC, all **class-names$_{85}$** for the correct character set, and so on.

RECOMMENDATION

- Use the **class** condition to verify item contents to prevent an abend caused by alpha data being in a numeric item or other character errors.

The **condition-name** condition is used in conjunction with 88 levels. The simple syntax is

IF   condition-name

where **condition-name** is an 88 level defined in the DATA DIVISION.

A readable and easy-to-maintain program should contain many IF **condition-name** statements.

RECOMMENDATION

- Use IF **condition-name** statements and 88 levels freely to improve readability and maintainability.

The **switch-status[nr]** condition determines the on/off status of vendor-defined switches. As previously discussed, many old CPUs had external switches that could be set by the operator and read by programs. Most current mainframes do not have external switches but have preserved the concept with external software switches.[16] External switches are static information in a dynamic world.

RECOMMENDATION

● Do not use IF **switch-status**[nr] statements.

The **sign** condition tests an arithmetic expression for POSITIVE/NEGATIVE/ZERO.

        IF   arithmetic-expression   IS [NOT] POSITIVE/NEGATIVE/ZERO

The **sign** condition IF is also useful in defensive programming. An elementary numeric item that must be + should be tested for POSITIVE; an item that must be −, tested for NEGATIVE; and so on.

RECOMMENDATION

● Use IF **sign** condition statements to verify the value domain.

Single-term conditions can be combined to form combined conditions.

        IF   condition AND/OR   condition AND/OR   ...

AND and OR are logical operators used to determine whether the complex condition is TRUE or FALSE. AND evaluates TRUE only if all the single-term conditions are TRUE. OR evaluates TRUE if *any* of the single-term conditions are TRUE (OR can only evaluate FALSE if *all* the single-term conditions are FALSE). Table 10.3 is a truth table with three conditions.

TABLE 10.3 Truth table

Case	1	2	3	AND	OR
a	T	T	T	T	T
b	T	T	F	F	T
c	T	F	T	F	T
d	T	F	F	F	T
e	F	T	T	F	T
f	F	F	T	F	T
g	F	T	F	F	T
h	F	F	F	F	F

The NOT logical operator reverses the evaluation: If the condition evaluated TRUE without the NOT, the evaluation becomes FALSE; if the condition evaluated FALSE without the NOT, the evaluation becomes TRUE. Parentheses are important in the evaluation process. For instance,

        NOT (condition-1, condition-2, condition-3)

evaluates the complex condition within the parentheses without regard for the NOT. If the syntax were

NOT (condition-1 AND condition-2 AND condition-3)

the results in Table 10.3 would be reversed, as in Table 10.4.

TABLE 10.4   NOT (condition-1 OR condition-2 OR condition-3) evaluates to the OR column

Case	1	2	3	AND	OR
a	T	T	T	F	F
b	T	T	F	T	F
c	T	F	T	T	F
d	T	F	F	T	F
e	F	T	T	T	F
f	F	F	T	T	F
g	F	T	F	T	F
h	F	F	F	T	T

If the NOT precedes an arithmetic expression without a left parenthesis, the NOT applies only to that arithmetic expression. The syntax of

NOT condition-1 AND condition-2 AND condition-3

produces the results in Table 10.5.

TABLE 10.5   NOT condition-1 OR condition-2 OR condition-3 evaluates to the OR column

Case	1	2	3	AND	OR
a	T	T	T	F	T
b	T	T	F	F	T
c	T	F	T	F	T
d	T	F	F	F	F
e	F	T	T	T	T
f	F	F	T	F	T
g	F	T	F	F	T
h	F	F	F	F	T

Confused? Pity the poor maintenance programmer who encounters

IF a OR b AND NOT (c OR d OR e) AND . . .

or something worse. A tricky development programmer can make complex conditions even more confusing by using approved ANSI "abbreviations" that eliminate the subject (the first condition within a complex condition) or the subject and the relational operator. The syntax is

<u>IF</u>   subject   relational-operator   object

Here are some examples from the ANSI X3.23-1985 manual:

Condition	Equivalent
a > b AND NOT < c OR d	((a > b) AND (a NOT < c)) OR (a NOT < d)
a NOT EQUAL b OR c	(a NOT EQUAL b) OR (a NOT EQUAL c)
NOT a = b OR c	(NOT (a = b)) OR (a = c)
NOT (a GREATER b or < c)	NOT ((a GREATER b) OR (a < c))
NOT (a NOT > b AND c AND NOT d)	NOT ((((a NOT > b) AND (a NOT > c)) AND (NOT (a NOT > d))))

It is amazing that ANSI would use such unintelligible examples since COBOL is supposed to be easy to read and self-documenting. Flexibility is nice—but it isn't everything!

RECOMMENDATIONS

- Use a maximum of three simple conditions combined by only AND/OR connectors:

    condition-1 AND/OR condition-2 AND/OR condition-3

- Decompose complicated complex conditions to simpler complex conditions.
- Avoid NOT; do not combine it with AND/OR.
- Do not use abbreviated combined relation conditions[nr].

So far we have described the possible conditions in the basic syntax

<u>IF</u>   condition
$THEN_{85}$ statement-1/ ... /<u>NEXT</u> <u>SENTENCE</u>
<u>ELSE</u>   statement-2/ ... /<u>NEXT</u> <u>SENTENCE</u>
$END\text{-}IF_{85}$

IF the condition evaluates TRUE, **statement-1** or NEXT SENTENCE is executed; otherwise, control is transferred to the ELSE clause if present. Some compilers permit the use of the word $THEN_{85}$ (IF condition THEN...) or $OTHERWISE_{os}$ for ELSE.

RECOMMENDATION

- Do not use $THEN_{85}$ or $OTHERWISE_{os}$ for reasons of portability.

The NEXT SENTENCE phrase directs the computer to transfer control to the first executable statement following the next period and space or END-IF$_{85}$ (end of the IF conditional sentence). Gotoless proponents usually permit NEXT SENTENCE. NEXT SENTENCE is a GO TO; it transfers control without triggering a return.

The ANSI syntax of **statement-1** . . . may be misleading since there can be many statements:

> IF   condition statement-1, statement-2, statement-3, ...

All statements between the condition and the ELSE phrase are executed. If any of the statements transfers control, control is transferred as specified. If there is no transfer of control, the ELSE phrase is ignored and execution continues with the next executable statement following the period and space or END-IF$_{85}$.

```
IF      condition
        statement-1
        statement-2
        statement-3
        PERFORM (or GO TO or CALL)
ELSE
        statement-4. (or END-IF₈₅)

        next physical executable statement
```

If the condition is TRUE, **statement-1, statement-2,** and **statement-3** are executed, and control is transferred by the PERFORM with the return invoking the next physical executable statement after the ELSE or END-IF$_{85}$.

```
IF      condition
        statement-1
        statement-2
        statement-3
ELSE
        statement-4. (or END-IF₈₅)

        next physical executable statement
```

If the condition is TRUE, **statement-1, statement-2,** and **statement-3** are executed. The ELSE phrase is ignored, and control is transferred to the next physical executable statement following the period and space or END-IF$_{85}$.

If the condition is FALSE, **statement-1, statement-2,** and **statement-3** are not executed, and control is transferred to the statement following the ELSE (**statement-4**). Execution then continues with the next physical executable statement.

Nested IF Statements.   Any statement can be another IF statement. Multiple IF statements are "nested":

```
IF  condition-1
   IF  condition-2
      IF  condition-3
         IF  condition-4
            IF  condition-5
               IF  condition-6
                  IF  condition-7
                     IF  condition-8
                        IF  condition-9
                           IF  condition-10
```

There is no specified limit for nested IF statements (an article in *Computerworld* reported a nested IF that required 37 pages!). Each IF should be paired with an ELSE:

```
IF  condition-1
   IF  condition-2
      IF  condition-3
           statement-3-1
           statement-3-2
           statement-3-3
      ELSE
           statement-3-4
           statement-3-5
           statement-3-6
   ELSE
        statement-2-1
        statement-2-2
        statement-2-3
ELSE
     statement-1-1
     statement-1-2
     statement-1-3
END-IF85
```

next physical executable statement

Indentation with each IF-ELSE pair starting in the same column is recommended. There should always be an ELSE, even if it is ELSE NEXT SENTENCE.

Nesting should be limited to three levels for readability and maintainability.

RECOMMENDATIONS

- Limit nesting to three levels.
- Indent each nest with the IF-ELSE pair starting in the same column.
- Always use ELSE.

- Use END-IF$_{85}$ to explicitly terminate IF statements if supported; otherwise, insert it as a comment (* in column 7).

There is one exception to the guideline of three nested IF statements: the case structure.

Nested IF statements imply that any of the conditions can be true and be true simultaneously. In the most recent example, **condition-1** could be true and **condition-2** and **condition-3** false, or **condition-1** and **condition-2** could be true, or all three conditions could be true.

The case structure states that only one condition of a set of conditions can be true for each evaluation. For instance, a person can only have a single marital status at any point in time: single, married, separated, divorced, or widowed. The case structure (using 88 levels) is as follows:

```
IF      single
        single-statements
ELSE
IF      married
        married-statements
ELSE
IF      separated
        separated-statements
ELSE
IF      divorced
        divorced-statements
ELSE
IF      widowed
        widowed-statements
ELSE
        PERFORM   invalid-marital-status-routine. (or END-IF₈₅)
```

IF and ELSE are not indented to indicate that only one condition can be true per evaluation. The last ELSE is the defensive programming statement to prevent runaway.

RECOMMENDATION

- Use unindented case structure IF statements with 88 levels wherever possible.

EVALUATE$^{nr}_{85}$ ANSI describes the EVALUATE$^{nr}_{85}$ statement as a "multi-branch, multi-join structure" that "can use multiple conditions to be evaluated" (ANSI X3.23-1985). That description alone should condemn it; the following syntax certainly should:

```
EVALUATE    identifier-1/literal-1/expression-1/TRUE/FALSE
[ALSO       identifier-2/literal-2/expression-2/TRUE/FALSE], ...
[WHEN       ANY/condition-1/TRUE/FALSE
[NOT]       identifier-3/literal-3/arithmetic-expression-1
```

            [THRU   identifier-4/literal-4/arithmetic-expression-2]
            [ALSO   ANY/condition-2/TRUE/FALSE
            [NOT]   identifier-5/literal-5/arithmetic-expression-3
            [THRU   identifier-6/literal-6/arithmetic-expression-4]], ...
                               imperative-statement-1], ...
            [WHEN OTHER   imperative-statement-2]
            [END-EVALUATE]

It is difficult to understand the syntax, much less decipher what it really means when encountered in a real program. IF statements and 88s are easier to use, read, and maintain.

RECOMMENDATION

- Do not use EVALUATE$_{85}$; use IF statements and 88s for readability, maintainability, and portability.

Arithmetic

The following common phrases apply to arithmetic statements:

- CORRESPONDING^{nr}
- SIZE ERROR and NOT ON SIZE ERROR$_{85}$
- ROUNDED

As previously explained under MOVE, CORRESPONDING^{nr} should not be used.

The SIZE ERROR phrases should always be used to check for overflow. If SIZE ERROR is not used, the value in the overflowed identifier is undefined. Errors occur (usually in user reports).

The ROUNDED phrase adds 1 to the least significant digit of the identifier as defined by its PIC clause if the next digit to its right that is in the computer's computation area is 5 or more. For consistency, rounding should be used at all times or never. Since the U.S. Internal Revenue Service and COBOL agree on rounding, its use is recommended.

ADD   The ADD statement has three formats:

1. ADD   identifier-1/literal-1, [identifier-2/literal-2],...
   TO   identifier-3 [ROUNDED], [identifier-4 [ROUNDED]],...
   [ON SIZE ERROR   imperative-statement-1]
   [NOT ON SIZE ERROR imperative-statement-2$_{85}$]
   [END-ADD$_{85}$]
2. ADD   identifier-1/literal-1, [identifier-2/literal-2]$_{85}$,...
   TO$_{85}$ identifier-3$_{85}$ [ROUNDED]
   GIVING identifier-4 [ROUNDED], [identifier-5 [ROUNDED]],...
   [ON SIZE ERROR   imperative-statement-1]

[<u>NOT</u> ON <u>SIZE</u> <u>ERROR</u> imperative-statement-2_{85}]
[<u>END-ADD</u>$_{85}$]

3. <u>ADD</u> <u>CORRESPONDING</u>^{nr} identifier-1
   <u>TO</u>   identifier-2 [<u>ROUNDED</u>]
   [<u>ON</u> <u>SIZE</u> <u>ERROR</u>   imperative-statement-1]
   [<u>NOT</u> ON <u>SIZE</u> <u>ERROR</u>   imperative-statement-2_{85}]
   [<u>END-ADD</u>$_{85}$]

Format 1 adds all the identifiers preceding the TO together and then adds that sum to each identifier following the TO. Format 2 adds all the identifiers preceding the TO_{85} or the GIVING together and then that sum *replaces* the current value in each of the identifiers following the GIVING. Format 2_{74} requires at least two identifiers or literals before the GIVING. Format 2_{85} requires at least one identifier or literal before the TO_{85} and one identifier or literal after the TO_{85}. The Format 2 TO_{85} was not part of the syntax of $COBOL_{74}$, probably an oversight, which $COBOL_{85}$ has rectified. Format 3^{nr} is not recommended.

RECOMMENDATIONS

- Do not use literals.
- Do not use CORRESPONDING^{nr}.

SUBTRACT   SUBTRACT has the same basic formats as ADD, except the sum calculated by adding the identifiers preceding the FROM is subtracted from the identifiers following the FROM and the result replaces those identifiers (Format 1), or the result replaces the current values of the identifiers following the Format 2 GIVING ($COBOL_{74}$ uses FROM in its Format 2 GIVING syntax). The recommendations are the same as for ADD.

DIVIDE   The DIVIDE statement has five similar formats:

1. <u>DIVIDE</u>   identifier-1/literal-1
   <u>INTO</u>   identifier-2 [<u>ROUNDED</u>], [identifier-3 [<u>ROUNDED</u>]], ...
   [<u>ON</u> <u>SIZE</u> <u>ERROR</u>   imperative-statement-1]
   [<u>NOT</u> ON <u>SIZE</u> <u>ERROR</u> imperative-statement-2_{85}]
   [<u>END-DIVIDE</u>$_{85}$]

2. <u>DIVIDE</u>   identifier-1/literal-1
   <u>INTO</u>   identifier-2 [<u>ROUNDED</u>], [identifier-3 [<u>ROUNDED</u>]], ...
   <u>GIVING</u>   identifier-3 [<u>ROUNDED</u>], [identifier-4 [<u>ROUNDED</u>]], ...
   [<u>ON</u> <u>SIZE</u> <u>ERROR</u>   imperative-statement-1]
   [<u>NOT</u> ON <u>SIZE</u> <u>ERROR</u> imperative-statement-2_{85}]
   [<u>END-DIVIDE</u>$_{85}$]

3. <u>DIVIDE</u>   identifier-1/literal-1
   <u>BY</u>   identifier-2 [<u>ROUNDED</u>], [identifier-3 [<u>ROUNDED</u>]], ...
   <u>GIVING</u>   identifier-3 [<u>ROUNDED</u>], [identifier-4 [<u>ROUNDED</u>]], ...
   [<u>ON</u> <u>SIZE</u> <u>ERROR</u>   imperative-statement-1]

> [NOT on SIZE ERROR imperative-statement-2$_{85}$]
> [END-DIVIDE$_{85}$]

4. DIVIDE   identifier-1/literal-1
   INTO   identifier-2 [ROUNDED], [identifier-3 [ROUNDED]], ...
   GIVING   identifier-4 [ROUNDED]
   REMAINDER   identifier-5

   [ON SIZE ERROR   imperative-statement-1]
   [NOT ON SIZE ERROR imperative-statement-2$_{85}$]
   [END-DIVIDE$_{85}$]

5. DIVIDE   identifier-1/literal-1
   BY   identifier-2 [ROUNDED], [identifier-3 [ROUNDED]], ...
   GIVING   identifier-4 [ROUNDED]
   REMAINDER   identifier-5
   [ON SIZE ERROR   imperative-statement-1]
   [NOT ON SIZE ERROR imperative-statement-2$_{85}$]
   [END-DIVIDE$_{85}$]

*REMAINDER cannot be ROUNDED

In Format 1, the divisor (**identifier-1/literal-1**) is divided INTO the dividend (**identifier-2**), and after the division calculation, the quotient replaces the dividend. In the remaining GIVING formats, the quotient replaces the value in the GIVING identifier(s) and the dividend value is unchanged. The GIVING format is recommended since it provides more information in a memory dump upon an abend (divisor, dividend, and quotient instead of just divisor and quotient).

The INTO/BY formats are essentially identical except the divisor and dividend identifiers are interchanged. Each organization should standardize on either INTO or BY (personal preference is BY because the standard equation is *a/b*).

Formats 4 and 5 store the REMAINDER in the REMAINDER identifier. A standard use of the REMAINDER phrase is to determine if a year is a leap year.

```
DIVIDE      year
BY          four
GIVING      who-cares
REMAINDER leap-year-value
```

A value of zero in REMAINDER defines the year as a leap year unless it is a century year not divisible by 400 (1900 was not a leap year; 2000 will be).

A common ON SIZE error is to DIVIDE by zero; the algebraic answer is infinity.

RECOMMENDATIONS

- Do not use literals.
- Do *not* use Format 1^{nr} (no GIVING phrase).
- Use Formats 3 and 5 (BY phrase).

MULTIPLY   The MULTIPLY statement has only two formats:

1. <u>MULTIPLY</u> identifier-1/literal-1
   <u>BY</u>   identifier-2 [<u>ROUNDED</u>], [identifier-3 [<u>ROUNDED</u>]], ...
   [ON <u>SIZE</u> <u>ERROR</u>   imperative-statement-1]
   [<u>NOT</u> ON <u>SIZE</u> <u>ERROR</u> imperative-statement-2$_{85}$]
   [<u>END</u>-MULTIPLY$_{85}$]
2. <u>MULTIPLY</u> identifier-1/literal-1
   <u>BY</u>   identifier-2/literal-2
   <u>GIVING</u>   identifier-3 [<u>ROUNDED</u>], [identifier-4 [<u>ROUNDED</u>]], ...
   [ON <u>SIZE</u> <u>ERROR</u>   imperative-statement-1]
   [<u>NOT</u> ON <u>SIZE</u> <u>ERROR</u> imperative-statement-2$_{85}$]
   [<u>END</u>-MULTIPLY$_{85}$]

In Format 1 the multiplicand (**identifier-1/literal-1**) is multiplied by the multiplier (**identifier-2**), and after the multiplication calculation, the product *replaces* the multiplier. In Format 2, the product replaces the current value(s) in the GIVING identifier(s), and the multiplier is unchanged.

RECOMMENDATIONS

- Do not use literals.
- Use Format 2 only (more information available in memory dump).

COMPUTE^{nr}   The COMPUTE^{nr} statement is COBOL shorthand for combining arithmetic verbs. The basic syntax is

   <u>COMPUTE</u>^{nr} identifier-1 [ROUNDED], [identifier-2 [ROUNDED]], ...
                   = arithmetic-expression
   [ON <u>SIZE</u> <u>ERROR</u>   imperative-statement-1]
   [<u>NOT</u> ON <u>SIZE</u> <u>ERROR</u> imperative-statement-2$_{85}$]
   [<u>END</u>-COMPUTE$_{85}$]

The arithmetic-expression is the same as previously discussed under IF. Again, the arithmetic-expression can be exceedingly complex; for example, it would require significant effort for a maintenance programmer to understand the following calculation:

   COMPUTE^{nr} a = $-$b / c $*$ d + (e $-$ f) $**$ g / ((h $**$ i / j) + (k $-$ l))
   ON SIZE ERROR PERFORM compute-overflow-routine
   END-COMPUTE^{nr}

It would be easier to understand if it were decomposed into its simpler arithmetic statements. Another problem is that it is difficult to isolate the actual calculation that caused the overflow, whereas the simpler arithmetic statements isolate overflow.

   The compiler parses the arithmetic expression from left to right, scanning for a left parenthesis (. After a (has been isolated, scanning continues, looking for either another (or a right parenthesis). If another (is isolated before a), there are parentheses within parenthesis (nested). Eventually, a) is found, and the expression within the paired parentheses is scanned from left to right, looking for operators. ANSI has defined an evaluation sequence for arithmetic operators:

- unary^{nr} The term following the unary^{nr} operator is multiplied by $+1$ ($+a$) or -1 ($-a$).
- exponentiation   The term preceding $**$ is raised to the power specified by the term following ($a**b$).
- multiplication   The term preceding the $*$ or $/$ is multiplied or divided by the division   term following ($a*b$ or a/b).
- addition   The term following the $+$ or $-$ is added to or subtracted from subtraction   the term preceding ($a + b$ or $a - b$).

After all parentheses have been evaluated, scanning resumes from the leftmost character following the equal sign looking for operators as specified above.

The presence or absence of parentheses is important and can drastically alter the results. Consider the following examples.

$$\text{COMPUTE}^{nr} \quad a = b ? c ? d ? e$$

where $? =$ an unspecified arithmetic operator, all terms have a PIC clause of S999V9, and the current values of the terms are

$$b = +002.0 \qquad c = +004.0 \qquad d = +008.0 \qquad e = +016.0$$

If $?$ is replaced by $+$, then

$$\text{COMPUTE}^{nr} \quad a = b + c + d + e$$

$a = +030.0$. Since all terms are positive and all operators are positive, parentheses would not alter the result:

$$\text{COMPUTE}^{nr} \quad a = (b + c) + (d + e)$$

$$\text{COMPUTE}^{nr} \quad a = b + (c + d + e)$$

$$\text{COMPUTE}^{nr} \quad a = (b + c + d) + e$$

All yield the same result, $a = +030.0$. If $?$ is replaced by $-$, then

$$\text{COMPUTE}^{nr} \quad a = b - c - d - e$$

and $a = -026.0$ instead of -030.0. The reason is that the evaluation of $+02b - +04c = -02$, the next evaluation of $-02 - +08d = -10$, and finally, the last evaluation of $-10 - +16e = -26$. Achieving -030.0 requires a negative unary^{nr} operator preceding b:

$$\text{COMPUTE}^{nr} \quad a = -b - c - d - e$$

Parentheses do make a difference: $a = +006.0$ if

$$\text{COMPUTE}^{nr} \quad a = (b - c) - (d - e)$$

because $(b - c)$ evaluates to -02, $(d - e)$ evaluates to -08, $-02 - -08 = +06$ (a double negative evaluates *positive*,) and $-02 + 08 = +006.0$.
$a = +022.0$ if

$$\text{COMPUTE}^{nr} \quad a = b - (c - d - e)$$

and $a = -026.0$ if

$$\text{COMPUTE}^{nr} \quad a = (b - c - d) - e$$

If the equation is

$$\text{COMPUTE}^{nr} \quad a = b - c + d - e$$

$a = -010.0$ in the unparenthesized COMPUTE^{nr}. a also equals -010.0 for

$$\text{COMPUTE}^{nr} \quad a = (b - c) + (d - e)$$

and

$$\text{COMPUTE}^{nr} \quad a = (b - c + d) - e$$

but $a = +006.0$ if

$$\text{COMPUTE}^{nr} \quad a = b - (c + d - e)$$

(another instance of double minus).

Arithmetic statements force the programmer to define the precedence of arithmetic operators explicitly; the COMPUTE^{nr} statement does not and in fact provides many opportunities to calculate incorrect results.

RECOMMENDATION

• Do not use COMPUTE^{nr}.

Data Movement

STRING^{nr} and UNSTRING^{nr}   The STRING^{nr} verb takes specified characters from many sending fields and places them in a left-to-right sequence in a single receiving field. The UNSTRING^{nr} verb takes specific characters from a single sending field and places them in left-to-right sequence in many receiving fields. The characters to be transmitted are selected by DELIMITED BY identifiers. The character(s) in the DELIMITED BY phrase is used to terminate the scan; for example, if the transmitting field contained

abcdefghijklmnopqrstuvwxyz

and the DELIMITED BY contained an *e, abcd* would be moved; if the DELIMITED BY contained a *z*, everything but the *z* would be transmitted (assuming that the receiving field had sufficient capacity).

Both STRING^{nr} and UNSTRING^{nr} have an optional POINTER that allows the programmer to specify the starting position in the receiving field. UNSTRING^{nr} also has numerous COUNT and TALLYING optional phrases.

STRING^{nr} and UNSTRING^{nr} are usually used to process variable-length fields or to effect editing. Variable-length fields and editing have been recommended against. In any case, STRING^{nr} and UNSTRING^{nr} can be "decomposed" into simpler and easier-to-understand INSPECT and/or MOVE statements.

RECOMMENDATION

- Do not use STRING^{nr} or UNSTRING^{nr}; use INSPECT or MOVE for readability and maintainability.

If you must use STRING^{nr} or UNSTRING^{nr}, remember the defensive programming rule of always coding the optional OVERFLOW phrase. Any STRING^{nr} or UNSTRING^{nr} statement should also be subjected to code inspection.

STRING^{nr} and UNSTRING^{nr} remind me of my programming days on the RCA 501. The RCA 501 was a variable-length computer that used a bullet as an information separator symbol much like the DELIMITED BY identifiers. It also reminds me of my good friend Gordon Etherington, who had the responsibility for maintaining original RCA 501 programs for over 30 years through emulation (a hardware/software technique that permits one CPU to run another CPU's object code without modification).

Input-Output

ANSI divides files into three types:

- SEQUENTIAL
- RELATIVE
- INDEXED

A SEQUENTIAL FILE is composed of RECORDS that are stored in adjacent physical locations. KEY is not required, and the only ACCESS MODE is SEQUENTIAL.

A RELATIVE FILE is composed of RECORDS that are also stored in adjacent physical locations but are accessible by a RELATIVE KEY. The RELATIVE KEY is the physical storage number. ACCESS MODE can be SEQUENTIAL, RANDOM, or DYNAMIC (a combination of SEQUENTIAL and RANDOM in the same program).

An INDEXED FILE is also composed of RECORDS that are in adjacent physical locations[17] but are accessible by a unique primary index defined by the RECORD KEY clause of the FILE CONTROL entry. The RECORD KEY clause defines a data field within the RECORD, such as **student-number,** as the unique primary key. ACCESS MODE can be SEQUENTIAL, RANDOM, or DYNAMIC.

The ANSI high INDEXED I-O module permits access by secondary indices defined by the ALTERNATE RECORD KEY clause of the FILE CONTROL entry. A secondary index does not have to be unique, and duplicate values are allowed by the DUPLICATES phrase.

A RECORD KEY or an ALTERNATE RECORD KEY without DUPLICATES returns the single RECORD with the specified value from the FILE to the program. An ALTERNATE RECORD KEY with DUPLICATES returns the first RECORD that was written (first in, first out) with the specified value. Subsequent INDEXED READ statements with the same ALTERNATE KEY return all RECORDS with the specified value. The end of the chain is indicated by the RETURN STATUS of NO SUCH RECORD.

ANSI provides five INPUT-OUTPUT statements:

START   READ   REWRITE   DELETE   WRITE

The START statement positions a FILE to a specified position. The READ statement obtains the NEXT logical RECORD (SEQUENTIAL) or the specified RECORD (RANDOM).[18] The REWRITE statement replaces the current logical RECORD (SEQUENTIAL) or the specified RECORD (RANDOM) with a modified RECORD. The DELETE statement removes the current logical RECORD (SEQUENTIAL) or the specified RECORD (RANDOM).[19] The WRITE statement places a new logical RECORD in the next adjacent physical location (SEQUENTIAL or RANDOM).[20] There is a special WRITE format for printers.

The various INPUT-OUTPUT statements and formats can "trap" the exception conditions of END and INVALID KEY.

END can be

- END of FILE (EOF)
- OPTIONAL INPUT FILE not present[85]
- RELATIVE RECORD number > RELATIVE RECORD KEY[85]

INVALID KEY can be

- sequence error
- duplicate KEY
- no RECORD found
- boundary violation
- OPTIONAL INPUT FILE not present[85]
- RELATIVE RECORD number > RELATIVE RECORD KEY[85]

Each INPUT-OUTPUT statement can and should return a FILE STATUS (see Chapter 5).

Table 10.6 is a summary of exception conditions by statement by INPUT-OUTPUT type.

TABLE 10.6   Exception conditions

STATEMENT	I/O	INV KEY	AT END
START	REL	MND	—
READ	SEQ	—	MND
	RAN	MND	—
REWRITE	SEQ	—	—
	RAN	MND	—
DELETE	RAN	MND	—
WRITE	PRT	—	EOP
	SEQ	—	—
	RAN	MND	—
where	SEQ	= SEQUENTIAL	
	RAN	= RANDOM (RELATIVE or INDEXED)	
	PRT	= printer (SEQUENTIAL)	
	—	= not applicable or invalid	
	MND	= mandatory	
	EOP	= END OF PAGE	

ANSI considers the conditions specified mandatory as optional because a DECLARATIVES SECTION[nr] can be used instead of INVALID KEY or AT END for trapping. A DECLARATIVES SECTION[nr] must be generalized since all INVALID KEY or AT END conditions must transfer control to the same starting statement. Specific INVALID KEY or AT END clauses allow transfer to specific exception processing routines. Structured programming theory requires that a module process a specific function—such as what to do when an invalid duplicate KEY is detected—rather than a general routine that must determine what the actual condition is before processing. Another reason not to use DECLARATIVES[nr] is that it requires the program to be coded in sections.

RECOMMENDATION

- Always use INVALID KEY or AT END; do not use DECLARATIVES[nr].

The ANSI INPUT-OUTPUT statements plus additional non-ANSI statements added by vendors for specific hardware and/or access methods (such as ISAM or VSAM) have many formats with many optional clauses and phrases.

Each INPUT-OUTPUT statement required should be coded by a systems programmer and copied into the program. The systems programmer should also provide for each INPUT-OUTPUT statement:

- The specific INVALID KEY or AT END routine
- A specific routine to test FILE STATUS for other abnormal conditions
- Specific routines to process each possible abnormal condition

All should be in the COPYLIB.

Another symptom of spaghetti programs is a proliferation of INPUT-OUTPUT statements, which make it difficult to ascertain how data was READ or written. An easy-to-understand program contains one and only one INPUT-OUTPUT statement type per FILE, with each statement in a separate paragraph.

Consider a typical batch master/transaction updating program that has three files consisting of master, transaction, and error. The master FILE must be READ, rewritten, deleted, and written based on the transaction FILE. The transaction FILE must be READ; the error FILE must be written. Only the following common performable paragraphs should exist:

```
PC01-read-master-record.

PC02-rewrite-master-record.

PC03-delete-master-record.

PC04-write-new-master-record.

PC05-read-transaction-record.

PC06-write-error-record.
```

Other nefarious practices include using LOW-VALUES^{nr} and HIGH-VALUES^{nr} and numerous switches for BOF and EOF conditions to control processing.

Using LOW-VALUES^{nr}, HIGH-VALUES^{nr}, switches, and so forth causes confusion and errors when unusual but predictable processing conditions arise. These techniques are not required if the programmer uses the logical structure of the program and the control information available. The general processing logic for the batch master/transaction updating program is as follows (it assumes a sequential disk—the SAM of ISAM or VSAM stands for *sequential access method*):

```
IF master-record-key < transaction-record-key
    READ  master-record
     INTO   master-record-ws
ELSE
```

```
IF master-record-key = transaction-record-key
    IF transaction-code = update
        PERFORM  update-validation
        REWRITE  master-record
        FROM       transaction-record-ws
        READ       transaction-record
        INTO        transaction-record-ws
    ELSE
    IF transaction-code = delete
        DELETE  master-record
        READ     master-record
        INTO      master-record-ws
        READ     transaction-record
        INTO      transaction-record-ws
ELSE
IF master-record-key > transaction-record-key
    PERFORM  add-validation
    WRITE       new-master-record
    FROM        transaction-record-ws
    READ        transaction-record
    INTO         transaction-record-ws
END-IF
```

The programmer must cope with the following conditions:

- That the correct master, transaction, and error FILES are available
- That both the master and transaction FILES—even if openable—contain at least one record
- EOF on the transaction FILE
- INPUT-OUTPUT errors

The programmer should follow minimal auditing principles of balancing the INPUT-OUTPUT:

```
total-master-records       = master-record-read
                           + master-records-added
                           − master-records-deleted

total-transaction-records  = master-records-added
                           + master-records-deleted
                           + master-records-modified
                           + transaction-error-records-written
```

The following is a program shell (sometimes called skeleton) for a simple batch master/transaction update using a sequential disk.

```
SEQ     DISPLAY OF MSTUPD    FROM LIBRARY: ZADP05.ERIC.COBOL                                          COPY
NUMBER  1 . . . 5 . . . 10 . . . 15 . . . 20 . . . 25 . . . 30 . . . 35 . . . 40 . . . 45 . . . 50 . . . 55 . . . 60 . . . 65 . . . 70 . . . 75 . . . 80   MEMBER

  1   000100   IDENTIFICATION DIVISION.                                            00010001
  2   000200                                                                       00020001
  3   000300   PROGRAM ID.           Mstupd.                                       00030011
  4   000400                                                                       00040001
  5   000500                         Shell for a sequential disc                   00050012
  6   000600                         master/transaction update program.           00060006
  7   000700                                                                       00070001
  8   000800   AUTHOR.               Eric Garrigue Vesely.                         00080002
  9   000900                                                                       00090001
 10   001000   INSTALLATION.         The Analyst Workbench.                        00100002
 11   001100                                                                       00110001
 12   001200   DATE-WRITTEN.         1 May 1987.                                   00120012
 13   001300                                                                       00130001
 14   001400   DATE-COMPILED.                                                      00140001
 15   001500                                                                       00150001
```

```
SEQ     DISPLAY OF MSTUPD   FROM LIBRARY: ZADP05.ERIC.COBOL                                                                 COPY
NUMBER  1 . . 5 . . . 10 . . . 15 . . . . 20 . . . 25 . . . 30 . . . 35 . . . 40 . . . 45 . . . 50 . . . 55 . . . 60 . . . 65 . . . 70 . . . 75 . . . 80   MEMBER

16  001600         REMARKS                                                          00160012
17  001700         IF master-record-key < transaction-record-key                    00170001
18  001800             READ    master-record                                        00180001
19  001900             INTO    master-record-ws                                     00190001
20  002000         ELSE                                                             00200001
21  002100         IF master-record-key = transaction-record-key                    00210001
22  002200             IF transaction-code = update                                 00220001
23  002300                 PERFORM    update-validation                             00230001
24  002400                 REWRITE    master-record                                 00240006
25  002500                     FROM   transaction-record-ws                         00250006
26  002600                 READ       transaction-record                            00260001
27  002700                     INTO   transaction-record-ws                         00270001
28  002800             ELSE                                                         00280001
29  002900             IF transaction-code = delete                                 00290001
30  003000                 DELETE    master-record                                  00300001
31  003100                 READ      master-record                                  00310001
32  003200                     INTO  master-record-ws                               00320001
33  003300                 READ      transaction-record                             00330001
34  003400                     INTO  transaction-record-ws                          00340001
```

```
SEQ      DISPLAY OF MSTUPD   FROM LIBRARY: ZADP05.ERIC.COBOL                                           COPY
NUMBER  1 . . . 5 . . . 10 . . . 15 . . . 20 . . . 25 . . . 30 . . . 35 . . . 40 . . . 45 . . . 50 . . . 55 . . . 60 . . . 65 . . . 70 . . . 75 . . . 80   MEMBER

  36    003600       ENVIRONMENT DIVISION.                                                             00360001
  37    003700                                                                                         00370001
  38    003800             COPY master-update-environment-div.                                         00380001
  39    003900                                                                                         00390001
```

```
SEQ      DISPLAY OF MSTUPD    FROM LIBRARY: ZADP05.ERIC.COBOL              COPY
NUMBER   1 . . . 5 . . . 10 . . . 15 . . . 20 . . . 25 . . . 30 . . . 35 . . . 40 . . . 45 . . . 50 . . . 55 . . . 60 . . . 65 . . . 70 . . . 75 . . . 80    MEMBER

  41     004100   DATA DIVISION.                                                                                                00410001
  42     004200                                                                                                                 00420001
  43     004300   FD   master-record                COPY master-record.                                                        00430001
  44     004400                                                                                                                 00440001
  45     004500   FD   transaction-record           COPY transaction-record.                                                   00450001
  46     004600                                                                                                                 00460001
  47     004700   FD   error-record                 COPY error-record.                                                         00470001
  48     004800                                                                                                                 00480001
  49     004900   WORKING-STORAGE SECTION.                                                                                      00490001
  50     005000                                                                                                                 00500001
  51     005100   01   program-unique-data.                                                                                     00510001
  52     005200        02   FILLER                  PIC A(8)              VALUE "COUNTERS".                                      00520001
  53     005300        02   program-record-counters.                                                                           00530001
  54     005400             03   total-master-records                                                                           00540001
  55     005500                                     PIC 9(6)V             USAGE COMP                                            00550006
  56     005600                                                           VALUE ZERO.                                           00560001
  57     005700             03   master-records-read                                                                            00570001
  58     005800                                     PIC 9(6)V             USAGE COMP                                            00580006
  59     005900                                                           VALUE ZERO.                                           00590001
  60     006000                  88   no-master-records                  VALUE ZERO.                                            00600001
  61     006100             03   master-records-added                                                                           00610001
  62     006200                                     PIC 9(6)V             USAGE COMP                                            00620006
  63     006300                                                           VALUE ZERO.                                           00630001
  64     006400             03   master-records-deleted                                                                         00640001
  65     006500                                     PIC 9(6)V             USAGE COMP                                            00650006
  66     006600                                                           VALUE ZERO.                                           00660001
  67     006700             03   total-transaction-records                                                                      00670001
  68     006800                                     PIC 9(6)V             USAGE COMP                                            00680006
  69     006900                                                           VALUE ZERO.                                           00690001
  70     007000                  88   no-transaction-records             VALUE ZERO.                                            00700001
  71     007100                                                                                                                 00710001
  72     007200             03   master-records-modified                                                                        00720001
  73     007300                                     PIC 9(6)V             USAGE COMP                                            00730006
  74     007400                                                           VALUE ZERO.                                           00740001
  75     007500             03   error-records-written                                                                          00750001
  76     007600                                     PIC 9(6)V             USAGE COMP                                            00760006
  77     007700                                                           VALUE ZERO.                                           00770001
  78     007800                                                                                                                 00780001
```

```
SEQ     DISPLAY OF MSTUPD   FROM LIBRARY: ZADP05.ERIC.COBOL                                      COPY
NUMBER  1...5...10...15...20...25...30...35...40...45...50...55...60...65...70...75...80         MEMBER

 79   007900        02  FILLER                            PIC A(8)     VALUE "KEYFIELD".          0079001
 80   008000            03  master-record-key-field                                              0080001
 81   008100                                               PIC 9(?)V    VALUE ZERO.               0081006
 82   008200            03  transaction-record-key-field                                          0082001
 83   008300                                               PIC 9(?)V    VALUE ZERO.               0083006
 84   008400  *master-record-key-field is compared to the transaction-record-                    0084001
 85   008500  *key-field to control processing.                                                  0085001
 86   008600                                                                                      0086001
 87   008700    01  master-record-read-into.                                                      0087001
 88   008800        02  FILLER                                         VALUE "MASTER".            0088001
 89   008900                                                                                      0089001
 90   009000    01  master-record-ws                                  COPY master-record-ws.      0090001
 91   009100                                                                                      0091001
 92   009200    01  transaction-record-read-into.                                                 0092001
 93   009300        02  FILLER                            PIC A(8)     VALUE "TRANSACTION".        0093001
 94   009400                                                                                      0094001
 95   009500    01  transaction-code-field.                                                       0095001
 96   009600        02  FILLER                            PIC A(8)     VALUE "TRANCODE".           0096001
 97   009700        02  transaction-code                  PIC A        VALUE SPACE.               0097001
 98   009800                88  add                                    VALUE "A".                 0098001
 99   009900                88  delete                                 VALUE "D".                 0099001
100   010000                88  update                                 VALUE "U".                 0100001
101   010100                88  null                                   VALUE SPACE.               0101001
102   010200                                                                                      0102001
103   010300    01  transaction-record-ws                             COPY transaction-record-ws. 0103001
104   010400                                                                                      0104001
105   010500    01  file-status-fields.                                                           0105001
106   010600        02  FILLER                            PIC A(8)     VALUE "FILESTAT".           0106001
107   010700  *cobol-85 file statuses                                                             0107001
108   010800        02  master-file-status-field          PIC XX.                                 0108001
109   010900                88  successful-completion                  VALUE ZERO.                0109001
110   011000  *sc = successful completion                                                         0110001
111   011100                88  sc-duplicate-key                       VALUE "02".                0111001
112   011200                88  sc-record-length-incorrect             VALUE "04".                0112001
113   011300                88  sc-optional-file-not-present           VALUE "05".                0113001
114   011400                88  sc-magtape-for-nonreel-unit            VALUE "07".                0114001
115   011500                88  at-end-of-file                         VALUE "10".                0115001
```

```
SEQ                                                                                                              COPY
NUMBER      DISPLAY OF MSTUPD     FROM LIBRARY: ZADP05.ERIC.COBOL                                                 MEMBER
            1 . . . 5 . . . 10 . . . 15 . . . 20 . . . 25 . . . 30 . . . 35 . . . 40 . . . 45 . . . 50 . . . 55 . . . 60 . . . 65 . . . 70 . . . 75 . . . 80

116    011600 *ae = at end condition                                                                             0116001
117    011700    88 ae-optional-file-not-present          VALUE "10".                                            0117001
118    011800    88 ae-relative-rec-number-too-big        VALUE "14".                                            0118001
119    011900    88 invalid-key-sequence-error            VALUE "21".                                            0119001
120    012000 *ik = invalid key condition                                                                        0120001
121    012100    88 ik-duplicate-key                      VALUE "22".                                            0121001
122    012200    88 ik-record-not-found                   VALUE "23".                                            0122001
123    012300    88 ik-boundary-violation                 VALUE "24".                                            0123001
124    012400    88 permanent-error                       VALUE "30".                                            0124001
125    012500 *pe = permanent error condition                                                                    0125001
126    012600    88 pe-boundary violation                 VALUE "34".                                            0126001
127    012700    88 pe-non-optional-file-not-prsnt        VALUE "35".                                            0127001
128    012800    88 pe-open-mode-incorrect                VALUE "37".                                            0128001
129    012900    88 pe-file-is-locked                     VALUE "38".                                            0129001
130    013000    88 pe-conflict-btwn-files-attrib         VALUE "39".                                            0130001
131    013100    88 logic-error-file-open                 VALUE "41".                                            0131001
132    013200 *le = logic error condition                                                                        0132001
133    013300    88 le-file-not-open                      VALUE "42".                                            0133001
134    013400    88 le-required-read-not-ok               VALUE "43".                                            0134001
135    013500    88 le-boundary-violation                 VALUE "44".                                            0135001
136    013600    88 le-eof-or-bad-read-or-start           VALUE "46".                                            0136001
137    013700    88 le-file-notopen-in-input-or-io        VALUE "47".                                            0137001
138    013800    88 le-file-notopen-in-out-or-exte        VALUE "48".                                            0138001
139    013900    88 le-notopen-in-io                      VALUE "49".                                            0139001
140    014000                                                                                                    0140001
141    014100    88 invalid-codes                         VALUE "01",                                            0141001
142    014200                                                    "03",                                           0142001
143    014300                                                    "06",                                           0143001
144    014400                                              "08" THRU "09",                                       0144001
145    014500                                              "11" THRU "13",                                       0145001
146    014600                                              "15" THRU "20",                                       0146001
147    014700                                              "25" THRU "29",                                       0147001
148    014800                                              "31" THRU "33",                                       0148001
149    014900                                                    "36",                                           0149001
150    015000                                                    "40",                                           0150001
151    015100                                                    "45",                                           0151001
152    015200                                              "50" THRU "99".                                       0152001
153    015300                                                                                                    0153001
154    015400 *the file statuses should be copied with appropriate prefixes for                                 0154001
155    015500 *each file.                                                                                        0155001
156    015600                                                                                                    0156001
157    015700 01  working-storage-end.                                                                           0157001
158    015800    02 FILLER             PIC A(8)           VALUE "WSEND".                                          0158001
```

```
SEQ      DISPLAY OF MSTUPD   FROM LIBRARY: ZADP05.ERIC.COBOL                                        COPY
NUMBER   1...5...10...15...20...25...30...35...40...45...50...55...60...65...70...75...80          MEMBER

160      016000  PROCEDURE DIVISION.                                                               01600001
161      016100                                                                                    01610001
162      016200  P101-initialization.                                                              01620001
163      016300 ****************************************************                                01630002
164      016400 *   perform initialization                                                         01640001
165      016500 *                                                                                  01650001
166      016600 * @IN    None                                                                      01660010
167      016700 * @OUT   None                                                                      01670010
168      016800 * @OUT   CONTROL=None                                                              01680010
169      016900 ****************************************************                                01690002
170      017000 *                                                                                  01700001
171      017100 *      initialization statements                                                   01710011
172      017200                                                                                    01720001
173      017300      OPEN I-O       master-file                                                     01730001
174      017400                                                                                    01740001
175      017500      OPEN INPUT     transaction-file                                                01750001
176      017600                                                                                    01760001
177      017700      OPEN OUTPUT    error-file                                                      01770012
178      017800                                                                                    01780001
179      017900 *      CONTINUE                                                                     01790012
180      018000                                                                                    01800001
181      018100  P102-mainline.                                                                     01810002
182      018200 ****************************************************                                01820002
183      018300 *   compares master-record-key-filed (M) to transaction-                           01830001
184      018400 *   record-key-field (T) to control processing.                                    01840001
185      018500 *      IF M < T then    READ M;                                                     01850001
186      018600 *      IF M = T then    update M                                                    01860001
187      018700 *      IF M > T then    READ T;                                                     01870001
188      018800 *                       WRITE M from T                                              01880001
189      018900 *                       READ T.                                                     01890001
190      019000                                                                                    01900001
191      019100 * @IN   Master-record-key-field                                                     01910010
192      019200 * @IN   Transaction-record-key-field                                                01920010
193      019300 * @OUT  NONE                                                                        01930010
194      019400 * @OUT  CONTROL=None                                                                01940010
195      019500 ****************************************************                                01950002
```

```
SEQ        DISPLAY OF  MSTUPD    FROM LIBRARY: ZADP05.ERIC.COBOL                                              COPY
NUMBER   1 . . . 5 . . . 10 . . . 15 . . . 20 . . . 25 . . . 30 . . . 35 . . . 40 . . . 45 . . . 50 . . . 55 . . . 60 . . . 65 . . . 70 . . . 75 . . . 80   MEMBER

 196   019600                                                                                                         01960001
 197   019700                                                                                                         01970001
 198   019800        IF              master-record-key-field                               <                          01980001
 199   019900                        transaction-record-key-field                                                     01990001
 200   020000        PERFORM         PC01-read-master-record                                                          02000001
 201   020100            THRU        PC01-X                                                                           02010001
 202   020200        ELSE                                                                                             02020001
 203   020300        IF              master-record-key-field                               =                          02030001
 204   020400                        transaction-record-key-field                                                     02040001
 205   020500        PERFORM         P211-update-master-record                                                       02050001
 206   020600            THRU        P211-X                                                                           02060001
 207   020700        ELSE                                                                                             02070001
 208   020800        IF              master-record-key-field                               >                          02080001
 209   020900                        transaction-record-key-field                                                     02090001
 210   021000        PERFORM         P212-write-new-master-record                                                    02100001
 211   021100            THRU        P212-X                                                                           02110001
 212   021200        ELSE                                                                                             02120001
 213   021300        GO TO           PCXX-program-abort                                                               02130001
 214   021400        END-IF                                                                                           02140001
 215   021500                                                                                                         02150012
 216   021600                                                                                                         02160002
 217   021700        GO TO           P102-mainline.                                                                   02170012
```

```
SEQ      DISPLAY OF MSTUPD   FROM LIBRARY: ZADP05.ERIC.COBOL                                                      COPY
NUMBER   1...5...10...15...20...25...30...35...40...45...50...55...60...65...70...75...80                         MEMBER

219      021900 P103-termination.                                                                                02190002
220      022000 ************************************                                                              02200002
221      022100 *    perform termination                                                                         02210001
222      022200 *                                                                                                 02220001
223      022300 *@IN           None                                                                              02230010
224      022400 *@OUT          None                                                                              02240010
225      022500 *@OUT     CONTROL=None                                                                           02250010
226      022600 ************************************                                                              02260002
227      022700 *                                                                                                 02270001
228      022800            COPY termination-routine.                                                              02280002
229      022900 *Installation standard routine which includes balancing                                          02290002
230      023000 *control fields                                                                                   02300002
231      023100                                                                                                   02310001
232      023200            CLOSE      master-file                                                                 02320001
233      023300                       transaction-file                                                            02330001
234      023400                       error-file                                                                  02340001
235      023500                                                                                                   02350001
236      023600            STOP       RUN.                                                                        02360001
237      023700                                                                                                   02370001
239      023900 P211-update-master-record.                                                                        02390001
240      024000 ****************************************                                                          02400002
241      024100 *    validate that transaction code is update or delete                                          02410001
242      024200 *    if update then validate transaction-record                                                  02420001
243      024300 *                   rewrite master-record                                                         02430001
```

```
SEQ       DISPLAY OF MSTUPD    FROM LIBRARY: ZADP05.ERIC.COBOL           COPY
NUMBER    1 . . . 5 . . . 10 . . . 15 . . . 20 . . . 25 . . . 30 . . . 35 . . . 40 . . . 45 . . . 50 . . . 55 . . . 60 . . . 65 . . . 70 . . . 75 . . . 80    MEMBER

244       024400                                        read next transaction-record                                          02440001
245       024500 *  If delete then delete current master-record                                                              02450001
246       024600 *                            read next master-record                                                         02460001
247       024700 *                            read next transaction-record                                                    02470001
248       024800 *                                                                                                            02480001
249       024900 * @IN         Transaction-code                                                                               02490010
250       025000 * @OUT        None                                                                                           02500010
251       025100 * ©OUT        CONTROL=error-condition                                                                        02510010
252       025200 ***************************************************                                                          02520002
253       025300 *                                                                                                            02530001
254       025400                                                                                                              02540001
255       025500             IF             update                                                                            02550001
256       025600                 PERFORM    PC07-validate-transaction-rec                                                     02560001
257       025700                 PERFORM    PC02-rewrite-master-record                                                        02570001
258       025800                 PERFORM    PC05-read-transaction-record                                                      02580002
259       025900             ELSE                                                                                             02590001
260       026000             IF             delete                                                                           02600001
261       026100                 PERFORM    PC03-delete-master-record                                                         02610001
262       026200                 PERFORM    PC01-read-master-record                                                          02620001
263       026300                 PERFORM    PC05-read-transaction-record                                                      02630001
264       026400             ELSE                                                                                             02640001
265       026500                                                                                                             02650001
266       026600 * transaction-code is initialized to null. After                                                            02660001
267       026700 * initialization, M = T and P212 is invoked. The                                                            02670001
268       026800 * null "primes the pump".                                                                                   02680001
269       026900                                                                                                             02690001
270       027000             IF             null                                                                            02700001
271       027100                 PERFORM    PC01-read-master-record                                                          02710001
272       027200                 PERFORM    PC05-read-transaction-record                                                      02720001
273       027300             ELSE                                                                                             02730001
274       027400                 PERFORM    P321-invalid-update-transcode                                                     02740001
275       027500                 THRU       P321-X                                                                           02750001
276       027600             END-IF                                                                                           02760001
277       027700                                                                                                             02770002
```

```
 SEQ      DISPLAY OF MSTUPD    FROM LIBRARY: ZADP05.ERIC.COBOL                            COPY
NUMBER   1 . . . 5 . . . 10 . . . 15 . . . 20 . . . 25 . . . 30 . . . 35 . . . 40 . . . 45 . . . 50 . . . 55 . . . 60 . . . 65 . . . 70 . . . 75 . . . 80   MEMBER

 278    027800 P211-X.                                                                   02780001
 279    027900                       EXIT.                                               02790001
 280    028000           GO TO       PRUN-runaway-abort.                                 02800008
 281    028100 *defensive goto that will only be invoked if EXIT has not been            02810001
 282    028200 *triggered                                                                02820001
 283    028300 *may require paragraph depending on compiler                              02830001
 284    028400                                                                           02840002
```

```
SEQ      DISPLAY OF MSTUPD    FROM LIBRARY: ZADP05.ERIC.COBOL                                        COPY
NUMBER   1 . . . 5 . . . 10 . . . 15 . . . 20 . . . 25 . . . 30 . . . 35 . . . 40 . . . 45 . . . 50 . . . 55 . . . 60 . . . 65 . . . 70 . . . 75 . . . 80   MEMBER

286   028600  P212-write-new-master-record.                                                          02860002
287   028700 ***********************************************                                          02870002
288   028800 *    validate that transaction code is add                                              02880001
289   028900 *      if add then        validate transaction-record                                   02890001
290   029000 *                         write master-record from transaction-record                  02900001
291   029100 *                         read next transaction-record                                  02910001
292   029200 *                                                                                        02920001
293   029300 * @IN        Transaction-code                                                            02930010
294   029400 * @OUT       None                                                                        02940010
295   029500 * @OUT       CNTRL = bndry-viol-or-othr-err-cd                                           02950010
296   029600 ***********************************************                                          02960002
297   029700                                                                                          02970001
298   029800       IF        add                                                                      02980001
299   029900          PERFORM        PC07-validate-transaction-rec                                    02990001
300   030000          PERFORM        PC04-write-new-master-record                                     03000001
301   030100          PERFORM        PC05-read-transaction-record                                     03010001
302   030200       ELSE                                                                               03020001
303   030300          PERFORM        P332-invalid-add-transaction                                     03030003
304   030400          THRU           P332-X                                                           03040001
305   030500       END-IF                                                                             03050001
306   030600                                                                                          03060002
307   030700  P212-X.   EXIT.                                                                         03070001
308   030800                                                                                          03080002
309   030900       GO TO     PRUN-runaway-abort.                                                      03090008
310   031000                                                                                          03100002
```

```
SEQ                                                                                          COPY
NUMBER   DISPLAY OF MSTUPD   FROM LIBRARY: ZADP05.ERIC.COBOL                                 MEMBER
         1 . . . 5 . . . 10 . . . 15 . . . 20 . . . 25 . . . 30 . . . 35 . . . 40 . . . 45 . . . 50 . . . 55 . . . 60 . . . 65 . . . 70 . . . 75 . . . 80

312      031200  P321-invalid-update-transcode.                                              03120002
313      031300  ***********************************************                             03130002
314      031400  *  installations should have standard error routine                        03140002
315      031500  *  which is copied into the program.                                        03150002
316      031600  *                                                                           03160002
317      031700  *@IN   Invalid-update-transaction-code                                      03170010
318      031800  *@OUT  Installation-error-report                                            03180010
319      031900  *@OUT  CONTROL=None                                                         03190010
320      032000  ***********************************************                             03200002
321      032100                                                                              03210002
322      032200          COPY   inv-update-transcode-routine.                                03220002
323      032300                                                                              03230002
324      032400  P321-X.                                                                     03240002
325      032500          EXIT.                                                               03250002
326      032600          GO TO  PRUN-runaway-abort.                                          03260008
327      032700                                                                              03270002
```

```
 SEQ      DISPLAY OF MSTUPD    FROM LIBRARY: ZADP05.ERIC.COBOL                              COPY
NUMBER   1 . . . 5 . . 10 . . 15 . . 20 . . 25 . . 30 . . 35 . . 40 . . 45 . . 50 . . 55 . . 60 . . 65 . . 70 . . 75 . . 80    MEMBER

  329    032900  P332-invalid-add-transaction.                                             03290003
  330    033000 *******************************************************                    03300002
  331    033100 *    installations should have standard error routine                      03310002
  332    033200 *    which is copied into the program.                                      03320002
  333    033300 *                                                                           03330002
  334    033400 *@IN        Invalid-add-transaction-code                                    03340010
  335    033500 *@OUT       Installation-error-report                                       03350010
  336    033600 *@OUT       CONTROL=None                                                    03360010
  337    033700 *******************************************************                    03370002
  338    033800                                                                             03380002
  339    033900           COPY      inv-add-transcode-routine.                              03390002
  340    034000                                                                             03400002
  341    034100  P332-X.                                                                    03410003
  342    034200            EXIT.                                                            03420002
  343    034300            GO TO     PRUN-runaway-abort.                                    03430008
  344    034400                                                                             03440002
```

```
SEQ        DISPLAY OF MSTUPD   FROM LIBRARY: ZADP05.ERIC.COBOL                              COPY
NUMBER   1 . . . 5 . . . 10 . . . 15 . . . 20 . . . 25 . . . 30 . . . 35 . . . 40 . . . 45 . . . 50 . . . 55 . . . 60 . . . 65 . . . 70 . . . 75 . . . 80   MEMBER

  346   034600 PC01-read-master-record.                                                                  03460002
  347   034700 ************************************************                                           03470002
  348   034800 * read next master record                                                                 03480001
  349   034900 * check for AT END and FILE STATUS error conditions                                        03490001
  350   035000 * add one to master-record-read                                                            03500001
  351   035100 * move master-record-actual-key to master-record-key-field                                03510001
  352   035200 *                                                                                          03520001
  353   035300 *@IN    None                                                                               03530010
  354   035400 *@OUT   Next-master-record                                                                 03540010
  355   035500 *@OUT   CONTROL=EOF-or-othr-err-cond                                                        03550010
  356   035600 ************************************************                                           03560002
  357   035700 *                                                                                          03570001
  358   035800                                                                                            03580001
  359   035900          READ        master-file        RECORD                                            03590001
  360   036000          INTO        master-record-ws                                                      03600001
  361   036100          AT END      GO TO      PC01a-master-file-eof                                      03610001
  362   036200          END-READ                                                                          03620002
  363   036300                                                                                            03630002
  364   036400          IF          master-successful-completion                                          03640001
  365   036500                      NEXT SENTENCE                                                          03650001
  366   036600          ELSE                                                                              03660001
  367   036700          PERFORM                 PC01b-master-filestatus-inv                               03670002
  368   036800                      THRU        PC01b-X                                                   03680001
  369   036900          END-IF                                                                            03690001
  370   037000                                                                                            03700002
  371   037100          ADD         one                                                                   03710001
  372   037200          TO          master-record-read                                                    03720001
  373   037300          END-ADD                                                                           03730001
  374   037400                                                                                            03740002
  375   037500          MOVE        master-record-actual-key                                              03750001
  376   037600          TO          master-record-key-field                                               03760001
  377   037700                                                                                            03770001
  378   037800 PC01-X.      EXIT.                                                                         03780008
  379   037900                                                                                            03790001
  380   038000 *no EJECT statement since the three paragraphs perform a                                   03800001
  381   038100 *logical function.                                                                         03810001
  382   038200                                                                                            03820001
```

```
SEQ       DISPLAY OF MSTUPD    FROM LIBRARY: ZADP05.ERIC.COBOL                    COPY
NUMBER    1 . . . 5 . . . 10 . . . 15 . . . 20 . . . 25 . . . 30 . . . 35 . . . 40 . . . 45 . . . 50 . . . 55 . . . 60 . . . 65 . . . 70 . . . 75 . . . 80    MEMBER

383       038300 PC01a-master-file-eof.                                          03830002
384       038400 ******************************************************          03840002
385       038500 *    check for legitimate master-file EOF                       03850001
386       038600 *    writes any remaining transaction-file-records with add     03860001
387       038700 *    transaction code to master-file                            03870001
388       038800 *                                                               03880001
389       038900 *@IN      Master-records-read                                   03890010
390       039000 *@OUT     None                                                  03900010
391       039100 *@OUT     CONTROL=None                                          03910010
392       039200 ******************************************************          03920002
393       039300 *                                                               03930001
394       039400                                                                 03940001
395       039500    IF             no-master-records                             03950001
396       039600       GO TO        PCXX-program-abort                           03960001
397       039700    ELSE                                                         03970001
398       039800       PERFORM      P212-write-new-master-record                 03980001
399       039900         UNTIL      transaction-eof                              03990001
400       040000 *transaction-eof is a "dummy"; loop is terminated by the        04000001
401       040100 *AT END clause of the transaction-file read.                    04010001
402       040200    END-IF                                                       04020001
403       040300 PC01a-X.            EXIT.                                        04030002
404       040400                                                                 04040001
405       040500 PC01b-master-filestatus-inv.                                    04050003
406       040600 ******************************************************          04060002
407       040700 *    Paragraph only invoked if master file status is invalid    04070002
408       040800 *    each installation should have standard error routines      04080002
409       040900 *    which are copied into programs                             04090002
410       041000 *                                                               04100002
411       041100 *@IN      Incorrect-master-file-status                          04110010
412       041200 *@OUT     Installation-error-report                             04120010
413       041300 *@OUT     CONTROL=None                                          04130010
414       041400 ******************************************************          04140002
415       041500 *                                                               04150002
416       041600                                                                 04160001
417       041700    COPY           mf-status-wrong-routine.                      04170008
418       041800                                                                 04180002
419       041900 PC01b-X.            EXIT.                                        04190002
```

```
SEQ       DISPLAY OF MSTUPD   FROM LIBRARY: ZADP05.ERIC.COBOL                              COPY
NUMBER    1 . . . 5 . . . 10 . . . 15 . . . 20 . . . 25 . . . 30 . . . 35 . . . 40 . . . 45 . . . 50 . . . 55 . . . 60 . . . 65 . . . 70 . . . 75 . . . 80   MEMBER

420   042000                                                                              04200002
421   042100            GO TO       PRUN-runaway-abort.                                    04210008
422   042200                                                                               04220002
424   042400   PC02-rewrite-master-record.                                                 04240002
425   042500 ************************************************                              04250002
426   042600 *  rewrite master-record from the transaction-record                          04260001
427   042700 *  check for FILE STATUS error conditions                                     04270001
428   042800 *  add one to master-records-modified                                         04280001
429   042900 *                                                                             04290001
430   043000 *@IN    New-master-record                                                     04300010
431   043100 *@IN    Transaction-record                                                    04310010
432   043200 *@OUT   None                                                                  04320010
433   043300 *@OUT   CONTROL=error-conditions                                              04330010
434   043400 ************************************************                              04340002
435   043500 *                                                                             04350001
436   043600                                                                               04360001
437   043700            REWRITE     master-record                                          04370008
438   043800            FROM        transaction-record-ws                                  04380008
439   043900            END-REWRITE                                                        04390008
440   044000                                                                               04400002
441   044100            IF          master-successful-completion                           04410008
442   044200                         NEXT SENTENCE                                         04420008
443   044300            ELSE                                                               04430008
444   044400                PERFORM      PC01b-master-filestatus-inv                       04440008
445   044500            END-IF                                                             04450008
446   044600                                                                               04460002
447   044700            ADD         one                                                    04470008
448   044800            TO          master-records-modified                               04480008
449   044900            END-ADD                                                            04490008
450   045000                                                                               04500002
451   045100   PC02-X.  EXIT.                                                               04510002
452   045200                                                                               04520002
453   045300            GO TO       PRUN-runaway-abort.                                    04530008
454   045400                                                                               04540002
```

```
SEQ
NUMBER  DISPLAY OF MSTUPD    FROM LIBRARY: ZADP05.ERIC.COBOL                        COPY
        1 . . . 5 . . . 10 . . . 15 . . . 20 . . . 25 . . . 30 . . . 35 . . . 40 . . . 45 . . . 50 . . . 55 . . . 60 . . . 65 . . . 70 . . . 75 . . . 80   MEMBER

456   045600  PC03-delete-master-record.                                           04560002
457   045700  ****************************************                             04570002
458   045800  *    delete current master-record                                    04580001
459   045900  *    check for FILE STATUS error conditions                          04590001
460   046000  *    add one to master-records-deleted                               04600001
461   046100  *                                                                    04610001
462   046200  *@IN    None                                                         04620010
463   046300  *@OUT   None                                                         04630010
464   046400  *@OUT   CONTROL=None                                                 04640010
465   046500  ****************************************                             04650002
466   046600  *                                                                    04660001
467   046700                                                                       04670001
468   046800          DELETE    master-file        RECORD                          04680001
469   046900          END-DELETE                                                   04690002
470   047000                                                                       04700002
471   047100          IF    master-successful-completion                          04710001
472   047200                NEXT-SENTENCE                                          04720001
473   047300          ELSE                                                         04730001
474   047400                PERFORM       PC01b-master-filestatus-inv              04740002
475   047500                   THRU       PC01b-X                                  04750002
476   047600          END-IF                                                       04760002
477   047700                                                                       04770002
478   047800          ADD    one                                                   04780001
479   047900          TO    master-records-deleted                                04790001
480   048000          END-ADD                                                      04800001
481   048100                                                                       04810002
482   048200  PC03-X.      EXIT.                                                   04820002
483   048300                                                                       04830002
484   048400          GO TO    PRUN-runaway-abort.                                04840008
485   048500                                                                       04850002
```

```
SEQ                                                                              COPY
NUMBER    DISPLAY OF MSTUPD    FROM LIBRARY: ZADP05.ERIC.COBOL                    MEMBER
          1 . . . 5 . . . 10 . . . 15 . . . 20 . . . 25 . . . 30 . . . 35 . . . 40 . . . 45 . . . 50 . . . 55 . . . 60 . . . 65 . . . 70 . . . 75 . . . 80

487    048700                                                                    04870002
488    048800    PC04-write-new-master-record.                                   04880002
489    048900 * ********************************************************          04890002
490    049000 *    write new master-record from transaction-record               04900001
491    049100 *    check for FILE STATUS error conditions                        04910001
492    049200 *    add one to master-records-added                               04920001
493    049300 *                                                                  04930001
494    049400 * @IN    New-master-record                                         04940010
495    049500 * @IN    Transaction-record                                        04950010
496    049600 * @OUT   None                                                      04960010
497    049700 * @OUT   CONTROL=error-conditions                                  04970010
498    049800 * ********************************************************          04980002
499    049900 *                                                                  04990001
500    050000                                                                    05000001
501    050100          WRITE    master-file                                      05010001
502    050200          FROM     transaction-record-ws                           05020008
503    050300          END-WRITE                                                 05030001
504    050400                                                                    05040002
505    050500          IF       master-successful-completion                    05050001
506    050600                   NEXT SENTENCE                                    05060001
507    050700          ELSE                                                      05070001
508    050800                   PERFORM    PC01b-master-filestatus-inv           05080004
509    050900                   THRU       PC01b-X                               05090004
510    051000          END-IF                                                    05100001
511    051100                                                                    05110002
512    051200          ADD      one                                             05120001
513    051300          TO       master-records-added                           05130001
514    051400          END-ADD                                                   05140001
515    051500                                                                    05150002
516    051600    PC04-X.                                                         05160002
517    051700          EXIT.                                                     05170002
518    051800          GO TO    PRUN-runaway-abort.                             05180008
519    051900                                                                    05190002
```

```
              DISPLAY OF MSTUPD    FROM LIBRARY: ZADP05.ERIC.COBOL
 SEQ                                                                                    COPY
NUMBER   1 ...5 ...10 ...15 ...20 ...25 ...30 ...35 ...40 ...45 ...50 ...55 ...60 ...65 ...70 ...75 ...80  MEMBER

 521   052100                                                                                            05210002
 522   052200   PC05-read-transaction-record.                                                            05220002
 523   052300  **************************************************                                        05230001
 524   052400  *  read next transaction-record                                                           05240001
 525   052500  *  check for EOF and FILE STATUS error conditions                                         05250001
 526   052600  *  add one to total-transaction-records                                                   05260001
 527   052700  *  move transaction-record-actual-key to                                                  05270001
 528   052800  *          TRANSACTION-RECORD-KEY-FIELD                                                    05280001
 529   052900  *                                                                                         05290001
 530   053000  *  @IN       None                                                                         05300010
 531   053100  * @OUT       Next-transaction-record                                                      05310010
 532   053200  * @OUT       CONTROL = EOF-and-othr-err-cond                                              05320010
 533   053300  **************************************************                                        05330002
 534   053400  *                                                                                         05340001
 535   053500                                                                                            05350001
 536   053600       READ        transaction-file        RECORD                                           05360001
 537   053700       INTO        transaction-record-ws                                                    05370001
 538   053800       AT END      GO TO      PC05a-transaction-file-eof                                    05380001
 539   053900       END-READ                                                                             00539001
 540   054000                                                                                            05400002
 541   054100       IF          trans-successful-completion                                              05410001
 542   054200                   NEXT SENTENCE                                                            05420001
 543   054300       ELSE                                                                                 05430001
 544   054400       PERFORM     PC05b-trans-filestatus-invalid                                           05440001
 545   054500                   THRU       PC05b-X                                                       05450001
 546   054600       END-IF                                                                               05460002
 547   054700                                                                                            05470001
 548   054800       ADD         one                                                                      05480001
 549   054900       TO          total-transaction-records                                                05490001
 550   055000       END-ADD                                                                              05500002
 551   055100                                                                                            05510001
 552   055200       MOVE        transaction-record-actual-key                                            05520001
 553   055300       TO          transaction-record-key-field                                             05530001
 554   055400                                                                                            05540002
 555   055500   PC05-X.                                                                                  05550002
 556   055600                   EXIT.                                                                    05560001
```

```
SEQ     DISPLAY OF MSTUPD    FROM LIBRARY: ZADP05.ERIC.COBOL                          COPY
NUMBER  1 . . 5 . . 10 . . 15 . . 20 . . 25 . . 30 . . 35 . . 40 . . 45 . . 50 . . 55 . . 60 . . 65 . . 70 . . 75 . . 80    MEMBER

557     055700  PC05a-transaction-file-eof.                                          05570002
558     055800  ********************************************                         05580002
559     055900  * read legitimate transaction-file-EOF.                             05590001
560     056000  * terminate run by going to P103-termination.                       05600001
561     056100  *                                                                    05610001
562     056200  *@IN     Total-transaction-records                                   05620010
563     056300  *@OUT    None                                                        05630010
564     056400  *@OUT    CONTROL=None                                                05640010
565     056500  ********************************************                         05650002
566     056600  *                                                                    05660001
567     056700                                                                       05670001
568     056800          IF          no-transaction-records                           05680001
569     056900             GO TO    PCXX-program-abort                               05690001
570     057000          ELSE                                                         05700001
571     057100             GO TO    P103-termination                                 05710001
572     057200          END-IF                                                       05720001
573     057300                                                                       05730002
574     057400  PC05a-X.      EXIT.                                                   05740002
575     057500                                                                       05750002
576     057600             GO TO    PRUN-runaway-abort.                              05760008
577     057700                                                                       05770002
```

```
SEQ    DISPLAY OF MSTUPD    FROM LIBRARY: ZADP05.ERIC.COBOL                            COPY
NUMBER 1 . . . 5 . . . 10 . . . 15 . . . 20 . . . 25 . . . 30 . . . 35 . . . 40 . . . 45 . . . 50 . . . 55 . . . 60 . . . 65 . . . 70 . . . 75 . . . 80   MEMBER

579    057900                                                                         05790002
580    058000  PC05b-trans-filestatus-invalid.                                        05800002
581    058100 *******************************************                             05810002
582    058200 *   Paragraph only invoked if transaction file status invalid.          05820002
583    058300 *   Each installation should have standard error routine               05830002
584    058400 *   which is copied into the program.                                   05840002
585    058500 *                                                                       05850002
586    058600 *@IN     Invalid-transaction-file-status                               05860010
587    058700 *@OUT    Installation-error-report                                      05870010
588    058800 *@OUT    CONTROL=None                                                   05880010
589    058900 *******************************************                             05890002
590    059000 *                                                                       05900002
591    059100                                                                         05910002
592    059200           COPY    transaction-status-invalid-routine.                   05920002
593    059300                                                                         05930002
594    059400  PC05b-X.                                                               05940008
595    059500                                                                         05950002
596    059600           GO TO   PRUN-runaway-abort.                                   05960008
597    059700                                                                         05970002
```

```
SEQ      DISPLAY OF MSTUPD    FROM LIBRARY: ZADP05.ERIC.COBOL                        COPY
NUMBER   1 . . . 5 . . . 10 . . . 15 . . . 20 . . . 25 . . . 30 . . . 35 . . . 40 . . . 45 . . . 50 . . . 55 . . . 60 . . . 65 . . . 70 . . . 75 . . . 80    MEMBER

599      059900                                                                                       05990002
600      060000  PCO7-validate-transaction-rec                                                        06000002
601      060100 ********************************************************                               06010002
602      060200 *  Each installation should have standard validation routine                          06020002
603      060300 *  which is copied into the program.                                                   06030002
604      060400 *                                                                                      06040002
605      060500 * @IN    Transaction-record                                                            06050010
606      060600 * @OUT   Transaction-file-status-field                                                 06060010
607      060700 * @OUT   Control=None                                                                  06070010
608      060800 ********************************************************                               06080002
609      060900 *                                                                                      06090002
610      061000                                                                                        06100002
611      061100          COPY      validate-transaction-routine.                                       06110002
612      061200                                                                                        06120002
613      061300  PCO7-X.                      EXIT.                                                     06130008
614      061400                                                                                        06140002
615      061500          GO TO     PRUN-runaway-abort.                                                 06150008
616      061600                                                                                        06160002
```

```
SEQ      DISPLAY OF  MSTUPD    FROM LIBRARY: ZADP05.ERIC.COBOL                          COPY
NUMBER   1 . . . 5 . . . 10 . . . 15 . . . 20 . . . 25 . . . 30 . . . 35 . . . 40 . . . 45 . . . 50 . . . 55 . . . 60 . . . 65 . . . 70 . . . 75 . . . 80   MEMBER

618      061800                                                                                    06180002
619      061900  PCXX-program-abort.                                                               06190002
620      062000 *****************************************                                          06200002
621      062100 * Paragraph only invoked if mainline < = > comparison fails.                       06210002
622      062200 * Each installation should have standard program abort routine                     06220002
623      062300 * which is copied into the program.                                                06230002
624      062400 *                                                                                  06240002
625      062500 *@IN     Transaction-record                                                        06250010
626      062600 *@OUT    Transaction-file-status-field                                             06260010
627      062700 *@OUT    Control=None                                                              06270010
628      062800 *****************************************************                              06280002
629      062900 *                                                                                  06290002
630      063000                                                                                    06300002
631      063100         COPY        program-abort-routine.                                         06310002
632      063200                                                                                    06320002
633      063300         STOP RUN.                                                                   06330002
634      063400                                                                                    06340002
```

```
SEQ     DISPLAY OF  MSTUPD    FROM LIBRARY: ZADP05.ERIC.COBOL                                  COPY
NUMBER  1 . . . 5 . . . 10 . . . 15 . . . 20 . . . 25 . . . 30 . . . 35 . . . 40 . . . 45 . . . 50 . . . 55 . . . 60 . . . 65 . . . 70 . . . 75 . . . 80    MEMBER

636     063600                                                                                06360002
637     063700  PRUN-runaway-abort.                                                           06370002
638     063800 ***********************************************                                06380002
639     063900 * Paragraph only invoked if runaway happens.                                   06390002
640     064000 * Each installation should have standard program abort routine                 06400002
641     064100 * which is copied into the program.                                            06410002
642     064200 *                                                                              06420002
643     064300 * @IN    Transaction-record                                                    06430010
644     064400 * @OUT   Transaction-file-status-field                                          06440010
645     064500 * @OUT   Control=None                                                           06450010
646     064600 ***********************************************************                     06460002
647     064700 *                                                                              06470002
648     064800                                                                                06480002
649     064900      COPY        program-runaway routine.                                       06490002
650     065000                                                                                06500002
651     065100      STOP RUN.                                                                  06510002
652     065200                                                                                06520002
```

PROGRAM NOTES

1. No LOW-VALUES[nr], HIGH-VALUES[nr], EOF switches[nr], or ... were required.

2. **P102-mainline** is a **doinfinite** loop that is terminated by the external condition of **transaction-file EOF.**

3. Most programmers would question the defensive programming ELSE in **P102-mainline** because there are only three possible conditions [<=>] and all were tested for; this defensive ELSE is there not to test for the improbable condition that the computer hardware actually failed but rather to catch a maintenance programmer inadvertently coding a period and space (.) somewhere in the case IF.

4. The "pump priming" was accomplished by initializing both key fields to ZERO and initializing **transaction-code** to null.

5. All common routines (PCnn, PCXX, PRUN) should be copied. Why have common routines unless all programmers use them in all appropriate programs?

6. An EJECT statement is not used between the input-output paragraph and its error paragraphs because they form one logical unit.

RECOMMENDATIONS

- Always use control totals to audit the quantity of input-output transactions.
- The termination paragraph should balance the control totals and report the results (good or bad) to the control clerk.[21]
- Use the information supplied by "mandatory" audit fields and the control information supplied by the compiler to control processing; do not use artificial constructs.
- Use simple statements, narratives, comments, and EJECT statements to produce easy-to-read, maintainable programs.

A structure chart, profile chart, narratives, and additional information are provided in Appendix E.

Table Handling

SEARCH (ALL)   The SEARCH statement compares each element (field) in a named one-dimensional table (list) against one or more specified conditions. The SEARCH begins at a designated element and stops when the condition is satisfied or AT END. The SEARCH statement has two formats:

```
1. SEARCH    identifier-1
   [VARYING identifier-2/index-name-1]
   [AT END    imperative-statement-1]
   WHEN     condition-1  imperative-statement-2/NEXT SENTENCE
   [WHEN    condition-2  imperative-statement-3/NEXT SENTENCE],...
   [END-SEARCH₈₅]
```

2. <u>SEARCH</u> <u>ALL</u> identifier-1
   [AT <u>END</u>   imperative-statement-1]
   <u>WHEN</u>   condition-name-1/data-name-1 $=$ identifier-2/literal-1/
                                         arithmetic-expression-1
   [<u>AND</u>   condition-name-2/data-name-2 $=$ identifier-3/literal-2/
                                         arithmetic-expression-2]
   [<u>AND</u>   ...]
                imperative-statement-2/<u>NEXT</u> <u>SENTENCE</u>
   [END-SEARCH$_{85}$]

Format 1 is the serial SEARCH, and **identifier-1** is a one-dimensional table with both an OCCURS clause and one or more INDEXED BY phrases. The index used to control the search is either of the following:

- The index-name specified by the first INDEXED BY phrase if the optional VARYING phrase is not used
- **index-name-1** in the VARYING phrase if that index-name is specified by an INDEXED BY phrase associated with the **identifier-1** table (otherwise it is again the index-name specified by the first INDEXED BY clause)

If **identifier-2** or a nonassociated index-name is used in the VARYING phrase, that item is incremented by the same amount as the **identifier-1** index whenever that index is incremented. This permits synchronization of two tables.

RECOMMENDATIONS

- Always use the VARYING phrase to specify the index associated with the **identifier-1** table (otherwise index is selected by default).
- Use SET to keep two or more tables in synchronization.

A common problem of a Format 1 SEARCH is that the index is SET to the wrong offset (physical element location). Unlike PERFORM, where the program can inadvertently exceed the table limits, SEARCH always stops AT END. This prevents runaway but does not guarantee that the index is SET correctly.

RECOMMENDATIONS

- Always use a SET statement immediately preceding the Format 1 SEARCH, even if it is

        SET index-name   TO one

- Always comment on how, to what, and why the index is SET.

The AT END clause is optional but should always be used because the compiler continues with the next executable statement if the end of the table is reached before a condition is satisfied (another instance of defensive programming).

There can be any number of WHEN phrases, and each WHEN is treated independently of the others. The WHEN phrases are evaluated sequentially in the order that they are written, and the SEARCH terminates WHEN any condition has been satisfied. This is actually a COBOL version of the case IF (see discussion under IF).

The conditions can be any of the conditions described under the IF statement. The IF condition recommendations apply equally to WHEN.

Format 2 is the binary SEARCH. The binary SEARCH is more efficient than the serial SEARCH if the table elements are in ASCENDING or DESCENDING collating sequence. Consider the following table:

```
01  binary-search-example-table.
    02  table-element          PIC S999V USAGE IS COMP
                               OCCURS 128 TIMES
         ASCENDING KEY IS  table-element-number
         INDEXED BY        binary-search-index.
```

Assume that **table-element-1** has a value of 1 and the next value is incremented by 1 so that the table is a continuous sequence of values from 1 to 128. Further assume that each number has an equal chance of occurring. A serial SEARCH would require an average of 64 compares (128/2). The binary SEARCH starts at value 64 and divides the table in half (binary) after each unsuccessful compare. Assume **WHEN data-name-1** has an actual value of 128. The binary SEARCH would progress as follows:

```
      SET binary-search-index to table half    128/2          64
1  WHEN satisfied: no: data-name-1 >  64   64/2    32      96
2  WHEN satisfied: no: data-name-1 >  96   32/2    16     112
3  WHEN satisfied: no: data-name-1 > 112   16/2     8     120
4  WHEN satisfied: no: data-name-1 > 120    8/2     4     124
5  WHEN satisfied: no: data-name-1 > 124    4/2     2     126
6  WHEN satisfied: no: data-name-1 > 126    2/2     1     127
7  WHEN satisfied: no: data-name-1 > 127
      SET table to END                                    128
8  WHEN satisfied: ok: data-name-1 = 128                  128
```

This binary search required 8 compares and will never require more than 8 compares for a table containing 128 elements.[2] Since each number has an equal chance of occurring, the average number of compares for the binary SEARCH is 4 (8/2). This is 16 times better than 64 compares! Efficient coding should be used when it does not jeopardize readability or maintainability.

The examples just given assumed that each value had an equal chance of occurring. Usually there are certain values that occur more frequently than others. For instance, if $a = 50\%$, $b = 25\%$, and $c = 15\%$, the other 125 elements had an equal chance, and the table was arranged $a, b, c, \ldots$, the average number of compares would be about 8.[23] This is better than the standard serial SEARCH but worse than the binary SEARCH. Careful thought should be given to the type of SEARCH and the arrangement of the values in the table.

Format 2 does not have a VARYING clause because the binary SEARCH always uses the first index associated with the **identifier-1** table. The AT END should always be coded (defensive programming).

The Format 2 WHEN is different from the WHEN in Format 1. Each KEY defined in the ASCENDING/DESCENDING clause must be either the WHEN data-name or the WHEN identifier. The relation test can only be equal (=). Condition-name is an 88 level associated with a KEY. These simple compares can be combined using AND, which requires that all compares be true to invoke **imperative-statement-2.**

RECOMMENDATIONS

- Use condition-names (88s) where possible.
- Do not use literals or arithmetic expressions.
- Do not use more than two AND clauses.

The SEARCH statement, though complicated, is the best way to process a table. PERFORMING VARYING can be used, but it is more prone to logic errors—the programmer must SET and increment (BY) the indices, specifically check for index value exceeding TIMES, and so on.

RECOMMENDATIONS

- Use SEARCH rather than PERFORM VARYING for one-dimensional tables.
- Subject any SEARCH to code inspection.

SUMMARY OF RECOMMENDATIONS FOR SEARCH

- Determine the occurrence frequency for all table elements.
- If occurrence frequencies are skewed, determine if a serial SEARCH starting at the most frequent value is more efficient than a binary SEARCH.
- If occurrence frequencies are not skewed or if binary SEARCH is more efficient, arrange table values in ASCENDING or DESCENDING sequence.
- Do not use PERFORM VARYING as a substitute for SEARCH.
- Inspect all SEARCH statements.
- For Format 1:
    Always use VARYING to specify the index.
    Use SET to initialize the index (with comments on how and why) and to synchronize other tables.
    The WHEN conditions should conform to the IF statement recommendations.
- For Format 2:
    Use 88s (condition-names).
    Do not use literals or arithmetic expressions.
    Do not use more than two AND.
- Both Formats:
    Always use AT END (defensive programming).

Multidimensional Tables

The ANSI SEARCH statement does not process multidimensional tables; typically, two SEARCH statements are required for two-dimensional tables and three for three-dimensional ones. COBOL$_{VS}$ permits nested$_{VS}$ SEARCHs.

RECOMMENDATIONS

- Determine that multidimensional tables are required; processing and maintainability are exponentially simplified if one-dimensional tables can be used.
- If multidimensional tables are required, determine if a serial SEARCH of all dimensions would be more efficient than a binary SEARCH of each dimension.
- Use PERFORM VARYING if serial SEARCH is better; otherwise, use binary SEARCH on each dimension.
- Coding should be done by a senior programmer with a multitude of explanatory comments (remember that the original senior programmer is probably not going to maintain the program).

Interprogram Module

COBOL$_{85}$ has made substantial changes to the Inter-Program Communication module, which contains the CALL and CANCEL statements. COBOL$_{74}$ is described first, and the described features are supported in COBOL$_{85}$. The changes made by COBOL$_{85}$ are then described.

CALL$_{74}$ The CALL statement allows a program (the calling program) to invoke another program (the called program). The called program can be in almost any other language (PL/1, FORTRAN, BAL, etc.), but this text only discusses the COBOL-to-COBOL CALL. Some definitions:

run unit   All object programs—including the main program—that have been invoked and are in memory[24].

main program   The first COBOL program invoked in the run unit.

load modules   All the object programs that are placed (loaded) into memory in a single executable program (module).

linkage editor   Software utility that converts object programs into load modules and saves them.

loader   Software utility that converts object programs into a load module and then loads and invokes that module[25].

The linkage editor saves the load module for later invocation; the loader invokes immediately and does not save the load module. The linkage editor is used for production programs and the loader for programs in test.

The CALL statement format is as follows:

CALL literal/identifier-1 [USING identifier-2,
                                [identifier-3]], ...
       [ON OVERFLOW   imperative-statement]

The CALL literal can be either a static CALL or a dynamic CALL; the CALL **identifier-1** is always a dynamic CALL.

A static CALL is link-edited into the same load module as the calling program. A static CALL is in effect a PERFORM to an overlayable fixed SEGMENT$_{74}$ SECTION (see previous discussion in this chapter). There are two major differences:

- The called program must be a program; it must have an IDENTIFICATION DIVISION, ENVIRONMENT DIVISION$_{74}$, DATA DIVISION$_{74}$, AND PROCEDURE DIVISION$_{74}$.

- The only items (data) that the called program can access directly are the items specified in the USING clause.

A dynamic CALL is link-edited in its own load module and is loaded into memory when requested by a calling program CALL statement. The dynamic called program becomes part of the main program run unit as long as it is in memory. A dynamic called program can be deleted from memory by a CANCEL statement (discussed later).

A dynamic CALL *without* CANCEL is again in effect a PERFORM to an overlayable fixed SEGMENT$_{74}$ SECTION. The major difference between the static CALL and the dynamic CALL without CANCEL is that the static CALL is in the same load module as the main program and the dynamic CALL is in a separate load module.

A dynamic CALL *with* CANCEL is in effect a PERFORM to an independent SEGMENT$_{74}$ SECTION. Table 10.7 summarizes SEGMENTs$_{74}$ and CALLs. *Reinitialized* means that all items in the DATA DIVISION are set to the value specified in the VALUE clause; *uninitialized* leaves whatever values were placed there by the previous execution of the program.[26]

Table 10.7 Segments and Calls

SEGMENT or CALL type	Overlayable	Reinitialized
permanent fixed	no	no
overlayable fixed	yes	no
static CALL		
dynamic CALL without CANCEL		
independent	yes	yes
dynamic CALL with CANCEL		

The question that arises from Table 10.7 is why use a static CALL (or dynamic CALL without CANCEL) if the subprogram is in the same load module and/or run unit and not reinitialized? The answer lies in structured programming theory, which requires data (items) to be passed in restricted storage. *Restricted storage* means that the module (in this case the subprogram) can access only that data (the items defined in the USING clause). Any statement in the PROCEDURE DIVISION in the calling program can access any item in its DATA DIVISION, which is global storage. ''Pure'' structured programming theory requires that all COBOL modules be invoked by CALL statements rather than PERFORM statements. Restricted storage is not normally worth the effort of writing separate subprograms, for three reasons:

- The run unit is harder to read and therefore to maintain than a simple program using PERFORM.
- Logical data partitioning (see discussion in WORKING-STORAGE SECTION) plus defensive programming practices can effect quasi-restricted storage.
- Unless defensive programming is used, a called subprogram can affect other items in the calling program if tables and/or indices (subscripts) are defined in the USING clause.

These statements are true for most—if not all—virtual memory computers; they may not be true for stack architecture CPUs.

CALL statements have their uses. My guidelines for uncommon routines (function is only required by a single module) are as follows:[27]

1 to 10 statements:	Use in-line$_{85}$ PERFORM or lexical inclusion.
11 to 20 statements:	Use out-of-line PERFORM.
More than 20 statements:	Use CALL.

My guidelines for common routines within a single program are as follows:

1 to 20 statements:	Use out-of-line PERFORM.
More than 20 statements:	Use CALL or COPY.

If a routine is common to more than one program, always use CALL.

Only dynamic CALL statements with CANCEL should be used. The ''black box'' theorem of structured programming states:

- A module should always be entered at the top (first statement).
- A module should always execute in the same way (each execution is first time).
- A module should always return to the calling program unless an error causes a fatal abend.

The theorem is based on maintainability. How does a maintenance programmer know what the initial state of a subprogram is if it was uninitialized and left in its previous state? (Performed paragraphs should also always be in the first-time state whenever invoked.)

RECOMMENDATION

- Use dynamic CALL with CANCEL.

Literal-1/identifier-1 can be either the PROGRAM-ID of the subprogram or, in some compilers, a (non-ANSI) ENTRY point within the subprogram. Again the black box theorem rejects the ENTRY statement because it permits the subprogram to be invoked at other than the first statement. The reason again is maintainability—how does the maintenance programmer know what part of the subprogram is executed if there are ENTRY points?

RECOMMENDATION

- Do not use the non-ANSI ENTRY statement.

Use the literal (surprise!) syntax with a compiler directing statement to make the CALL dynamic ($DYNAM_{vs}$). The CALL **identifier-1** syntax is analogous to the Format 3 GO TO (GO TO where or CALL what). The objective of good coding is readability. In this rare case, the literal is more readable.

Impact analysis is not a factor, for these reasons:

- This is a procedure name, not data.
- Source-driven documentation usually has special options for finding procedures and/or CALL statements.

RECOMMENDATIONS

- Use the literal syntax with a compiler directing option to make the CALL dynamic.
- The statement immediately following the CALL should always be a CANCEL.

The COBOL$_{74}$ USING clause passes the address of the identifiers to the called subprogram. The subprogram must have a USING clause in its PROCEDURE DIVISION statement and a LINKAGE SECTION in its DATA DIVISION.

The compiler checks only that both USING clauses have the same number of identifiers; it does not do any name checking. The identifier addresses are passed in one-to-one positional correspondence.

        CALL literal USING   a, b, c

        PROCEDURE DIVISION USING x, y, z

would pass the address of a to x, b to y, and c to z.

The LINKAGE SECTION describes the items to the subprogram. Many compilers do not verify that the PIC clauses in both programs yield the same length. With these compilers it is possible for the subprogram inadvertently to modify other items in the calling program.

RECOMMENDATIONS

- MOVE the LINKAGE items to a single 01 in WORKING-STORAGE; that is, logically partition the data for subprograms as recommended for paragraphs.
- Use a single COPY statement in both programs.

The ON OVERFLOW optional clause provides a programmer-defined exit for the condition of insufficient memory to store the called subprogram. Most and probably all virtual memory compilers do not support this clause because there is always enough memory in virtual memory. Defensive programming requires this clause if supported.

RECOMMENDATION

- Use ON OVERFLOW if supported.

Subprograms can be program terminated by either EXIT PROGRAM or STOP RUN. EXIT PROGRAM returns to the next executable statement following the CALL statement in the calling program. This statement should always be a CANCEL statement.

STOP RUN returns to the invoker of the main program. This is usually the operating system, and it normally causes the termination of the run unit. Subprograms should not terminate run units. Subprograms should always EXIT PROGRAM with a status code defining the completion status of the subprogram.

The status code should be defined in the USING clause with all statuses defined by 88s. $COBOL_{vs}$ permits access to a special RETURN-CODE[nr] register, which is set to successful completion (value of 0) by the compiler before termination. Unsuccessful RETURN-CODES may be moved into the register by the subprogram. Again, this is non-ANSI and should not be used.

RECOMMENDATION

- Do not use the non-ANSI RETURN-CODE[nr] special register.

A main program should use only STOP RUN because EXIT PROGRAM is non-operational. Consequently, defensive programming requires a GO TO abort statement or paragraph after every EXIT PROGRAM to prevent runaway.

IBM compilers have a GOBACK[nr] statement that can be used in either main programs or subprograms. The effect is the same—return to the invoking program. In the case of the main program, this would normally be the operating system and would terminate the run unit.

RECOMMENDATION

- Do not use GOBACK[nr].

CALL statements cannot be recursive; that is, a calling program cannot be called by another program. For instance, a CALL b   b CALL c   c CALL d

d cannot CALL *a, b,* or *c,* as this is a recursive CALL and terminates the run unit.

Subprograms can be serially reusable or reentrant. A serially reusable subprogram can be used by many programs but only by a single program at any instant of time. The serially reusable subprogram must terminate before another program can invoke it. If programs *a, b,* and *c* all need serially reusable subprogram *z* simultaneously, three separate copies of *z* must be loaded, each attached to the appropriate run unit.

A reentrant subprogram can be used by many programs simultaneously. In the example just given, *a, b,* and *c* would all use a single copy of *z.* ANSI requires only serial reusability, but many compilers, such as COBOL$_{VS}$, support reentrancy. Reentrancy does not adversely affect portability.

RECOMMENDATION

- Use reentrant subprograms if supported.

CANCEL   The CANCEL statement unlinks the identified subprogram from the run unit and releases the memory to the operating system. Here is the CANCEL statement format:

CANCEL   literal-1/identifier-1, [literal-2/identifier-2], ...

RECOMMENDATION

- Use only CANCEL **literal-1** syntax.
- A CANCEL statement should always immediately follow its associated dynamic CALL statement:

```
CALL     literal-1 USING   identifier-1
CANCEL   literal-1
```

SUMMARY OF RECOMMENDATIONS FOR CALL AND CANCEL

- Use dynamic CALL with CANCEL.
- Do not use ENTRY (non-ANSI).
- Always use the literal syntax for readability.
- The next physical statement immediately following the CALL should always be a CANCEL.
- Use a compiler directing option to make the CALL dynamic.
- Use a compiler directing option to make the dynamic CALL reentrant if supported.
- Logically partition the LINKAGE data in WORKING-STORAGE.
- Use only a single USING clause.
- Use a single COPY statement for both the WORKING-STORAGE in the calling program and the LINKAGE SECTION in the called subprogram.

- Use ON OVERFLOW if supported (defensive programming).
- Subprograms should use only EXIT PROGRAM.
- Place a defensive programming GO TO or paragraph abort after EXIT PRO-GRAM.
- Do not use GOBACK[nr].
- Subprograms should return completion status code in the single 01 identifier in the USING clause.
- Define the completion codes with 88 levels.
- Do not use the RETURN-CODE[nr][vs] special register.
- Place CALL statements in segmented$_{74}$ main programs in a permanent fixed segment$_{74}$.

The COBOL$_{85}$ high Inter-Program Communication module has added the following features over and above COBOL$_{74}$:

- sharing$_{85}$ of files
- EXTERNAL$_{85}$ attributes
- GLOBAL$_{85}$ names
- nesting$_{85}$ of source programs

Nested$_{85}$ Source Programs

COBOL$_{74}$ defines a syntactically correct source program as one that contains an IDEN-TIFICATION DIVISION, ENVIRONMENT DIVISION, DATA DIVISION, and PRO-CEDURE DIVISION with all required entries present (see the world's smallest COBOL$_{74}$ program in Chapter 14). COBOL$_{85}$ defines a correct COBOL source program as a syn-tactically correct set of COBOL statements. This new definition permits all DIVISIONS other than IDENTIFICATION to be optional and for numerous programs to be contained in a single source listing. A nested$_{85}$ program is *directly* contained if there is but a single occurrence; it is *indirectly* contained if there is more than one occurrence (i.e., if another nested$_{85}$ program contains it). For example, in

```
program-a
   program-b
END PROGRAM₈₅ program-a.
```

program-a is the containing program, and **program-b** is directly contained within **program-a**. In

```
program-a
   program-b
   program-c
      program-d
      program-e
```

```
                        program-f
                        program-b
                        program-e
                  END-PROGRAM₈₅ program-a.
```

program-a is again the containing$_{85}$ program, and it directly contains programs c, d, and f and indirectly[nr] contains programs b and e because programs b and e occur more than once. The problem with indirectly[nr] contained programs is duplication. Each occurrence wastes memory and can cause substantial maintenance problems when a program modification must be made. The maintenance problems include these:

- Finding each occurrence of the program
- Determining if that particular program occurrence should be changed
- Making the required changes
- Debugging all the changed and unchanged modules to verify that they work correctly.

Indirectly[nr] contained programs can also cause significant data-name qualification problems with identical data-names. COBOL$_{85}$ prescribes a lengthy set of qualification rules, but Murphy's law guarantees that sooner or later COBOL$_{85}$ will make the wrong interpretation.

RECOMMENDATION

- Do not nest$_{85}$ indirectly[nr] contained programs.

COBOL$_{85}$ has made it easy to avoid the indirectly[nr] contained program by adding a COMMON$_{85}$ attribute for nested$_{85}$ programs:

```
      PROGRAM-ID.  program-name  [IS COMMON₈₅ PROGRAM].
```

The preceding example would be changed to

```
                  program-a
                     program-b COMMON₈₅
                     program-c
                     program-d
                     program-e COMMON₈₅
                     program-f
                  END PROGRAM₈₅ program-a.
```

Programs b and e can be called by programs a, c, d, and f; programs b and e can also CALL each other as long as the CALL is not recursive (b CALLs e, which CALLs b).

COMMON$_{85}$ was added to facilitate the writing of subprograms or functions that could be invoked by any program in a single source listing.

RECOMMENDATION

- Any program that is to be invoked by more than one program within a single source listing should be COMMON$_{85}$.

Each contained$_{85}$ program, COMMON$_{85}$ or not, can be INITIAL$_{85}$. An INITIAL$_{85}$ program is initialized whenever called. Initialization means that the following criteria are met:

- All data items with a VALUE clause are assigned that VALUE (all other data items are initialized to an undefined VALUE).
- All internal files are opened.
- All PERFORM control mechanisms are set to their initial state.

INITIAL$_{85}$ guarantees the maintenance programmer that the program (module) always functions the same way and that the source listing is an accurate picture of its operation. INITIAL$_{85}$ enforces the structured programming black box theorem that a module should always execute identically.

RECOMMENDATION

- Always use INITIAL$_{85}$ for every contained$_{85}$ program.

COBOL$_{85}$ allows FILE, RECORD, and data-name to be classified as GLOBAL$_{85}$ or local$_{85}$ within a single source listing. A GLOBAL$_{85}$ item can be referenced by any program within the source listing, a local$_{85}$ item only by the program that defines it as local$_{85}$ within its DATA DIVISION. GLOBAL$_{85}$ must be explicitly defined; otherwise, the item is local$_{85}$.

COBOL has often been described as a "bad" language because its DATA DIVISION is GLOBAL storage accessible to every data referencing statement in the program. It could take painstaking research and debugging to determine how each data-item might be modified by program execution. Significant maintenance activity is devoted to determining how incorrect values were placed into data-items. GLOBAL$_{85}$ is the ANSI COBOL$_{85}$ solution: Unless an item is explicitly declared GLOBAL$_{85}$, it is local$_{85}$ and can only be modified by the data referencing statements in the program that declared that item in its DATA DIVISION. If the source listing is a single program, a COBOL$_{85}$ program is equivalent to a COBOL$_{74}$ program.

```
IDENTIFICATION DIVISION.  IDENTIFICATION DIVISION.
PROGRAM-ID.  COBOL74     PROGRAM-ID.  COBOL85
ENVIRONMENT DIVISION.     ENVIRONMENT DIVISION.
     ...                       ...
DATA DIVISION.            DATA DIVISION.
     ...                       ...
PROCEDURE DIVISION.       PROCEDURE DIVISION.
     ...                       ...
```

The COBOL$_{74}$ DATA DIVISION is "global" since any data-item may be referenced by any appropriate statement in its PROCEDURE DIVISION. The COBOL$_{85}$ DATA DIVISION is "local" because there are no GLOBAL$_{85}$ clauses; however, any appropriate statement in its PROCEDURE DIVISION can reference any data-item, thereby making its DATA DIVISION "global." The net result is that the DATA DIVISION of any single COBOL$_{85}$ program is global, even if the GLOBAL$_{85}$ clause is omitted. To effect data isolation requires that performable paragraphs be converted to contained$_{85}$ programs with local$_{85}$ DATA divisions:

```
IDENTIFICATION DIVISION.     IDENTIFICATION DIVISION.
PROGRAM-ID. COBOL₇₄         PROGRAM-ID. COBOL₈₅
ENVIRONMENT DIVISION.        ENVIRONMENT DIVISION.
    ...
DATA DIVISION.               DATA DIVISION.
    ...                          ...
PROCEDURE DIVISION.          PROCEDURE DIVISION.
paragraph-a                  IDENTIFICATION DIVISION.
    ...                      PROGRAM-ID. program-a INITIAL.
    ...                      DATA DIVISION. (no GLOBAL)
    ...                      PROCEDURE DIVISION
    ...
    ...                      END PROGRAM program-a.
paragraph-b                  IDENTIFICATION DIVISION.
    ...                      PROGRAM-ID. program-b INITIAL.
    ...                      DATA DIVISION. (no GLOBAL)
    ...                      PROCEDURE DIVISION
    ...
    ...                      END PROGRAM program-b.
paragraph-c                  IDENTIFICATION DIVISION.
    ...                      PROGRAM-ID. program-c INITIAL.
    ...                      DATA DIVISION. (no GLOBAL)
    ...                      PROCEDURE DIVISION
    ...
    ...                      END PROGRAM program-c.
```

Any data referencing statements in paragraphs *a*, *b*, or *c* can modify the COBOL$_{74}$ DATA DIVISION, whereas program *a* can modify only its DATA DIVISION, program *b* only its DATA DIVISION, and program *c* only its DATA DIVISION. Limited data isolation has been achieved.

COBOL$_{85}$ allows data to be isolated to a single source listing or referenceable by any program in the associated run unit by the use of the EXTERNAL$_{85}$ clause. EXTERNAL$_{85}$ items can be GLOBAL$_{85}$ or local$_{85}$. The basic formats are as follows:

```
FD  file-name-1
    [IS EXTERNAL₈₅]
    [IS GLOBAL₈₅]
    [...]
```

or

```
01  data-name-1/FILLER
    [IS EXTERNAL₈₅]
    [IS GLOBAL₈₅]
    [...]
```

SUMMARY

- Any item declared EXTERNAL$_{85}$ and GLOBAL$_{85}$ can be referenced by any applicable statement in any program in any source listing in the run unit that declares that item by including its FD or 01 in any DATA DIVISION.

- Any item declared EXTERNAL$_{85}$ and local$_{85}$ can be referenced by any applicable statement in any program in the run unit that specifically declares that item by including its FD or 01 in its DATA DIVISION.

- Any item declared internal$_{85}$ and GLOBAL$_{85}$ can be referenced by any applicable statement in any program in the source listing.

- Any item declared internal$_{85}$ and local$_{85}$ can only be referenced by the specific program that declared it in its DATA DIVISION.

COBOL$_{85}$ has introduced another data isolation mechanism with the BY CONTENT$_{85}$ phrase in the CALL statement. CALL$_{74}$ always passes any parameters declared in the USING phrase by reference, which in effect means that the called program has access to those parameters in the calling program DATA DIVISION. USING parameters passed BY CONTENT$_{85}$ have their current values placed into an implementor-defined area that is accessible by the called program. The net result is that the called program cannot change the parameter value in the calling program's USING phrase.

CALL$_{85}$ syntax is as follows:

```
CALL    identifier-1/literal-1
[USING  BY [REFERENCE₈₅]/CONTENT₈₅ identifier-2, ...]
[ON OVERFLOW/EXCEPTION₈₅  imperative-statement-1]
[NOT ON EXCEPTION₈₅          imperative-statement-2]
[END-CALL⁸⁵]
```

The brackets [] around REFERENCE$_{85}$ mean that it is optional and is the default or assumed clause if CONTENT$_{85}$ is omitted. As before, never assume.

OVERFLOW refers to the specific condition that the called program could not fit into available memory; EXCEPTION$_{85}$ refers to any condition that makes the called program unavailable.

RECOMMENDATIONS

- Always use literals for readability and maintainability.
- Always use the BY REFERENCE$_{85}$ or BY CONTENT$_{85}$ clause, even if the USING parameters are to be passed BY REFERENCE$_{85}$ (never assume).

- Always use the EXCEPTION$_{85}$ phrase (defensive programming).
- Always use END-CALL$_{85}$.

The CANCEL statement remains functionally unchanged in COBOL$_{85}$.

RUN UNIT PLANNING

COBOL$_{74}$ has a simple run unit construction:

- All programs in a run unit are independent, comprise a single source listing, and are individually compiled.
- All performable modules are out-of-line paragraphs or sections.
- The DATA DIVISION is "global" to its own program and "local" (not referenceable by other programs in the run unit).
- The only restricted storage is the parameters passed by reference in the USING phrase.

COBOL$_{85}$ has a complex run unit construction:

- Any program in a run unit can be nested$_{85}$ within another program, and any number of programs can comprise a single source listing and be jointly compiled; any nested$_{85}$ program can be COMMON$_{85}$ and/or INITIAL$_{85}$.
- Any performable module can be in-line$_{85}$ or out-of-line.
- DATA DIVISION FDs and 01s can be declared GLOBAL$_{85}$, thereby making them accessible to any program in the same source listing; FDs and 01s can be declared EXTERNAL$_{85}$, thereby making them accessible to any program in the run unit.
- DATA DIVISION FDs and 01s are local$_{85}$ unless specifically declared GLOBAL$_{85}$ and/or EXTERNAL$_{85}$.
- CALL USING parameters can be passed BY CONTENT$_{85}$, which prohibits change by the called program.

Careful run unit planning must be performed prior to coding to make effective use of the new COBOL$_{85}$ techniques. The basic issues are the protection of data and the use of INITIAL modules. Two maintenance defects of COBOL$_{74}$ are the use of GLOBAL storage and the fact that any paragraph, SECTION, or subprogram can be left in any state after invocation.

The maintenance problems include the difficulty of deriving from the source listing the actual data being used by any paragraph or SECTION and the impossibility of determining the state of any paragraph, SECTION, or subprogram when invoked.

Knowledge of actual data modification is difficult because of group MOVE statements, CORRESPONDING phrases, indexing, and the like. COBOL$_{85}$ provides the development programmer with the ability to protect all data and guarantee that all modules are in INITIAL state. Programs written using these defensive programming techniques available in COBOL$_{85}$ would be a boon to preventive maintenance. They could halt the maintenance dragon dead in its tracks![28]

Figure 10.11 is a COBOL$_{74}$ example.

```
IDENTIFICATION DIVISION.
PROGRAM-ID.   COBOL₇₄.
...
ENVIRONMENT DIVISION.
DATA DIVISION.
...
FD      file-1.
FD      file-2.
FD      file-3.
...
WORKING-STORAGE SECTION.
...
    02  P201-local-data.
    02  P202-local-data.
    02  P203-local-data.
    02  P204-local-data.
...
PROCEDURE DIVISION.
...
    PERFORM  P201-???.
    PERFORM  P202-???.
    PERFORM  P203-???.
    PERFORM  P204-???.
    CALL        "common-routine-only-used-by-this-program"
    USING       ...
    END-CALL
    CANCEL   "common-routine-only-used-by-this-program"
    CALL        "common-routine-used-by-other-programs"
    USING       ...
    END-CALL
    CANCEL   "common-routine-used-by-other-programs"
...
STOP RUN.
```

Figure 10.11   COBOL$_{74}$ run unit (... indicates a break in the source code sequence).

All data in the DATA DIVISION is GLOBAL and therefore can be modified by any data modification statement anywhere in the PROCEDURE DIVISION. The called programs cannot explicitly modify any data other than that included in the USING phrases, but there are numerous methods, as previously discussed, for called programs implicitly to modify data that is outside the USING phrases. COBOL$_{85}$ defensive programming techniques can completely eliminate these anomalies and protect all data.

The defensive programming technique is to make all performable paragraphs into directly$_{85}$ contained$_{85}$ nested$_{85}$ programs within the same source listing with all programs having local$_{85}$ storage except for the results that each program produces being placed into its own GLOBAL$_{85}$ WORKING-STORAGE. Figure 10.12 is the preliminary COBOL$_{85}$ version.

```
          IDENTIFICATION DIVISION.
          PROGRAM-ID. COBOL₈₅.
          ENVIRONMENT DIVISION.
     ...
          DATA DIVISION.
          *the entire DATA DIVISION including WORKING-STORAGE is local₈₅
          *storage since there are no GLOBAL₈₅ clauses
     ...
          FD        file-1.
     ...
          FD        file-2.
     ...
          FD        file-3.
     ...
          WORKING-STORAGE SECTION.
     ...
              02   P201-using-parameters.
     ...
              02   P202-using-parameters.
     ...
              02   P203-using-parameters.
     ...
              02   P204-using-parameters.
     ...
              02   common-routine-only-used-by-this-program-using-parameters
     ...
              02   common-routine-used-by-other-programs-using-parameters
     ...
          PROCEDURE DIVISION.
     ...
              CALL      "P201-???"
              USING   P201-using-parameters   BY CONTENT
           *
          *BY CONTENT is used to protect all data within the calling program
           *
          *CANCEL not required since program is INITIAL and within same source
          *listing
           *
              END-CALL
     ...
              CALL      "P202-???"
              USING     P202-using-parameters   BY CONTENT
              END-CALL
```

```
...
        CALL        "P203-???"
        USING       P203-using-parameters  BY CONTENT
        END-CALL
...
        CALL        "P204-???"
        USING       P204-using-parameters  BY CONTENT
        END-CALL
...
        CALL   "common-routine-only-used-by-this-program"
...
```

*COBOL$_{74}$ CALL "common-routine-only-used-by-this-program" would be
*treated exactly as the performable programs converted to nested$_{85}$
*programs and it would also be a nested$_{85}$ program with the
*COMMON$_{85}$ clause to permit it to be used by the other nested$_{85}$
*programs

```
...
        CALL            "common-routine-used-by-other-programs"
        USING           common-routine-used-by-other-programs-parameters
        BY REFERENCE
*never assume
        END-CALL
        CANCEL          "common-routine-used-by-other-programs"
...
```

*COBOL$_{74}$ CALL "common-routine-used-by-other-programs" could be a
*program used by only programs within the run unit or a systemwide
*program—such as a date conversion routine—that can be used by
*any program in the site inventory.
*the USING parameters would be treated exactly as before; however,
*the program would not be contained$_{85}$ within the source listing
*of COBOL$_{85}$
*
*CANCEL required since program is not within same source listing or
*part of original load module
*

```
...
        STOP RUN.
```

```
IDENTIFICATION DIVISION.
PROGRAM-ID.  P201-???   INITIAL.
```
*INITIAL reinitializes the program prior to each invocation, which
*means that a maintenance programmer can rely on the program to
*execute identically each time it is invoked
*
*ENVIRONMENT DIVISION is omitted$_{85}$ since all nested$_{85}$ programs

```
*should use the containing₈₅ program ENVIRONMENT DIVISION
*
 DATA DIVISION.
*the nested₈₅ program should not have any FDs; all FDs should be
*under the control of the containing₈₅ program; also, FDs are
*placed into unopen status whenever an INITIAL₈₅ program is
*invoked
*
 WORKING-STORAGE SECTION.
 01 P201-local-parms.
*all data specific to a particular program is moved from the
*containing₈₅ program WORKING-STORAGE to the nested₈₅ program
*WORKING-STORAGE;
*
*the omission of GLOBAL₈₅ means that this data is local₈₅ and
*cannot be modified in any other program in the source listing or any other
*program in the run unit
*
 01 P201-return-parameters   GLOBAL
*program moves its results into this GLOBAL₈₅ storage, which then
*provides the calling program with the latest values for its
*operations
...
 LINKAGE SECTION.
 01 P201-using-parameters.
*both the USING parameters in the calling program and the called
*program should use a single COPY to keep them in sync
...
 PROCEDURE DIVISION.
...
     MOVE   results
     TO     P201-return-parameters
*program moves results to GLOBAL₈₅ WORKING-STORAGE, which provides
*the calling program with the latest values for its processing
...
     EXIT   PROGRAM.
     GO TO  P???-abort-procedure
*the defensive GO TO is even more important in COBOL₈₅ nested₈₅
*source listing since a runaway (untriggered EXIT PROGRAM) could
*cause serious damage; may require paragraph, depending on compiler
     END PROGRAM   P201-???.
     EJECT

 IDENTIFICATION DIVISION.
 PROGRAM-ID.   P202-???   INITIAL.
*the statements for P202, P203, and P204 would follow the same
*pattern as for P201
```

```
...
IDENTIFICATION DIVISION.
PROGRAM-ID.   common-routine-only-used-by-this-program
              INITIAL
              COMMON.
...
*the statements for common-routine-only-used-by-this-program would
*follow the same pattern as the other nested₈₅ programs
*
*the major difference is COMMON₈₅, which permits this nested₈₅
*program to be invoked by any other nested₈₅ program in the
*same source listing
...
```

Figure 10.12   COBOL₈₅ run unit (... indicates a break in the source code sequence).

The source listing syntax is

```
COBOL₈₅
   P201
   P202
   P203
   P204
   common-routine-only-used-by-this-program   [COMMON]
```

This style of COBOL$_{85}$ defensive programming provides the benefits of protecting all data either directly (local$_{85}$) or by providing the latest values of GLOBAL$_{85}$ data to the calling program and by guaranteeing that each performable paragraph is initialized upon each invocation. The development programmers will undoubtedly scream, but maintenance of COBOL$_{85}$ defensive programs will be significantly decreased, thereby beginning to make inroads into the maintenance dragon that consumes over 50 percent of current DP personnel budgets. Part 2 contains recommendations that should quiet some of the screams.

RECOMMENDATIONS for COBOL$_{85}$ DEFENSIVE PROGRAMMING CONSTRUCTION

- IDENTIFICATION DIVISION:
  PROGRAM-ID: All nested$_{85}$ programs use INITIAL$_{85}$ clause; all common$_{85}$ programs use COMMON$_{85}$ clause.
- ENVIRONMENT DIVISION: COPY into main (containing$_{85}$) program; should be omitted$_{85}$ in any nested$_{85}$ program.
- DATA DIVISION:
  COPY into main program with local$_{85}$ construct (GLOBAL$_{85}$ clause omitted).
  FDs should be omitted$_{85}$ in any nested$_{85}$ program.
  All READ and WRITE use INTO/FROM with single 01 construct; INTO/ FROM is local$_{85}$ storage.

WORKING-STORAGE SECTION:

Main program does not contain any nested[85] program local[85] data.

Nested[85] program local data is in local[85] storage.

Nested[85] program return parameters are placed into GLOBAL[85] storage for use by the calling program.

LINKAGE SECTION should use the same COPY statement as the main program.

- PROCEDURE DIVISION:

    All CALL USING are BY CONTENT[85].

    Nested[85] programs return results by moving to their own GLOBAL[85] WORKING-STORAGE.

    Defensive GO TO or paragraph after each EXIT PROGRAM.

These COBOL[85] defensive programming techniques will quell the maintenance dragon!

COMPILER DIRECTING

This text subdivides compiler directing statement and options into three types:[29]

- Source: Statement or option affects only the source listing, does *not* affect the source or object code.
- Object: Statement or option affects only the object code, does not affect the source code or listing.
- Both: Statement or option affects the source code and listing and the object code.

Source

The only ANSI statement that affects the source listing is the slash / in column 7, which causes an eject to the top of the next source listing page. / is generally not supported, whereas non-ANSI EJECT is.

RECOMMENDATION

- Use / if supported; otherwise, use EJECT if supported to separate paragraphs onto individual pages for easier readability.

An interesting experiment is to see what your compiler does with

```
/  EJECT
```

Many compilers have statements or options that affect the source listing but not the source code or the object code. These options usually do not adversely affect portability and should be used freely.[30] Here are some COBOL$_{VS}$ compiler directing statements and options:

- FLAG   Produces embedded error messages and/or a listing of the error message at the end of the source listing, depending on the parameters selected.
- LINECOUNT   Specifies the number of lines per page for the source listing.
- LIST   Produces an assembly language expansion of the source code, including global tables, literal pools, WORKING-STORAGE characteristics, and program statistics.
- NUMBER   Sequence-checks columns 1–6 and prints that number in error messages, MAP, XREF, and LIST.
- OFFSET   Produces a condensed LIST.
- QUOTE   Uses " (ANSI standard) as literal delimiter.
- TERMINAL   Sends progress and diagnostic messages to SYSTEM (usually the CRT that the programmer is using during an online compile).
- TITLE   Prints PROGRAM-ID, compilation date and time, page number, and up to 65 characters of user-defined text on each source listing page.
- XREF   Produces a sorted cross-reference listing of all data names and procedure names in alphanumeric order.

RECOMMENDATIONS

- Always use QUOTE if supported.
- Always use TITLE if supported.

Object

ENTER$^{nr}_{74}$ The ENTER$^{nr}_{74}$ statement allows the incorporation of other languages (PL/1, FORTRAN, BAL, etc.) into COBOL programs. Most compilers do not support ENTER$^{nr}_{74}$.

RECOMMENDATION

- Do not use ENTER$^{nr}_{74}$; use CALL if a foreign-language routine is required.

USE   The USE statement permits specific user-defined asynchronous processing of exception conditions. The ANSI USE conditions are as follows:

- User-defined input-output error handling after standard procedures have been executed.

- User-defined procedures invoked before the REPORT WRITER[nr] produces a report group.
- User-defined items that are to be monitored if the debug module is active.

All ANSI and non-ANSI USE statements other than USE FOR DEBUGGING have not been recommended and are not discussed further.

USE FOR DEBUGGING$_{74}$ USE FOR DEBUGGING$_{74}$ allows the programmer to specify that certain items be traced (monitored) during the execution of the program. The USE FOR DEBUGGING$_{74}$ format is as follows:

```
USE FOR DEBUGGING74 ON  cd-name-1nr
                        [ALL REFERENCE OF] identifier-1
                        file-name-1
                        procedure-name-1
                        ALL PROCEDURES
                        [cd-name-2
                        [ALL REFERENCES OF] identifier-2
                        file-name-2
                        procedure-name-2
                        ALL PROCEDURES]
                        ...
```

cd-name[nr] is the name of a communication description **entry**[nr] in the COMMUNICA-TION SECTION[nr], which was not recommended. **identifier** is any item in the DATA DIVISION. **file name** is any file defined by an FD in the FILE SECTION of the DATA DIVISION. **procedure-name** is any paragraph or SECTION name in the PRO-CEDURE DIVISION.

The trace information is maintained by a DEBUG-ITEM$_{74}$ special register. The DEBUG-ITEM$_{74}$ special register has the following implicit description:

```
01   DEBUG-ITEM.
     02  DEBUG-LINE     PIC X(6).
     02  FILLER         PIC X     VALUE SPACE.
     02  DEBUG-NAME     PIC X(30).
     02  FILLER         PIC X     VALUE SPACE.
     02  DEBUG-SUB-1    PIC S9999 SIGN IS LEADING SEPARATE CHARACTER.
     02  FILLER         PIC X     VALUE SPACE.
     02  DEBUG-SUB-2    PIC S9999 SIGN IS LEADING SEPARATE CHARACTER.
     02  FILLER         PIC X     VALUE SPACE.
     02  DEBUG-SUB-3    PIC S9999 SIGN IS LEADING SEPARATE CHARACTER.
     02  FILLER         PIC X     VALUE SPACE.
     02  DEBUG-CONTENTS PIC X(n).
```

Even ANSI does not use PIC A for FILLER, even though SPACE is part of the domain of PIC A; nor does it use V for integers.

DEBUG-LINE$_{74}$ identifies the source statement associated with DEBUG-ITEM$_{74}$.

DEBUG-NAME$_{74}$ contains the name that invoked the debugging section. DEBUG-SUB-1/2/3$_{74}$ contains the current value of any subscripts associated with an identifier.

- **procedure-name**   Blank unless an ALTER$_{74}$ statement was used, in which case the value is **procedure-name-2** of ALTER$_{74}$; *or* **procedure-name** was invoked by a fallthrough, in which case the value is FALLTHROUGH; *or* **procedure-name** was invoked by USE, in which case the value is USE PROCEDURE; *or* START PROGRAM on initial entry.
- **file-name**   Blank unless a READ statement was used, in which case DEBUG-CONTENTS contains the entire record read; **n** is set to the largest possible size.
- **identifier**   Current value (contents).

Vendors can add additional debugging features by using D in column 7 (debugging line). For instance, ANSI specifies a batch DEBUG, whereas COBOL$_{VS}$ provides extensive online and batch debugging tools.[31]

RECOMMENDATION

- Use all debugging tools available with your compiler.

The ANSI USE FOR DEBUGGING$_{74}$ is triggered by adding the WITH DEBUGGING MODE$_{74}$ phrase to the SOURCE-COMPUTER paragraph of the CONFIGURATION SECTION of the ENVIRONMENT DIVISION:

SOURCE-COMPUTER.   [computer-name] WITH DEBUGGING MODE$_{74}$.

A programmer-coded debugging SECTION is incorporated as the first SECTION if there is no DECLARATIVES SECTION or the second SECTION if there is a DECLARATIVE SECTION. The debugging SECTION can access the DEBUG-ITEM$_{74}$ special register and do whatever is necessary to debug the program.

Many compilers treat the debugging SECTION as optional and allow the rest of the PROCEDURE DIVISION to be coded with paragraphs rather than sections as specified by ANSI (if any SECTION is used, all paragraphs must be part of a SECTION).

RECOMMENDATION

- Use paragraphless sections to take advantage of USE FOR DEBUGGING$_{74}$ if required by your compiler.

In fact, a programmer should use every available software tool to assist in debugging.[32]

Many compilers have options that affect object code but not the source code. Portability is not affected because the source code is pure. The following COBOL$_{VS}$ compiler directing options should be used freely:

- DYNAM   Makes all CALL literal statements into DYNAMIC CALLS.
- NOCOMPILE   Checks the syntax of the source code only; does not produce object code. There is no reason to waste computer resources producing bad object code until the source code is syntactically correct.
- OPTIMIZE   Optimizes syntactically correct object code. The OPTIMIZE option eliminates unnecessary transfers of control, simplifies inefficient branches, simplifies PERFORM object code, eliminates duplicate computations, eliminates constant computations, and combines MOVE statements of contiguous items of the same length into a single MOVE where possible.
- RENT   Produces reentrant object code.
- SSRANGE   Produces object code to validate that all subscripts and indices at execution time have values that are within their assigned storage area.
- TEST   Invokes the VS COBOL II debugging option.

RECOMMENDATION

- Always use SSRANGE or its equivalent source code to prevent runaways (defensive programming).

Both Source and Object

COPY   The COPY statement affects the source code because whatever is copied is inserted into the source listing;[33] it affects the object code by generating instructions caused by the insertion of the copied material into the source program.

The COPY statement should be the most used compiler directing statement in any program and in the program library. Unfortunately, COPY statements are rare and are usually used only in the DATA DIVISION. COPY statements have the following advantages:

- They significantly reduce both the keystroking effort and the coding effort.
- COPY material can be standardized, scrutinized, and subject to intensive code inspections.
- Modifications to COPY material are made only once in the COPYLIB.
- COPY statements in a source program are easy to locate with software tools, thereby providing a list of programs requiring recompilation automatically.
- Data naming standards can be enforced.
- Logical partitioning of WORKING-STORAGE can be enforced.

- Standard INPUT-OUTPUT routines including error and exception processing can be developed, standardized, maintained, and enforced.
- USING and LINKAGE SECTIONS can be kept in sync.
- Reusable modules (another objective of structured programming) can be developed, standardized, maintained, and enforced.
- Debugging is easier and faster because the copied material has already been thoroughly debugged.
- Maintenance is easier because the only bug that should occur is either in the source code unique to the program or the interface to the copied material.

RECOMMENDATIONS

- Use the COPY statement.
- *Use the COPY statement.*
- USE THE COPY STATEMENT!

The general format of the COPY statement is as follows:

```
COPY          text-name [OF/IN LIBRARY-NAME]
[REPLACING  = = pseudo-text-1 = = identifier-1/literal-1/word-1
BY            = = pseudo-text-2 = = identifier-2/literal-2/word-2], ...
```

Generally, a compiler scans a source program for COPY statements and inserts **text-name** into the location beginning with the reserved word COPY.

The copied text is usually kept in a COPYLIB. There can be more than one COPY-LIB, in which case the OF/IN qualification is required.

A COPY statement without the optional REPLACING phrase inserts the text into the source program unchanged. The REPLACING phrase allows specified text to be modified.

pseudo-text	Any character string enclosed in pseudo-text delimiters ($==$); **pseudo-text-1** must contain at least one text word; **pseudo-text-2** can be null.
identifier	Any standard COBOL statement.
literal	Any character string not enclosed by pseudo-text delimiters.
word	Any user-defined word, system-name, or reserved word.

I know of no use for pseudo-text, and REPLACING identifiers and words or reserved words would cause aliases. The only good use for REPLACING is to provide qualification of generic data-names as described in the DATA DIVISION. This requires a literal prefix or suffix of $X(n)$ where **n** equals the number of REPLACING characters. For instance, if personnel records were maintained for students, instructors, alumni, and deans and those records contain generic data-names such as

name   home-address   home-phone-number

and so on, each one of those generic data-names could have a four-character prefix of PPPP—

PPPP-name   PPPP-home-address   PPPP-home-phone-number   ...

and the COPY statement would be

```
COPY        personnel-record
REPLACING   PPPP-[34]
BY          STDN- or INST- or ALMN- or DEAN-
```

RECOMMENDATION

• The REPLACING phrase should be used in the DATA DIVISION only if generic data-names are required (the data naming standard previously recommended has an entity type prefix that distinguishes generic data-names).

COPY AND CALL   A static CALL or a dynamic CALL without CANCEL is link-edited into the same load module as the calling program and is not reinitialized. The CALL major benefit is restricted storage, and that is a sufficient benefit.

RECOMMENDATION

• If you must choose between a static CALL and a COPY, use CALL.

nested COPY$^{nr}_{VS}$ COBOL$_{V5}$ permits COPY statements within COPY statements. IBM recommends nested COPY for top-down programming.[35] Each high-level module is coded with COPY statements that ''stand in'' for the lower-level code (usually called stubs). The stubs are then replaced by the real code. The technique is good but nested COPY statements are specifically prohibited by ANSI. Here is the easy way to code stubs and conform to ANSI standards:

```
P???-high-level-paragraph-1.
    statement
    statement
    ...
    PERFORM P???-stub-1.
    ...
        P???-stub-1.
        P???-X.   EXIT.
                  EJECT
```

There may be some interesting uses for nested COPY statements besides top-down coding, but for now, avoid them.

RECOMMENDATION

• Do not use nested$_{VS}$ COPY statements (non-ANSI).

Replace[85] permits source pseudo-text to be replaced BY the specified pseudo-text. The syntax is

<u>REPLACE</u> ==pseudo-text-1== <u>BY</u> ==pseudo-text-2==
              [==pseudo-text-3== <u>BY</u> ==pseudo-text-4==],...

REPLACE[85] was added to ease the conversion between COBOL[74] and COBOL[85]. The REPLACE[85] function can be terminated by

<u>REPLACE</u> <u>OFF</u>

Chapter 11 provides the acceptable syntax for all acceptable verbs. This replaces the normal summary of recommendations found at the end of most chapters.

NOTES

1. It is possible for COBOL programs to be invoked by and to invoke programs in other languages (PL/1, FORTRAN, assembler, etc.). This text is concerned only with COBOL-to-COBOL CALL verbs.
2. Virtual storage combines computer main memory and some amount of auxiliary storage to provide sufficient space for executing programs.
3. "Although VS COBOL II allows segmentation language, you won't improve storage allocation by using it, because VS COBOL II does not perform overlay." (*VS COBOL II Application Programming Guide*, Publication No. 8C26-4045-0, San Jose, Calif.: IBM, 1984)
4. Stack architecture places the executable code into a stack, with the top of the stack being the next executable instruction. There is a maximum stack size.
5. A swap involves moving a write/read program image to/from auxiliary storage.
6. For instance, see E. Yourdon, C. Gane, T. Sarson, and T. Lister, *Learning to Program in Structured COBOL* (New York: Yourdon Press, 1976).
7. Edsger Dijkstra, "GO TO Statement Considered Harmful," *Communications of the ACM*, 1968.
8. *Computerworld*, June 15, 1981.
9. Technically, the terminating GO TO is a network GO TO because it transfers control to a different paragraph (EXIT); however, the EXIT paragraph is logically and functionally a part of its parent paragraph, and the terminating GO TO is in fact a local GO TO.
10. Developer of Structured Retrofit software, which assists maintenance programmers in structuring unstructured COBOL programs.
11. *Inspections in Applications Development*, IBM, GC70-2000-0.
12. COBOL[74] provides for only out-of-line execution, while COBOL[85] provides for either out-of-line or in-line[85]. Also, COBOL[85] has reversed the FROM/BY steps. The ANSI justification is that the COBOL[85] sequence properly processes "half of a matrix along the diagonal," whereas COBOL[74] did not. **Caution:** ANSI has stated that current COBOL[74] programs could

be affected but believes the number to be small. (*Note:* ANSI has not provided flowcharts for PERFORMS of more than three levels.) These comments also apply to Figure 10.9.

13. COBOL$_{85}$ de-edits$_{85}$ (converts) a sending (identifier-1) numeric edited operand to its unedited numeric value before moving it to a numeric or numeric edited receiving field.

14. IBM provides a non-ANSI return code for returning status.

15. The arithmetic verbs abend if alpha is present in a numeric item.

16. IBM allows switch-type information to be passed in the PARM parameter of the EXEC statement in execution-time JCL.

17. Many access methods store RECORDS in convenient physical locations rather than adjacent physical locations. However, the access method maintains some sort of list that permits SEQUENTIAL processing.

18. As described in the BLOCK CONTAINS clause, there can be many logical RECORDS to a physical RECORD. A READ obtains the NEXT logical RECORD from the CPU buffer. A physical READ is executed only if the CPU read buffer is exhausted.

19. Some access methods remove the RECORD only logically by setting a flag that prohibits a READ of that RECORD. This permits deleted RECORDS to be recovered in case of error; it also requires reorganization to recover the lost space of deleted RECORDS for future use.

20. The logical RECORD is placed in the next physical location of the CPU write buffer. A physical WRITE is executed only if the CPU write buffer is full.

21. Most mainframe data processing organizations have designated persons to review control information and reports for accuracy. These persons are usually called control clerks or input-output clerks.

22. The formula for the number of binary SEARCH compares is to determine what power of 2 exceeds the table TIMES. $2^7 = 128$ which does not exceed 128, but 2^8 does (256). Therefore, the maximum number of compares is 8 (if the TIMES was 127, the maximum number of compares would be 7).

23. The formula is $(1*.50) + (2*.25) + (3*.15) + (63*.10)$ where the integer is the number of compares required and the fractions equal the percent of occurrence.

24. The original COBOL code is the source program. The compiler translates the source program into an object program. The object program becomes executable after being placed into a load module. Most of the programs are probably in mass storage that is part of the CPU's virtual memory.

25. *Load module, linkage editor,* and *loader* are IBM terms.

26. The programmer is also responsible for reinitializing ALTER GO TO statements, data items without VALUE clauses, PERFORM statements, and the like.

27. A guideline is not an absolute rule. If 15 statements are more readable in-line$_{85}$ than in a PERFORM paragraph, use in-line!

28. Three clients sponsored a Kyota dragon in the Sydney Toranga Zoo with a dedication plaque stating that they were "taming the maintenance dragon."

29. Statements are coded within source code; options are coded outside the source code.

30. Not adversely affecting portability means that another compiler might issue an error diagnostic and not implement the option. This would not affect the source code or the object code produced from the source code.

31. For more information, see IBM's *VS COBOL II Application Programming: Debugging Guide* (SBOF-1191).

32. Here is a selection of references and the tools they discuss:

HARDY, LEONG-HONG, and FIFE, *Software Tools: A Building Block Approach*, National Bureau of Standards (SP 500-14).

Abort diagnosis	Full or selective dump of memory on abend
Breakpoint control	Ability of programmer to specify a pause at a specified point with control returned to the programmer
Data auditing	Analysis of data for consistency and validity
Error analysis	Production of meaningful error messages
Error recovery	Permitting execution to continue after abend
Program formating	Rearranging source code for improved readability
Program monitor	Collecting statistical data during execution
Test generator	Generating test data

HOWDEN, *A Survey of Dynamic Analysis Methods*, IEEE Computer Society.

Branch testing	Identification of untested branches
Expression test	Validation of arithmetic expressions by algebraic theory
Path testing	Identification of untested logical paths
Statement testing	Identification of untested statements

HOWDEN, *A Survey of Static Analysis Methods*, IEEE Computer Society.

Design analysis	Analysis of software design for consistency and correctness
Expression analysis	Analysis of programs for common errors
Interface analysis	Analysis of data consistency between modules
Reference analysis	Analysis of reference anomalies

RAMAMOORTHY AND HO, *Testing Large Software with Automated Software Evaluation Systems* (Englewood Cliffs, N.J.: Prentice-Hall, 1983).

Documentation generation	Source-driven documentation
Program restructuring	Restructuring programs for better maintainability

33. COPY is in the $COBOL_{74}$ $Library_{74}$ module, which has been replaced by the Source Text $Manipulation_{85}$ module in $COBOL_{85}$.

34. The number of characters replaced does not require the same length as the replacing characters.

35. IBM, *VS COBOL II Application Programming Guide* (SC26-4045-0).

11

Verb Syntax

This chapter contains the recommended syntax for all acceptable verb formats.

GENERAL OBSERVATIONS

- All verbs except for EXIT and nested IFs begin in column 12 of the coding form.
- Clauses and phrases begin in column 12 unless otherwise shown (readability places some clauses and phrases in other columns).
- The verb object begins in column 28, except for nested IFs.

Column 7	Column 12	Column 28	Column 60
ACCEPT			
	ACCEPT	identifier	
	FROM	DATE/DAY/DAY-OF-WEEK$_{85}$/TIME	
ADD			
	ADD	identifier-1	
		[identifier-2]	
		...	

Column 7	Column 12	Column 28	Column 60
	TO	identifier-m	ROUNDED
		[identifier-n	ROUNDED]
		...	
	ON SIZE ERROR	imperative-statement-1	
*and/or			
	NOT ON SIZE ERROR₈₅		
		imperative-statement-2	
	END-ADD₈₅		
	ADD	identifier-1	
		[identifier-2]₈₅	
		[identifier-3]	
		...	
	TO₈₅	identifier-m₈₅	ROUNDED
		...	
	GIVING	identifier-n	ROUNDED
		[identifier-o	ROUNDED]
		...	
	ON SIZE ERROR	imperative-statement-1	
*and/or			
	NOT ON SIZE ERROR₈₅		
		imperative-statement-2	
	END-ADD₈₅		
CALL			
	CALL	literal	
	[USING	[BY REFERENCE₈₅/CONTENT₈₅]	
		identifier]	
		imperative-statement-1	
	ON OVERFLOW		
*and/or			
	ON EXCEPTION₈₅	imperative-statement-2	
*and/or			
	NOT ON EXCEPTION₈₅	imperative-statement-3	
*Use the EXCEPTION₈₅ clause if supported.			
	END-CALL₈₅		
CANCEL			
	CANCEL	literal	
CLOSE			
	CLOSE	file-name-1	
	[REEL/UNIT [FOR REMOVAL WITH NO REWIND/LOCK]]		
		[file-name-2]	
	[REEL/UNIT [FOR REMOVAL WITH NO REWIND/LOCK]]		
		...	
	CLOSE	file-name-1	[WITH LOCK]
		[file-name-2	[WITH LOCK]]
		...	
CONTINUE			
	CONTINUE₈₅		

*Use only as a replacement for a dummy GO TO in mainline.

Column 7	Column 12	Column 28	Column 60

COPY

	COPY	text-name	
	[OF	library-name]	
	[REPLACING	literal-1	
	BY	literal-2]	

*REPLACING BY should be used only in the DATA DIVISION to qualify
*generic-data names.

DELETE

| | DELETE | file-name | RECORD |
| | INVALID KEY | imperative-statement-1 | |

*and/or

| | NOT INVALID KEY$_{85}$ | imperative-statement-2 | |
| | END-DELETE$_{85}$ | | |

DIVIDE

	DIVIDE	identifier-1	
	BY	identifier-2	
	GIVING	identifier-3	ROUNDED
		[identifier-4	ROUNDED]
		...	

*Only one GIVING identifier can be specified if REMAINDER is specified.

| | [REMAINDER | identifier-m] | |
| | ON SIZE ERROR | imperative-statement-1 | |

*and/or

	NOT ON SIZE ERROR$_{85}$		
		imperative-statement-2	
	END-DIVIDE$_{85}$		

EJECT

| | EJECT | | |

*Non-ANSI but usually supported whereas the ANSI / is not usually supported;
*use / EJECT if your compiler accepts it.

END PROGRAM

| | END PROGRAM$_{85}$ | program-id. | |

*Must be used as termination of every nested program.

EXIT

| | | EXIT. | |

*EXIT starts in column 16 because the prescribed format is **P???-X. EXIT.**
*The period and space (.) are required.
*EXIT should always be the final sentence of an invocable module, followed by an abort paragraph or
statement.

EXIT PROGRAM

| | EXIT PROGRAM | | |

*Should be used only in subprograms.
*Should always be the final sentence of a subprogram, followed by an abort paragraph or statement.

GO TO

| | GO TO | procedure-name | |

*Only local and abort GO TOs are allowed.

Column 7	Column 12	Column 28	Column 60
IF			
	IF	condition	
		statement-1/.../<u>NEXT</u> <u>SENTENCE</u>	
	<u>ELSE</u>	statement-2/ ... /<u>NEXT</u> <u>SENTENCE</u>	
	<u>END-IF</u>$_{85}$		

*Allowable condition: relation condition

	<u>IF</u>	identifier-1/arithmetic-expression-1/
		index-name-1$_{85}$
	IS [<u>NOT</u>]	$\underline{>}/\underline{<}/\underline{=}/\underline{>=}_{85}/\underline{<=}_{85}$
		identifier-2/arithmetic-expression-2/
		index-name-2$_{85}$
	<u>END-IF</u>$_{85}$	

*Allowable condition: arithmetic expressions

a + or − or * or /
b + or − or * or /
c

*Allowable condition: class condition

	<u>IF</u>	identifier
	IS [<u>NOT</u>]	<u>NUMERIC</u>/<u>ALPHABETIC</u>/<u>ALPHABETIC-LOWER</u>$_{85}$/
		<u>ALPHABETIC-UPPER</u>$_{85}$/class-name$_{85}$
	<u>END-IF</u>$_{85}$	

*Allowable conditions: sign condition

	<u>IF</u>	arithmetic-expression

*Same rules for arithmetic expressions.

	IS [<u>NOT</u>]	<u>POSITIVE</u>/<u>NEGATIVE</u>/<u>ZERO</u>
	<u>END-IF</u>$_{85}$	

*Allowable condition: condition-name condition

	<u>IF</u>	condition-name
	<u>END-IF</u>$_{85}$	

*Should be the most used IF statement.
*Allowable condition: combined condition

	<u>IF</u>	condition
	<u>AND/OR</u>	condition
	<u>AND/OR</u>	condition
	<u>END-IF</u>$_{85}$	

*Do not use NOT in conjunction with AND/OR; avoid NOT in all cases.

	<u>IF</u>	condition-1
	<u>IF</u>	condition-2
	<u>IF</u>	condition-3
		statement-3-1
		statement-3-2
		...
	<u>ELSE</u>	
		statement-3-m
		statement-3-n
		...
	<u>END-IF</u>$_{85}$	

*There must be a matching ELSE and END-IF$_{85}$ if supported for each IF.

Column 7	Column 12	Column 28	Column 60
	ELSE		
		statement-2-1	
		statement-2-2	
		...	
	END-IF$_{85}$		
	ELSE		
		statement-1-1	
		statement-1-2	
		...	
	END-IF$_{85}$		

*Nested IF statements are limited to three levels.
*Each nested level is indented by four characters.
*Any statement can be NEXT SENTENCE except ELSE NEXT SENTENCE if END-IF$_{85}$ is also used
*(ANSI restriction).
*Case construct IF statements are not indented.
*There is no limit on the number of case IF statements.

INSPECT

Column 7	Column 12	Column 28	Column 60
	INSPECT	identifier-1	TALLYING
		identifier-2	
	FOR ALL/LEADING/CHARACTERS		
		identifier-3	
	[BEFORE/AFTER	identifier-4...]	
	INSPECT	identifier-1	REPLACING
	CHARACTERS BY	identifier-2	
	[BEFORE/AFTER	identifier-3]	
	ALL/LEADING/FIRST	identifier-4	
	BY	identifier-5	
	[BEFORE/AFTER	identifier-6...]	

*TALLYING and REPLACING can be combined into a single INSPECT.

Column 7	Column 12	Column 28	Column 60
	INSPECT	identifier-1	
	CONVERTING$_{85}$	identifier-2	
	TO	identifier-3	
	[BEFORE/AFTER	identifier-4 ...]	

*Use CONVERTING$_{85}$ to translate alphabets.
*Code-inspect all INSPECT statements.

MOVE

Column 7	Column 12	Column 28	Column 60
	MOVE	identifier-1	
	TO	identifier-2	
		[identifier-3]	
		...	

MULTIPLY

Column 7	Column 12	Column 28	Column 60
	MULTIPLY	identifier-1	
	BY	identifier-2	
	GIVING	identifier-3	ROUNDED
		[identifier-4	ROUNDED]
	ON SIZE ERROR	imperative-statement-1	
*and/or			
	NOT ON SIZE ERROR$_{85}$		
		imperative-statement-2	
	END-MULTIPLY$_{85}$		

Column 7	Column 12	Column 28	Column 60
OPEN			
	OPEN INPUT	file-name-1	[REVERSED] [NO REWIND]
		[file-name-2	[REVERSED] [NO REWIND]]
		...	
	OPEN OUTPUT	file-name-1	[NO REWIND]
		[file-name-2	[NO REWIND]]
		...	
	OPEN I/O	file-name-1	
		[file-name-2]	
		...	
	OPEN EXTEND	file-name-1	
		[file-name-2]	
		...	

PERFORM

        PERFORM   [procedure-name-1]

*Out-of-line procedure-names should always be paragraphs whenever possible.

        [THRU   procedure-name-2]

*The THRU phrase is mandatory for out-of-line PERFORM statements and must be an EXIT paragraph
*that immediately follows the last statement of the paragraph.

        END-PERFORM$_{85}$

*END-PERFORM$_{85}$ must be specified for in-line$_{85}$ PERFORM statements.

        PERFORM   [procedure-name-1]
        [THRU   procedure-name-2]
        UNTIL   condition

*Condition must follow the same rules as IF conditions

        TEST$_{85}$ BEFORE$_{85}$/AFTER$_{85}$

*TEST BEFORE$_{85}$/AFTER$_{85}$ must always be used if permitted by syntax.

        END-PERFORM$_{85}$
        PERFORM   [procedure-name-1]
        [THRU   procedure-name-2]
        VARYING   index-name-1
        FROM   identifier-1/index-name-2
        BY   identifier-2
        UNTIL   condition-1

*Conditions must follow the same rules as IF conditions.

        [AFTER   index-name-3
        FROM   identifier-3/index-name-4
        BY   identifier-4
        UNTIL   condition-2]
        [AFTER   index-name-5
        FROM   identifier-5/index-name-6
        BY   identifier-6
        UNTIL   condition-3]
        ...
        END-PERFORM$_{85}$

*Code-inspect all PERFORM VARYING statements.

Column 7	Column 12	Column 28	Column 60

READ

	READ	file-name	[NEXT] RECORD
	INTO	identifier	

*INTO phrase is mandatory.

	[KEY IS	data-name]
	AT END/INVALID KEY	imperative-statement-1

*and/or

	NOT AT END$_{85}$/NOT INVALID KEY$_{85}$	
		imperative-statement-2
	END-READ$_{85}$	

REPLACE

	REPLACE$_{85}$	==pseudo-text-1==
	BY	==pseudo-text-2==
		...

*Should only be used in converting COBOL$_{74}$ to COBOL$_{85}$.

	REPLACE OFF$_{85}$

REWRITE

	REWRITE	record-name
	FROM	identifier

*FROM phrase is mandatory.

	[INVALID KEY	imperative-statement-1]

*and/or

	[NOT INVALID KEY$_{85}$	imperative-statement-2]

*INVALID KEY clause must be used when allowed by format.

	END-REWRITE$_{85}$

SEARCH

	SEARCH	identifier
	VARYING	index-name-1
	AT END	imperative-statement-1
	WHEN	condition-1

*Conditions must follow the same rules as IF conditions.

		imperative-statement-2/NEXT SENTENCE
	[WHEN	condition-2
		imperative-statement-3/NEXT SENTENCE]
	...	
	END-SEARCH$_{85}$	
	SEARCH ALL	identifier-1
	AT END	imperative-statement-1
	WHEN	data-name-1
		= identifier-2/arithmetic-expression-1

*Arithmetic-expressions must follow the same rules as IF.

	[AND	data-name-2
		= identifier-3/arithmetic-expression-2]
	[AND	data-name-3
		= identifier-4/arithmetic-expression-3]
		imperative-statement-2/NEXT SENTENCE
	END-SEARCH$_{85}$	

*Code-inspect all SEARCH statements.

Column 7	Column 12	Column 28	Column 60
SET			
	SET	identifier-1/index-1	
		[identifier-2/index-2]	
		...	
	TO	identifier-3/index-3	
	SET	index-name-1	
		[index-name-2]	
		...	
	UP BY/DOWN BY	identifier	
START			
	START	file-name	
	[KEY	=/>/NOT </>=$_{85}$	data-name]
	[INVALID KEY	imperative-statement-11	
*and/or			
	[NOT INVALID KEY$_{85}$	imperative-statement-2]	
	END-START$_{85}$		

*Should only be used if external storage media requirement.

STOP RUN			
	STOP RUN		

*Should only be used in main program.

SUBTRACT			
	SUBTRACT	identifier-1	
		[identifier-2]	
		...	
	FROM	identifier-m	ROUNDED
		[identifier-n	ROUNDED]
	ON SIZE ERROR	imperative-statement-1	
*and/or			
	NOT ON SIZE ERROR$_{85}$	imperative-statement-2]	
	END-SUBTRACT$_{85}$		
	SUBTRACT	identifier-1	
		[identifier-2]	
		...	
	FROM	identifier-m	
	GIVING	identifier-n	ROUNDED
		[identifier-o	ROUNDED]
		...	
	ON SIZE ERROR	imperative-statement-1	
*and/or			
	NOT ON SIZE ERROR$_{85}$	imperative-statement-2	
	END-SUBTRACT$_{85}$		
TITLE			
	TITLE	user-defined-text	

*Non-ANSI; should always be used if supported.

USE FOR DEBUGGING			
	USE FOR DEBUGGING$_{74}$		
		[ALL REFERENCES OF] identifier/file-name/	
		procedure-name/ALL PROCEDURES	
		...	

Column 7	Column 12	Column 28	Column 60

WRITE

| | WRITE | record-name | |
| | FROM | identifier | |

*FROM phrase is mandatory.

| | [INVALID KEY | imperative-statement-1] | |

*and/or

| | [NOT INVALID KEY$_{85}$ | imperative-statement-2] | |

*INVALID KEY clause must be used when allowed by format.

END-WRITE$_{85}$

Miscellaneous allowable syntaxes:

indexing

data-name-1/condition-name-1
[index-name-1, [index-name-2],...)

*Relative addressing is not allowed.
*Subscripts are not allowed unless absolutely necessary.
*All subscripts are to be bound to a single table.
*Subscripts and indices cannot be intermixed$^{nr}_{85}$.

qualification

COPY   text-name
OF   library-name

*Only COPY statement qualification is allowed.

Combining the approved verb syntax with the other recommendations will provide the high-quality software described in Chapter 1.

12

Compiler Message Codes

Every COBOL compiler flags syntax errors in source programs, providing the following details:

- Line number of the source statement in which the error was detected
- An error message identifier
- Severity level of the error
- Error message text

Initially, the compiler error messages were placed at the end of the source listing. Some compilers, such as COBOL$_{vs}$, permit the compiler error messages to be embedded within the source code listing and/or the end of the source code listing (FLAG option).

Each compiler has its own format for compiler error messages. The COBOL$_{vs}$ format is as follows:

LINE ID	MESSAGE CODE	MESSAGE TEXT
nnnnnn	IGVppxxxx-1	text of message

where

nnnnnn	is the line number of the last statement parsed and processed by the compiler preceding the compiler error message[1]

and

IGV   is the mnemonic for a COBOL compiler error message

and

PP   is the phase of the compiler that discovered the error

and

xxxx   is a four-digit compiler error message identifier

and

1   is the severity level of the error

and

text of message is an understandable description of the error.[2]

There are five severity levels:

1. Informational (I)   Program will execute as coded, but statement is either inefficiently coded or contains a slight syntax error.

2. Warning (W)   Statement is syntactically correct but may cause erroneous execution.

3. Error (E)   Statement is syntactically incorrect and the compiler has attempted correction; program *may* execute as coded.

4. Severe (S)   Statement is syntactically incorrect and the compiler has attempted correction; program *might* execute as coded.

5. Unrecoverable (U)   Statement syntax was so bad that the compiler aborted.

All compiler error messages must be corrected before a program is loaded for testing and debugging. A possible exception is an I or W error message that does not affect the object code but whose correction would affect readability and maintainability. For instance, some compilers print an I or W message if PERFORM with a THRU phrase is used with paragraphs instead of sections. It is better to accept this I or W error message than to recode the program with sections.

RECOMMENDATIONS

- Embed error messages if possible (it is easier to debug the source listing).
- Correct all I and W error messages unless a specific error message does not affect the object code and its correction would affect maintainability.
- Correct all E, 8, and U error messages.

NOTES

1. It is possible that the error actually occurred in a preceding statement but the error condition was not detected until a later statement, which becomes the error statement.
2. A bane of programmers is the gibberish that is often printed as an informational message.

13

ANSI and FIPS

$COBOL_{74}$ is divided into 12 functional modules, each containing two or three levels, null, low, and high. A full (complete) $COBOL_{74}$ compiler must contain all the language elements, statements, and formats in all levels of all modules. I do not believe that a full $COBOL_{74}$ compiler exists.

Anything less is a legitimate subset if it includes at least all the language elements, statements, and formats of the lowest levels of all modules. Nine $modules_{74}$ contained null levels (relative I/0, indexed I/0, sort-merge[nr], report writer[nr], segmentation, library, debug, interprogram communication, communication[nr]); thus the smallest legitimate $COBOL_{74}$ subset consists of the low levels of the remaining three modules (nucleus, table handling, sequential I/0).

ANSI does not have any enforcement powers, but the United States government has certification powers. The Department of Commerce issued a Federal Information Processing Standard (FIPS) to evaluate the ANSI status of any COBOL compiler.[1] Any COBOL compiler proposed or sold to the U.S. government must contain a FIPS flagger that evaluates that compiler as nonconforming, low, low intermediate, high intermediate, or high.

Most $COBOL_{74}$ compilers contain the FIPS flagger, which can be turned on at compile time so that you can obtain your own rating.

TABLE 13.1   COBOL$_{85}$ Module Summary

COBOL SUBSETS	REQUIRED MODULES (Required in Subsets)								OPTIONAL MODULES (Not Required in Subsets)		
	Nucleus	Sequential I/O	Relative I/O	Indexed I/O	Interprogram Communication	Sort-Merge	Source Text Manipulation	Report Writer	Communication	Debug	Segmentation
High	2 NUC 1,2	2 SEQ 1,2	2 REL 0,2	2 INX 0,2	2 IPC 1,2	1 SRT 0,1	2 STM 0,2	1 RPW 0,1	2 COM 0,2	2 DEB 0,2	2 SEG 0,2
Inter-mediate	1 NUC 1,2	1 SEQ 1,2	1 REL 0,2	1 INX 0,2	1 IPC 1,2	1 SRT 0,1	1 STM 0,2	1 RPW 0,1	2 COM 0,2	2 DEB 0,2	2 SEG 0,2
Mini-mum	1 NUC 1,2	1 SEQ 1,2	Null	Null	1 IPC 1,2	Null	Null		1 COM 0,2	1 DEB 0,2	1 SEG 0,2

RECOMMENDATION

- Use the FIPS flagger to rate your COBOL$_{74}$ compiler.

COBOL$_{85}$ combined the nucleus and table-handling modules and made the report writer[nr], communication[nr], debug, and segmentation modules optional (it also renamed the library module as source text manipulation). Table 13.1 gives a summary.

COBOL$_{85}$ has defined three subsets—high, intermediate, and minimum. The high subset must contain all the language elements, statements, and formats shown in the high row of Table 13.1. A high subset does not have to contain any language elements from any of the optional modules.[2] An intermediate subset is the intermediate row, and a minimum subset is the minimum row. Again, no optional modules need be included. The COBOL$_{85}$ minimum subset permits basic operations, table handling, sequential I/0, and COBOL inter-program communication.

A conforming compiler implementation fully supports any subset, and a conforming source program cannot contain any language element not specified by COBOL$_{85}$. ANSI has adopted the FIPS flagger principle and requires that a conforming compiler have the capability to flag any nonstandard and obsolete language elements at compile time.

RECOMMENDATIONS

- Rate your COBOL$_{85}$ compiler with both the ANSI and FIPS flaggers.
- Develop a site standard that specifies which flagged language elements are forbidden.
- Enforce standards with a production turnover software checker that prohibits any program with proscribed language elements from entering production.

NOTES

1. Publication No. 21-1-1975. Testing is performed at the Federal Compiler Testing Center of the General Services Administration.
2. All COBOL$_{85}$ reserved words must be reserved, even if they are part of nonsupported modules.

14

The World's Smallest COBOL Programs

A fitting end to Part 1 is the world's smallest syntactically correct COBOL programs:

```
COBOL74
        IDENTIFICATION DIVISION.
        PROGRAM-ID   smlcbl.
        ENVIRONMENT DIVISION.
        DATA DIVISION.
        PROCEDURE DIVISION.
            STOP RUN.


COBOL85
        IDENTIFICATION DIVISION.
        PROGRAM-ID.   smlcbl.
```

P.S. The programs do not do anything except compile correctly!

Part 2 HOW to RESTRUCTURE EXISTING SPAGHETTI COBOL PROGRAMS

15

Maintenance

For a friend assigned to a maintenance group:

> The fellow who designed it
> Is working far away;
> The spec's not been updated
> For many a livelong day.
> The guy who implemented it is
> Promoted up the line;
> And some of the enhancements
> Didn't match to the design.
> They haven't kept the flowcharts.
> The manual's a mess.
> And most of what you need to know,
> you'll simply have to guess.
>
> We do not know the reason,
> Why the bugs pour in like rain,
> But don't just stand here gaping!
> Get out there and MAINTAIN!

David H. Diamond, *Datamation*, June 1976.

And now, a few aphorisms for the office wall:

What can go wrong, will go wrong.

All programs will have to be changed some day.

Sooner or later someone else is going to have to understand the programs you write.

Programs must be written for people as well as for computers.

Knowing that a program can be understood and amended by someone else ought to be one of the programmer's criteria for success.

Programmers who write non-communicative programs should be drummed out of the profession.

Mick Punter, 1975

In my opininon, there is nothing in the programming field more despicable than an uncommented program. A programmer can be forgiven many sins and flights of fancy . . . ; however, *no* programmer, no matter how wise, no matter how experienced, no matter how hardpressed for time, no matter how well-intentioned, should be forgiven an uncommented and undocumented program.

If this seems an unreasonably venomous attack, you are invited to debug, maintain, or change someone else's uncommented program; you will find that it is worse than having no program at all. Only a fool would venture into an unknown forest without leaving trailmarkers behind. Writing an uncommented program is roughly the same as crawling blindfolded into the jungles of the Amazon. Though there are no firm rules in this area, a good guideline to follow is four or five lines of comment for every subroutine (or COBOL SECTION, etc.), and an average of one comment for every two or three lines of source code.

Edward Yourdon, Techniques of Program
Structure and Design (Englewood Cliffs, N.J.:
Prentice-Hall, 1975).

These are a few comments on maintenance drawn from the very few articles on maintenance. Various authorities have concluded that only about one book out of 20 on computer programming is devoted to maintenance, even thought maintenance takes up to 80 percent of the real-world programming effort! They have also concluded that this has occurred because maintenance is considered to be the lowest rung on the programming ladder. Only trainees and people who really cannot program are given the job of maintenance. This theory assumes that all maintenance programmers cannot wait until their "penitence" is over and they can do something meaningful in the development arena. The perception is true; the reality is not. Statistics previously quoted indicate that most programmers, trainee or senior, do maintenance programming on a regular basis. Current trends indicate that their percentage of maintenance programming will continue to increase until most programmers will devote all their time to maintenance unless something is done. Part 2 discusses some techniques to quell the maintenance dragon.

Most maintenance articles that I have read do not actually discuss how to do maintenance. They usually fall into the following categories:

- Proving that maintenance is a real problem
- Proving that structured techniques can reduce future maintenance
- Proving that software tools can help the maintenance programmer
- Proving that someday ''structured engines'' will be able to structure unstructured programs

Despite that fact that ''everybody'' knows that maintenance is a serious problem, it is swept under the rug because admitting that it exists means that data processing has done a poor job. The unfortunate truth is that most DP shops have done a poor job. They have allowed programmers to do whatever without reviewing their code. The DP rationale is that reviewing code is an insult to the programmers, which in turn may mean that programmers might leave for other employment. The DP fear is founded; statistics indicate that the average programmer stays only 18 months in any employment. The programmer rationale is that 18 months provides significant experience on a résumé, which in turns means more salary. Programmers know that they are still in high demand and can move easily. Until supply exceeds demand or until most DP shops start enforcing standards, the problem will continue. However, DP shops must bite the bullet in order to start reducing the enormous cost of maintenance.

The chapters in this part provide some answers.

Part 1 featured recommendations for writing readable COBOL. Using these recommendations will reduce future maintenance.

Software tools can assist, and structured engines are now available. This part of the book provides, to the best of my knowledge, the first comprehensive treatment of using computer software to assist harried maintenance programmers in their difficult task.

Most of this part is based on the experience of the following companies and individuals:

- The Analyst Workbench (AWB—my company)
- ADPAC Corporation (AWB designs new tools and extensions to existing tools, which are then programmed and marketed by ADPAC)
- The Catalyst Group of Peat Marwick (especially friends and coworkers of Cris Miller, developer of the structured engine, and Al Travis, senior manager)

This does not imply that work being performed by other persons and companies in this field are less important, only that I am more familiar with my own work and that of my colleagues.

Analysts are usually taught that the most important first step is to scope the problem. The problem is software maintenance, and therefore the question is, What is software maintenance? The literature abounds with definitions and distinctions. The simplist definition is ''Software maintenance is any change to any system for any reason.''[1] Therefore, once the system is accepted by the user, it is in maintenance, and any change or enhancement is maintenance.

The following statistics again underscore the cost of maintenance:

- Maintenance as a percentage of resources: 49%[2]
- Number of U.S. programmers by 1990: 1 million[3]
- Number of maintenance programmers: 490,000 (49% × 1 million)
- Annual cost of a programmer in the United States: $40,000[4]
- Annual U.S. maintenance bill: $19.6 billion

Another study provides percentages for various maintenance activities:[5]

Study code	33%	
Study request	25%	
Study documentation	4%	
Study subtotal		62%
Implement	20%	
Test	15%	
Update documentation	3%	
Implementation subtotal		38%
Total		100%

The interesting percentages are for documentation—maintenance programmers basically do not use external documentation and do not keep it up to date. The usual reason for this sad state of affairs is that the original development programmers provided poor or no external documentation.

Ed Yourdon provided a list of excuses for not documenting:

- I don't have enough time.
- I have to do my own keypunching, and I don't type well.
- I type my programs into a time-sharing terminal, and I get charged for connect time—and since I don't type well . . . .
- My program is self-documenting.
- Any *competent* programmer can understand my code without comments.
- My program is only going to be used once, so documentation is not necessary.
- The program will certainly be changed drastically during the testing and debugging phase, so the documentation will be obsolete by the time the program is finished.
- I understand perfectly well what my program does—so why should I have to document it?
- I don't like to document or comment.

PROFILE

PFM: PERFORM   PFMT: TIMES   PFMJ: UNTIL   PFMV: VARYING
COM: COMMON   LEX: FALLTHRU

RPT=SEQUENTIAL LINE ON THIS REPORT

HOW=INVOCATION METHOD
  @PM =OPERATING SYSTEM
  PFM =PERFORM
  PFMT=PERFORM THRU
  CALL=CALL
  FALL=FALLTHRU

USE=NUMBER OF INVOCATION STATEMENTS FOR A COMMON MODULE.

LINE NO=COBOL LINE NUMBERS

COM=MODULE CAN BE INVOKED BY MULTIPLE STATEMENTS

LVL=LEVEL THAT MODULE IS ON IF DISPLAYED AS A CONSTANTINE STRUCTURE CHART.

RPT LINE	HOW	INVK USE	LINE NO INVOKE	LINE NO LOCATE	COM	LVL USE NO.	MODULE IDENT AND TITLE
1	@PM					00	NEWDB COBOL PROGRAM
2	PFM			000380		01	P001-MAIN-LINE
3	CALL		000402			02	MMOPEN UNFOUND MODULE ***
4	PFM		000408	000430		02	P102-CALL-MESSAGE-HANDLER
5	CALL		000439			03	MMINPST UNFOUND MODULE ***
6	CALL		000442			03	MMRECV UNFOUND MODULE ***
7	PFM		000444	000473		03	P202-PROCESS-MESSAGE
8	PFM		000483	000532		04	P301-CHECK-FOR-ACTIVE-PCB
9	PFM		000493	000570		04	P401-PROCESS-SIGNON
10	PFM		000494	000620		04	P402-OPEN-DOCUMENT
11	PFM	2	000637	003219	COM	05	P903-ALLOCATE-CACHE
12	CALL		003260		COM	06	MMALLOC UNFOUND MODULE ***
13	PFM		003273	003080	COM	06	P800-PROCESS-I-O
14	PFMT		003290	000412	COM	06	P099-ABORT-HANDLEDB
15	PFM	10	000645	003302	COM	05	P904-DEALLOCATE-CACHE
16	PFM		003326	004973	COM	06	P940-FIND-CPT-ENTRY
17	PFM		004989	003219	COM	07	P903-ALLOCATE-CACHE /SEE LINE 11
18	PFM		004997	000412	COM	07	P099-ABORT-HANDLEDB
19	PFM		005004	008804	COM	07	P1017-FIND-CPIB-ENTRY
20	PFM	4	005015	003080	COM	07	P800-PROCESS-I-O
21	PFM		005021	004973	COM	07	P940-FIND-CPT-ENTRY /SEE LINE 16
22	PFM		005042	008873	COM	07	P1018-FIND-CPDB-ENTRY
23	PFM		003336	003219	COM	06	P903-ALLOCATE-CACHE /SEE LINE 11
24	PFM		003345	004722	COM	06	P936-ALLOCATE-BMT-ENTRY
25	PFM		004736	003219	COM	07	P903-ALLOCATE-CACHE /SEE LINE 11
26	PFM		004744	008038	COM	07	P1009-ALLOCATE-BMIB-ENTRY
27	PFM	3	004752	003080	COM	07	P800-PROCESS-I-O
28	PFM		004758	004722	COM	07	P936-ALLOCATE-BMT-ENTRY /SEE LINE 24
29	PFM		004770	008067	COM	07	P1010-ALLOCATE-BMDB-ENTRY
30	PFM		008090	008104		08	SET-BIT
31	PFM	2	003350	003080	COM	08	P800-PROCESS-I-O
32	PFM		003358	007288	COM	06	P960-INSERT-CPT-ENTRY
33	PFM	3	007304	003219	COM	07	P903-ALLOCATE-CACHE /SEE LINE 11
34	PFM		007313	004291	COM	07	P925-ALLOCATE-CACHE-BLOCK
35	PFM		004307	004722	COM	08	P936-ALLOCATE-BMT-ENTRY /SEE LINE 24
36	PFM		004316	003219	COM	08	P903-ALLOCATE-CACHE /SEE LINE 11
37	PFM		004329	003080	COM	08	P800-PROCESS-I-O
38	PFM	7	007323	003473	COM	07	P1017-FIND-CPIB-ENTRY
39	PFM	2	007358	008804	COM	07	P099-ABORT-HANDLEDB
40	PFMT	7	007402	000412	COM	07	P903-ALLOCATE-CACHE
41	PFM	7	007409	008873	COM	07	P1018-FIND-CPDB-ENTRY
42	PFM	3	007417	010507	COM	07	P1102-MERGE-BEFORE
43	PFM	2	007433	010431	COM	07	P1100-MERGE
44	PFM		007453	003473	COM	07	P910-SPLIT-BLOCK
45	PFM		007543	009430	COM	07	P1050-INSERT-CPIB-ENTRY
46	PFM	4	009447	003219	COM	08	P903-ALLOCATE-CACHE /SEE LINE 11
47	PFM	8	009453	008804	COM	08	P1017-FIND-CPIB-ENTRY
48	PFMT		009468	000412	COM	08	P099-ABORT-HANDLEDB
49	PFM	3	009485	010507	COM	08	P1102-MERGE-BEFORE
50	PFM	2	009503	010431	COM	08	P1100-MERGE
51	PFM	8	009512	003080	COM	08	P800-PROCESS-I-O
52	PFM		009520	003473	COM	08	P910-SPLIT-BLOCK
53	PFM		009611	004291	COM	08	P925-ALLOCATE-CACHE-BLOCK /SEE LINE 34
54	PFM		009623	010534	COM	08	P1121-MOVEBYTE

Figure 15.1   A level report (also called a snake report) provides a static analysis of the level of each module in the hierarchy by tracing fallthrus, gobacks, ALTER, CALL, EXIT, GO TO, and PERFORM statements.

- It's not good to have too many comments—it obscures the important ones.
- If I put in too many comments, my program will take longer to compile.
- My source program will take up too much room.
- Who reads the documentation anyway?[6]

The last question completes the circle—no one reads the documentation because manual documentation is usually poor and almost never kept up to date. As recommended in Part 1:

- Use *REMARKS$_{68}$ to document the program function.
- Use meaningful data and paragraph names.
- Define the data and control parameters for each paragraph.
- Comment any unusual code.
- Use source-driven documentation to provide cross reference reports, level reports (see Figure 15.1), Constantine structure charts, and the like.

All this should substantially reduce the study time of 62 percent. A reduction in study time by 25 percent would result in an annual saving of about \$3 billion (\$19.6 billion $\times$ 62% $\times$ 25%). Placed in a smaller perspective, a DP department with 100 programmers would annually save about \$300,000 (100 $\times$ 49% $\times$ \$40,000 $\times$ 62% $\times$ 25%). Source-driven documentation packages offer great return on investment.

Here's one last comment from Ed Yourdon on the maintenance problem:

> The number of bugs *remaining* in large programs and systems (after they have supposedly been thoroughly tested) is rather immense. It has been estimated in references that each new release of OS/360 (IBM operating system) contains over one thousand errors; Tom Gilb, an EDP consultant in Oslo, Norway, claims to have counted over *eleven thousand* bugs in a recent release of OS![7]

NOTES

1. Nicholas Zvegintzov, coord., *Software Maintenance: Tools, Techniques, and Management Strategies*, Symposium, UCLA, 1982.

2. B. P. Lientz and E. B. Swanson, *Software Maintenance Management: A Study of the Maintenance of Computer Application Software in 487 Data Processing Organizations* (Reading, Mass.: Addison-Wesley, 1980).

3. Girish Parikh, "In Defense of the Maintenance Programmer," *Infosystems*, January 1985.

4. Source EDP, *Annual EDP Salary Survey*, 1987.

5. R. K. Fjeldstad and W. T. Hamlen, *Application Program Maintenance Study: Report to Our Respondents*, White Plains, N.Y.: IBM, 1979.

6. E. Yourdon, *Techniques of Program Structure and Design* (Englewood Cliffs, N.J.: Prentice-Hall, 1975).

7. Ibid.

16

Program Inventory

Peter Harris, founder and president of ADPAC, has proved over and over again that most DP departments cannot provide a list of their executable programs. This is the documentation problem applied to operations instead of programming. Operational run books are usually updated, but hardly anything else is. Most of Ed Yourdon's reasons listed in Chapter 15 apply to operational documentation.

Equally true for operational documentation is that most operators will not refer to external manually produced documentation because it does not exist or is out of date. Therefore, the question is, How do you know what programs to fix if you do not know the programs?

ADPAC has a simple solution.

WHERE

There WHERE command of

    @PM INPUT: @PM.JOB ALL,CATAL=ALLPROGS

produces a complete listing of all programs listed in any IBM job control language (JCL).[1]

The CATAL clause requests that the "system vector" (list of all programs) be saved (cataloged) for future use.

This is source-driven documentation carried to its ultimate. The only source code for executable programs is the JCL, and that is what WHERE analyzes. The program inventory must be correct because it is derived from the source code that must be used to invoke any program that can be loaded for computer execution. Figure 16.1 is an example.

The next interesting question for most DP organizations is, What is the hierarchical structure of the executable programs (what programs invoke what programs)? If a DP organization could tell you what executable programs they had, it is improbable they could tell you the hierarchical relationships. The WHERE command of

```
@PM INPUT:
           @PM.MODEL          JCL=JOBCNTL,ALL
           @PM.STRUCTURE      MODULE=PGM
           @PM.DIAGRAM        RPT=(IDENT,TITLES,BOX)
```

Standard Documentation Runs

```
@PM INPUT:
    ===> @PM.JOB MEMBER=RA10001,CATALOG=T1
MEMBER=RA10001
    The jobcontrol library member to be processed.
CATALOG=T1
    Saves the output of the run as a JCLIST (Job list) in the PMLIB under the name
    T1.
```

JCLIST RPT LINE	USER CODES	JOBCNTL NAME	JOB IDENT	JOB STEP	PROC NAME	PROC STEP	PGM IDENT
	-----11-----	-----21-----	---31---	---41---	---51---	---61---	
1	00001 1J	RA10001	RA10001	RAG001	RAG001	PSCOPY1	PSCOPY
2	00002 1J	RA10001	RA10001	RAG001	RAG001	GENEOF1	GENEOF
3	00003 1J	RA10001	RA10001	RAG001	RAG001	PSCOPY2	PSCOPY
4	00004 1J	RA10001	RA10001	RAG001	RAG001	GENEOF2	GENEOF
5	00005 1J	RA10001	RA10001	RAG001	RAG001	PSCOPY3	PSCOPY
6	00006 1J	RA10001	RA10001	RAG001	RAG001	GENEOF3	GENEOF
7	00007 1J	RA10001	RA10001	RAG002	RAG002	CB609	CB609
8	00008 1J	RA10001	RA10001	RAG002	RAG002	ST845	SYNCSOR
9	00009 1J	RA10001	RA10001	RAG002	RAG002	CB610	CB610
10	00010 1J	RA10001	RA10001	RAG002	RAG002	PSCOPY1	PSCOPY
11	00011 1J	RA10001	RA10001	RAG002	RAG002	PSCOPY2	PSCOPY
12	00012 1J	RA10001	RA10001	RAG002	RAG002	FPRINT1	FPRINT

Figure 16.1 JCL listing.

produces Figure 16.2. This command analyzes all JCL (ALL clause) for programs and then analyzes each program to determine if there are any CALL statements within that program to establish the hierarchical relationships.

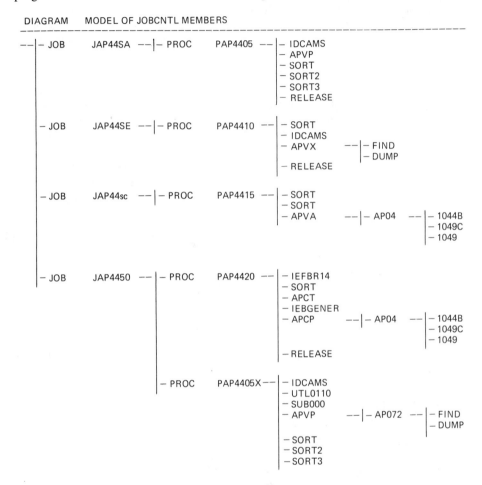

DIAGRAM   MODEL OF JOBCNTL MEMBERS

Figure 16.2 System diagram. A complete system diagram (model) can be prepared automatically, driven by the data in the JOBCNTL and procedure libraries, through the primary and alternate source library's programs—up to 28 nest levels deep. Some large systems may actually contain 500 to 1000 or more separate JOB PROCS and programs. Many users who have been in charge of maintaining a system for many years have reported that the invocation diagram provided by PM/SS is the first time they ever saw the complete system on one piece of paper (which is now their office wallpaper).

This book is interested in retrofitting COBOL programs, so the WHERE command of

```
@PM INPUT:
        @PM.LIST   MLIST=ALLPROGS,CATAL=ALLCOBOL
        @PM        SELECT=(8,C)
```

is required to isolate all the executable COBOL programs. (The original command identified the program language—A = assembler, C = COBOL, and so on—and placed that code in column 8 of the system vector.) The SELECT clause extracts from the system vector any MEMBER NAME that has a C in column 8.

RECOMMENDATION

- Use a JCL analyzer to produce a COBOL program inventory with hierarchical relationships.

NOTE

1. JCL controls the sequencing of jobs through the computer. Each job consists of one or more job steps, each invoking a program or a procedure. Each invoked program can invoke other programs with CALL statements. A procedure is a set of JCL statements that can contain one or more job steps. WHERE works only on IBM mainframes or compatibles. More information about WHERE can be found in Appendix A.

17

Reformatting

The JCL analyzer recommended in Chapter 16 provides a list of all executable COBOL programs in your DP shop. There is a simple software package that yields 10 to 50 percent maintenance programmer productivity improvement.[1] That simple software package is a reformatter.[2]

Poorly written COBOL code is characterized by the following flaws:

- No page EJECT verbs
- Levels not indented in the DATA DIVISION
- Multiple statements per coding line in the PROCEDURE DIVISION
- IF statements are not indented and not matched with ELSE statements
- Lack of blank lines between statements, sentences, paragraphs, and so on
- Inconsistent starting column positions for verbs, clauses, phrases, and the like

A reformatter program merely takes poorly written code and reformats it to make it *cosmetically* more readable (it's still spaghetti; it just looks more edible).

The ideal reformatter would perform the following functions:

IDENTIFICATION DIVISION

- Expand ID to IDENTIFICATION.
- Note $AUTHOR_{74}$ if missing and supported.
- Place standard installation name into $INSTALLATION_{74}$ if desired and missing and supported.
- Insert reformatting date and the term **reformatted** into $DATE\text{-}WRITTEN_{74}$ if supported.
- Insert $DATE\text{-}COMPILED_{74}$ if missing and supported.
- Flag (highlight) $SECURITY^{nr}_{74}$ if present.
- Flag $REMARKS_{74}$ if present or substitute * in column 7 as per installation standard; note $REMARKS_{74}$ or comment lines defining function if not present.
- Insert EJECT (or / if supported) after last entry if missing.
- Align all area A entries in column 8; align all area B entries in column 24.

ENVIRONMENT DIVISION

- Replace computer-name in SOURCE-COMPUTER and OBJECT-COMPUTER with standard installation name if desired.
- Insert WITH DEBUGGING $MODE_{74}$ in SOURCE-COMPUTER if missing and desired and supported.
- Flag MEMORY SIZE IS_{74}, SEGMENT LIMIT IS_{74}, PROGRAM COLLATING SEQUENCE, **system-name** IS^{nr}, $SWITCH^{nr}$ ON STATUS IS, **alphabet-name** IS, CURRENCY SIGN IS, DECIMAL-POINT IS if present.
- Flag $OPTIONAL^{nr}$ and $RESERVE^{nr}$ AREAS if present.
- Note FILE STATUS IS if missing and insert FILE STATUS IS **file-status-word;** reformatter should be customizable so that it inserts two characters for ANSI compilers and four characters for $COBOL_{vs}$.
- Insert FILE STATUS error recovery routine in appropriate places in the PROCE-DURE DIVISION if missing.
- Flag RERUN ON^{nr}_{74}, MULTIPLE FILE TAPE $CONTAINS_{74}$, $POSITION_{74}$ if present.
- Insert EJECT or / after last entry if missing.
- Flag any entry that was not copied.
- Align all area A entries in column 8; align all area B entries in column 24.

DATA DIVISION

- Flag LABEL RECORD IS $OMITTED_{85}$ for any mountable media peripherals; flag any nonstandard LABEL $RECORD_{74}$ clauses.

- Insert BLOCK CONTAINS **one** RECORD if missing; flag BLOCK CONTAINS **integer-1 to integer-2**[nr] RECORDS (variable[nr] length records) if present; flag CHARACTERS[nr] if present; note RECORD CONTAINS is missing and insert RECORD CONTAINS **integer** CHARACTERS (reformatter calculates **integer** from the 01 description); flag RECORD CONTAINS **integer-1 to integer-2**[nr] CHARACTERS[nr] (variable[nr] length) if present.

- Note DATA RECORD[74] if missing and supported.

- Flag VALUE[nr] OF, CODE-SET IS, LINAGE[nr] IS, WITH FOOTING[nr], LINES[nr] AT TOP, LINES[nr] AT BOTTOM, SD[nr] or RD[nr] or CD[nr] level indicators if present.

- Resequence the level numbers so that they are contiguous (01, 02, 03, 04, etc.) if required and desired.

- Indent each higher-level number by **n** where **n** is the installation standard (default is four spaces).

- Change all PICTURE IS clauses to PIC clauses.

- Align all PIC clauses in column 44.

- Flag any edited PIC clauses.

- Calculate and insert replication factor where applicable.

- Insert S (sign) into all numeric PIC clauses where required.

- Insert V (assumed decimal point) as the rightmost symbol for all numeric integer PIC clauses.

- Flag all P[nr] (assumed decimal scaling position).

- Flag all non-ANSI COMP clauses.

- Flag all SIGN[nr] IS LEADING/TRAILING SEPARATE CHARACTER, BLANK[nr] WHEN ZERO, SYNCHRONIZED LEFT/RIGHT, JUSTIFIED clauses.

- Flag all REDEFINES[nr], 66[nr] levels (RENAMES[nr]), and 77[nr] levels.

- Count and print the number of 88 levels and VALUE clauses; note that the quantity of 88 levels and/or VALUE clauses is below the installation standard.

- Flag all OCCURS clauses; flag all TIMES DEPENDING[nr] ON clauses.

- Flag all FILLER clauses [explicit or implicit[85]]

- Flag all figurative constants except ZERO/ZEROS/ZEROES and SPACE/SPACES.

- Flag REPORT SECTION[nr] and COMMUNICATION SECTION[nr] if present.

- Insert a WORKING-STORAGE SECTION FILLER tracer at the beginning and end of the WORKING-STORAGE SECTION and other eye-catcher constants if required.

- Insert READ INTO and WRITE FROM 01 levels into the WORKING-STORAGE SECTION if required; change appropriate FD to a single 01 level with no subordinate items if required; modify the appropriate PROCEDURE DIVISION input/output statements.

- Note any items that are not copied.
- Flag any item that is not reference by a PROCEDURE DIVISION statement; change **data-name** to FILLER and insert the data-name on the next line as a comment.
- Insert EJECT (or / if supported) after each completed FD or SD^{nr}, WORKING-STORAGE SECTION, LINKAGE SECTION, COMMUNICATION SECTION^{nr}, and REPORT SECTION^{nr} if required.

PROCEDURE DIVISION

- Flag any DECLARATIVES.
- Flag all sections^{nr}; flag **priority-number**$_{74}$ (**segmentation**$_{74}$); flag any paragraphs within sections^{nr}.
- Insert sequential paragraph or SECTION^{nr} number if required; abbreviate all names that exceed the COBOL limit of 30 characters.
- Note any paragraph or SECTION^{nr} that does not have comments preceding the first executable statement (lack of narrative); flag any paragraph or SECTION^{nr} that does not have any comments in the code; count and print the number of comments; note that quantity of comments is below the installation standard.
- Flag any identical^{nr} paragraph names (qualification^{nr}).
- Insert and flag dummy GO TO or CONTINUE$_{85}$ as the last SENTENCE in any paragraph or SECTION^{nr} that invokes the next module by fallthru except in the mainline.
- Insert blank line and EJECT or / after the last SENTENCE of each paragraph or SECTION^{nr} if required.
- Flag any literals^{nr} other than the CALL literal.
- Eliminate any unnecessary^{nr} periods and spaces (.).
- Flag any network^{nr} GO TO; flag any GO TO that is the target of an ALTER^{nr}; flag any Format 3 GO TO$^{nr}_{74}$; flag any DEPENDING^{nr} ON; insert defensive IF test for valid range of DEPENDING^{nr} ON value with abend if invalid.
- Flag any ALTER$^{nr}_{74}$.
- Flag any PERFORM **n**^{nr} TIMES; flag any multiple^{nr}-condition UNTIL; flag **switch-status**^{nr} condition UNTIL; flag any NOT condition UNTIL; insert defensive IF to validate that index or subscript^{nr} is within range and to abend if out of range (alternatively, insert compiler option such as SSRANGE$_{vs}$ to do range validation); flag any multidimensional PERFORM VARYING; flag any THRU or THROUGH unless it is to an EXIT paragraph of the invoked module.
- Flag any INSPECT.
- Flag any CORR^{nr} or CORRESPONDING^{nr} phrase.
- Flag any group^{nr} MOVE; flag any MOVE where the source and receiving PIC clauses are of different^{nr} types (A to 9; X to 9, etc.); flag any MOVE where the receiving field size is smaller^{nr} than the sending field size; flag any MOVE where

the sending PIC has an S (sign) and the receiving field does not[nr]; flag any MOVE that has overlapping[nr] fields; flag any field that is not moved in a MOVE CORR[nr].

- Flag any STOP RUN in a subprogram[nr] (called program); flag any STOP literal[nr]; insert a defensive abend GO TO or paragraph after any EXIT PROGRAM to prevent runaway; flag any GOBACK[nr] (non-ANSI).

- Flag any ACCEPT FROM mnemonic-name[nr] or MESSAGE COUNT[nr].

- Flag any uncopied OPEN and CLOSE statements.

- Flag any DISPLAY[nr].

- Flag any DISABLE[nr], ENABLE[nr], RECEIVE[nr], and SEND[nr] statements.

- Flag any MERGE[nr], RELEASE[nr], RETURN[nr], and SORT[nr] statements.

- Flag any GENERATE[nr], INITIATE[nr], SUPPRESSS[nr], and TERMINATE[nr] statements.

  Flag any IF that compares a numeric PIC field to a nonnumeric[nr] PIC field; flag any unary[nr] operators; flag any relational condition that has more than three[nr] elementary items; flag any IF where the nonnumeric fields are of unequal[nr] length; flag any **switch-status**[nr] IF; flag any IF that has more than two[nr] AND/OR connectors; flag any IF that has NOT connectors; flag any noncase IF statements that are nested more than three[nr] levels; flag any THEN[nr] or OTHERWISE[nr] (non-ANSI) phrases.

- Expand any abbreviated[nr] conditions; insert a matching ELSE NEXT SENTENCE and/or END-IF[85] where ELSE is missing.

- Insert SIZE ERROR phrase with abend into all arithmetic statements that require it; insert ROUNDED phrase or delete ROUNDED phrase as per installation standard; flag any Format 1 DIVIDE or MULTIPLY statement; flag any COMPUTE[nr] statement; flag any COMPUTE[nr] that has no parentheses.

- Flag any STRING[nr] and UNSTRING[nr] statements; insert ON OVERFLOW to abend in any STRING[nr] or UNSTRING[nr] that requires it.

- Flag all input-output statements; insert AT END and/or INVALID KEY with abend in all input-output statements that require them; insert FILE STATUS and FILE STATUS subroutine into all input-output statements that require them (FILE STATUS subroutine should be copied); change all READ statements to READ INTO where required; change all WRITE statements to WRITE FROM where required.

- Flag all SEARCH statements; flag all VARYING identifier phrases; flag any WHEN condition that would be flagged if it was part of an IF statement; flag any arithmetic-expression in a Format 2 SEARCH; insert AT END to abend where required.

- Flag any CALL identifier[nr] statement; flag any CALL with more than one[nr] identifier in the USING phrase; flag any static[nr] CALL if possible; flag any dynamic CALL without[nr] CANCEL if possible; insert ON OVERFLOW to abend if required and supported; flag any CALL to an ENTRY[nr] if possible; flag any CALL whose calling subprogram has a USING phrase and/or LINKAGE SEC-

TION that does not conform[nr] to the called program if possible; flag any RETURN-CODE[nr] (non-ANSI).

- Flag any ENTER[nr] statements.
- Flag any USE statements except USE FOR DEBUGGING.
- Count and print the number of COPY statements; note that the quantity of COPY statements is below the installation standard; flag any REPLACING BY.
- Flag any REPLACE$_{85}$.
- Flag any statement that uses qualification[nr], subscripts[nr], or relative indexing[nr] or intermixes$_{85}$ subscripts[nr] and indices.
- Align all statements as recommended in Chapter 11.

GENERAL

- Flag anything non-ANSI except EJECT.
- Insert sequence numbers if required; resequence sequence numbers if required.
- Substitute double quotation marks ('') for single quotation mark (') if required and possible.
- Substitute * in column 7 for any NOTE$_{68}$ statements.
- Insert a blank line where applicable.
- Insert END$_{85}$ scope terminators in any allowable syntax; insert as a comment if not supported.
- Insert blank lines for any SKIP$_{os/vs}$ and delete SKIP$_{os/vs}$.
- Insert PROGRAM-ID on the first line of each page in the identification area if area is blank and possible or use TITLE$_{vs}$ if supported.
- Provide a FIP rating and/or ANSI rating$_{85}$.

Strictly speaking, a reformatter would basically only realign the source code as per the aligning recommendations of this text or some other standard. The flags (highlighting a potential problem) and the notes (highlighting that the absence of something poses a potential problem) are the beginning of a rating system that evaluates how bad or how good a particular program is. As with any COBOL compiler, the flags and notes should be classified according to severity.

My evaluation as to the severity level of the flags and notes listed in this chapter are presented in Chapter 18. All reformatted inserts, deletions, and changes should be commented.

NOTES

1. Girish Parikh, *Techniques of Program and System Maintenance* (Lincoln, Nebr.: Ethnotech, Inc., 1980).
2. Five years ago, thirty people were engaged in programming and maintenance. Today, with more work than ever, fifteen people keep up with the whole operation [because of a reformatter]. Nick Kaluger, systems development manager of Olin Ecusta Paper Division, quoted in Parikh, *Techniques*.

Client studies of The Analyst Workbench, ADPAC, and Catalyst.

18

Rating a Program

Chapter 17 provided rating specifications. Different people have differing views on the severity level of some of the flags and notes, but most people in the restructuring field would produce the same overall program rating.

ADPAC produces a listing of the flags and notes without a severity level or a total rating report for a group of COBOL programs. Catalyst produces several reports that deal with the program complexity of the PROCEDURE DIVISION. The most interesting is the "quadrant report," illustrated in Figure 18.1.

COMPLEX GOOD ARCHITECTURE	COMPLEX POOR ARCHITECTURE
NOT COMPLEX GOOD ARCHITECTURE	NOT COMPLEX POOR ARCHITECTURE

Figure 18.1 A quadrant report.

Program complexity is derived from an analysis of logic level depth, length of logic path, number of verbs, and percentage of control logic in the program. Architecture is determined through an evaluation of program packaging. That is, how the program is organized and how control flow is directed by the use of go to's, occurrences of fall-thru logic, use of alter verbs, and usage of perform thru and perform constructs. The horizontal line represents the complexity threshold; those programs above the line are complex, while those below the line are not. The vertical line represents the threshold for acceptable architecture; programs that fall into the left quadrants have good architecture, while those to the right do not. By reviewing PROFILE [the Catalyst report generator that produces the quadrant report], we can make smart decisions about program maintenance, enhancement and maintenance staffing levels, and we can determine which programs can be salvaged and improved.[1]

Quadrant 1 (not complex, good architecture) is a "happy" program;[2] quadrant 2 (not complex, poor architecture) is a "somewhat happy" program; quadrant 3 (complex, good architecture) is a "somewhat unhappy" program; quadrant 4 (complex, poor architecture) is an "unhappy" program. This permits maintenance managers to make smart decisions about which programs to attack first. Quadrant 1 programs can be left alone; quadrant 2 programs can be left on the back burner or given to new maintenance programmers for on-the-job training; quadrant 3 and 4 programs are candidates for restructuring.

Gerry Weinberg has made numerous client studies that indicate that 80 percent of the maintenance effort is caused by 20 percent of the programs, in some cases 90 percent by 10 percent and in one extreme case 80 percent by 2 percent![3] Weinberg proposes many methods for isolating the worst programs, but the only automated method is to record the recompilation time of all programs in production.[4] Matching monthly (quarterly, semi-annual, or annual) recompilation times with quadrant 3 or 4 programs should yield a good approximation of the procedurally complex and/or poorly architected programs that need restructuring in a priority sequence.

However, neither ADPAC nor Catalyst nor any other rating system that I know of rates data complexity. Data complexity is the most important—if you have all the data, you can always use that data to prepare any user report required by using appropriate programming methods; if you do not have all the data, the most sophisticated programming technique cannot produce a user report requiring that uncaptured data.

I like the concept of the quadrant report and propose the data complexity quadrant report in Figure 18.2. It differs from the Catalyst procedure quadrant report in that it measures on a scale of 1 to 4 rather than a combination of architecture and complexity.

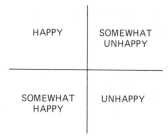

Figure 18.2   Data complexity quadrant report.

The mode (the quadrant that has the greatest number of entries) is the plot point. The mean should also be plotted for information.

Two data complexity quadrant reports are required because data transcends programs and must be evaluated on a system basis and must also be evaluated within the context of each program.

SYSTEM DATA COMPLEXITY

The first system data complexity measure is to make a rough guess as to the quantity of homonyms[nr], synonyms, aliases, and/or redundant data present in the system. This requires two counts:

- The number of COBOL programs
- The number of unique elementary items

A unique elementary item is any elementary item that has a unique name and a unique logical length. Logical length is the number of placeholder symbols in a PIC clause and is not influenced by the USAGE IS clause. For instance:

```
02 abc  PIC S999V99      USAGE IS COMP.
05 abc  PIC X(5)         USAGE IS DISPLAY.
10 abc  PIC $ZZ9.99CR   USAGE IS DISPLAY.
```

is counted as one unique elementary item because the dataname is the same (abc) and the number of placeholder symbols is the same (99999, XXXXX, ZZ999). By contrast,

```
02 xyz  PIC A       USAGE IS DISPLAY.
05 xyz  PIC A(30)   USAGE IS DISPLAY.
```

is counted as two unique elementary items even though the datanames are the same because the number of placeholder symbols is unequal.

The third term required for the calculation is the standard number of unique elementary items expected per COBOL program. This is the "rough guess"; my experience of creating logical databases by using normalization indicates that the total number of unique elementary items for a system is the number of COBOL programs times 20. Therefore, a system of ten COBOL programs should, on the average, have 200 unique elementary items. The excess of unique elementary items over this threshold represents potential homonyms[nr], synonyms, aliases, and/or redundant data. The quadrant scoring is as follows:

Quadrant 1 Unique elementary item count within 100% of calculation
Quadrant 2 Unique elementary item count within 500% of calculation
Quadrant 3 Unique elementary item count within 1000% of calculation
Quadrant 4 Unique elementary item count greater than 1000% of calculation

Aliases and redundant[nr] data cannot be detected automatically, but homonyms[nr] and synonyms can. Homonyms[nr] are two or more elementary items that have the same dataname but different logical lengths (number of placeholder symbols is unequal). There are two distinct types of homonyms[nr]:

- True   Numeric homonyms[nr] with a logical length difference more than 3 or nonnumeric homonyms[nr] with any logical length difference
- Numeric   Numeric homonyms[nr] with a logical length difference of 3 or less are usually the same elementary item with different magnitude PIC clauses

The true homonym[nr] is a catastrophe! Two or more users or programmers can interpret the value in the homonym[nr] differently, based on their definition of what the dataname means to them. Programmers may and usually do change the wrong elementary item when performing maintenance.

Numeric homonyms[nr] are time bombs. The effect of differing magnitudes is that truncation will sooner or later occur. The truncation is normally in the high-order digits, thereby typically causing mistakes in the millions. It is difficult to explain rounding errors to users; it is impossible to explain truncation errors to users. The quadrant rating is as follows:

Quadrant 1 No homonyms[nr]

Quadrant 2 (Does not apply.)

Quadrant 3 Fewer than five numeric homonyms[nr]; no true homonyms[nr]

Quadrant 4 More than four numeric homonyms[nr] and/or any true homonyms[nr]

Synonyms are elementary items with identical names and identical logical lengths but different PIC clauses. Certain synonyms are valid because of the need for different formats for different procedures. An elementary item could have a storage PIC of S999V99, a print PIC of $ZZ9.99CR, a display PIC of 99999-, and so on. The use of synonyms is desirable; however, they must be identified for future transfer to the mainframe data dictionary. The lack of synonyms indicates poor naming conventions, which result in increased maintenance. The quadrant rating is as follows:

Quadrant 1 Synonyms are >20% of total unique elementary items

Quadrant 2 Synonyms are between 10% and 20%

Quadrant 3 Synonyms are under 10%

Quadrant 4 There are no synonyms

Many old COBOL programs use a naming standard of prefixing a specific combination of letters to a dataname to indicate the role that elementary item is playing in that program. For instance, the prefix MSTIN- could be used to indicate MASTER-IN; MSTOUT- would be MASTER-OUT, TRSIN- would be TRANSACTION-IN, and so forth. The initial analysis should be repeated, eliminating prefixes and the results rated as before.

Literals[nr] are constants hard-coded in the PROCEDURE DIVISION. There are "innocent" literals[nr] that are basically "figurative" or report[nr] headings. There are dangerous literals[nr] that are actually hard-coded system literals[nr] such as **date, account-number,** and **userid.**

Figurative literals[nr] include 0, 1, 2, 3, . . . or MON, TUE, WED, ... The figurative literal[nr] that is a time bomb is any date literal[nr]. The use of 0–9 to represent year or 00–99 to represent decade will cause programs to abend and/or cause incorrect results when **year+1** occurs (all good DP people realize the chaos that is going to happen in 1999 and particularly on January 1, 2000).

Report[nr] headings are not dangerous per se but should be identified and redefined as WORKING-STORAGE literals[nr] for ease in identifying reports[nr] that must be changed when maintenance is performed.

The dangerous system literals[nr] are rarely changed when the real-world conditions change because they are too hard to find. This again places a time bomb into the system that will explode when real-world conditions provide data that activates the literal[nr]. Hard-coded literals[nr] also provide the hacker with the opportunity to bypass security by using a "back door." The quadrant rating is as follows:

Quadrant 1 No literals[nr]

Quadrant 2 Report[nr] literals[nr] only (alpha literals[nr] up to ten characters)

Quadrant 3 Any figurative literals[nr] (because of the possibility of date)

Quadrant 4 Any numeric literals[nr] within quotes (because of the possibility of system literals[nr])

The ratings score data complexity over the entire system being profiled.

PROGRAM DATA COMPLEXITY

The program ratings are divided into two sections dealing with data in the DATA DIVISION and the PROCEDURE DIVISION.

DATA DIVISION

Most old COBOL batch programs fall into the following categories:

Editing	Unedited transaction FILE in.
	Edited transaction FILE out.
	Incorrect transaction FILE out.
Update	Master FILE in.
	Edit transaction FILE in.
	Updated master FILE out.
	Incorrect transaction FILE out.

Report[nr]   Print FILE in.
              Print FILE out.

The preceding indicates that a "standard" program should have four or fewer files in and/or out. The quadrant rating is as follows:

Quadrant 1 One to four files
Quadrant 2 Five or six files
Quadrant 3 Seven files
Quadrant 4 More than seven files or zero files (zero files indicates that all input-output is performed with ACCEPT or DISPLAY statements, which is unacceptable for production programs)

FILE can be sequential or random. A FILE can also be declared OPTIONAL[nr] (an OPEN of a nonexistent OPTIONAL[nr] FILE will not cause an abend). SEQUENTIAL FILE processing is easier than RANDOM. However, neither SEQUENTIAL or RANDOM FILE processing causes significant data complexity by itself. However, an OPTIONAL[nr] FILE does significantly complicate the data complexity because an operator can control the program processing by mounting or not mounting the OPTIONAL[nr] FILE. OPTIONAL[nr] FILES should not be allowed. The quadrant rating is as follows:

Quadrant 1 SEQUENTIAL FILE processing only
Quadrant 2 RANDOM FILE processing
Quadrant 3 (Does not apply.)
Quadrant 4 One or more OPTIONAL[nr] files

The use of COPY statements indicates that standard data definitions have been used; lack thereof indicates that each programmer used his or her own data definitions. Use of COPY reduces homonyms[nr], synonyms, and aliases; nonuse increases their number. All items in the DATA DIVISION, other than program-specific literals[nr], should be in copy-libs. The quadrant rating is as follows:

Quadrant 1 All items in COPYLIB
Quadrant 2 Some items in COPYLIB; only one FILE undefined
Quadrant 3 Some items in COPYLIB; more than one FILE undefined
Quadrant 4 No items defined in COPYLIB

Homonyms[nr] and synonyms per se cannot exist in a single COBOL program. However, it is possible to have the identical item name in more than one place in the DATA DIVISION. If this occurs, each time the item is used, it must be qualified[nr] by an IN or OF connector. The danger of qualification[nr] is that many COBOL compilers only issue an intermediate warning (warning or error) and allow the program to be compiled and executed using the first occurrence of the qualified[nr] item. Any program with qualification[nr] should be examined to determine if a qualification[nr] error could exist (PROCEDURE DIVISION statement accesses a qualified[nr] item without or with insufficient qualification[nr]). The quadrant rating is as follows:

Quadrant 1 No qualification[nr]

Quadrant 2 All items requiring qualification[nr] have sufficient qualification[nr]

Quadrant 3 (Does not apply.)

Quadrant 4 Any items requiring qualification[nr] have insufficient qualification[nr]

The OCCURS clause allows repeating groups (a data structure, or group of related items, that can occur any number of times per single occurrence of a FILE). There are two OCCURS formats:

```
OCCURS integer            TIMES
OCCURS integer-1 to integer-2 TIMES DEPENDING[nr] ON data-name
```

The second format permits the repeating group to occur a variable number of TIMES; the actual TIMES at any moment of time is defined by the DEPENDING[nr] ON **data-name** variable. The DEPENDING[nr] ON **data-name** variable can be predefined or can actually be a variable defined in the FILE and read in at program execution.

OCCURS clauses are obsolescent because of the trend to relational databases, which require flat files. OCCURS clauses with hard-coded integer literals[nr] cannot be listed in cross-reference reports; OCCURS clauses with DEPENDING[nr] ON where the variable is read are violating the structured programming concept of "scope of control" (each module—in this case the program—should make all decisions that affect its processing). The quadrant rating is as follows:

Quadrant 1 No OCCURS clause

Quadrant 2 OCCURS clauses with predefined DEPENDING[nr] ON phrase

Quadrant 3 OCCURS clauses with hard-coded integers

Quadrant 4 OCCURS clauses with DEPENDING[nr] ON **data-name** variable read in by program.

The REDEFINES[nr] clause permits a data structure or elementary item to be given a different PIC for different processing. For instance, **data** could be defined as 999999 and redefined as **month** 99: **day** 99: **decade** 99. There is no theoretical limit to number of REDEFINES[nr] (either total or multiple per data structure, although some compilers impose limits). A single REDEFINES[nr] where the redefined logical length equals the target logical length does not cause significant data complexity. REDEFINES[nr] that have different logical lengths indicate data and/or processing complexity. Multiple REDEFINES[nr] that have overlapping fields also indicate significant data and/or processing complexity. The quadrant rating is as follows:

Quadrant 1 No REDEFINES[nr]

Quadrant 2 Single REDEFINES^{nr} per data structure with consistent logical lengths

Quadrant 3 Single REDEFINES^{nr} per data structure with inconsistent logical lengths and/or multiple REDEFINES^{nr} with consistent logical lengths and no overlap

Quadrant 4 Multiple REDEFINES^{nr} with inconsistent logical length or overlap

The RENAMES^{nr} clause (66^{nr} level) permits multiple data structures to be redefined (REDEFINES^{nr} works only on a single data structure). The same basic rules apply to RENAMES^{nr} that apply to REDEFINES^{nr} except that RENAMES^{nr} is inherently more complex because of the multiple data structures. The quadrant rating is as follows:

Quadrant 1 No RENAMES^{nr}

Quadrant 2 (Does not apply.)

Quadrant 3 (Does not apply.)

Quadrant 4 Any RENAMES^{nr}

77^{nr} levels permit elementary items with no internal structure to be placed into the WORKING-STORAGE. The preferred elementary item definition is to place 77^{nr} elementary items into WORKING-STORAGE as parameters under a general 01 level. 77^{nr} levels are easy to spot, and placing them into WORKING-STORAGE is not difficult. The quadrant rating is as follows:

Quadrant 1 No 77^{nr} levels

Quadrant 2 Any 77^{nr} levels

Quadrant 3 (Does not apply.)

Quadrant 4 (Does not apply.)

88 levels permit the use of meaningful names for possible values of an elementary item. The presence of 88s indicates a program that is easier to understand and maintain; 88s can also be placed in a data dictionary for easy cross-referencing. The quadrant rating is as follows:

Quadrant 1 20 or more 88 levels

Quadrant 2 10 to 19 88 levels

Quadrant 3 1 to 9 88 levels

Quadrant 4 No 88 levels

PROCEDURE DIVISION

The major data villain is the homonym^{nr}. Statements that reference system homonyms^{nr} have the potential for causing the greatest errors. Numeric homonyms^{nr} that have the maximum magnitude may not cause problems since a truncation cannot happen in the program (it could already have happened, depending on the overall program sequence). The quadrant rating is as follows:

Quadrant 1 No system homonyms[nr] referenced

Quadrant 2 (Does not apply.)

Quadrant 3 Only system numeric homonyms[nr] with maximum magnitude

Quadrant 4 Any true homonym[nr] and/or numeric homonym[nr] with less than maximum magnitude

Unreferenced items are not a problem in the current program. Unreferenced items are typically caused by the standard procedure in old COBOL programs of reading entire records regardless of how many of the items were required. There are two future problems:

- A program can always modify an unreferenced item, thereby allowing a program to make unknown or unauthorized modifications. The danger of an accidental modification increases substantially if the program uses CORRESPONDING[nr], table operations, STRING[nr] or UNSTRING[nr], or INSPECT with REPLACING.
- The trend to logical records (each program reads only the items it needs for processing) by the major DBMS vendors (IBM, ADR, Cullinet, Cincom) and the trend to relational databases have made unreferenced items obsolescent; programs will require modification, recompilation, and testing to conform to logical records.

The quadrant rating is as follows:

Quadrant 1 No unreferenced items

Quadrant 2 Up to 25% of items unreferenced

Quadrant 3 Up to 50% of items unreferenced

Quadrant 4 Over 50% of items unreferenced

Data must typically be read into a program by READ statements. Data is typically written by WRITE statements. Structured programming theory requires that nonprint files have one READ, one WRITE, and, for RANDOM access, one update statement per program. SEQUENTIAL WRITE files can also have an EOF (end-of-file) WRITE. Multiple READ or WRITE statements for nonprint files indicate poor programming practices and can result in either missing or duplicate I/O (print files can have multiple WRITE statements because of top-of-page and/or bottom-of-page conditions). The quadrant rating is as follows:

Quadrant 1 Each nonprint FILE has one READ statement; each SEQUENTIAL nonprint FILE has a maximum of one WRITE statement and a maximum of one EOF WRITE statement; each update FILE has one READ, one REWRITE, and one WRITE statement

Quadrant 2 One violation of the criteria for quadrant 1

Quadrant 3 Two violations of the criteria for quadrant 1

Quadrant 4 More than two violations of the criteria for quadrant 1

READ statements can have INTO phrases that move the data from the FD input area into WORKING-STORAGE; WRITE statements can have FROM phrases that move data from WORKING-STORAGE to the FD output area. The data continues to be available in the INTO or FROM areas. The major reason to use INTO or FROM is for debugging. The original data is always available to ascertain what the program was attempting to process when it abended. The quadrant rating is as follows:

Quadrant 1 All READ or WRITE statements have INTO or FROM phrases

Quadrant 2 More than 50% of the READ or WRITE statements have INTO or FROM phrases

Quadrant 3 Up to 50% of the READ or WRITE statements have INTO or FROM phrases

Quadrant 4 No READ or WRITE statements have INTO or FROM phrases

ANSI standards allows the INVALID KEY condition to be omitted to permit the programmer more extensive error processing by specifying a USE statement in the DECLARATIVES[nr] SECTION. Omitting both the INVALID KEY condition and the USE statement typically causes the INVALID KEY error to be ignored with uncertain results. The quadrant rating is as follows:

Quadrant 1 All I-O statements have INVALID KEY where syntactically possible

Quadrant 2 USE statement exists for omitted INVALID KEY conditions

Quadrant 3 (Does not apply.)

Quadrant 4 Any omitted INVALID KEY condition occurs with a corresponding omitted USE statement

The MOVE statement and the arithmetic statements can have a CORR[nr] or CORRESPONDING[nr] phrase. The CORRESPONDING[nr] phrase permits the programmers to specify multiple moves, adds, and the like by having the compiler compare the data structures specified for "identicalness" (the rules are complex) and MOVE the elementary items in data structure A to its "twin" in data structure B. The objective of the CORRESPONDING[nr] phrase is to reduce the "wordiness" of COBOL. Its typical effect is data corruption because of the pairing complexity rules. The quadrant rating is as follows:

Quadrant 1 No CORRESPONDING[nr] phrases

Quadrant 2 (Does not apply.)

Quadrant 3 Only one CORRESPONDING[nr] phrase

Quadrant 4 More than one CORRESPONDING[nr] phrase

Another subtle cause of truncation problems is the use of unsigned[nr] PIC clauses for elementary items involved in computations. Truncation or inaccurate results happen when a negative result occurs. The actual effect of the negative result (what does the computer do with the minus sign?) is dependent on the compiler, the selected compiler options, and the operating system). In any case, the result is inaccurate data. The quadrant rating is as follows:

Quadrant 1 All computational elementary items S (signed)

Quadrant 2 One or two unsigned computation elementary items

Quadrant 3 Three to five unsigned computation elementary items

Quadrant 4 More than five unsigned computation elementary items

The arithmetic statements permit the use of ROUNDED phrase to add 1 to the least significant digit if the fraction to be dropped is 5 or more. The purpose of rounding is to adjust the "pennies." Rounding should be used consistently; that is, every computation in every program in the entire system should either use rounding or not use rounding. The quadrant rating by program is as follows:

Quadrant 1 All computations use ROUNDED or do not use ROUNDED

Quadrant 2 (Does not apply.)

Quadrant 3 ROUNDED phrases are used inconsistently

Quadrant 4 (Does not apply.)

The arithmetic statements also permit the specification of an error routine if the result of the calculation exceeds the magnitude of the result PIC clause. Failure to specify the SIZE ERROR phrase typically results in the error being ignored and the value in the GIVING elementary item being unpredictable. The quadrant rating is as follows:

Quadrant 1 All computations have SIZE ERROR phrases

Quadrant 2 One computation does not contain a SIZE ERROR phrase

Quadrant 3 Two computations do not contain SIZE ERROR phrases

Quadrant 4 More than two computations do not contain SIZE ERROR phrases

COBOL contains some sophisticated table-handling and character string statements. When used correctly, they save a considerable number of simpler COBOL statements. Unfortunately, these statements are often misused and cause data corruption.

The TRANSFORM (non-ANSI) statement permits a series of values to be converted to another alphabet. The normal use of TRANSFORM is to convert ASCII (standard alphabet for most non-IBM mainframes) to EBCDIC (IBM mainframe alphabet) or the reverse. If the source data alphabet changes, then the converted data is wrong. This means that any program that uses TRANSFORM violates the structured programming concept of scope of control since the source data alphabet is outside the program's control. Nevertheless, language translations must be done, and steps should be taken to isolate the use of TRANSFORM. The recommended method is to isolate it in an edit program that performs only the translation. COBOL has added an INSPECT CONVERT$_{85}$ clause to provide language translation; the same comments apply. The quadrant rating is as follows:

Quadrant 1 No TRANSFORM or CONVERT$_{85}$ statements
Quadrant 2 Program with up to three files and up to 100 statements
Quadrant 3 Program with up to three files and 100 or more statements
Quadrant 4 Program with more than three files

The Format 1 SEARCH statement (nonbinary) permits a table of values to be searched for a specific value or values. The major problem is the setting of the index that controls the SEARCH. Improper setting of the index causes problems. A SET statement should always immediately precede the SEARCH statement. The quadrant rating is as follows:

Quadrant 1 One SEARCH statement with preceding SET statement
Quadrant 2 More than one SEARCH statement, all with preceding SET statements
Quadrant 3 One SEARCH statement without a preceding SET statement
Quadrant 4 More than one SEARCH statement without preceding SET statements

The INSPECT statement is used to count the number of times a specified character appears in a target data field and/or replace the character with another character. The problem is similar to the CORRESPONDING^{nr} problem. The INSPECT rules are complex, as are the TALLYING and REPLACING rules. INSPECTs, though nice, are dangerous. The quadrant rating is as follows:

Quadrant 1 No more than one INSPECT statement
Quadrant 2 Two INSPECT statements
Quadrant 3 Three INSPECT statements
Quadrant 4 More than three INSPECT statements

The STRING^{nr} and UNSTRING^{nr} statements permit a data field to be parsed or put together from many fields. The rules are exceedingly complex and easy to misapply. Like INSPECT, these statements are nice but dangerous. The quadrant rating is as follows:

Quadrant 1 No more than one STRING^{nr} or UNSTRING^{nr} statement
Quadrant 2 Two STRING^{nr} or UNSTRING^{nr} statements

Quadrant 3 Three STRING^{nr} or UNSTRING^{nr} statements

Quadrant 4 More than three STRING^{nr}or UNSTRING^{nr} statements

As previously stated, ADPAC and Catalyst have numerous reports to document the programming and architectural complexity of programs. The factors they consider include these:

- **Logic level depth:** What is the deepest level in the program? (The snake report displayed in Figure 15.1 has ten levels.)
- **Logic path length:** How tortuous is the path to get to the deepest level? (Sometimes a level other than the deepest has the most tortuous path.)
- **Number of verbs:** The more verbs, the more complicated the program.
- **Control logic percentage:** How many transfer-of-control statements are there? The greater the number of control statements, the more complex the program.
- **Number of network^{nr} GO TOs:** The more network^{nr} GO TOs, the more spaghetti (program complexity).
- **Number of ALTER^{nr} statements:** The more ALTER^{nr} statements, the more spaghetti.
- **Number of fallthrus:** The more fallthrus, the more spaghetti.
- **Deadcode^{nr} percentage:** Deadcode^{nr} consists of executable statements that cannot be reached by an executable path in the program; the higher the percentage, the greater the complexity because the maintenance programmer cannot tell from the source listing that the code cannot be executed. Cris Miller has estimated that production programs contain 32 percent deadcode^{nr}![5]
- **Runaway^{nr} logic:** An executable path that can execute the last physical sentence or invoke an unaltered Format 3^{nr} GO TO (causes abend); Cris Miller has estimated that 12 percent of production programs have runaway logic![6]
- **Range^{nr} violation:** A range^{nr} violation can be a GO TO out of the range of a PERFORM or PERFORM statements that are overlaping^{nr}, thereby causing program complexity.
- **Number of PERFORM THRU:** A PERFORM THRU to a non-EXIT paragraph^{nr} provides the possibility of multiple^{nr} entries, which increases program complexity.
- **Number of sections^{nr} with paragraphs:** Sections^{nr} with paragraphs again provide the possibility of multiple entries^{nr}.
- **Number of ENTRY^{nr}:** ENTRY^{nr} again provides the possibility of multiple entries^{nr}.
- **IF analysis:** Determines the deepest level (any noncase IF containing more than three^{nr} levels is complex); determines how many IF statements do not^{nr} have matching ELSE statements, which can cause incorrect branching; counts the number of Boolean operands (AND, OR, NOT), which increase program complexity.

- **Percentage of common modules:** A high percentage of common routines indicates a well-structured program that decreases program complexity.

- **Percentage of copied modules:** A high percentage of copied routines indicates a well-structured program.

- **Paragraph size analysis:** Determines the number of statements in the largest paragraph ($SECTION^{nr}$); determines the average statement size of executable paragraphs; counts the paragraphs that have over 50 statements (modular programming theory states that a good module should have 50 or fewer statements).

- **Percentage of comments:** A higher percentage of comments indicates a well-documented program, which is an indicator of a readable program.

Contact ADPAC and Catalyst for more details on how they rate these factors (addresses can be found in Appendix E). My quadrant ratings are given in Chapter 19.

The combination of the data complexity quadrant report and the processing complexity quadrant report and the recompilation time per program provides the information to rank preliminarily the priority in which the programs should be restructured. The equation is as follows:

$$\text{Rank} = \text{program data complexity mode factor} \times$$
$$\text{program processing complexity factor} \times$$
$$\text{program recompilation time}$$

Use the same time period for all programs.

NOTES

1. A. J. Travis, *Reengineering Business Systems* (Chicago: Peat Marwick, 1984).

2. I was responsible for the manufacturing reporting system while working at Intel. The system was "real time" in that it provided the next-shift manufacturing managers with information on how the previous manufacturing shift had done. The first page of the report was the "face" page, which was a computer-generated face that summarized the previous shift results:

3. G. M. Weinberg, "Worst First Maintenance," in *Techniques of Program and System Maintenance.* ed. G. Parikh (Lincoln, Nebr.: Ethnotech, Inc., 1980).

4. IBM and most other hardware vendors provide system accounting software that records for each account the amount of "wall clock" time (actual elapsed time), CPU time used, connect time,

I/O requests, and the like. This can be used to generate charges in a chargeback accounting program in which each user pays for the computer system on the basis of resources consumed.

5. J. C. Miller, in *Software Maintenance: Tools, Techniques, and Management Strategies*, symposium, coord. N. Zvegintzov, UCLA, 1982.

6. Ibid.

19

Summary of Quadrant Ratings

SYSTEM DATA COMPLEXITY QUADRANT RATINGS

Quadrant 1 (Happy)

- Unique elementary item count is within 100 percent of theoretical calculation
- No homonyms[nr]
- Synonyms comprise more than 20 percent of the total unique elementary items
- No literals[nr]

Quadrant 2 (Somewhat Happy)

- Unique elementary item count is within 500 percent of theoretical calculation
- Synonyms comprise 10 to 20 percent of the total unique elementary items
- Only report literals[nr]

Quadrant 3 (Somewhat Unhappy)

- Unique elementary item count is within 1000 percent of theoretical calculation
- Fewer than five numeric homonyms[nr] and no true homonyms[nr]

- Some synonyms, but they comprise less than 10 percent of the total unique elementary items
- The presence of any figurative literals[nr]

Quadrant 4 (Unhappy)

- Unique elementary item count is greater than 1000 percent of theoretical calculation
- More than four numeric homonyms[nr] and/or any true homonyms[nr]
- No synonyms
- The presence of any numeric literals[nr]

PROGRAM DATA COMPLEXITY QUADRANT RATINGS

Quadrant 1

- One to four files
- Only SEQUENTIAL FILE processing
- All elementary items in COPYLIB
- No item qualification[nr]
- No OCCURS clauses
- No REDEFINES[nr] clauses
- No 66[nr] levels (RENAMES[nr]) clauses
- No 77[nr] levels
- 20 or more 88 levels
- No system homonyms[nr] referenced
- No unreferenced elementary items
- Each nonprint FILE has a maximum of one READ, WRITE, EOF WRITE, and REWRITE statement
- All READ or WRITE statements have INTO or FROM phrases
- All I-O statements have INVALID KEY phrases if syntactically possible
- No CORRESPONDING[nr] phrases
- All computational elementary items are S (signed)
- All computations use ROUNDED or all do not use ROUNDED
- All computations have SIZE ERROR phrases
- No TRANSFORM$_{OS}$ or CONVERT$_{85}$ statements
- One SEARCH statement with preceding SET statement
- No more than one INSPECT statement
- No more than one STRING[nr] or UNSTRING[nr] statement

Quadrant 2

- Five or six files
- RANDOM FILE processing
- Some elementary items in COPYLIB with only one FILE undefined
- Elementary items that require qualification[nr], but qualification[nr] is sufficient
- OCCURS clauses with predefined DEPENDING[nr] phrases
- Single REDEFINES[nr] per data structure with consistent logical lengths
- Any 77[nr] levels
- 10 to 19 88 levels
- Less than 25 percent of the elementary items are unreferenced
- A nonprint FILE has more than one READ, WRITE, or REWRITE statement
- More than 50 percent of READ or WRITE statements have INTO or FROM phrases
- There is a USE[nr] statement for any omitted INVALID KEY phrase
- One computation does not contain a SIZE ERROR phrase
- There are one or two unsigned computational elementary items
- TRANSFORM[os] statement(s) but fewer than three files and under 100 statements
- More than one SEARCH statement, but all have preceding SET statements
- Two INSPECT statements
- Two STRING[nr] or UNSTRING[nr] statements

Quadrant 3

- Seven files
- Some elementary items in COPYLIB, but more than one FILE is undefined
- OCCURS clauses with hard-coded literals[nr]
- Single REDEFINES[nr] per data structure, but the logical lengths are inconsistent, and/or multiple REDEFINES[nr] with consistent logical lengths and no overlap
- One to five 88 levels
- Any numeric system homonym[nr] that is referenced has a maximum magnitude PIC clause
- Up to 50 percent of the elementary items are unreferenced
- A nonprint FILE has more than two READ, WRITE, or REWRITE statements
- Up to 50 percent of the READ or WRITE statements have INTO or FROM phrases
- Only one CORRESPONDING[nr] phrase
- Three to five unsigned computational elementary items
- ROUNDED phrase used inconsistently

- Two computations that do not contain SIZE ERROR phrases
- $TRANSFORM_{OS}$ or $CONVERT_{85}$ statements with fewer than three files but more than 100 statements
- One SEARCH statement without a preceding SET statement
- Three INSPECT statements
- Three STRING[nr] or UNSTRING[nr] statements

Quadrant 4

- More than seven files or zero files
- One or more OPTIONAL[nr] files
- No elementary items defined in a COPYLIB
- At least one elementary item requiring qualification[nr] that has insufficient qualification[nr]
- At least one OCCURS clause with the DEPENDING[nr] ON **data-name** variable read in by the program
- Multiple REDEFINES[nr] with inconsistent logical length or overlap
- 66[nr] level (RENAMES[nr])
- No 88 levels
- Program references a true system homonym[nr] and/or any numeric system homonym[nr] that has a less than maximum magnitude PIC clause
- More than 50 percent of the elementary items are unreferenced
- A nonprint FILE that has more than two READ, WRITE, or REWRITE statements
- No READ or WRITE statement that has an INTO or FROM phrase
- At least one I-O statement that has an omitted INVALID KEY condition and does not have a USE[nr] statement
- More than one CORRESPONDING[nr] phrase
- More than five unsigned[nr] computational elementary items
- More than two computations that do not contain SIZE ERROR phrases
- $TRANSFORM_{OS}$ or $CONVERT_{85}$ statements and more than three files
- More than one SEARCH statement that does not have a preceding SET statement
- More than three INSPECT statements
- More than three STRING[nr] or UNSTRING[nr] statements

My quadrant ratings for program complexity and architecture follow. These ratings are again on a 1 (happy) to 4 (unhappy) basis and are not combinational, as the Catalyst ratings are.

PROGRAM COMPLEXITY AND ARCHITECTURAL QUADRANT RATINGS

Quadrant 1

- No DECLARATIVES[nr] SECTION[nr]
- No sections[nr]
- All paragraphs or sections[nr] have correct numerical sequential prefixes
- All paragraphs or sections[nr] have narratives (comments preceding any statements that define the function of the module)
- No paragraphs requiring qualification[nr]
- No module is invoked by fallthru[nr] (lexical inclusion)
- The entire program is properly formatted including blank lines and EJECT verbs (or /)
- No literals[nr] in the PROCEDURE DIVISION other than CALL literals[nr]
- No unnecessary periods (.) or semicolons (;)
- No network[nr] GO TO statements
- No ALTER[nr] statements
- No PERFORM TIMES[nr] statements
- No multiple condition, **switch-status[nr]**, or NOT condition PERFORM UNTIL statements
- No PERFORM VARYING statements
- No THRU clauses except to EXIT paragraphs
- No group[nr] MOVEs; all MOVEs have identical PIC types; all receiving fields have a length equal to or greater than the sending field; all signed fields are moved to a receiving field with a signed PIC; no overlapping[nr] fields
- No ACCEPT FROM **mnemonic-name[nr]** or MESSAGE[nr] COUNT statements
- No DISPLAY[nr] statements
- No COMMUNICATION[nr] statements
- No REPORT[nr] WRITER statements
- NO SORT[nr] or MERGE[nr] statements
- No IF statements that compare numeric fields to nonnumeric fields; all relational conditions have three or fewer elementary items; all nonnumeric comparison fields have the same logical length; no condition has more than two AND/OR connectors or any NOT connector; no abbreviated[nr] conditions; no noncase IF has more than three nested levels; all IF statements have matching ELSE statements
- No SEARCH WHEN conditions that would violate any IF statement rules
- No COMPUTE[nr] statements
- All I/O statements retrieve FILE STATUS and test it for all possible conditions

- All CALL statements have no USING phrase or a USING phrase with one data-name; all USING data-names have the same logical length as the called program LINKAGE SECTION; all CALL statements are dynamic and are immediately followed by a CANCEL statement
- No subscripting^{nr} or relative^{nr} indexing or intermixed$^{nr}_{85}$ subscripts^{nr} and indices

Quadrant 2

- One DECLARATIVES^{nr} SECTION^{nr}
- All sections^{nr} are paragraphless
- All paragraphs or sections^{nr} have narratives but insufficient comments
- Any fallthru^{nr} or CONTINUE$_{85}$ invocation is in the "mainline"
- Entire program is properly formatted but may not have blank lines or EJECT verbs
- Fewer than five literals^{nr} in the PROCEDURE DIVISION
- Fewer than five unnecessary periods and semicolons
- At least one PERFORM TIMES^{nr} statement
- All PERFORM VARYING have only one VARYING phrase
- At least one ACCEPT FROM **mnemonic-name^{nr}** or MESSAGE^{nr} COUNT statement
- At least one DISPLAY^{nr} statement
- At least one IF statement that contains four or five elementary items or three AND/OR connectors or one NOT connector
- At least one SEARCH WHEN condition that contains four or five elementary items or three AND/OR connectors or one NOT connector
- At least one noncase IF statement that is nested to four levels and/or does not have a matching ELSE and END-IF$_{85}$ if supported
- One COMPUTE^{nr} statement that does have parentheses
- At least one CALL statement that has two USING data-names

Quadrant 3

- Two DECLARATIVES^{nr} SECTIONs^{nr}
- Paragraphs or sections^{nr} do not have numerical prefixing or have incorrect numerical prefixing
- Only some modules have narratives or sufficient comments
- Some paragraphs require qualification^{nr}
- Between five and ten literals^{nr} in the PROCEDURE DIVISION
- Between five and ten unnecessary periods and semicolons
- At least one PERFORM UNTIL statement with multiple conditions or a **switch-status^{nr}** condition

- At least one PERFORM VARYING statement with two VARYING phrases
- At least one PERFORM THRU or THROUGH clause that does not go to an EXIT paragraph
- At least 1 group[nr] MOVE statement or any MOVE that has different sending and receiving PIC types
- A COMMUNICATION[nr] SECTION[nr]
- A REPORT[nr] WRITER
- A SORT[nr] or MERGE[nr] statement
- At least one IF statement that compares a numeric field to a nonnumeric field or two nonnumeric fields of unequal logical length or containing four AND/OR connectors
- At least one noncase IF statement that has five nested levels and/or two unmatched ELSEs and END-IFs[85] if supported
- At least one SEARCH WHEN condition that has four AND/OR connectors
- Two COMPUTE[nr] statements, both with parentheses
- Any static[nr] CALL statements or dynamic CALL statements without matching CANCEL statements or any CALL to an ENTRY[nr]
- Any tables that can be accessed by multiple subscripts[nr]

Quadrant 4

- More than two DECLARATIVES[nr] SECTIONs[nr]
- Any SECTION[nr] that has paragraphs
- Most paragraphs or sections[nr] have insufficient narratives or comments
- Any nonmainline module invoked by fallthru[nr] or CONTINUE[85]
- Multiple statements per source line, inadequate blank lines or EJECT verbs (program looks like spaghetti)
- More than ten literals[nr] in the PROCEDURE DIVISION
- More than ten unnecessary periods and semicolons
- Any network[nr] GO TO statement
- Any ALTER[nr] statement
- Any PERFORM VARYING statements with three or more VARYING phrases or a range violation
- Any MOVE statement where the receiving field is smaller in logical length than the sending field
- Any IF statement that has relation conditions with more than seven elementary items or more than four AND/OR connectors or more than two NOT connectors, or any abbreviated[nr] conditions
- Any noncase IF statement that is nested more than five levels or has more than two unmatched ELSEs and END-IFs[85] if supported
- Any SEARCH WHEN condition that has more than seven elementary items or

more than four AND/OR connectors or more than two NOT connectors, or any abbreviated[nr] conditions

- More than two COMPUTE[nr] statements or any COMPUTE[nr] without parentheses
- Any I-O statement that does not retrieve FILE STATUS or test for all FILE STATUS conditions
- Any CALL statement that has more than three USING data-names or where the logical length of any data-name differs from the logical length of the called program LINKAGE SECTION
- Any relative[nr] indexing or intermixed[nr][85] subscripts[nr] and indices

You should be aware by now that most programs will be at least "somewhat unhappy."

20

Restructuring a Program

The ranking algorithm has selected a program and the reformatter has made it cosmetically pretty with problems flagged and noted. The problem now is to turn the spaghetti into readable and more easily maintainable code. Much of this tedious work can be done by so-called structured engine software, and such software is commercially available (see vendor list in Appendix E). A structured engine cannot perform miracles—a bug is a bug is a bug. What it can do is isolate a bug by making the program readable and therefore the bug more easily correctable. This chapter describes the basic procedures that a generic structured engine would perform in restructuring a spaghetti COBOL program.

The first programs to be restructured are the worst programs. After restructuring five or so of these "tin gods," the rest will seem easy.

All true system homonyms[1] are renamed **true-system-homonym-n** where **n** is a sequential odometer or an installation default name. The actual data-name is a comment line following the substitution line and appropriately highlighted for further analysis by a restructuring programmer.[2] Requisite changes are made to the PROCEDURE DIVISION.

The numeric system homonyms' PIC clauses are flagged whenever the PIC clause is not of the maximum magnitude for further analysis.

All PROCEDURE DIVISION literals (other than CALL literals) are transferred to WORKING-STORAGE under a single 01 level. Report literals have the data-name **report-literal-n** (**n** = odometer) or installation default standard. Figurative literals have the data-name **figurative-literal-n** (**n** = odometer) or installation default standard. Numeric literals within quotes have the data-name **dangerous-literal-n** (**n** = odometer) or installation default standard. Requisite changes are made to the PROCEDURE DIVISION.

All qualifiable data-names with insufficient qualification are made sufficient using the same default logic as the installation compiler. The substitution is flagged for further analysis.

Any OCCURS clause with hard-coded integers is changed to OCCURS DEPENDING ON **dataname-1** (**integer-1**) TO **dataname-2** (**integer-2**) if supported by the installation compiler (non-ANSI). All multiple indexed OCCURS data structures are changed to single indexed tables. Requisite changes are made to the PROCEDURE DIVISION (such as changing PERFORM VARYING to SEARCH).

All REDEFINES and 66-level (RENAMES) data structures are transferred to WORKING-STORAGE with requisite changes to the PROCEDURE DIVISION.

All 77 levels are renumbered to 02 and transferred to WORKING-STORAGE under a single 01 level with data-name **program-77-level-n** (**n** = odometer).

All unreferenced data elements (structured engine must verify that the data-name is not referenced by a CORRESPONDING phrase) have their data-name changed to FILLER. The actual data-name becomes a comment line after the substitution line.

All distinct I-O statements (READ, WRITE, EOF, WRITE, REWRITE) per file are combined into a single I-O statement in a common performable paragraph. Appropriate PERFORM statements are substituted in the PROCEDURE DIVISION. Any READ statement without an INTO phrase is modified to include an INTO phrase. The FD 01 description is transferred to WORKING-STORAGE, and a single 01 level without any elementary items is substituted for the transferred FD. A suffix of -WS is appended to the original FD 01 group data-name and any statement that accesses it. FROM phrases are inserted into WRITE statements in the same manner. Any I-O statement that can have an INVALID KEY has one (a USE statement is acceptable). Insert an INVALID KEY to abend whenever it or an applicable USE statement is not present.[†3] All I-O statements shall retrieve FILE STATUS and test for all possible conditions. Insert appropriate statements where required, including abend, for any error or exception condition that the original program did not test for.[†]

Decompose all CORRESPONDING phrases into their simple MOVE and arithmetic statements.

Insert S (sign) into all computational data element PIC clauses. Insert IF data element IS NEGATIVE to abend after any computation statement that uses the data element.[†]

Insert a ROUNDED phrase into all computation statements if any computational statement in the application has a ROUNDED phrase (alternatively, delete all ROUNDED phrases).[†]

Insert ON SIZE ERROR to abend in all computation statements where applicable.[†]

Insert an EXHIBIT$_{OS}$ statement or equivalent preceding any Format 1 serial

SEARCH statement to print the value of the index or subscript value controlling the SEARCH.[4] This assists the restructuring programmer in further debugging.

Eliminate SECTION headings if possible; change any invocation statements to transfer control to the first paragraph following the original SECTION heading. If sections cannot be eliminated, delete all paragraph headings that are not directly accessed. Add an odometer suffix to any paragraph-name requiring qualification, and change the corresponding transfer statements. Insert EXIT paragraphs whenever possible; insert EJECT (or /) after EXIT.

Insert a dummy GO TO or $CONTINUE_{85}$ statement in any module that is invoked by fallthru (lexical inclusion). Insert a TRACE statement or equivalent to obtain the actual flow of a program during execution.[5]

Change all GO TO DEPENDING ON statements to case IF statements using 88 levels. The 88-level data-names are **value-1**, **value-2**, **value-3**,... The last ELSE clause is a GO TO abend to prevent a runaway if the data value is invalid.[†]

All alterable GO TO statements are changed to GO TO DEPENDING ON. The ALTER statements are changed to MOVE statements that place a DEPENDING ON value into a WORKING-STORAGE area created by the structured engine. The GO TO DEPENDING ON is changed to a case IF as previously described, with the 88-level names being the original ALTER module named.

Insert IF statements in the target module of any PERFORM VARYING to verify that each index or subscript is within the table range as specified by the OCCURS clause; abend if index or subscript is out of range. Insert an EXHIBIT statement to display the value of each index or subscript. All PERFORMS TIMES statements are changed to PERFORM UNTIL with the UNTIL condition being > TIMES (TIMES is defined in WORKING-STORAGE). All PERFORM THRU statements that span physical modules are flagged.

Decompose any complex relation condition (more than three elementary items or more than two AND/OR/NOT connectors) into simple relation conditions. Expand any abbreviated conditions and decompose if complex. Convert any NOT condition to positive test if possible and readable.

Flag any MOVE statement where the receiving field is smaller in logical length than the sending field or when an operational sign is lost.

Decompose all COMPUTE statements into the component arithmetic statements. Flag any arithmetic statements that were derived from a COMPUTE statement without parentheses.

Insert ELSE NEXT SENTENCE or $END-IF_{85}$ for any unmatched IF. Flag any noncase IF statements with nesting level greater than three; flag any IF statement that compares numeric to nonnumeric or two nonnumeric data elements of unequal logical length.

Combine all CALL USING multiple data-names into a single data-name, and modify each appropriate LINKAGE SECTION. Insert $EXHIBIT_{OS}$ to print CALL parameters. Flag both a CALL USING statement and any associated LINKAGE SECTION that have different logical lengths.

Convert all relative indexing to a SET statement with the value defined in WORKING-STORAGE. Convert all subscripts to indices if possible.

NOTES

1. The [nr] (not recommended) superscript will be omitted throughout Part 3 to make the text easier to read.

2. The restructuring programmer is a new type of programmer who does maintenance by restructuring.

3. Most commercial structured engines would not make the changes marked † because the restructured program could produce different (incorrect) results from those of the original program. Structured engine vendors normally prove that the restructured programs produce the same results as the original program by doing an automated file compare on the results produced by a test case. I believe that it is better to abort an incorrect execution with sufficient explanatory comments than to continue with bad data or results.

4. Most compilers have debugging features in addition to an ANSI COBOL DEBUG module. EXHIBIT is a debugging statement available for IBM $COBOL_{OS}$ compilers (see *IBM OS Full American National Standard COBOL Compiler and Library Programmer's Guide*, Publication No. SC29-6456, and *IBM OS COBOL Interactive Debug Terminal User's and Reference Guide*, Publication No. SC28-6465, among others). Many compilers permit the debugging statements and options to be placed into a "debugging packet" that can be removed after the program has been successfully debugged.

5. TRACE is another debugging statement available for the $COBOL_{OS}$ compiler.

——— 21 ———

Data-Name Rationalization

Data-Name rationalization is a term coined by Cris Miller to describe the process of purifying existing data-names in COBOL applications. The basic process is to perform the following functions:

- Identify homonyms, synonyms, and aliases
- Decide on the standard data-name
- Determine which synonyms and aliases will be permitted to remain
- Globally change all the bad data-names to the selected data-name

Data-name rationalization can be done before, concurrent with, or after program restructuring. The basic definitions are as follows:

Homonym   Same data-name for two or more different elementary items.
Synonym   Different PIC clauses for the same elementary item.
Alias   Two or more different data-names for the same elementary item.

Data-name rationalization is difficult to perform manually. Organizations have spent calendar years trying to isolate all occurrences of elementary items such as ZIP codes so that they could be changed to ZIP+4 or employee numbers so that the field size could be increased. Consider the McAuto quotation in note 1 of the Preface in which President

A. J. Quackenbush stated that his company had 26,000 COBOL programs of an average of 2000 instructions each. That amounts to approximately 50 million lines of code! How long would it take you to analyze 50 million lines manually to isolate ZIP codes given a ratio of 20 bad data-names for each elementary item? At a second per line, it would take about 14,000 hours, or about seven working years—and that is only for *one* elementary item! How about for two, three, or all the elementary items? The power of the computer to perform clerical tasks quickly must be used to perform data-name rationalization. The basic computer steps are as follows.

1. Construct the system vector (an inventory of all programs that are to participate in the data-name rationalization process). The procedure is to analyze the JCL as previously described.

2. Print a listing of all the data-names in the system vector for reference.

3. Extract unique data-names from the complete list. Uniqueness is determined by logical length (the number of placeholder symbols in the PIC clause). Two or more elementary items having the same data-name—such as **abc**—are considered unique if their logical length is different.

4. Homonyms are automatically identified (identical data-names with different logical lengths) for resolution by the data analyst.[1] Many homonyms are numeric—the difference in logical length is due to different magnitude PIC clauses. A magnitude difference will sooner or later cause a truncation problem in the high-order digits. The solution is simple: Change all PICs to the maximum magnitude. The implementation, however, is difficult because changing the logical length of a field affects record size, which in turn affects existing master records, which in turn affects other aspects. The ripple effect assumes tidal-wave proportions. The short-range solution is to make sure that all arithmetic statements involving the numeric homonym have ON SIZE ERROR clauses to trap truncation before it actually causes any damage. The long-range solution is to substitute logical records containing maximum magnitude. This solution is discussed further in Chapter 22.

   The true homonym is a catastrophe (or a potential one). Somehow the same data-name has been used to identify two or more different elementary items. For instance, the data-name **grade** was used for both the grade received by the student and issued by the instructor to rate the student and for the grade issued by the student to rate the instructor's performance as a teacher. How does a program, 4GL, query language, or the like know which grade is wanted when **grade** is requested? This particular homonym is particularly insidious, since it will probably have the same logical length for students and instructors and graduate student/instructors. Grades will be difficult to distinguish by humans, much less ''dumb'' computers. The data analyst must resolve true homonyms, and their data-names must be globally changed.

5. Synonyms are automatically identified (identical data-names with identical logical lengths but different physical PIC clauses). There are valid reasons for synonyms. It is more efficient for the computer to have different physical representations of a data-name, depending on how the data-name is being used. For example, a dollar

elementary item that does not exceed hundreds and has cents could have the following PIC clauses:

dollar-item-with-cents   PIC S999V99

and USAGE COMP could be used for computation and storage, whereas

dollar-item-with-cents   PIC ZZZ.99CR

could be used for a printed report where "check protection" (leading zeros replaced by spaces) was not required, and

dollar-item-with-cents   PIC ***.99CR

could be used for a printed report where check protection (leading zeros replaced by astericks) was required.

Basically, synonyms are desirable in limited quantities. The limited quantity is one per usage format. There should be one PIC clause per usage:

- **Computational storage**: Typically, a PIC with a USAGE IS COMP clause also represents the smallest (without compaction) storage space; if this is not true on your CPU, there could be a separate storage PIC clause.
- **Display**: A PIC for display on a CRT.
- **Zero suppression (space)**: A PIC with Zs so that any leading zeros are replaced by spaces.
- **Zero suppression (∗)**: A PIC with ∗s so that any leading zeros are replaced by asterisks (the normal symbol for check protection).

There are many COBOL compilers with many options (ANSI and non-ANSI) and many operating systems; it is therefore impossible to determine the actual number of allowable synonyms. However, a definitive algorithm is possible: **synonyms-number-total** = maximum number of unique physically different PIC clauses allowed by your compiler and CPU; any **synonyms-number-total** that exceeds this computational limit is redundant and should be modified to a standard synonym name.

Aliases are the real problem. Aliases are different data-names for the same elementary item. For instance, ZIP code could be all of the following:

zipcode   postal-code   postal-zip-code   postoffice-code
a-five-digit-code-representing-a-specific-area-in-the-united-states-for-delivery-of-mail
del1964[2]   sue[3]   code-of-zip   zipper   that-[expletive-deleted]-postoffice-code
zip+4   zipcode+4   zipcode+four   zipcode-plus-4   zipcode-plus-four
it-cost-me-three-months-to-replace-the-good-old-american-zipcode-with-a-seven-x-pic-to-

handle-that-crazy-english-postal-code   state-code   united-states-post-office-code
local-postmaster-code

Aliases cannot be isolated in any reasonably sized system or application by manual procedures. Aliases can only be reasonably isolated by a combination of a human being working with the superb clerical powers of a computer. Most of the vendors listed in Appendix E have software to assist; I am most familiar with the WHERE module of ADPAC PM/SS. WHERE has virtually unlimited searching and sorting algorithms to assist the data analyst in isolating aliases in COBOL programs. Some of these algorithms permit the following tasks:

- All data-names can be sorted by their logical length (number of placeholder symbols) in alphabetical sequence. This provides a report of all elementary items of a given character length that can be visually scanned.

   The report can be further refined by using the data type—alphabetic (A), numeric (9), alphanumeric (X), alphanumeric edited (X + editing symbols), numeric edited (9 + editing symbols)—as an extraction parameter. For example, printing all elementary items that had five 9 placeholder symbols should isolate almost all of the elementary items that could be ZIP code.

- In a COBOL program aliases are most often caused by MOVE statements:

      MOVE a TO b
      MOVE b TO c
      MOVE c TO z
      MOVE z TO a

WHERE has an algorithm that identifies and traces these MOVE aliases across all programs in the system vector, providing a report listing of all the paired data-names (items) with a reference to the MOVE line number in each program.

- WHERE can provide a KWIC (*key word in context*) report that prints the PROCEDURE DIVISION invocation line and a user-specified number of lines before and after the invocation line for any suspect data-name. This information should normally be sufficient for a senior programmer to determine what the item really represents.

WHERE can strip off prefixes and/or suffixes where a role naming standard was used:

       MSTRIN-   (master record in)

       -MSTROUT   (master record out)

       TRANS-...-IN   (transaction record in)

This permits the real or generic data-name to be used in all analysis. The Analyst Workbench uses WHERE extensively in performing data-name rationalization for its clients. A more complete description of using WHERE is provided in Appendix A.

How many aliases should there be? Ideally, none. However, the real world is not ideal, and there are some legitimate aliases:

zipcode	Most users
zcd	Programmer shorthand[4]
c.zip	OF language (**code of zip**)
postal-code	Sue has been managing the shipping department for 30 years and that's the name she wants.

The last statement reflects the real world. Users have the right to use names that are familiar and meaningful to them. The computer—which is supposed to be the user's servant—can easily keep track of these names by user and provide each user with his or her pet name. This is an inexpensive method for DP to build goodwill with its customers (users).

The foregoing analysis has isolated all the homonyms, synonyms, and aliases. The data administrator (person charged with the organizational responsibility to control data) has established the basic data-name for each elementary item and which synonyms and aliases for that elementary item will be allowed. The problem is now to change all the bad data-names in all programs to allowable data-names.

This is not an easy task, even with computer assistance. Consider the McAuto inventory of 26,200 COBOL programs and a ratio of 20 bad data-names. This means that at least 500,000 changes must be made. Most, if not all, word replacement software changes explicit references only; that is, a bad data-name is changed to a good data-name in all lines of all programs wherever the bad data-name is actually coded. Unfortunately, COBOL can reference elementary items *implicitly* with CORRESPONDING phrases, group MOVEs, subscripts and indices, REDEFINES and RENAMES clauses, and other statements.

Using a single good data-name does not work because this would cause qualification problems within a program:

```
MOVE bad-dataname-a   TO   bad-dataname-b
```

would be changed to

```
MOVE good-dataname   TO   good-dataname
```

The COBOL compiler should issue either an E (error) or S (severe) warning message after compiling this statement. The operative word is *compiling*. Most, if not all, COBOL compilers try to be nice to programmers and create executable objective code for syntactically incorrect statements other than unrecoverable that might be what the programmer intended. My COBOL compiler gives an S warning and executable object code that moved the value in the first occurrence of the good data-name in the DATA DIVISION to the *first* occurrence of the good data-name in the DATA DIVISION—in other words, a recursive or do-nothing MOVE. This is certainly not what the programmer intended, and the revised program could cause incorrect results or abend.

    A possible COBOL solution is to qualify each good data-name:

```
MOVE good-dataname  TO  good-dataname
```

would be changed to

```
MOVE good-dataname  IN/OF  level9-group-good-dataname
                    IN/OF  level8-group-good-dataname
                    IN/OF  level7-group-good-dataname
                    IN/OF  level6-group-good-dataname
                    IN/OF  level5-group-good-dataname
                    IN/OF  level4-group-good-dataname
                    IN/OF  level3-group-good-dataname
                    IN/OF  level2-group-good-dataname
                    IN/OF  level1-group-good-dataname

                    TO     good-dataname
                    IN/OF  level9-group-good-dataname
                    IN/OF  level8-group-good-dataname
                    IN/OF  level7-group-good-dataname
                    IN/OF  level6-group-good-dataname
                    IN/OF  level5-group-good-dataname
                    IN/OF  level4-group-good-dataname
                    IN/OF  level3-group-good-dataname
                    IN/OF  level2-group-good-dataname
                    IN/OF  level1-ws-good-dataname
```

Admittedly, this works. Admittedly, a "smart" word replacement program could perform the requisite analysis and produce the code. But why? Besides destroying many trees, it would make most programs unreadable, and the point of this exercise is to make programs readable!

    The recommendation is to add an odometer suffix to each good data-name, thereby changing

```
MOVE good-dataname  TO  good-dataname
```

to

```
MOVE good-dataname-01  TO  good-dataname-02
```

Of course, this also requires that the data-name replacement program be smart. The program must affix the correct odometer suffix correctly to all data-names.

    The odometer suffix permits the data administrator to assign a unique generic

COBOL program data-name for all elementary items in all programs; each program should be more readable, since there is a unique generic data-name with a distinguishing odometer suffix that the human eye can easily ignore.

The smart data-name replacement program should also resolve any implicit references, thereby retaining the original program integrity.

Security of data from either accidental or deliberate modification is becoming increasingly more important as more organizations place more of their valuable data into computer databases. This data can only be modified by some sort of computer program. COBOL is the most prevalent computer language, and therefore every effort should be made to limit COBOL program data modifications to the data that it is authorized to modify. The ultimate answer is a logical record and a logical record facility (LRF) that permits the COBOL program to access only data that is modifiable. The LRF must also be smart enough to permit the program to "view" data that it needs for parameters, search keys, and the like but is not authorized to modify.

A short-range solution is for the smart data-name replacement program to replace any unreferenced (explicit or implicit) data-name with FILLER. A programmer maintaining this type of program would have to bypass the FILLER security deliberately to modify a FILLER item. This is sabotage (possibly innocent because the programmer did not want to go through the bureaucratic red tape of obtaining modification authorization). The innocent saboteur should get a severe reprimand; the guilty saboteur should get worse.

Data security can be further enhanced by placing all data-names (including FILLER) into COPYLIBs and having a required precompiler for all programs requiring compilations that ensures the following:

- That all data-names are in COPYLIBs
- That there are no implicit references that could modify a FILLER item
- That the COBOL compiler can be invoked only by the precompiler.

ANSI COBOL does permit a FILLER elementary item to be a conditional variable with 88 levels defining the permissible domain values. This permits a status elementary item, such as marital status, to be read by a program that cannot explicitly modify that elementary item:

```
0?  FILLER          PIC A.
    88 single        VALUE "s."
    88 married       VALUE "m."
    88 divorced      VALUE "d."
    88 widowed       VALUE "w."
    88 unknown       VALUE "u."
    88 valid-values  VALUES "s," "m," "d," "w," "u."
```

This construct prohibits the program from changing the marital status by explicit statements such as

```
MOVE "u" TO marital-status
```

Consequently, the smart data-name replacement program can either retain existing 88 levels or create 88 levels for status elementary items that are not modified. For instance, a program could contain

```
GO TO               P???-single
                    P???-married
                    P???-divorced
                    P???-widowed
                    P???-unknown
                    P???-invalid-marital-status
DEPENDING ON        marital-status
```

The smart data-name replacement program should change **marital-status** to FILLER and create the following 88 levels:

```
0? FILLER                       PIC S9V.
   88 single                    VALUE 1.
   88 married                   VALUE 2.
   88 divorced                  VALUE 3.
   88 widowed                   VALUE 4.
   88 unknown                   VALUE 5.
   88 invalid-marital-status    VALUES 0, 6 THRU 9.
```

The smart data-name replacement program (or the restructuring engine) should change the GO TO DEPENDING ON to a case IF:

```
IF       single     PERFORM P???-single-marital-status
ELSE
IF       married    PERFORM P???-married-marital-status
ELSE
IF       divorced   PERFORM P???-divorced-marital-status
ELSE
IF       widowed    PERFORM P???-widowed-marital-status
ELSE
IF       unknown    PERFORM P???-unknown-marital-status
ELSE                PERFORM P???-invalid-marital-status
END-IF
```

Each program should now be syntactically correct, be very readable, and produce the intended results. The corrected program may produce different results from those of the original program because error traps (ON SIZE, AT END, etc.) have been inserted in all appropriate places, thereby trapping logically erroneous results—such as a magnitude truncation problem trapped by an ON SIZE ERROR phrase. The corrected program may also abend because runaways have been prevented.

As stated before, I would rather trap incorrect execution with sufficient explanatory comments than have the corrected program produce the same incorrect results as the original program.

A different approach is as follows:

1. Save on computer media the input and output for a normal execution of the program to be corrected; this will be used to test the corrected program.

2. Reformat the program cosmetically:
- Compile the reformatted program.
- Perform a software file compare on the reformatted object code and the original object code. The object code should be the same, and further testing is not required.[5]

3. Perform data-name rationalization:
- Compile the rationalizations program.
- As before, perform a file compare on the object code; as before, the object code should be same, and further testing is not required.

4. Insert a class of trap; for example, insert only ON SIZE ERROR phrases rather than all traps:
- Compile the trapped program.
- Execute the trapped program with the input media previously saved in step 1, placing the output on computer media.[6]
- Perform a file compare on the trapped output against the original output previously saved in step 1.
- Resolve any differences.

5. Repeat step 4 for each trap class until the program is "perfect."

The perfect program is still probably obsolescent—most old COBOL programs use the VSAM (or ISAM) disk access method, whereas most organizations have installed a database management system (DBMS). The problem now is to modernize the perfect program by using extended retrofit.

NOTES

1. The data analyst is responsible for the following tasks, among others:
   - Creating and maintaining the logical database
   - Assigning the correct data-name to each item and determining what synonyms and aliases shall be allowed
   - Eliminating homonyms
   - Determining the correct domain of values for each item
   - Determining why incorrect values were produced by any program
2. **Data element 19 identified in 1964**; I actually had a client who used this data-naming standard. It does make program readability and maintainability difficult. Some of the data-names created by assembler-to-COBOL translators are as cryptic.
3. Or any other personal names. Some programmers can be maddeningly creative when it comes to data names!

4. A programmer's task should be to write readable programs. Readable programs require mean-ingful data-names, and *unexpandable* shorthand, abbreviations, or mnemonics should not be allowed. However, to ease the writing or typing chore, each programmer should be provided with a list of acceptable abbreviations. The abbreviations are expanded to the full meaningful data-names by the previously recommended precompiler.

5. The original COBOL program is the source code; the code created by the COBOL compiler from the source code is the object code. Object code can be executed; source code is not directly executable.

     If the corrected object code does not match the original object code, it is probable that the reformatter committed a mistake. A possible solution is to make only single changes and to perform the code comparison after each change. Sooner or later, the change that caused the difference will be revealed for resolution.

6. The trapped program could also abend because of the new traps. In this case, a senior restruc-turing (maintenance) programmer must determine the cause of the abend and make appropriate changes. If the abend was caused by data, the data analyst and a knowledgeable user must be consulted to determine the proper course of action.

22

Extended Retrofit

Extended retrofit is a term I coined to describe the process of converting COBOL program I-O statements to database CALL statements. The structured engine has reduced and isolated all I-O commands so that they are easy to find. The smart data-name replacement program has converted all unreferenced item data-names to FILLER, thereby making the definition of the logical record easy. The problem now is to establish the proper CALLs for the organizational database management system (DBMS).[1]

The top-down decomposition of the problem is as follows:

- Development of a physical schema[2]

which contains

- Subschemas and maybe logical records[3]

which requires

- a logical database[4]

which requires

- entity type attributes (COBOL items) to be normalized[5]

which requires

- attributes clustered to their entity types

which requires

- the identification of entity types in the application to which extended retrofit is being applied[6]

NOTES

1. A database management system (DBMS) is a generalized tool for manipulating large databases; it is made available through special software for the interrogation, maintenance, and analysis of data. Its interfaces generally provide a broad range of language to aid all users—from clerk to data administrator. (T. Teorey and J. Fry, *Design of Database Structures*, Englewood Cliffs, N.J.: Prentice-Hall, 1982.)

   A database is a computerized collection of stored operational data that serves the needs of multiple users within an organization or some defined subset of the organization. (Ibid.)

2. The CODASYL definition is that a schema consists of DDL (Data Definition Language) entries and is a complete description of the areas, set occurrences, and associated data items and data aggregates as they exist in the database. (J. Martin, *Strategic Data Planning Methodologies*, Englewood Cliffs, N.J.: Prentice-Hall, 1982.)

   CODASYL (Conference on Data System Languages) is the organization that specified a set of manufacture-independent, application-independent languages designed to form the basis of database management. (Ibid.)

   CODASYL DBTG (Data Base Task Group) is a special committee of CODASYL formed in the late 1960s to propose a standard for modern database management systems. (Teorey and Fry, *Design.*)

   A data aggregate is a named collection of data items (data elements) within a record. (C. Gane and T. Sarson, *Structured System Analysis: Tools and Techniques*, Englewood Cliffs, N.J.: Prentice-Hall, 1979.)

3. A subschema is a map of a programmer's view of the data he uses. It is derived from the global logical view of the data. (Teorey and Fry, *Design.*)

   A logical record is a view of the physical database that is independent of the physical structure. (E. Vesely, *The Practitioner's Blueprint to Logical and Physical Database Design*, Englewood Cliffs, N.J.: Prentice-Hall, 1986.)

4. A logical database is a database as perceived by its users; it may be structured differently from the physical database structure (schema). (J. Martin, *Methodologies.*)

5. An entity type is a class of objects that an enterprise desires to maintain independent data elements (attributes, COBOL items) about. (Vesely, *Blueprint.*)

   Normalization is the decomposition of complex data structures into a set of one or more flat files (relations); analysis of functional dependencies is necessary to formulate the different levels of normalization (i.e., normal forms). (Teorey and Fry, *Design.*)

6. More definitions are in this book's glossary and a complete description of entity type analysis, attribute clustering, normalization, logical database design, and physical database design can be found in Vesely, *Blueprint.* The next chapter is a summary of the relevant chapters of that book.

23

Extended Retrofit Procedure

ENTITY TYPE IDENTIFICATION

In COBOL terms, entity types are master RECORDS because the master RECORDS contain items (attributes) that define something about an object that the enterprise wishes to maintain independent data about. At this point, the structured engine and the retrofitter have purified all the data-names including the SELECT and FD file-names and 01 record-names. The input FDs are software extracted for analysis by the data analyst. It should be simple for the data analyst to determine the actual entity type from the FD and 01 data-names. If this is not possible, an analysis of the item data-names should be sufficient to identify the actual entity type (if not, somebody has devised a poor naming standard and/or the naming standard has not been implemented). In any case, it is the data analyst's responsibility to identify the enterprise entity types involved in the application being extended-retrofitted from the input FDs.

ATTRIBUTE CLUSTERING

A good data analyst likes to analyze data. It is easy for the data analyst to fall into the trap of manually analyzing each item within an 01 record description to determine which identified entity types it is describing (is an attribute of). Data analysts can spend hours, days, weeks, or even longer in this subjective analysis. An objective of normalization is to place all attributes (items) in the proper table within an identified entity type set of tables. Normalization is a set of precise mathematical rules derived from set theory that places all attributes *objectively* in the correct table if the rules are correctly applied. Objective analysis is better than subjective analysis. Objective analysis is also faster and less prone to error if a computer can be used to perform the multitude of clerical tasks involved in objective data analysis.

RECOMMENDATIONS

- Use software to cluster all attributes (items) within an 01 record description to the entity type identified for that 01 record.
- Use software to change all attribute names to the standard name.
- Use software to combine all attributes attributed to a single entity type from all 01 record descriptions assigned to that entity type; eliminate all identical attributes.
- Use software to identify, where possible, the primary key and/or to list all keys for each entity type by analyzing the various COBOL KEY clauses.[1]
- Use software to identify all repeating groups for each entity type by highlighting any group item (data aggregate) that has an OCCURS clause.[2]
- Print and/or display results.

The recommended procedures have *automatically*—without human intervention other than to start the software—produced an unnormalized listing of all attributes by each entity type with both potential candidate keys and repeating groups identified.[3] The recommended procedures have automatically prepared the input for normalization.

NORMALIZATION

The set rules for normalization are precise but probably undecipherable for most nonmathematicians. Many authors, including myself, have translated the set rules to a less precise but simpler-to-understand English syntax. The rationale is to demystify normalization and concentrate on its important functions of reducing the attributes to the minimum (minimal cover) and eliminating all storage anomalies.[4]

Normalization has many "forms," and nobody agrees on how many forms there are. There does have to be a final form, and I have coined the phrase *final normal form* (FNF) to represent that ultimate. The following is a brief English description of the forms and the recommended procedures for attaining them.[5]

First Normal Form (1NF)

The steps in performing 1NF are as follows:

1. Identify the candidate keys for each entity type. The data analyst interacts with an interactive program using a display (CRT) to verify the candidate keys selected by the software and/or identify other keys.
2. Identify the primary key from the candidate key set. The data analyst verifies the primary key selected by the software or selects one or more other attributes to be the primary key for this entity type.
3. Identify the repeating groups within each entity type. The data analyst verifies the repeating groups identified by the software and identifies any other repeating groups not identified by the software.
4. Remove the repeating groups, thereby establishing new tables. The data analyst instructs the software to create new tables for all of the identified repeating groups, including creating a table-name that is the concatenation of the original table-name and the repeating group name and inserting the primary key of the original table into the new table.
5. Identify the primary key of the new table.

The primary key of the original table can never be the complete primary key of the newly created table because the new table represents a one-to-many relationship. A many relationship (which is defined as zero to n where n is the maximum number of occurrences) means that some other attribute is required to identify a single occurrence of the new table. For instance, the simplified unnormalized listing of the student entity type could include

```
student  P  student-number
            student-name
         R  course-history
         X  course-number
         X  semester-taken
         X  course-hours-taken
         X  course-hours-earned
         X  course-grade-earned
```

where

```
P = the primary key
R = the repeating group name
X = an item within the repeating group
```

student-number is the primary key because it identifies a single occurrence of the student entity type. **course-history** is a repeating group because it can occur zero times (an entering freshman) to **n** times (whatever is the maximum number of courses any student can take at Logic University). **course-history** would be removed to a separate table with a table name of **student.course-history** (a concatenation of the original table name, **student**, and the repeating group name, **course-history**). A period is used between student and course instead of a hyphen to indicate that this is a relationship table; that is, it could not exist unless two or more separate entity types entered into a relationship, such as entity type **student** taking entity type **course**.

The new table in Codd relational notational is

student.course-history (<u>student-number</u>, course-number,

semester-taken, course-hours-taken,

course-hours-earned, course-grade-earned)

student-number was inserted into the new table because it was the primary key of the original table. Does **student-number** always identify a single occurrence of the **student.course-history** table? (No, because a student can take many courses.) Do **student-number** and **course-number** always identify a single occurrence of the **student.course-history** table? (No, because a student can take a single course many times—for example, fail, audit, fail, pass.) Do **student-number**, and **course-number**, and **semester-taken** always identify a single occurrence? (Yes, because a student cannot take the same course twice in the same semester.)

The new table in 1NF is

student.course-history (<u>student-number</u>, <u>course-number</u>,

<u>semester-taken</u>, course-hours-taken,

course-hours-earned, course-grade-earned)

RECOMMENDATION

- Have the data analyst identify interactively with the program the additional attributes necessary to identify a single occurrence of the new table.

It is probable that some repeating groups have repeating groups within them. Assuming that multiple instructors can teach the same course and that the retention of the information is important, the new **student.course-history** table is

student.course-history (<u>student-number</u>, <u>course-number</u>,

<u>semester-taken</u>, course-hours-taken,

course-hours-earned, course-grade-earned,

instructor-number, instructor-name)

where **instructor-number** and **instructor-name** are attributes within a repeating group of **instructors-teaching.course**. **instructors-teaching.course** should be removed to a new table:

student.course.instructor-history (<u>student-number</u>, <u>course-number</u>,

<u>semester-taken</u>, <u>instructor-number</u>,

instructor-name)

Oil companies can have complicated primary keys:

region

which contains

                                          areas

which contains

                                        subareas

which contains

                                          fields

which contains

                                          wells

which contains

                                          holes

which contains

                                          depth

which contains

                                         stratus

which contains

                                         product

which contains yet further items. To identify a single occurrence of this key would require

                oil-data (<u>region</u>, <u>area</u>, <u>subarea</u>, <u>field</u>, <u>hole</u>, <u>depth</u>, <u>stratus</u>,
                          <u>product</u>, <u>...</u>, attribute-1, attribute-2, attribute-3, ...)

RECOMMENDATION

- The software analyzes the existing COBOL code for OCCURS clauses and produces a preliminary 1NF, which the data analyst reviews and interactively corrects.

Second Normal Form (2NF)

Second normal form describes a normalized table in which all the nonkey attributes are fully functionally dependent on the primary keys.

Check each nonkey attribute to each individual key attribute to determine if there is a one-to-one relationship.

RECOMMENDATIONS

- 2NF requires the data analyst to be thoroughly familiar with the attributes and how the user uses each attribute. Software cannot by itself do 2NF; however, it can assist. The DESIGN software of ADPAC produces a "decision table" (see Figure 27.8 in Chapter 27) to provide that assistance.
- Use software to assist the data analyst in performing 2NF.[6]

Third Normal Form (3NF)

Third normal form is a normalized table in which all the nonkey attributes are fully functionally dependent on the primary key and all the nonkey attributes are mutually independent.

The theoretical step of identifying the attributes that can be derived or calculated from other nonkey attributes sounds easy but is manually very difficult in the real world. 1NF and 2NF analyzed attributes within the same table; 3NF requires all nonkey attributes regardless of the table they are in. If there were 2000 nonkey attributes in the application under analysis, it would require 2000! (factorial) comparisons—a finite but very large number. Many organizations that believe in normalization do not perform 3NF or perform only a cursory 3NF if it must be done manually because of the enormous number of clerical operations involved. The key word is *clerical* because a computer is good at doing clerical chores.

RECOMMENDATIONS

- Have the reformatter or other software highlight all attributes calculated in all the PROCEDURE DIVISIONs in the application being extended-retrofitted. For instance, in the COBOL statement

MULTIPLY a BY b GIVING c

  c is a calculated attribute.
- Use software to transfer the algorithm for calculating each calculable attribute to the organizational data dictionary.[7]
- Use software to eliminate all calculable attributes from the nonnormalized listing. (Why bother to carry attributes through 1NF and 2NF when they will be eliminated in 3NF?)

The recommended procedures eliminate calculable attributes but do not eliminate derivable attributes. For instance, in the table

course.instructor-can-teach (<u>course-number</u>, instructor-number, instructor-name)

instructor-name is functionally dependent on **course-number** since each course can be taught by only one instructor. If the logical database also contained

instructor-data (<u>instructor-number</u>, instructor-name, ...)

instructor-name could be derived from **instructor-number**. In this specific case, **instructor-name** is said to be *transitively* dependent on the **course-number** key attribute in the **course.instructor-can-teach** table because it can be derived from **instructor-number**. The 3NF procedure is to eliminate **instructor-name** from the **course.instructor-can-teach** table. Again, this is a difficult clerical chore but one that is easy for the computer.

- Use cross-referencing software to highlight any nonkey attribute that is duplicated.
- Use software to identify the transitively dependent attribute by analyzing foreign key attributes within the tables containing the duplicated nonkey attribute. A foreign key is an attribute that provides a logical pathway to another entity set. **instructor-number** in the **course.instructor-can-teach** table is a foreign key because it references the primary key attribute in the **instructor-data** table (another entity set) and therefore **instructor-name** can be derived by using **instructor-number** to reference the **instructor-data** table.

The software eliminates all transitively dependent attributes from the logical database.

Fourth Normal Form (4NF)

4NF is a 3NF relation (table) without key data element (attribute) anomalies. The previous forms have analyzed nonkey attributes to key attributes (2NF) and analyzed all nonkey attributes to all other nonkey attributes (3NF). No previous form has analyzed key attributes to key attributes. There can be transitive dependencies between key attributes just as there are between nonkey and key attributes. The copyright page of this book contains an ISBN (International Standard Book Number). A table about book data could be constructed as follows:

book-data (ISBN, author, title, list-price)

ISBN is treated as an elementary item, but it is really a group item consisting of four elementary items:

- Country where published
- Publisher
- Book identifier
- Check digit

The **book-data** table should read as follows:

book-data (country-where-published, publisher, book-identifier,
check-digit, author, title, list-price)

check-digit is a ''hash'' digit calculated by a specific algorithm applied to other digits within the item. In ISBN, the last or check digit is calculated from the preceding digits. The purpose of the check digit is to discover entry and/or transmission errors. An ISBN with a transposed digit should produce a check digit different from the predicted check digit and should be trapped as an error by an edit program. Check digits are necessary for entry, but they need not be stored. The procedure is to eliminate the **check-digit** attribute from the **book-data** table.

Unfortunately, software cannot help. The data analyst must analyze all key attributes to determine if they are group or elementary items. The data analyst must decompose any group items to their subordinate elementary items.

RECOMMENDATION

- Decomposition should be done before normalization; otherwise, normalization will have to be redone if a group attribute is discovered. Redoing normalization is time-consuming, costly, and frustrating.

Final Normal Form (FNF)

Since no one can agree on how many forms there are, I define final normal form as the "last" level of normalization. To achieve the last level requires optimization and generalization.

Optimization. It is quite possible in performing normalization to create tables that have the same set of key attributes; for instance,

abc-table (a̲, b̲, c̲, d, e, f,...)
bac-table (b̲, a̲, c̲, d, e, f,...)
cab-table (c̲, a̲, b̲, d, e, f,...)

are really the same table because all three tables have the same key attributes, albeit in a different sequence (sequence is of no importance in normalization). The procedure is to combine all tables with the same set of key attributes into a single table.

RECOMMENDATION

- Use software to perform optimization.

Generalization. Inaccurate entity type analysis can cause entity instances to be identified as entity types. Logic University has three master RECORDS:

student   instructor   alumnus

It is possible for the same person to be a student and/or instructor and/or alumnus simultaneously. This means that common items such as name, address, phone number, and social security number could be stored three times rather than once. An objective of normalization is to achieve minimal cover, and obviously this has not been achieved. The problem is that **student**, **instructor**, and **alumnus** are entity instances instead of independent entity types. Specifically, they are subtypes of a supertype (persons involved with courses) and should be combined into a multityping set.[8] Software can help.

RECOMMENDATIONS

- Use software to derive the generic name for each attribute (usually requires simply removing prefixes and/or suffixes) and highlight all tables that have the same set of generic key attributes.
- Have the data analyst identify subtypes and have the software combine them into a multitype set.

All recommendations to this point have produced the FNF logical database in some form of relational notation. Most people like pictures, so the next step is to produce the FNF logical database in graphic format. The first step is to choose the graphic syntax. The most popular are Bachman (DBTG), bubble, and canonical.

- Use software to produce automatically a graphic model from the FNF logical database.

PHYSICAL SCHEMA

The graphic logical database and other required statistical information that can usually be derived from the programs, log files, and/or statistic files by software are given to the database designer for preparation of the schema.

RECOMMENDATION

- Provide the database designer with software that generates a first-cut physical schema and transaction timing software that permits ''what if'' queries. This software makes physical database design less difficult.

Subschema

The smart data-name replacement program has inserted FILLER into all unreferenced items in each DATA DIVISION in all the programs.

RECOMMENDATION

- Use software to generate the subschemas based on the programs' logical views as identified by the FILLER clauses.

Logical records.   Some DBMS vendors (ADR, Cullinet, IBM, and CINCOM among them) have introduced a logical record facility (LRF) into their DBMS to permit programs to request only the data each requires by the use of logical records. The FILLER clauses have in effect created logical records but reserved space because the data is actually read into the program.

RECOMMENDATION

- Use software to remove the FILLER references from all programs, thereby creating logical records.

CONVERTING ALL COBOL I-O TO DBMS CALLS

The foregoing procedures have completed all the preparations required to allow the COBOL I-O statements to be translated to DBMS CALLs. All DBMS use customized CALL statements to communicate between the COBOL program and the DBMS.

RECOMMENDATION

- Use software to translate COBOL I-O to DBMS CALL.

The procedures in Chapters 15–23 have converted tired old spaghetti-coded COBOL programs using obsolescent I-O statements to readable COBOL programs that use modern DBMS CALLs that are easy to maintain.

NOTES

1. A primary key uniquely identifies a single record, tuple, or table.
2. A repeating group is a data group that can have zero to many sets of data value per data store or table.
3. A candidate key is a key that uniquely identifies normalized record instances of a given type. A candidate key must have two properties: (1) Each instance of the record must have a different value on the key, so that given a key value one can locate a single instance, and (2) no attribute in the key can be discarded without destroying the first property. (J. Martin, *Strategic Data Planning Methodologies*, Englewood Cliffs, N.J.: Prentice-Hall, 1982.)
4. Irregularities and anomalies can result if a relation or table is not in normal form. For example, they could involve loss of information about a relationship between data items if the last occurrence of that relationship is deleted.
5. These descriptions are based on E. Vesely, *The Practitioner's Blueprint to Logical and Physical Database Design*, Englewood Cliffs, N.J.: Prentice-Hall, 1986.
6. See the vendor list in Appendix D for addresses of vendors that supply software to assist in the normalization process.
7. A data dictionary is a catalogue of all data types, giving their names and structures, and information about data usage. Advanced data dictionaries have a directory function which enables them to represent and report on the cross-references between components of data and business models. (Martin, *Methodologies*.)
8. A multityping data language permits each individual entity to be an instance of one or more entity types.

——— 24 ———

COBOL₈₅ Defensive Programs

Part 1 described defensive programming techniques available under COBOL$_{85}$, including these:

- Converting all performable paragraphs to directly contained$_{85}$ nested$_{85}$ programs within a single source listing
- Transferring all nested$_{85}$ program-specific data items from the main containing$_{85}$ program to local$_{85}$ WORKING-STORAGE in each nested$_{85}$ program
- Making all storage in the source listing local$_{85}$ except for parameters that are to be returned from a called program to the calling program, the return parameters for these being in the called program GLOBAL$_{85}$ WORKING-STORAGE
- Making all CALL USING clauses BY CONTENT$_{85}$, thereby rendering it impossible for the called program to change any data in the calling program
- Using the called program GLOBAL$_{85}$ WORKING-STORAGE to return parameters to the calling program rather than the USING clause
- Initializing all nested$_{85}$ programs so that they always perform identically

The rationale is total data protection with single-entry modules (programs) that are always initialized.

This additional restructuring should take place after the program has been restructured as previously discussed. It is an additional extension to ease maintenance and reduce its burden on DP shops.

PASS 1: PARAGRAPHS TO PROGRAMs

Isolate all performable paragraphs. Convert each paragraph to a nested$_{85}$ PROGRAM:

- Substitute IDENTIFICATION DIVISION for paragraph entry:

                              P212-compute-best-solution

becomes

                              IDENTIFICATION DIVISION.
                              PROGRAM-ID.   P212CBS
                              *P212-compute-best-solution

- Form PROGRAM-ID from the paragraph number plus the first letter of each syllable (letters between hyphens).
- Place the original paragraph name as a comment after PROGRAM-ID.
- Transfer paragraph narratives to *REMARKS$_{68}$.
- Insert COMMON$_{85}$ if PROGRAM is invoked from multiple PERFORMs.
- There never will be an ENVIRONMENT DIVISION.
- There is no DATA DIVISION on the first pass.
- Insert PROCEDURE DIVISION without USING before the first executable statement.
- Substitute EXIT PROGRAM for EXIT paragraph.

Here is a comparative example:

```
        P212-compute-best-solution          IDENTIFICATION DIVISION.
        **************************           PROGRAM-ID.  P212CBS.
        *narratives                          *P212-compute-best-solution
        *                                    *REMARKS.    narratives
        **************************           **************************
        *                                    PROCEDURE DIVISION.
            executable statements               executable statements
        ...                                  ...
        P212-X.    EXIT.                      EXIT PROGRAM
            GO TO    abort                       GO TO    abort
            EJECT                                EJECT
```

Data Referencing

No change on the first pass.

Invocation

- Simple PERFORM statements are changed to simple CALL statements:

        PERFORM P212-compute-best-solution

  becomes

                    CALL "P212CBS"

- PERFORM USING and VARYING are changed to <u>in-line</u>$_{85}$ PERFORM statements:

        PERFORM   P212-compute-best-solution
        THRU   P212-X
        WITH TEST BEFORE
        UNTIL   master-file-eof
        END-PERFORM
        ...

  becomes

        PERFORM   [in-line; no procedure name]
                       CALL "P212CBS"
                       WITH TEST BEFORE
                       UNTIL master-file-eof
        END-PERFORM
        ...

This should be a purely cosmetic change since all nested$_{85}$ programs have GLOBAL$_{85}$ access to all data and have not been initialized. The cosmetic change is simply to change paragraphs to programs. However, this cosmetic change would be onerous to accomplish manually; therefore, software should be used.

Program validation should be done with known test data as previously discussed (run new program with known input and do an automated file compare on the program results against the known results—there should be no difference). If differences arise, change one paragraph at a time and test. If correct, change the next paragraph until the offending paragraph is isolated. Determine the problem and correct it. Continue until all performable paragraphs have been converted to nested$_{85}$ programs.

PASS 2: CREATE LOCAL$_{85}$ STORAGE FOR NESTED$_{85}$ PROGRAMS

The second pass is to transfer all specific nested$_{85}$ data from the main program DATA DIVISION to the nested$_{85}$ program DATA DIVISION:

- Use software to isolate program-specific data.
- Insert DATA DIVISION and WORKING-STORAGE SECTION in nested$_{85}$ program with the GLOBAL$_{85}$ clause omitted (local$_{85}$ storage).
- Transfer data metadata.

Again, this should be a purely cosmetic change. Again, it would be onerous to accomplish manually, so software should be used. Again, program validation should be done as discussed previously.

PASS 3: CREATE USING CLAUSES AND LINKAGE SECTIONs

The third pass is to create the USING clauses and LINKAGE SECTIONs:

- Use software to isolate the data being used by each nested$_{85}$ program.
- Create and insert data-names in the appropriate CALL and PROCEDURE DIVISION USING clauses.
- Create and insert data-names in the appropriate LINKAGE SECTION.

This is another series of cosmetic changes that should be accomplished by software and validated.

PASS 4: COMPLETE DATA PROTECTION

The first three passes have performed only limited data isolation by moving program-specific data to program local$_{85}$ storage. This pass basically protects all data in a single source listing. The technique is to employ CALL USING BY CONTENT$_{85}$. BY CONTENT$_{85}$ passes the specific value to the called program rather than the reference address. It is impossible for the called program to modify any data in the calling program; it is also impossible for the called program to transfer data back to the calling program. The solution is to have the called program place the return parameters into its own GLOBAL$_{85}$ storage, thereby making it accessible to any program in the source listing. Although the GLOBAL$_{85}$ data values could be inadvertently modified by other programs, the values must be correct when control returns to the calling program. This guarantees that the calling program has access to the latest values and that all of its data has been protected. For example:

```
            IDENTIFICATION DIVISION.
            PROGRAM-ID.    P101PBS.
           *P101-produce-best-solution
   ...
            DATA DIVISION.   [all local₈₅ storage; no GLOBAL₈₅]
   ...
            PROCEDURE DIVISION.
   ...
               CALL "P212CBS" USING   good-input   BY CONTENT
               ON EXCEPTION  ???
               END-CALL
               any statements that wish to access solution which is in
               P212CBS GLOBAL₈₅ WORKING-STORAGE
   ...
               IDENTIFICATION DIVISION.
               PROGRAM-ID.    P212CBS.
           *P212-compute-best-solution
   ...
               DATA DIVISION.
               WORKING-STORAGE SECTION.
               01  solution         GLOBAL.
   ...
               01  P212-local-parms
   ...
```

All data other than the GLOBAL$_{85}$ WORKING-STORAGE is local$_{85}$ and is protected. The GLOBAL$_{85}$ WORKING-STORAGE contains the latest values (in this case the solution), and the calling program is guaranteed the latest values. The data is now protected.

PASS 5: THE LAST FRONTIER

Now the fun starts! The first four passes have protected all the data. The last frontier is to make each nested$_{85}$ program adhere to the structure theorem of always executing in the same way. In other words, initialized all programs. A significant maintenance problem in COBOL$_{74}$ is that the maintenance programmer does not know from reading the source listing what state each paragraph is in on each execution. The paragraph can only be guaranteed to be in a virgin state upon its first invocation. After that, who knows? The development programmer might have reinitialized, but maintenance statistics indicate that most do not. Trace debugging tools and memory dumps are often needed to determine the exact state of a paragraph when an abend or other erroneous event occurs.

The syntactic solution is easy: Just insert an INITIAL$_{85}$ clause into each nested$_{85}$ program. The result will probably be chaos, as many of the programs will be expecting a particular transitive state.

The solution is to insert the first INITIAL$_{85}$ clause and test. If OK, insert the second INITIAL$_{85}$ clause and test again. Continue until all nested$_{85}$ programs have INITIAL$_{85}$ clauses. The final program will be data-protected and its total functionality derivable from the source listing. Is it worth the effort? Calculate the cost of maintenance in your DP shop. This cost includes all of these expenses:

- The programmer cost (salary, vacation pay, sick pay, insurance) to do maintenance (current industry statistics indicate that 80 percent of a programmer's time is devoted to maintenance)
- The computer resources to compile, test, recompile, retest, re-recompile, re-retest, re-re-recompile,...
- The user time to check the test results and recheck the test results and re-recheck and...
- The costs to correct the database
- The costs to rerun the programs after being debugged
- The costs to the users for bad information, the waiting time, the manual procedures,...

Is it worth the effort?

Note: The defensive programmer software could take new programs that were developed as if using COBOL$_{74}$ and redo them in COBOL$_{85}$ defensive programming construct. This would ease the programming burden on the development programmers.

25

Selecting the Right Tool

Rapid application development using COBOL? You gotta be kidding! Everybody knows
that COBOL is a dinosaur that should have died out by now. 4GLs are the only way to go.
This is a prevalent attitude in many data processing shops.

4GLs, prototyping, and expert languages all have their place in the system development
life cycle (SDLC). Figure 25.1 is a simplified Gane and Sarson data flow diagram (dfd) of
a "typical" SDLC.[1] There are many SDLCs, but most of them follow the same general
pattern:

- Define the user requirements.
- Collect and verify the data necessary to process the user requirements.
- Define the entity types and their relationships.
- Create the logical data model using normalization.
- Integrate the new logical model into an existing organization data model, thereby
  creating modified subject databases.
- Transfer the metadata to the organizational data dictionary.
- Create a new schema or modify an existing schema for the new user transactions
  and data.

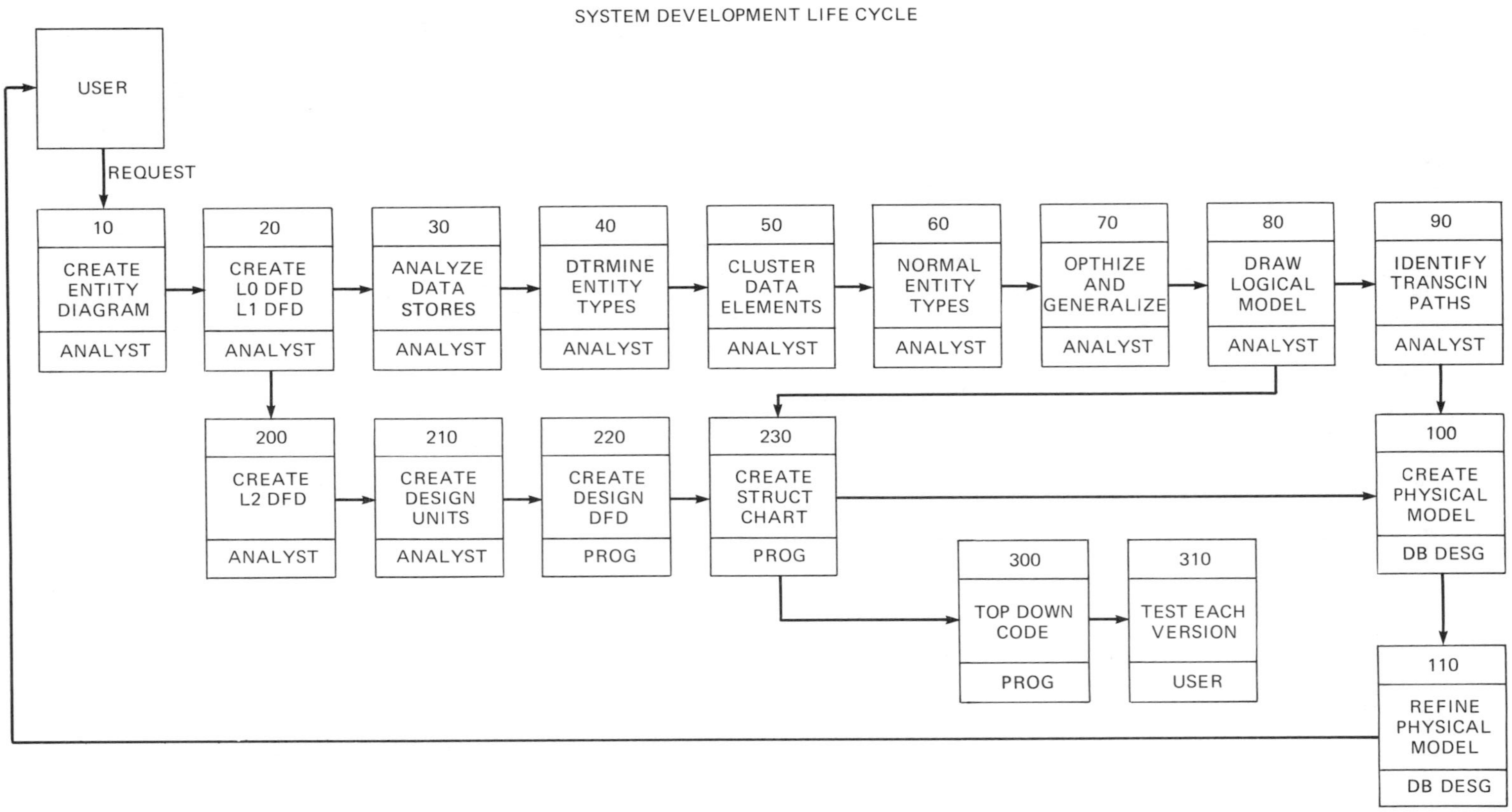

SYSTEM DEVELOPMENT LIFE CYCLE

Figure 25.1 System development life cycle data flow diagram.

- Create new subschemas for individual user views and/or programmer views.
- Test and refine the physical schema to provide optimum user response.
- Define the detailed business logic.
- Create the programming specification.
- Code and test the program to make optimum use of the optimum physical database.
- Provide source-driven documentation for the users, maintenance programmers, operations, data administration, system programmers, project team, and others.

4GLs and prototyping can assist in refining the user requirements, but users and analysts must initially determine the users' needs and whether those needs should be automated. Once the users' needs have been preliminarily defined, prototyping tools can be used to "paint" online screens providing the users with a feeling of how the online portion of the system will look and function.[2] This is an important advance in analysis in that it permits users to provide meaningful input early in the analysis cycle. This user input can shortcut the analysis cycle, but more important, it can and does specifically define the actual user requirements as opposed to perceived requirements either by the user or the analyst. This definition of actual user requirements saves countless months or years of effort in supplying the wrong answers to the users and in undoing those wrong answers. Protyping should be used in applications requiring online processing.

However, analysis and prototyping are but a small part of the entire SDLC. Collecting, verifying, and normalizing all the data (online and batch) into a logical database that can be converted to a physical database requires significant effort that is outside the realm of 4GLs and prototyping (expert languages may someday be useful, but they are not yet).

A program must be written by somebody in some language to actually use the data. 4GL vendors claim that 4GLs are the appropriate language because they are concise, nonprocedural,[3] and easy to use. Some are and some aren't. My intention is not to rate 4GLs but to try to describe their appropriate place in the SDLC. The simple 4GLs are for simple online queries by users. They take the simple query using sophisticated parsing techniques and the metadata contained in a data dictionary to navigate the physical database to provide the answer. The parsing, interfacing to the data dictionary, and database navigation require substantial and sophisticated programming in the 4GL itself, and it is a proven fact that 4GLs consume significant computer resources. But again, the use of computer resources is a small portion of the entire application cycle. If a user can in five minutes get an answer to an ad hoc query that would require a month of conventional programming (which presumably will be thrown away), the overall organizational cost is quantifiably cheaper. If the answer permits the querier favorably to affect the bottom line, the 4GL has definitely proved its worth.

The real problem is to place each tool into its proper perspective for each user request. What works for one application can easily bomb on the next application because of inadequate analysis of the application cycle needs. The application project manager must be aware of the tools available in the organizational tool kit and must pick the tools that are most applicable to the project under the manager's control. There should be tools for each SDLC step:

- Requirements definition
- Data collection and verification
- Normalization

or all the steps listed on the first page of this chapter.

However, I do have a significant disagreement with some of the current 4GL vendors. Current 4GLs should not be used as a substitute for production batch COBOL programs that manipulate large files or large databases.

The first reason is the rationale for the development of COBOL: the need to have a portable language that is compliable and executable on many different CPUs. Add to that requirement the modern need to be portable between many different DBMS, and you have an overwhelming reason not to use 4GLs for batch production: portability. McAuto has an inventory of 50 million lines of COBOL code (see note 1 of the Preface) which at the minimum cost of $10 per line equals $500 million and whose actual cost is probably closer to $2 billion! If McAuto used a production 4GL tied to a particular DBMS and it wanted to change to a different DBMS, you can imagine the extent of the catastrophe.

The second reason is another unstated rationale for COBOL: the creation of an environment that fostered a large population of programmers who could program in a common language and who would not need retraining. There are orders of magnitude more COBOL programmers than all of the 4GL programmers put together. Therefore, it is much easier and less expensive to recruit competent COBOL programmers than 4GL production programmers.

The third reason is practical. Current 4GLs are not designed for production batch programs. The following quotes from a *Computerworld* article should suffice:[4]

> A bureaucratic snafu of epic proportion has been created for New Jersey drivers, allegedly owing to a system design consultant's inappropriate use of a fourth-generation-language-based application.
> As a result, more than a million drivers have been unable to register their cars or have registered them and are incorrectly listed in the state's computers as operating unregistered vehicles. So many New Jersey drivers have been forced to drive without registrations that the state attorney general's office has ordered state police to cease citing drivers for the offense."

So what? you say. A COBOL application could have the same problems. True, but let's continue with the story.

> The Department of Motor Vehicles wanted to expand to 1,000 the number of terminals able to access the system. Instead, officials said, they found the new system floundering with 200 terminals. Response times went from the three to five seconds targeted to as long as five minutes.
> The new $6.5 million system "is simply not capable of handling the volume of work

generated each day. Even working overtime and on weekends, the system is not keeping up.''

COBOL would probably have done as badly if the COMMUNICATION module was used, since COBOL is the wrong language for online applications.

The 4GL used in this application was ADR's Ideal. Here are additional quotes:

> ''It was a barn-burner application and I'm not sure Ideal was the right technology to use,'' Jones [deputy administrator of the state Office of Telecommunications and Information Systems] said.
>
> Said ADR's Farrelly [vice-president for research and development], ''The batch sequential processing should have been written in COBOL.''

Thank you, Mr. Farrelly.

> Farrelly said it takes the same number of lines of code in Ideal to accomplish batch processing as in COBOL and that there was no inherent advantage in using Ideal in such a way.

Thank you very much, Mr. Farrelly.

> He [Farrelly] said that 20% of subsystems that required heavy processing should also have been written in COBOL rather than Ideal.

My cup runneth over.

The preceding is not a tirade against 4GLs but against using the wrong tool at the wrong time in the wrong place. The $6.5 million spent on the system is probably lost, and more money will be needed for a redo. Add to that the cost and inconvenience of the state police citing drivers incorrectly, the cost to the drivers to defend themselves, the cost to the law courts of hearing the cases, the cost of overtime, and you have the making of a multimillion-dollar fiasco. Acquisition of the appropriate software tools and their *intelligent* use is the answer.

SDLCs can be shortened, but they cannot be shortchanged. In other words, productivity tools can reduce the actual time required, but all the generic steps must be done.

NOTES

1. In *Structured Systems Analysis and Design* (Englewood Cliffs, N.J.: Prentice-Hall, 1979), C. Gane and T. Sarson define *data flow diagram* as ''a picture of the flows of data through a system of any kind, showing the external entities which are sources or destinations of data, the processes which transform data, and the places where the data is stored''.

2. There are many software products that allow application developers to design (paint) CRT screens. Some products, such as Cullinet's ADS/ONLINE, have a facility to sequence through screens based on the entered function. This prototyping feature permits application developers to set up the actual screens for the users to play with and, more important, comment on.

3. COBOL is a procedural language in that it requires up to four divisions and has many required entries. A nonprocedural language does not have any specific syntax and basically permits English queries such as

How many salespersons made over $25000 in commissions last year?

4. C. Babcock, "New Jersey Motorists in Software Jam," *Computerworld*, October 1985.

26

System Development Life Cycle

In Figure 25.1 in Chapter 25, process boxes (rounded rectangles 10 through 110 and 200 through 220) are part of the SDLC but do not involve application programming.[1] Rectangle 230 starts the process with the coding being actually done in rectangle 300 and tested (debugged) in 310. Coding is one process box out of 17 and represents less than 10 percent of the SDLC.

The process in box 200 recommends that the programmer (PROG) create a structure chart before coding. The structure chart is a hierarchical map of the programs functions, with each rectangle representing a single module performing a single function (see Figure 2.2 in Chapter 2). There are numerous software tools that can assist programmers in developing structure charts. The arrowhead lines indicate the parameters that are passed between modules, with the arrowhead indicating the flow direction. Each module (normally a COBOL paragraph) should contain a narrative describing the module function as described in Part 1. The structure chart with narratives should be reviewed with the user for business correctness and with DP people for computer correctness.

RECOMMENDATIONS

- Have the programming project manager create a high-level structure chart for the project where the modules are normally programs; each program should have a high-level narrative.

- Review the structure chart with the user for business correctness and with DP people for computer correctness.
- Have each programmer develop a structure chart for each assigned program with detailed narratives.
- Review each structure chart with users and DP people.

The structure chart is a programming view of whatever specifications were presented for implementation. An early review should catch serious misinterpretations and increase the probability that the delivered application will do what the users would like it to do.

TOP-DOWN CODING

The approved structure chart is the programming specification, which the programmer translates to top-down code (process box 300). The top-down coding approach breaks the programming requirement into smaller and more precise modules. The basic motto of top-down is divide and conquer.

The divide-and-conquer approach is a systematic plan of attack on the supplied programming specifications in which the major modules and their interfaces are coded first and subjected to stringent code inspections.

The characteristics of top-down coding include designing by level:

- Develop the program according to an approved hierarchical concept (structure chart).
- Develop the coding for the highest levels using stubs for lower levels.
- Verify the interfaces between the modules.

COBOL can have four divisions. Let us discuss the recommended coding procedure for each.

IDENTIFICATION DIVISION

The PROGRAM-ID should be given to the programmer. The name should be based on site standards with the complete name being the next comment line.

The rest of the IDENTIFICATION DIVISION should be coded as recommended in Part 1.

The following coding is based on Figure 2.2.

```
IDENTIFICATION DIVISION.

PROGRAM-ID.     prbssl.
*produce best solution

*AUTHOR.          eric garrigue vesely
```

```
*INSTALLATION.      the analyst workbench

*DATE-WRITTEN.      09 january 1988

 DATE-COMPILED.

*REMARKS.      read parameter-file
*              edit parameter-file for validity
*              compute best solution for the specific set of
*                  parameters based on supplied criteria
*              print output as per user report format 13-169

     EJECT
```

CODING TIME: 10 minutes ± 5 minutes. The coding time specified is for a typical program and not just for the sample coded program. In other words, the coding time for any typical IDENTIFICATION DIVISION should not exceed 15 minutes regardless of the size of the program.

DEBUGGING TIME: 30 minutes or less to cover for the possibility that the PROGRAM-ID is incorrect. Debugging time is the estimated time to uncover and completely fix any logic problems identified by the program testing procedures. It does not include correcting syntax problems such as AUHTOR.

ENVIRONMENT DIVISION

Any required language elements should be copied.

```
ENVIRONMENT DIVISION.

CONFIGURATION SECTION.

SOURCE-COMPUTER.      COPY awb-source-computer.

OBJECT-COMPUTER.      COPY awb-object-computer.

SPECIAL-NAMES.        COPY awb-special-names-format-3.

INPUT-OUTPUT SECTION.

FILE-CONTROL.    COPY awb-sequential-file-format-7.

     EJECT
```

CODING TIME: 10 minutes ± 5 minutes.

DEBUGGING TIME: One hour or less to cover for the possibility that the wrong SPECIAL-NAMES and/or FILE-CONTROL were copied.

DATA DIVISION

The DATA DIVISION is the ''wordy'' DIVISION and can require many hours or days to code if COPY is not used. Letting programmers create their own DATA DIVISION entries usually means problems, especially these:

- Data-names are meaningless. (Why write a 20+ character meaningful data-name when **abc** is shorter?)
- Data element metadata such as PIC clauses are different from other uses of the same data element.
- More aliases and homonyms are created.
- PROCEDURE DIVISION references are confusing because of the confusion in the DATA DIVISION.

Time now devoted to maintenance is above 50 percent. Probably about half—or more than 25 percent—is caused by confusion in the DATA DIVISION. The entire FILE SECTION and LINKAGE SECTION (if required) should be copied. All of the WORKING-STORAGE SECTION should be copied other than the specific parameters required by this specific program.

COBOL should be used for batch production programs. Production programs should use standard files. Standard files should be defined by COPY statements.

```
DATA DIVISION.

FILE SECTION.

FD      COPY parameter-file.

01      COPY parameter-record.

FD      COPY formatted-output-file.

01      COPY formatted-output-record.

WORKING-STORAGE SECTION.

01      COPY working-storage-skelton.

01      best-solution-specific-parms.
```

CODING TIME: 10 minutes per COPY plus 10 minutes per specific parameter.
DEBUGGING TIME: Substantially reduced because of standard data-names.

PROCEDURE DIVISION

The PROCEDURE DIVISION should be coded from the top down. This means that only higher modules should be coded first, with any directly invoked lower modules coded as stubs. Stubs can perform three functions:

- Provide status that it was invoked
- Provide a predefined input or output
- Provide a time delay

Time delays are occasionally required to provide realistic response or processing times when testing partially developed programs. A partially developed program could perform substantially faster because it was performing limited processing and editing. Allowing the user to test a fast-response-time system will cause dissatisfaction when the real response time manifests itself. Use a stub for delay to avoid user dissatisfaction.

This technique provides the programmer with a rare opportunity to be a software hero. The programmer could code a 10-second delay when the user objective was 5 seconds. The user would undoubtedly be concerned, but the programmer could state that "fine tuning" would achieve the desired response time. The fine tuning is taking out the delay.

The first step is to determine the higher modules. The simple technique is to "peel the onion." The outer "skin" of the structure chart (onion) is coded first. In Figure 2.2, that includes paragraphs P101, P211, P213, P311, and P334. P212, P312, and P333 are stubs because they are directly invoked by coded modules. PC01 and PC02 are not involved in the first implementation because they are invoked by currently uncoded modules.

Top-down coding for Figure 2.2 is as follows:

```
PROCEDURE DIVISION.

P101-produce-best-solution.

    PERFORM          P211-get-good-input
    THRU             P211-X
    END-PERFORM

    PERFORM          P212-compute-best-solution
    THRU             P212-X
    END-PERFORM

    PERFORM          P213-put-out-solution
    THRU             P213-X
    END-PERFORM

    EJECT
```

```
P211-get-good-input.

    PERFORM           P311-read-input
    THRU              P311-X
    END-PERFORM

    PEFORM            P312-edit-input
    THRU              P312-X
    END-PERFORM

P211-X.  EXIT.

    EJECT


P212-compute-best-solution.
*stub - return predefined solution to P101

    MOVE              predefined-solution
    TO                best-solution.

P212-X.  EXIT.

    EJECT


P213-put-out-solution.

    PERFORM           P333-format-output
    THRU              P333-X
    END-PERFORM

    PERFORM           P334-write-output
    THRU              P334-X
    END-PERFORM

P213-X.  EXIT.

    EJECT


P311-read-input.

    READ              parameter-record        RECORD
    INTO              parameter-record-ws
    AT END            STOP RUN
*eof should not occur in version 1 therefore stop
    END-READ

P311-X.  EXIT.

    EJECT
```

```
    P312-edit-input.
*stub - return input-ok to P211-edit-flag

        MOVE              input-ok
        TO                edit-flag.

    P312-X. EXIT.

        EJECT


    P333-format-output.
*stub - return predefined output to P213-formatted output

        MOVE              predefined-output
        TO                formatted-output.

    P333-X.  EXIT.

        EJECT


    P334-write-output.

        WRITE             P213-formatted-output
        FROM              P213-formatted-output-ws
        END-WRITE

    P334-X. EXIT.

        EJECT
```

A COBOL programmer realizes that a FILE must be OPEN for processing and that exception and error conditions must be tested for and each FILE must CLOSE before STOP RUN. The uncommented version should be as follows:[2]

```
    PROCEDURE DIVISION.

    P101a-initialization.

        OPEN INPUT        parameter-file
        OPEN OUTPUT       formatted-output-file

        CONTINUE

    P101b-produce-best-solution.

        PERFORM           P211-get-good-input
        THRU              P211-X
        END-PERFORM
```

```
        PERFORM          P212-compute-best-solution
        THRU             P212-X
        END-PERFORM


        PERFORM          P213-put-out-solution
        THRU             P213-X
        END-PERFORM


        CONTINUE

P101c-termination.

        CLOSE            parameter-file
                         formatted-output-file


        STOP RUN.


        EJECT

P211-get-good-input.

        PERFORM          P311-read-input
        THRU             P311-X
        END-PERFORM


        PERFORM          P312-edit-input
        THRU             P312-X
        END-PERFORM

    P211-X. EXIT.


        EJECT

    P212-compute-best-solution.
    *stub - return predefined solution to P101

        MOVE             predefined-solution
        TO               best-solution.

    P212-X. EXIT.


        EJECT

    P213-put-out-solution.

        PERFORM          P333-format-output
        THRU             P333-X
        END-PERFORM
```

```
            PERFORM          P334-write-output
            THRU             P334-X
            END-PERFORM


        P213-X. EXIT.


            EJECT


        P311-read-input.


            READ             parameter-record                        RECORD
            INTO             parameter-record-ws
            AT END           STOP RUN
        *eof should not occur in version 1 therefore stop
            END-READ


            COPY             sequential-input-filestatus.
        *there should be common file status routines for all file
        *types. program should only check for specific errors
        *required by program


            IF               parameter-file-status-not-ok
                             STOP RUN
        *first version should not have errors
            ELSE             NEXT SENTENCE
            END-IF


        P311-X. EXIT.


            EJECT


        P312-edit-input.
        *stub - return input-ok to P211-edit-flag


            MOVE             input-ok
            TO               edit-flag.


        P312-X. EXIT.


            EJECT


        P333-format-output.
        *stub - return predefined output to P213-formatted output


            MOVE             formatted-output
            TO               formatted-output.


        P333-X. EXIT.
```

```
        EJECT

    P334-write-output.

        WRITE           P213-formatted-output
        FROM            P213-formatted-output-ws
        END-WRITE

        COPY            sequential-output-file-status.

        IF              formatted-out-filestatus-notok
                        STOP RUN
    *first version should not have errors
        ELSE            NEXT SENTENCE
        END-IF

    P334-X. EXIT.

        EJECT
```

This version is now tested with predefined raw input that is valid, producing a predefined solution that has a predefined formatted output, which is written out. This version, when satisfactorily tested, will provide a basic test bed for the other module. The OK tested version 1 proves that the program can READ and WRITE good raw input.

Version 2 begins coding the stubs. For instance, P312 is the edit input module. This module should be coded with all the required validity checks. If other modules are needed—such as PC01 and PC02—they should be coded as stubs that returned valid flags.

Version 2.1 should again use only predefined valid raw input. This means that P312 should always return a valid edit flag to P211. If it does not, there is an error in P312 that should be easy to find.

Version 2.2 should use predefined invalid raw input that P312 should identify as invalid. If it does not, the error is again in P312, and again it should be easy to find.

Version 3 codes the next stubs with 3.1 using predefined valid raw input and 3.2 using invalid raw input. Version 4 codes the next stubs, and so on.

This top-down coding and testing method brings each module into a stable test bed, which restricts bugs to the new inserted module. Any recoding is limited to the new module. This procedure is prima facie better than coding the entire program before any testing and then trying to isolate bugs in the entire program when they occur. The complete program coding method can also require substantial rewrites of significant portions of the program once the bug has been identified.

CODING TIME: Substantially reduced because of standard data-names and COPY statements.

DEBUGGING TIME: Substantially reduced because each module is tested in a stable test bed with predefined input, results, and output.

RECOMMENDATIONS

- Prepare a structure chart before coding.

- Determine top-down versions by "peeling the onion."
- Use COPY for all common items.
- Test each version with version .1 using predefined valid input and .2 using predefined invalid input.

Many clients have used this general approach, using software tools to assist analysts and programmers in producing the right system for the user within budget and user time frame. Chapter 27 provides a survey of software productivity tools, and Chapter 28 is an independent productivity assessment of a database management system developed, programmed, and tested by my company, The Analyst Workbench.

STRUCTURED PROGRAMMING

There are many methods of programming—most of them poor. These poor programming methods have created the kilotons of spaghetti programs that are plaguing most DP shops around the world today. Patching spaghetti programs usually creates more spaghetti. Software should not inherently deteriorate because it has no moving parts, but it usually rapidly decays until it should be put out of its misery. Unfortunately, it cannot be put out of its misery because it performs a vital business function, such as payroll, accounts receivable, or material requirement planning. Part 2 described structuring engines that restructured spaghetti COBOL; the first part of this chapter described top-down programming. This section describes a programming style that produces efficient COBOL that is readable, maintainable, and portable. It is basically a combination of the theories of top-down programming *and* testing, structure (not gotoless), and modular using pseudo-COBOL and COPY statements for implementation. First, some definitions:

Linear programming   Immediately start writing code as it will appear when executed.
Bottom up   Design and code the lower components first and the upper levels later.
Inside out   Start in the middle of the program and work down and up at the same time.
Top down   Divide and conquer the program by breaking its goal into precisely stated subgoals.
Structured programming   Restrict control logic to sequence, selection, and iteration.

The problems of linear programming include the need to make specific, detailed decisions with little assurance that the solution is appropriate. This style is tempting in that peers, managers, and users see immediate activity, but the net result is almost always poor program design, with massive patches resulting in unreadable, unmaintainable spaghetti code.

Bottom-up is usually better than linear in that some consideration has been given to the ultimate program design. Unfortunately, the consideration has been given to program components that can be changed radically, depending on the final requirements of the higher-level modules that actually drive the problem solution. The net result is almost always poor program design, with massive patches resulting in unreadable, unmaintainable spaghetti code.

Many programmers have tried both linear and bottom-up and have concluded that there must be a better way. The next evolution is usually inside-out. This is normally better than the first two approaches in that the programmer usually has a general idea of the entire program, does some preliminary coding of the entire program, and then revises and revises and revises. This style can achieve reasonable programs but is normally inefficient in overall programming effort.

The superprogrammers usually use top-down combined with structured and modular programming theories and reusable code inserted into the program by COPYLIB. The superprogrammers produce readable and maintainable code; the fast and tricky programmers produce code that may solve the immediate problem, but their programs are totally unreadable and unmaintainable. A language analogy is APL (A Programming Language, developed by Ken Iverson). APL is to programming languages what shorthand is to the English language—quick but difficult to comprehend. The standard dictum about how to maintain APL programs is to throw the original program away and start over again. This is acceptable for a language that is used only for quick, intermittent solutions but totally unreasonable for production programs that have a life expectancy exceeding ten years subject to a multitude of changes.

The *automated* superprogrammer typically codes the first two levels of the program by writing pseudo-COBOL. The pseudo-COBOL details the logic of the normal paragraph function with stubs for the second level as described earlier in this chapter. Pseudo-COBOL allows for quick coding because correct syntax is not required.

The pseudo-COBOL is processed by a software package that generates structure charts, narratives, snake reports, cross-reference reports, and other documentation for an intensive code inspection (superprogrammers normally crave reviews so that they can produce the perfect maintainable and readable code on their first try). Corrections are made on the basis of the code inspection, and the first-level modules are coded in real COBOL using structured theory. The basic underpinning of structured theory is that all programs can be created from the following three structures:

- Sequence of functions
- Selection of function (IF-THEN-ELSE)
- Iteration (dowhile, dountil, doinfinite)

Combining these structures with top-down produces a structured program that can be easily read without much skipping around. Most of the other styles require the "four-finger approach." This approach requires placing the first finger in the listing where the first transfer of control occurs, the second finger where the second sequential transfer of control occurs, the third finger where the third sequential transfer of control occurs, the fourth finger where the fourth sequential transfer of control occurs, the fifth finger where the fifth sequential transfer of control occurs, the sixth finger where the sixth sequential transfer of control occurs, ...

A second underpinning of structured theory is that each module performs only a single function. Constraining a module to a single function makes it understandable. It also usually adheres to the modular programming theory that a single function should not exceed 50 lines of code (which is, conveniently, the normal size of a computer printout page).

The goal of modular programming is to prove that each module is by itself correct. Valid input provides valid output. A valid program is composed of valid modules providing valid input to each other by creating valid output.

Modular programming requires that each module execute a single correctly defined function. The function is defined by an algorithm that provides the valid domains for input and output.

In actual practice, can you construct a paragraph that exceeds 50 lines of executable statements to perform a single function? The answer should be no. I have written, reviewed, and/or code-inspected thousands of COBOL programs and have never found any paragraph that should have required more than 35 lines of executable statements (narratives, comments, formatted statements, and blank lines may make the module exceed 50 printed lines).

The properly structured program is structured. It oozes structure. The program is a delight to read precisely because you can read it. The data-names are meaningful and understandable. 88_s are used extensively; most of the program has been "written" by COPY statements. The paragraphs contain narrative and extensive comments. The paragraph prefixes represent the hierarchical program structure; defensive programming permeates the program. The program does not normally require bug correction because it has been thoroughly tested; enhancements requiring new functions can be incorporated with a minimum of fuss.

The advantages should be obvious:

- The program is easier to understand, which facilitates code checking, program testing, and debugging.
- The program is easier to read, which makes maintenance simpler, faster, and less expensive.
- Source-driven documentation is understandable.
- Programmers won't grumble (as much) when maintaining it.
- When combined with $COBOL_{85}$ defensive programming (described in Parts 1 and 2), it ensures correct user results, uncorrupted databases, minimal maintenance, and quick and easy enhancements.

A DETAILED DESCRIPTION OF STRUCTURED PROGRAMMING THEORY

The structure theorem is that any program in any language can be written by using only the logic structure of sequence (COBOL fallthru), selection (COBOL IF), and iteration (COBOL PERFORM).

A proper program or any of its invocable modules has exactly one entry point (COBOL callable programs without entry points, paragraphless sections, PERFORM statements without THRU except to EXIT) and *one* exit point (EXIT paragraph). There is no dead code, and there are no infinite loops.

Structured Programming Logic Structures

Sequence is simply the execution of each COBOL statement as it physically occurs in the source program until there is a transfer-of-control statement (CALL, GO TO, PERFORM, AT ..., ON ...). In other words, the program executes the first imperative statement in the PROCEDURE DIVISION, then the second imperative statement, then the third imperative statement, and so on, until a transfer-of-control statement occurs.

Figure 26.1

Figure 26.1 shows the simple sequence diagram. A can be something like MOVE **a** TO **b**, whereas B can be something like ADD **c** TO **d** GIVING **e**; any COBOL imperative statement suffices. The inappropriate COBOL use of sequence causes fallthru to a new module:

paragraph-a

imperative statements

paragraph-b

A new module (**paragraph-b**) should not be invoked by fallthru since it is an *implicit* transfer of control, whereas structured theory requires *explicit* transfer. Legitimate fallthru implementations should occur only in the mainline paragraph, and they can be effected by a dummy GO TO or CONTINUE$_{85}$.

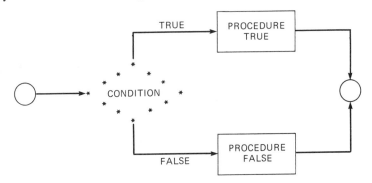

Figure 26.2

Selection is based on testing a given predicate (COBOL IF) for specific values. Figure 26.2 shows the selection flowchart.

Structured programming theory recognizes three iteration types:

dowhile   dountil   doinfinite

Figure 26.3 is the horizontal version of dowhile (see Figure 10.2b in Chapter 10 for the vertical version). The COBOL implementation is PERFORM UNTIL.

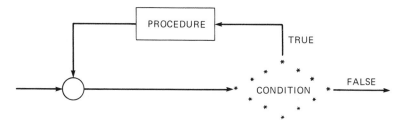

Figure 26.3

Figure 26.4 is the horizontal version of dountil (see Figure 10.2a in Chapter 10 for the vertical version). $COBOL_{74}$ can only implement this by two local GO TO statements as previously discussed, $COBOL_{85}$ with $TEST_{85}$ $AFTER_{85}$.

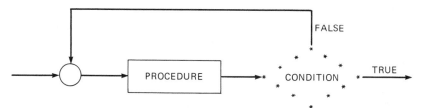

Figure 26.4

Doinfinite is not directly executable in any standard COBOL. It must be implemented by two local GO TO statements as previously discussed. Figure 26.5 is the horizontal version (see Figure 10.2c in Chapter 10 for the vertical version).

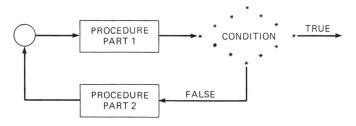

Figure 26.5

Structured theory also recognizes the CASE structure, which states that only one of a multiple set of conditions can be true at any single moment in time (marital status of divorced, married, single, or widowed, for example). The partial COBOL answer is GO TO DEPENDING ON; the better COBOL answer is using 88s with IF statements or sometimes SEARCH WHILE. Figure 26.6 is the horizontal version (see Figure 10.3 in Chapter 10 for the vertical version).

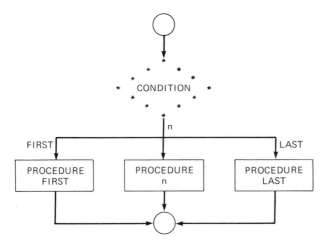

Figure 26.6

The appropriate segmentation structure is not arbitrary. The fact that I have not seen any single-function paragraph that exceeds 35 lines of executable statements does not mean that it is not possible. All paragraphs should execute a single function, and that single function should have one entry, one EXIT, and an EJECT or / after the EXIT regardless of the actual number of printed lines. The appropriate segmentation structure therefore divides the programs into logical single-function paragraphs that a software package can translate without problems into a structure chart representing the inherent hierarchical organization. All paragraphs define explicitly the parameters received, the parameters returned, and any control parameters returned (structure theory does not allow control to be passed down). These parameters are commented in the paragraph narratives.

The pseudo-COBOL and resultant COBOL source are indented for easy reading as shown here:

Pseudo-COBOL	COBOL
IF a	IF a
statement-1	statement-1
IF b	IF b
statement-2	statement-2
ELSE	ELSE
statement-3	statement-3
	END-IF
IF c	IF c
statement-4	statement-4
ELSE	ELSE
statement-5	statement-5
	END-IF
ELSE	ELSE
statement-6	statement-6
	END-IF

Indentation, matching ELSE statements and END-IF scope terminators provide the reader with prima facie documentation of the logic structure of the IF; not indenting requires that the reader usually draw some type of flowchart to understand the logic.

a, b, and **c** would have meaningful names such as **undergraduate, part-time,** and **full-time** and would be defined by 88s to provide easy readability.

Figure 10.3 in Chapter 10 illustrates the basic tenets of this programming style. The peel-the-onion approach isolates paragraphs P311, P211, P101, P213, P334 as the high-level modules and P312, P212, and P333 as first-level stubs.

P101 is the highest-level module. This is the mainline and is responsible for initiation, invoking the lower modules, and termination. It should look like this:

```
P101a-initialization.
*************************************************************
*pseudo-cobol
*narrative to
*describe initialization requirements
*
*@IN              *NONE*
*@OUT             *NONE*
*@OUT CONTROL   incorrent file status
*************************************************************
*
    initiation-statement-1
    initiation-statement-2
    initiation-statement-3
    initiation-statement-4
```

The initiation-statements are written in sequence and illustrate the simple COBOL implementation of the sequence logic structure.

```
        CONTINUE

P101b-produce-best-solution.
*************************************************************
*
```

CONTINUE is the $COBOL_{85}$ implementation of explicitly transferring control rather than implicitly by a fallthru sequence.

P101b-produce-best-solution must have some termination predicate (condition). Normally it is the transaction input EOF, and that predicate is used in this example. The dowhile logic structure (**do-P211-get-good-input WHILE there-is-input**) is implemented in $COBOL_{74}$ by a PERFORM UNTIL and in $COBOL_{85}$ by a PERFORM UNTIL WITH $TEST_{85}$ $BEFORE_{85}$.

```
P101b-produce-best-solution.
*************************************************************
*narratives
...³
*************************************************************
*

...
```

```
PERFORM            P211-get-good-input
THRU               P211-X
WITH TEST BEFORE
UNTIL              transaction-read-eof
END-PERFORM
```

Top-down testing begins after a successful code inspection of the documentation produced by the source documentation package. Top-down testing starts with predefined good input to determine if the program can display the expected output. If it can, the skeleton program executes correctly.

The IF-THEN-ELSE selection structured construct is directly implemented in COBOL$_{85}$ by IF THEN$_{85}$ ELSE and in COBOL$_{74}$ by IF ELSE. **P211-get-good-input** requires the selection of **good-input** or **bad-input**:

```
P211-get-good-input.
************************************************************
*narratives
...
************************************************************
*
...
    IF good-input
*defined by edit-flag 88
    THEN NEXT SENTENCE
    ELSE
    IF bad-input
*defined by edit-flag 88
    THEN PERFORM P???-bad-input
        GO TO P211-get-good-input
*assumes that the processing requirement is to get the next
*good input
    ELSE
    IF invalid-edit-flag
*defined by edit-flag 88
    THEN GO TO abort-procedure
*defensive programming
    END-IF
...


P211-X.   EXIT.

    GO TO abort-procedure.

    EJECT
```

The P211 IF is a case IF. P212 could be a "standard" IF.

```
 P212-produce-best-solution.
************************************************************
narratives
...
************************************************************
*
...
the good input record contains three fields
*  parm-1
*  parm-2
*  parm-3
*the parm fields are used to control the processing of
*determining the best solution
*each parm field can contain a y(es) or a n(o) with 3 nos wrong
*permissible values are
*     yes    yes    yes
*     yes    yes    no
*     yes    no     yes
*     yes    no     no
*     no     yes    yes
*     no     yes    no
*     no     no     yes
      IF  parameter-1
*parameter-1 defined by 88 in parm-1
           THEN IF parameter-2
*parameter-2 defined by 88 in parm-2
             THEN IF parameter-3
*parameter-3 defined by 88 in parm-3
*parm-1 = yes; parm-2 = yes; parm-3 = yes
                  PERFORM P??1-parm-1-best-solution
                  THRU     P??1-X
                  PERFORM P??2-parm-2-best-solution
                  THRU     P??2-X
                  PERFORM P??3-parm-3-best-solution
                  THRU     P??3-X
             ELSE
*parm-1 = yes; parm-2 = yes; parm-3 = no
                  PERFORM P??1-parm-1-best-solution
                  THRU     P??1-X
                  PERFORM P??2-parm-2-best-solution
                  THRU     P??2-X
             END-IF
           ELSE IF parameter-3
                THEN
```

```
*parm-1 = yes; parm-2 = no; parm-3 = yes
                    PERFORM P??1-parm-1-best-solution
                    THRU      P??1-X
                    PERFORM P??3-parm-3-best-solution
                    THRU      P??3-X
            ELSE
*parm-1 = yes; parm-2 = no; parm-3 = no
                    PERFORM P??1-parm-1-best-solution
                    THRU      P??1-X

        END-IF
        END-IF
        ELSE IF parameter-2
        THEN IF   parameter-3
*parm-1 = no; parm-2 = yes; parm-3 = yes
                    PERFORM P??2-parm-2-best-solution
                    THRU      P??2-X
                    PERFORM P??3-parm-3-best-solution
                    THRU      P??3-X

            ELSE
*parm-1 = no; parm-2 = yes; parm-3 = no
                    PERFORM P??2-parm-2-best-solution
                    THRU      P??2-X

        END-IF
        END-IF
        ELSE IF parameter-3
*parm-1 = no; parm-2 = no; parm-3 = yes
        THEN
                    PERFORM P??3-parm-3-best-solution
                    THRU      P??3-X

        ELSE
*parm-1 = no; parm-2 = no; parm-3 = no which is invalid
                    PERFORM P???-invalid-input-data
                    THRU      P???-X

        END-IF
        END-IF

    P212-X.  EXIT.

        GO TO     abort-procedure.

        EJECT
```

If the skeleton program fails, some form of trace is invoked to determine the actual program flow. The skeleton program flow for a single transaction should be as follows:

```
                        P101
                            P211
                                P311
                            P211
                                P312 (stub)
                            P211
                        P101
                            P212 (stub)
                        P101
                            P213
                                P333 (stub)
                            P213
                                P334
                            P213
                        P101
```

If the actual transaction flow was

```
                    P101
                        P211
                            P311
            abend
```

the bug is in either the invocation of P311 by P211 or within P311 itself. The bug should be easy to uncover, and retesting should be quick.

The next testing step after the output has been correctly displayed is to input a small set of known good input with predefined best solutions and predefined output formats to check the displayed output for correctness. If this works, the skeleton program is given a provisional OK for good input. P312 is now partially fleshed out by inserting the actual tests for determining good input. PC01 and PC02 are now coded as stubs or copied into the program if they are existing debugged edit routines. The same known set that provided the good input is processed again. If P312 works, it is provisionally OK for good input; if P312 fails, the bug must be within P312.

After P312 is debugged, P212 is completely coded, with the same set of input being processed again. P212 should provide the same answers as the predefined answers. If it does, fine; if not, . . .

Finally, P333 is fully coded. The same good set of input is processed again, and the formatted output should be the same as the predefined formatted outputs. If they are, good; if they are not, . . .

The next step is to test bad input in the same sequence as good input. After successful completion, the program is now ready for actual data. The actual data should have actual results if possible for complete testing.

Figure 10.3 does represent a small program, but the divide-and-conquer technique works even better as the application becomes more complex. Callable programs could be substituted for paragraphs, and the COBOL$_{85}$ defensive programming techniques discussed in Part 1 should be used. Programs invoked by the operating system required a different technique. Figure 16.2 in Chapter 16 is a partial system diagram graphically showing the hierarchical structure of an application using IBM's operating system JCL with four jobs having five procs and over 30 programs. Assuming that the procs represented actual object programs would provide the following sequential hierarchy:

```
PAP4405
PAP4410
PAP4415
PAP4420
PAP4405X
```

PAP4410 cannot execute before PAP4405, PAP4415 cannot execute before PAP4410 and PAP4405, and so on.

Each program usually outputs one or more files that are used as input by the next program (JCL analyzer software can provide complete FILE metadata). The major interface problem in a program is the data interaction between the modules; the major interface problem in an application is the data interaction between programs. FD COPY statements should always be used to keep each DATA DIVISION in sync. A single predefined FD for all common files should be created and copied into the WORKING-STORAGE of appropriate programs (VALUE is used to specified valid domains for each PIC item). A skeleton PAP4410 could look like this:

```
        IDENTIFICATION DIVISION.
        PROGRAM-ID.   PAP4410.
...
        DATA DIVISION.
...
        01      common-file-1    COPY            common-file-1.
...
        01      common-file-2    COPY            common-file-2.
...
        01      common-file-3    COPY            common-file-3.
...
        WORKING-STORAGE SECTION.
...
        01      common-file-1-test  COPY         common-file-1-test.
...
        01      common-file-2-test  COPY         common-file-2-test.
...
        01      common-file-3-test  COPY         common-file-3-test.
...
        PROCEDURE DIVISION.
...
            OPEN            common-file-1
            common-file-status  COPY            common-file-status.

            OPEN            common-file-2
            common-file-status  COPY            common-file-status.
```

```
            OPEN                    common-file-3
            common-file-status      COPY                    common-file-status.

    ...
            READ                    common-file-1
            common-file-status      COPY                    common-file-status.

            IF common-file-1        NOT EQUAL               common-file-test
            THEN                    DISPLAY                 common-file-1
                                                            common-file-1-test
            ELSE                    NEXT SENTENCE
    *       END-IF
    *else next sentence and end-if cannot be combined - ansi restriction

            READ                    common-file-2
            common-file-status      COPY                    common-file-status.

            IF common-file-2        NOT EQUAL               common-file-test
            THEN                    DISPLAY                 common-file-2
                                                            common-file-2-test
            ELSE NEXT SENTENCE
    *       END-IF
    *else next sentence and end-if cannot be combined - ansi restriction

            READ                    common-file-3
            common-file-status      COPY                    common-file-status.

            IF common-file-3        NOT EQUAL               common-file-test
            THEN                    DISPLAY                 common-file-3
                                                            common-file-3-test
            ELSE                    NEXT SENTENCE
    *       END-IF
    *else next sentence and end-if cannot be combined - ansi restriction

    ...
            STOP RUN.
```

All programs that do not DISPLAY can READ valid predefined data. After all programs in the application can successfully READ, the same basic procedure is used for WRITE. This seemingly trivial exercise can eliminate all future program interfacing problems, which normally show up at application testing time. Application testing time is near the project deadline—or usually after—and causes significant recoding, which results in many late hours, which causes more delays, which causes more recoding, which causes more delays . . .

These brief skeleton programs demonstrate if the parameter interface is working correctly. As stated before, a major cause of interprogram problems is the data interface—particularly when there are multiple programmers. Each programmer, after successful testing, knows that the parameters being passed are syntactically correct (domains will be tested later). Each program is now coded from the top down using structured, modular, and defensive programming theories as discussed. The data interface is retested after each program successfully passes each internal test.

This method of top-down and stepwise testing minimizes interfacing problems and quickly allows the detection of the offending program.

This programming approach provides intellectual control over complexity by combining divide-and-conquer strategy with functional decomposition. The characteristics include these:

- Top-down design and testing
- Structure theory logic structures
- Modular programming
- Pseudo-COBOL
- Software to produce source-driven documentation
- Code inspections

BLUEPRINT FOR SUCCESSFUL PROGRAM DEVELOPMENT

The blueprint for developing readable, maintainable, and efficient COBOL programs is as follows:

- Convert the programming specifications to pseudo-COBOL.
    Create structure charts and other documentation with software.
    Verify by code inspection.
- Determine the high-level modules by peeling the structure charts.
- Code the high-level modules.
    Each module should execute a single function.
    The module should be small and well documented.
    Only structure theory logic constructs should be used.
    Stubs should return predefined values or control; initially the values should be for good or normal data.
- Test with known, predefined good data with known, predefined results.
- After successful testing, structure theory logic constructs should be used to code the stubs.
    Bring in the next level modules as stubs.
- Repeat until all stubs have been coded for good data.
- Repeat the sequence for bad data.
- Test the program with actual data that has known results.
- Verify with the user.
- Place the program into production.

If the program is part of a multiple program application, retest the program-data interface after each successful internal test.

This chapter ends with a quotation from Professor E. Dijkstra:

> As a slow-witted human being I have a very small head and I had better learn to live with it and to respect my limitations and give them full credit, rather than to try to ignore them, for the latter vain effort will be punished by failure.[4]

NOTES

1. For more information, see E. Vesely, *The Practitioner's Blueprint for Logical and Physical Database Design* (Englewood Cliffs, N.J.: Prentice-Hall, 1986).
2. Each version should be commented as described in Part 1, especially the narratives.
3. ... indicates a break in the program source code sequence.
4. E. Dijkstra, *A Discipline of Programming* (Englewood Cliffs, N.J.: Prentice-Hall, 1976).

27

Survey of Software Productivity Tools

Most DP organizations are like the proverbial cobbler who does not have time to make shoes for the family members. They are so busy maintaining and developing programs manually that they do not have time to investigate and purchase (or write) productivity tools for their own use.

Figure 25.1 in Chapter 25 is a Gane-Sarson data flow diagram for a system development life cycle (SDLC). It is based on the Stradis methodology but is a general representation of the steps advocated by most SDLCs:[1]

- Define user requirements (process boxes 10 and 20).
- Collect and verify user data requirements (process box 30).
- Define the entity types required for this specific user application (process box 40).
- Create a logical data model using normalization rules (process boxes 50, 60, and 70).
- Convert Codd logical data model into a graphic model (process box 80).
- Identify the transaction paths and/or logical records required for this specific user application (process box 90).
- Develop a physical database to satisfy the user requirement (process box 100).[2]

- Repeatedly time and refine the physical database to satisfy the user timing requirements (process box 110).

and concurrently

- Define the business logic (process box 200).
- Create programming design unit (process box 210).[3]
- Create detailed programming specifications (process box 220).
- Create Constantine structure charts (process box 230).[4]
- Code the programs from the top down (process box 300).

Most methodologists recommend the use of some diagramming tool to define the user requirements.[5] The tools are roughly divided into two types:

- Functional decomposition
- Data decomposition

Functional decomposition decomposes functions (processes) until each process box can be defined by a minispec.[6] The leading tool kits are Gane-Sarson, SADT, and Yourdon.

Data decomposition begins with output reports and decomposes them to the atomic data elements necessary to satisfy the output. The leading tool kits are Jackson and Warnier/Orr.

DIAGRAM DRAWERS

There are many software packages that interface with analysts to draw diagrams interactively. There are also two types: PC and mainframe.

PC

The Excelarator software package is available for many PCs. It can draw any type of diagram but is most often used for Gane-Sarson and Warnier/Orr. Stradis-Draw (McAuto) is also available in a PC version.

Mainframe

Many mainframe software packages are available. DFDP (ADPAC) draws any type of diagram including JCL job step diagrams and organization charts. It uses standard 3270-type terminals with no enhancement and standard printers although microcode for laser printers is available. Figures 27.1 and 27.2 are examples.

Stradis-Draw uses 3278-type terminals with graphic enhancements and plotters for output. Stradis-Draw is used to support the Stradis methodology and the Gane-Sarson tool kit. Figure 27.3 is an example.

STRUCTURE(S) by Ken Orr and Associates prints Warnier/Orr diagrams from coded input forms. The software is available for many computers. Figure 27.4 is an example.

PDF by Michael Jackson Systems and PACT (3D SYSTEMS) are available for Jackson diagrams.

PSL/PSA by Meta Systems (also marketed by IBM) supports the PSA/PSL methodology and is available for many computers. Figure 27.5 is an example.

The productivity gains of these tools is not in the initial drawing of the original diagrams but in the maintenance of those diagrams and the ability to use the computer to cross-check and collect other information from the diagrams for later use in the SDLC.

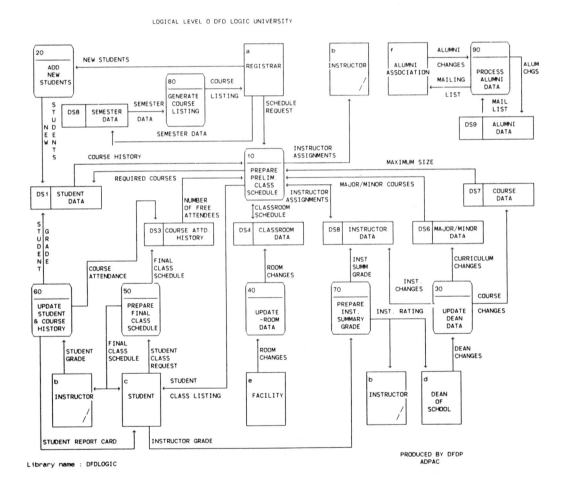

Figure 27.1 DFPD diagram.

Level 1: Prepare Final Class Schedule (Yourdon)

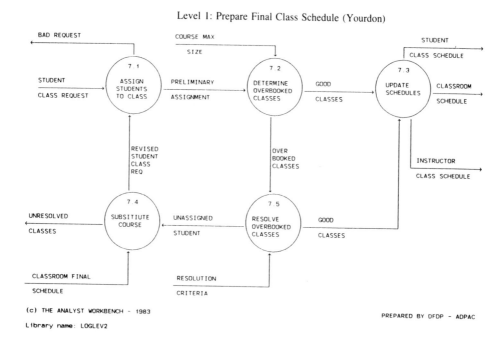

Figure 27.2   DFPD diagram.

New Applications

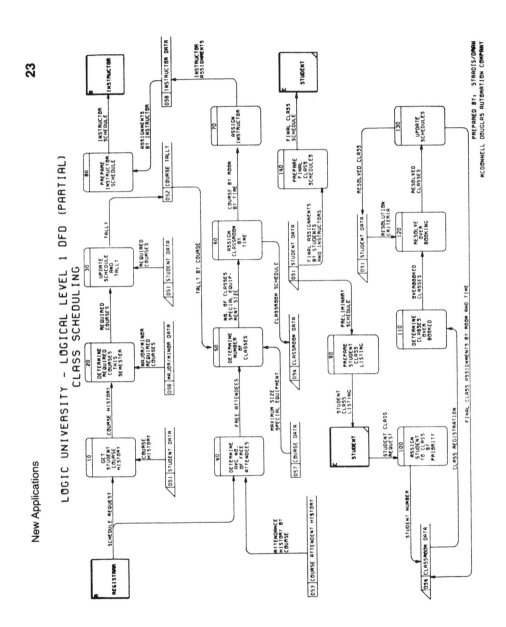

Figure 27.3 Stradis-Draw diagram.

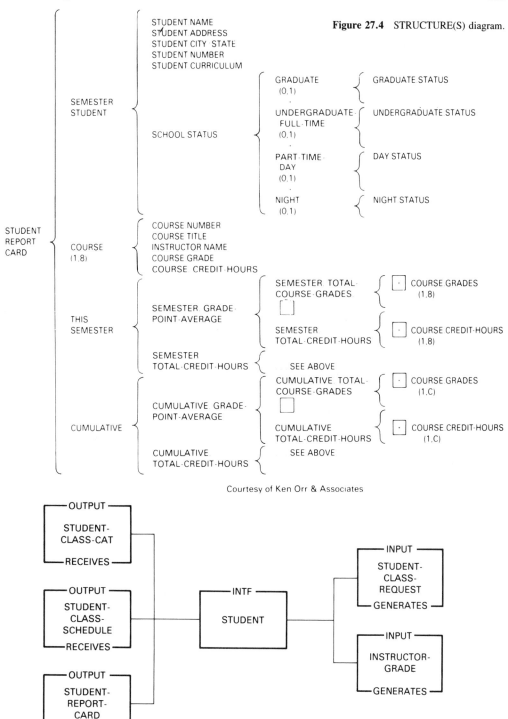

Figure 27.4 STRUCTURE(S) diagram.

Courtesy of Ken Orr & Associates

Figure 27.5 PSL/PSA diagram.

Most of the software mentioned allows the analyst to enter metadata into the library maintained by the software. For instance, each data flow can be decomposed into its component data elements, with each data element being defined. This permits most of the software to perform data verification automatically (is all data entered, maintained, and used either for output and/or as a parameter?). Exception reports are generated for resolution by analysts and users.

Metadata can also be derived from existing COBOL programs. The major problem in using existing programs is the proliferation of homonyms and aliases. The process of data-name rationalization can be used to purify the data. Available packages include WHERE (ADPAC), Data Composer (Composer Technology), and SCAN-370 (Group Operation).

No software that I know of performs automatic identification of entity tapes, but most produces documentation that should make entity type identification simple. Most software packages permit entity type identification to be maintained for later use.

ADPAC has an enterprise modeling option that assists a data analyst in identifying entity types from existing COBOL and PL/1 programs. WHERE automatically computes occurrence and affinity matrices from the identified entity types.

Normalization rules can be applied clerically. The problem in normalization is not the rules but the intimate knowledge of the data required to apply the rules. Software should and can assist in the normalization process by performing the clerical tasks, thereby permitting the data analyst to concentrate on the data itself. There are many software tools available: Data Designer (DDI), Design Manager (MSP), Facets (TSI), Information Builder (Holland Systems), PSA/PSL (Meta Systems and IBM), and DESIGN (ADPAC and The Analyst Workbench) among them.

Each software package can significantly assist in the normalization process. Some are based on the use of a data dictionary; others use canonical modeling; DESIGN uses decision tables and simple input. Figure 27.6 is the unnormalized listing of data elements by entity type created automatically by DESIGN; Figure 27.7 is first normal form (1NF) after the user input of P for primary key, repeating group name, and **x** for members of the repeating group. DESIGN creates a decision table (Figure 27.8) to assist the data analyst in determining which attributes are fully functionally dependent on the entire key. DESIGN performs second normal form (2NF) as illustrated by Figure 27.9. DESIGN can use a decision table for third normal form (3NF), but information already provided permits it to perform 3NF automatically. It also identifies transitive dependencies and foreign keys.

DISPLAY

```
NN    NN WW    WW LL      GGGGGG  UU     UU NN    NN
NNN   NN WW    WW LL      GGGGGGGG UU    UU NNN   NN
NNNN  NN WW    WW LL      GG    GG UU    UU NNNN  NN
NNNNN NN WW WW WW LL      GG       UU    UU NNNNN NN
NN NNNNN WW WW WW LL      GG  GGGG UU    UU NN NNNNN
NN  NNNN WWW  WWW LL      GG    GG UU    UU NN  NNNN
NN   NNN WW    WW LLLLLLL GGGGGGGG UUUUUUUU NN    NNN
NN    NN W     W LLLLLLL  GGGGGG    UUUU   NN    NN
```

```
SEQ       DISPLAY OF  NWLGUN    FROM LIBRARY: ADP.PM.A200.PMLIB
NUMBER    1...5...10...15...20...25...30...35...40...45...50...55...60...6
   1                STUDENT              STUDENT
   2                                     S-NUMBER
   3                                     S-NAME
   4                                     S-STATUS
   5                                     S-HOME-ADDRESS
   6                                     S-HOME-PHONE
   7                                     S-GRADUATION-EXPECTED-DATE
   8                                     S_I-NUMBER<ADVISOR>
   9                                     S_C-HISTORY
  10                                     S_C_T-TAKEN
  11                                     S_C-NUMBER-TAKEN
  12                                     S_C-TITLE
  13                                     S_C-HOURS-CREDIT-TAKEN
  14                                     S_C-HOURS-CREDIT-EARNED
  15                                     S_C-GRADE-EARNED
  16                                     S_M<MAJOR>
  17                                     S_M<MINOR>
  18                                     S-DEGREE-PREVIOUS
  19                                     S-DEGREE-TYPE-PREVIOUS
  20                                     S-GRADUATION-PREVIOUS-DATE
  21                                     S_R-NUMBER-ATTENDING
  22                                     S-DAYOFWEEK-ATTENDING
  23                                     S-TIME-START-ATTENDING
  24                                     S-TIME-END-ATTENDING
  25                                     S_I-NAME<TEACHING>
  26                                     S_H-NAME
  27                COURSE               COURSE
  28                                     C-NUMBER
  29                                     C-TITLE
  30                                     C_H-NAME-CURRICULUM
  31                                     C-HOURS-CREDIT-MINIMUM
  32                                     C-HOURS-CREDIT-MAXIMUM
  33                                     C-CLASSSIZE-MINIMUM
  34                                     C-CLASSSIZE-MAXIMUM
  35                                     C-HOURS-DURATION
  36                                     C-PREREQUSITE
  37                                     C-NUMBER<PREREQUISITE>
  38                                     C_E-SPECIAL
  39                                     C_E-EQUIPMENT-TYPE-SPECIAL
  40                                     C_T-TAKEN
  41                                     C_S-TALLY-TAKEN
  42                                     C_S-TALLY-MAJOR-TAKEN
```

Figure 27.6 Partial nonnormalized list of data elements clustered by entity type (DESIGN).

FIRST NORMAL FORM

RPT LINE	USER CODES	PARENT IDENT	SUBORD IDENT		DATA NAME
1--------	11-----	21------		31--------------------------	
1	A	STUDENT			STUDENT
2	A			P	S-NUMBER
3	A				S-NAME
4	A				S-STATUS
5	A				S-HOME-ADDRESS
6	A				S-HOME-PHONE
7	A				S-GRADUATION-EXPECTED-DATE
8	A				S_I-NUMBER<ADVISOR>
9	A				S_H-NAME
10	A	STUDENT	S_C-HIST		STUDENT.S_C-HISTORY
11	A			P	S-NUMBER
12	A			P	S_C_T-TAKEN
13	A			P	S_C-NUMBER-TAKEN
14	A				S_C-TITLE
15	A				S_C-HOURS-CREDIT-TAKEN
16	A				S_C-HOURS-CREDIT-EARNED
17	A				S_C-GRADE-EARNED
18	A	STUDENT	S_M-MAJR		STUDENT.S_M<MAJOR>
19	A			P	S-NUMBER
20	A			P	S_M<MAJOR>
21	A	STUDENT	S_M-MINR		STUDENT.S_M<MINOR>
22	A			P	S-NUMBER
23	A			P	S_M<MINOR>
24	A	STUDENT	S_DEG-PV		STUDENT.S-DEGREE-PREVIOUS
25	A			P	S-NUMBER
·26	A			P	S-DEGREE-TYPE-PREVIOUS
27	A				S-GRADUATION-PREVIOUS-DATE
28	A	STUDENT	S_R-#-AT		STUDENT.S_R-NUMBER-ATTENDING
29	A			P	S-NUMBER
30	A			P	S-TIME-START-ATTENDING
31	A			P	S-DAYOFWEEK-ATTENDING
32	A				S-TIME-END-ATTENDING
33	A				S_I-NAME<TEACHING>
34	B	COURSE			COURSE
35	B			P	C-NUMBER
36	B				C-TITLE
37	B				C_H-NAME-CURRICULUM
38	B				C-HOURS-CREDIT-MINIMUM
39	B				C-HOURS-CREDIT-MAXIMUM
40	B				C-CLASSSIZE-MINIMUM
41	B				C-CLASSSIZE-MAXIMUM
42	B				C-HOURS-DURATION
43	B	COURSE	C-PREREQ		COURSE.C-PREREQUSITE
44	B			P	C-NUMBER
45	B			P	C-NUMBER<PREREQUISITE>
46	B	COURSE	C_E-SPEC		COURSE.C_E-SPECIAL
47	B			P	C-NUMBER
48	B			P	C_E-EQUIPMENT-TYPE-SPECIAL
49	B	COURSE	C_T-TAKN		COURSE.C_T-TAKEN
50	B			P	C-NUMBER
51	B			P	C_T-GIVEN
52	B				C_S-TALLY-TAKEN

Figure 27.7 First normal form of the listing in Figure 27.6.

```
DISPLAY

NN    NN WW    WW LL       GGGGGG   222222   AAAA    DDDDD   TTTTTTT
NNN   NN WW    WW LL      GGGGGGGG 22222222  AAAAAA  DDDDDDD TTTTTTT
NNNN  NN WW    WW LL       GG   GG 22    22 AAA  AAA DD   DD    TT
NNNNN NN WW WW WW LL       GG           22 AA    AA DD   DD    TT
NN NNNNN WW WW WW LL       GG   GGGG   222  AAAAAAAA DD   DD    TT
NN  NNNN WWW  WWW LL       GG   GG    222  AAAAAAAA DD   DD    TT
NN   NNN WW    WW LLLLLLLL GGGGGGGG 22222222 AA    AA DDDDDD    TT
NN    NN W      W LLLLLLLL  GGGGGG  22222222 AA    AA DDDDD     TT

SEQ        DISPLAY OF  NWLG2ADT  FROM LIBRARY: ADP.PM.A200.PMLIB
NUMBER  1...5...10...15...20...25...30...35...40...45...50...55...60...65...70..
   1      1 RELATION: STUDENT.S_C-HISTORY          STUDENT.S_C-HIST
   2      2 ---------------------------------:---:-----------------------------
   3      3               KEY ITEM           :Y/N:        NON-KEY ITEM
   4      4 ---------------------------------:---:-----------------------------
   5      5 S-NUMBER                         : N : S_C-TITLE
   6      6 S_C_T-TAKEN                      : N :
   7      7 S_C-NUMBER-TAKEN                 : Y :
   8    NAME=S_C-TITLE                       ID=S_C-TIT
   9      9 S-NUMBER                         : Y : S_C-HOURS-CREDIT-TAKEN
  10     10 S_C_T-TAKEN                      : Y :
  11     11 S_C-NUMBER-TAKEN                 : Y :
  12    NAME=                                ID=
  13     13 S-NUMBER                         : Y : S_C-HOURS-CREDIT-EARNED
  14     14 S_C_T-TAKEN                      : Y :
  15     15 S_C-NUMBER-TAKEN                 : Y :
  16    NAME=                                ID=
  17     17 S-NUMBER                         : Y : S_C-GRADE-EARNED
  18     18 S_C_T-TAKEN                      : Y :
  19     19 S_C-NUMBER-TAKEN                 : Y :
  20    NAME=                                ID=

DISPLAY END:  NWLG2ADT
```

Figure 27.8   Decision table based on the listing in Figure 27.6.

SECOND NORMAL FORM

RPT LINE	USER CODES	PARENT IDENT	SUBORD IDENT	DATA NAME
1---------		11-----	21------	31----------------------------
1	A	STUDENT		STUDENT
2	A			P S-NUMBER
3	A			S-NAME
4	A			S-STATUS
5	A			S-HOME-ADDRESS
6	A			S-HOME-PHONE
7	A			S-GRADUATION-EXPECTED-DATE
8	A			S_I-NUMBER<ADVISOR>
9	A			S_H-NAME
10	A	STUDENT	S_C-HIST	STUDENT.S_C-HISTORY
11	A			P S-NUMBER
12	A			P S_C_T-TAKEN
13	A			P S_C-NUMBER-TAKEN
14	A			S_C-HOURS-CREDIT-TAKEN
15	A			S_C-HOURS-CREDIT-EARNED
16	A			S_C-GRADE-EARNED
17	A	S_C-TIT		S_C-TITLE
18	A			P S_C-NUMBER-TAKEN
19	A			S_C-TITLE
20	A	STUDENT	S_M-MAJR	STUDENT.S_M<MAJOR>
21	A			P S-NUMBER
22	A			P S_M<MAJOR>
23	A	STUDENT	S_M-MINR	STUDENT.S_M<MINOR>
24	A			P S-NUMBER
25	A			P S_M<MINOR>
26	A	STUDENT	S_DEG-PV	STUDENT.S-DEGREE-PREVIOUS
27	A			P S-NUMBER
28	A			P S-DEGREE-TYPE-PREVIOUS
29	A			S-GRADUATION-PREVIOUS-DATE
30	A	STUDENT	S_R-#-AT	STUDENT.S_R-NUMBER-ATTENDING
31	A			P S-NUMBER
32	A			P S-TIME-START-ATTENDING
33	A			P S-DAYOFWEEK-ATTENDING
34	A			S-TIME-END-ATTENDING
35	A			S_I-NAME<TEACHING>
36	B	COURSE		COURSE
37	B			P C-NUMBER
38	B			C-TITLE
39	B			C_H-NAME-CURRICULUM
40	B			C-HOURS-CREDIT-MINIMUM
41	B			C-HOURS-CREDIT-MAXIMUM
42	B			C-CLASSSIZE-MINIMUM
43	B			C-CLASSSIZE-MAXIMUM
44	B			C-HOURS-DURATION
45	B	COURSE	C-PREREQ	COURSE.C-PREREQUSITE
46	B			P C-NUMBER
47	B			P C-NUMBER<PREREQUISITE>
48	B	COURSE	C_E-SPEC	COURSE.C_E-SPECIAL
49	B			P C-NUMBER
50	B			P C_E-EQUIPMENT-TYPE-SPECIAL
51	B	COURSE	C_T-TAKN	COURSE.C_T-TAKEN

Figure 27.9 Second normal form of the listing in Figure 27.6.

Most of the software produces the logical database in some form of Codd relational notational, whereas most people would like some graphic model. DESIGN produces a DBTG (Bachman) model (Figure 27.10), and Data Designer produces a canonical model (Figure 27.11).

Various companies—such as Cincom with its Supra DBMS—have announced the availability of software tools to perform first-cut DBMS physical design from graphic models. AI devotees are also discussing the creation of an expert language to perform final physical design. Companies will also offer timing software to allow the database designer to perform "what if" studies to optimize the physical database.

The diagramming tools listed can be used to decompose the functions and/or data further to their atomic components, thereby providing the programming specification. Jackson, Orr, and 3D provide code generators to produce code automatically. I use pseudo-COBOL in combination with SS/80 (ADPAC) to produce structure charts (Figure 27.12), cross-reference reports, and snake reports (see Figure 15.1) as a programming specification.

As stated in Part 2, some companies have written structured engines to convert spaghetti COBOL code to structured code. These companies include Peat Marwick (Structure Engine), Group Operation (Super Structure), Language Technologies (Recoder), and IBM (Structuring Facility).

Many companies have software that produces source-driven documentation from existing COBOL programs.

SDLCs cannot be shortchanged, but they can be shortened by the intelligent use of software productivity tools.

NOTES

1. Stradis is a methodology marketed by McAuto; other methodologies include DSSD (Orr), Method 1 (Arthur Andersen), SDM-70 (Spectra), PSA/PSL (Meta Systems/IBM), and CONCEPT 90 (Deloitte, Haskins & Sells).

2. Physical database is used in its general sense; it could be a DBMS or a file access method such as VSAM.

3. A design unit is a unit of work to be performed by one clerk, one online transaction, or one batch program.

4. A structure chart is a graphic portrait of the hierarchy of a program structure; it can be done before coding as the programming specification and/or to display or verify the program structure.

5. A methodology is an SDLC blueprint; a tool is something that can be used within the blueprint for a specific purpose.

6. A minispec is usually a page of "structured English" used to describe the business processes required to fulfill a process box (function).

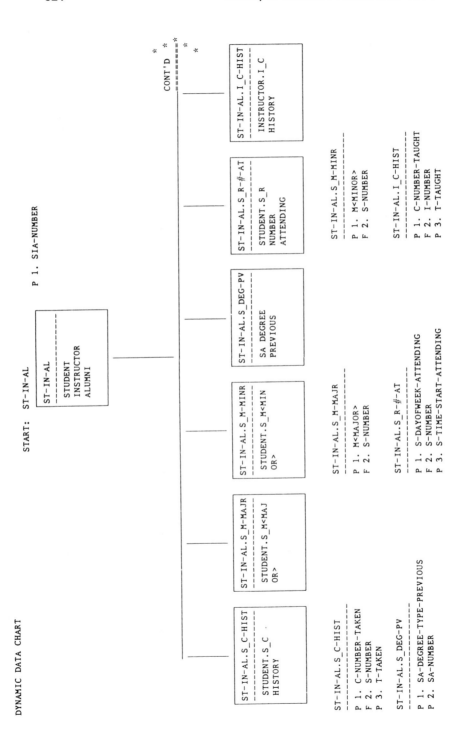

Figure 27.10 DBTG diagram (DESIGN).

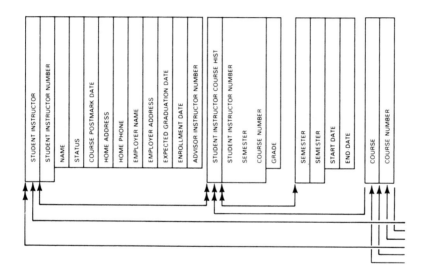

Figure 27.11 Canonical model (Data Designer).

STRUCTURE CHART – PROCESS 120 – LOGIC UNIVERSITY

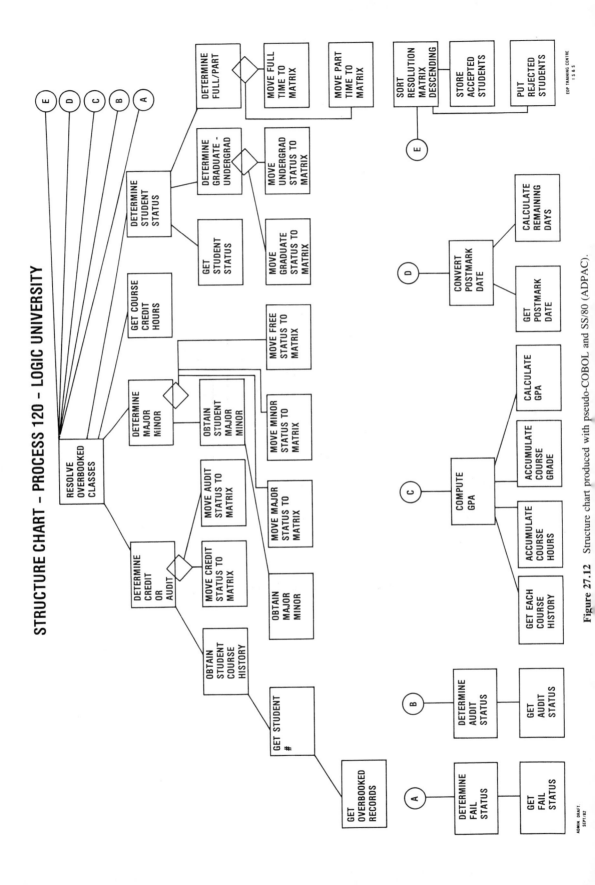

Figure 27.12 Structure chart produced with pseudo-COBOL and SS/80 (ADPAC).

EDP TRAINING CENTRE
I S & S

ADMIN DRAFT
SEP/82

28

Productivity Assessment

The independent productivity assessment abstract is included to provide outside proof that the rapid application development system described in Chapters 25–27 does produce quality software within budget and time frame. Many clients have used the same general approach, with similar results.

The project assessed was a DBMS designed, programmed, and tested by The Analyst Workbench to support an integrated office automation package (including word processing, spreadsheet, and graphics) for the AT&T 3B series computers.

The assessment speaks for itself; you or your company can achieve the same results through the intelligent use of software productivity tools to shorten the SDLC without shortchanging it!

PRODUCTIVITY ASSESSMENT OF A DATABASE MANAGEMENT SYSTEM

As part of our survey process we have performed a quantitative evaluation of your Database Management System.

The measures used in our assessment are:

- Productivity Index
- Manpower Buildup Index
- Source Statements per Manmonth
- Source Statements per Month
- Total Effort
- Schedule
- Average Manpower

DATABASE MANAGEMENT SYSTEM (TOTAL SIZE: 100,000 C)

Measure	Value	Assessment
Productivity Index	18	Very high—8 Higher than system software average
Manpower Buildup Index	2	Gradual buildup
Average Staffing	5 people	Lower than database average—efficient utilization of people
Effort	60 manmonths	Lower than database average—very cost-effective development
Schedule	12 months	Well below database average—very short delivery time
Code Production	8333 lines/month	Much higher than database average
Productivity	1666 lines/manmonth	Well above the database average

Summary

All quantitative measures on the Database Management System indicate that the developers were extremely efficient. This system would fall in the top 5% of all the Systems Software applications that QSM has measured in the US, Western Europe and Japan.

Douglas T. Putnam
Director of Marketing
Quantitative Software Management, Inc.

A

Programming Machine/Standard Solutions:[1] Application 4—Data Name Rationalization and Building the Data Dictionary

Data-name rationalization is the procedure used to identify all of the same physical data elements in a system of code, regardless of their given names, and reassigning each a unique self identify name. There are many steps in the complete procedure. Some of these PM/SS fully automates, others require man/machine interaction. Once a "clean" list of unique names has been prepared, they can be globally substituted throughout the system. As the final step, PM/SS automatically creates the particular input file required for virtually any data dictionary such as DATAMANAGER, DB/DC, IDMS, etc.

Most data dictionaries include procedures for converting existing COBOL record layouts into data dictionary input. Unfortunately, while there is a great deal of software available to perform this mechanical step, *it is undesirable to enter data elements into a dictionary in this manner.* The difficulty is that the existing COBOL programs contain the accumulated history of improper names (aliases) that, once entered into the dictionary, are difficult to remove. Thus, when these methods have been applied, the integrity of the data dictionary is compromised and, therefore, its usefulness diminished.

Application Nos. 3, 8, and 9 should also be read, since they contain additional analysis relevant to the subject of data dictionary development and other data administration functions.

Acknowledgments

Data-name rationalization, as this subject matter is now called, is an everyday assignment at The Catalyst Group of Peat Marwick. The general concepts outlined in this Application were expanded on, and made a very practical tool, by the following members of their organization.

Peat Marwick
The Catalyst Group
303 East Wacker Drive
Chicago, Ill. 60601
Tel: (312) 938–1000

Jon Cris Miller, Partner
Albert J. Travis, Senior Manager
Marc D. Gimbel, Analyst

Blue Cross and Blue Shield of Greater New York provided Adpac with a great deal of technical assistance in interfacing PM/SS to the DATAMANAGER dictionary. The following members of the BC/BS organization made significant contributions to the success of this phase of the application.

Blue Cross/Blue Shield of Greater New York
622 Third Ave.
New York, N.Y. 10017
Tel: (212) 490–4871

Harvey M. Smith, Jr., CDP, DBA Manager
Tony Gordon, Senior DA Analyst
William Colangelo, Analyst
Alexander Gollinge, DA Analyst

Functional Task List

1. Library member identification
2. Initial attribute list
3. Homonym identification
4. Synonym identification
5. Alias identification
6. Renaming
7. Preparing the WAS/IS list
8. Substitution of data-names
9. Substitution validation
10. Special problems
11. Entering the data elements into the dictionary
12. Entering other data into the dictionary
13. Entering process information into the dictionary

Glossary of Terms

Before beginning the procedural analysis it will be helpful to define some standard terms that will be used throughout this application.

Logical length   The length of the item that would result if all edit characters were removed from its PICTURE clause, except for the codes X, A, B, or 9. Thus an item's logical length is not affected by the picture codes V or P used to specify an implied decimal point, or any of the special edit characters such as: $, . ∗ CR DB, etc. Note also that an item's logical length is not affected by its COMP, SYNCH, OCCURS, or VALUE clauses.

Homonym   Two data elements with identical data-names but with *different logical lengths.*

Synonym   Two data elements with identical data-names and the *same logical lengths,* but with different picture clauses.

Alias   A single data element that has two or more data-names pertaining to the same physical element. Each data element will have the same logical length, regardless of the differences in their pictures.

Derived elements   An element that is operated upon in the Procedure Division and is the result of a data transfer or computation.

1. LIBRARY MEMBER IDENTIFICATION

The first task is to identify all of the members of the source library (programs) and Copylib members that pertain to the system being studied. Data elements may be located either in the COBOL programs or in separate Copylib (or Include) members. Furthermore, such members may be contained in one or more libraries resident throughout the entire operating system. In some cases, members may be all contained in one PDS, in other cases they are intermixed in a consolidated library masterfile such as PANVALET.

Before we can analyze all of the data elements that are contained in one system, we must first identify all of the members of the system. Refer to Application No. 2, Vector Processing, for a complete description of the various methods of performing this step.

2. INITIAL ATTRIBUTE LIST

Let us assume that we have now created a processing vector (MLIST), or have otherwise segregated all of the relevant members for processing in various PM/SS runs. The first run(s) are to create an Attribute List of data elements contained anywhere in the Data Division of all the members in the application system. This can be done by the following 2 runs:

Run 2a: @PM INPUT:

```
---> @PM. ATTRIBUTE  MLIST-SYSXC
---> @PM              SOURCE-COPYLIB
---> @PM              CATAL-SYSXATLC
```

MLIST-SYSXC: SOURCE-COPYLIB   SYSXC is the member name of the MLIST that contains the vector of all Copylib members. This Attribute List is based upon the elements found only in the Copylib members. If Include members (in the primary source library) are used in place of, or in addition to the Copylib, a second run using an appropriate MLIST should be done.

The following attributes will be retained for each data element.

1. Member name
2. Program Ident
3. Level number
4. Data name
5. Library indicator (C)
6. Record sequence number
7. Positional location
8. Logical length
9. Physical length
10. Occurs
11. Picture
12. Data format code
13. Value
14. 01 level record name
15. Next higher group level
16. Next higher group data-name
17. Redefines name
18. Indexed by name
19. 88 level data-names and values

Run 2b: @PM INPUT:

```
---> @PM ATTRIBUTE  MLIST-SYSXP
---> @PM             COPY-NO, INC-NO
---> @PM             CATAL-SYSXATLP
```

COPY-NO,INC-NO   This run is almost identical to Run 2a, except that it processes the Data Division of the programs in the MLIST-SYSXP, but excludes the "explosion" of their Copylib (and Include) members. Note that preparing two separate lists in this manner is more efficient than a single run involving all programs and expanding their COPY statements. Obviously, if this were done, each COPY statement would be unnecessarily reprocessed each time it was encountered. This would require an additional run to drop the duplicates.

3. HOMONYM IDENTIFICATION

Homonyms are two data elements with identical names but different logical lengths. PM/SS will automatically detect and mark homonyms in the Attribute list. Of all of the misnomers in a system of code, the homonym is the most offensive, and should be eliminated. Elements within the same name but different logical lengths are clearly different items, that can only add continued confusion to the maintenance programmers.

Run 3a: @PM INPUT:

```
---> @PM. LIST  ATLIST = (SYSXATLC,SYSXATLP)
---> @PM        CATAL = SYSXATL1
---> @PM        HOMONYM
```

LV No.	Data Name	Logical Length	From–To	Format Picture	N Y
03	CHRG-CODE	1	219	ALPNUM X	
03	CHRG-CODE	2	38–39	ALPNUM XX	H
07	CLASS-CODE	1	7	ALPNUM X	
03	RPT-CLIENT	12	17–28	ALPNUM X(12)	
03	RPT-CLIENT	14	29–42	ALPNUM X(14)	H
05	CC4-CLIENT-NAME	30	17–46	ALPNUM X(30)	
05	CC4-CLIENT-NAME	10	7–16	ALPNUM X(10)	H
07	CC4-CLIENT-NO	4	2–5	ALPNUM X(4)	
03	MS-COMMENT	36	357–392	ALPNUM X(36)	
03	TR4-COMMENT	30	17–46	ALPNUM X(30)	
03	RPT-COMMENT2	14	337–350	ALPNUM X(14)	
03	RPT-COMMENT2	30	47–76	ALPNUM X(30)	H

Homonym The letter H will be placed in position 68 of the homonym data-name record (Record-1) of the Attribute List.

A second homonym run can also be made if the record or program prefixing has been used. Record prefixes such as TR- (for transaction), IN- (for input), etc., are commonly found in older systems of Cobol code. The use of the PREFIX-IGNORE option marks the attribute list just as in Run 3a above, but the comparison ignores the prefix of each data-name. The option SUFFIX-IGNORE may also be used with or without the PREFIX option.

Run 3b: @PM INPUT:

```
---> @PM. LIST  ATLIST = SYSXATL1
---> @PM        CATAL = SYSXATL2
---> @PM        PREFIX = IGNORE
```

4. SYNONYM IDENTIFICATION

Synonyms are two data elements with identical data-names and logical lengths, but with different pictures. PM/SS will automatically mark synonyms. Synonyms are usually obvious variations in the same data element's picture to allow for different input/output formats required by the computer's processing language. Most dictionary systems have a means of carrying a synonym indicator field.

      Run 4a: @PM INPUT:

```
---> @PM. LIST  ATLIST = SYSXATL2
---> @PM        CATAL = SYSXATL3
---> @PM        SYNONYM
```

Synonym The letter S will be placed in position 68 of the synonym data-name record (Record-1) of the Attribute List.

      If record prefixing has been used, the same run (as in Run 4a) using the PREFIX-IGNORE option will frequently find many more synonyms, by ignoring data-name prefixes (or suffixes if the SUFFIX-IGNORE option is used).

5. ALIAS IDENTIFICATION

To begin with, it should be recognized that alias identification is more of an art than a science. For that reason, this description should not be regarded as a universal set of rules to be applied in all cases. Rather it shows a series of typical runs that can be made that should yield a very high percentage of successful alias name identifications.

      An alias is a single data element that has two or more data-names pertaining to the same physical element. Each data element will have the same logical length but need not have the same picture.

      It is agreed by most analysts that the identification of aliases is the most difficult problem to resolve in a system of programs. If the system has been maintained over a number of years, with many people adding to and modifying the programs, the same physical field may be known under many different names. Under these circumstances, the same physical element, with different names, may occur in many different record layouts and in different positional locations, etc.

      To further explain, let us take the case of a field that is called "zip code." When the programs were first developed, the name ZIP-CODE describing a five byte numeric field may have been a unique data-name. When other programmers added additional code, they may have used other abbreviations such as Z-CODE, etc. In many systems, a prefix was sometimes given to the same field to denote whether it is to be found on a transaction record or a master record, etc.

      Certainly it is not appropriate to enter all of these different names for the same field into the data dictionary. What we are trying to achieve here is to find all of the implied uses of the same physical field "zip code," and to find all variations in its name.

Alias identification here is based primarily upon the "data transfer rule." Under this rule, all pairs (or sets) of data-names involved in a data transfer instruction (MOVE) that are not homonyms or synonyms, are highly likely to be aliases. Furthermore, this pairing can be traced across program boundaries, so that all data transfer sets involving all common data elements may be collected into a single alias group. Consider the following case:

Program 1:

```
MOVE D-DESC TO D-FUNC
MOVE D-FUNC TO FUNC-CODE
```

Program 2:

```
MOVE FUNC-CODE TO CC2-DC-ID-PRE
```

Most analysts might agree that all of the data-names used above are probably aliases of each other. As will be seen this is a good first assumption, but it is not necessarily true of all such relations. The exceptions will be discussed later in this report (see Section 10), after the basic alias identification procedures have been presented.

Run 5a: @PM INPUT:

```
---> @PM. DNAMES  MLIST = SYSXP
---> @PM          DTRANS
---> @PM          CATAL = SYSXDNL1
```

DTRANS The DTRANS options cause the standard @PM.DNAMES function to modify its normal processing rules in the following ways:

1. Only the Procedure Division of each program will be processed.
2. Only MOVE instructions with two or more data-names will be provided.
3. The XREF field in the DNLIST, positions 62–67, are set to the line number of the data transfer MOVE instruction. Thus, even instructions in the form:

```
MOVE A TO B
          C
          D
```

will all have the same XREF number. This number will be used in the @PM.DTRANSFER run shown next, to identify each data transfer set.

Run 5b: @PM.INPUT:

```
---> @PM.DTRANS  DNLIST=SYSXDNL1
---> @PM         ATLIST=SYSXATL3
---> @PM         CATAL=SYSXATL4
```

DNLIST=SYSXDNL1; ATLIST=(SYSXATLC,SYSXATLP)   Both the data-name and the attribute lists previously created are now brought together to prepare the complete data transfer list. A unique 5 digit number is placed in position 2–6 of each ATLIST record of each alias group. Naturally, elements shown in the printed report that have their attributes displayed were taken from the ATLIST, while those that do not were taken from the DNLIST.

It is important that all data transfer elements of a group be shown in the list as all of its corresponding attributes, in order to facilitate the data administrator's analysis of those elements that are truly aliases, homonyms, synonyms, etc. Unlike the output of the earlier runs, this report should be printed. The printed report will make it somewhat easier to analyze the output of later runs that will be viewed using SPF Browse, Edit, and the Worksheets.

User Code	Member Name	Program Ident	LV No	Data Name	Logical Length
00001	PC34	PC34		CC1-EMP-FULL-NAME	
00001	PC34	PC34		CC1-EMP-FULL-NAME	
00001	PC34	PC34	05	D-EMP-NAME	30
00001	PC34	PC34	05	D-EMP-NAME	30
00002	PC34	PC34		CC2-DATA-CEN-NAME	
00002	PC34	PC34	03	DC-NAME	30
00003	PC34	PC34		CC2-DC-ID-SUF	
00003	PC34	PC34	03	DC-SUF	2
00004	PC34	PC34	05	D-DESC	42
00004	PC34	PC34	05	D-FUNC	2
00004	PC34	PC34	03	FUNC-CODE	40
00004	PC34	PC34		CC2-DC-ID-PRE	
00004	PC34	PC34	03	DC-PRE	2

Data Element Worksheets

To assist data administration in the very comprehensive task of identifying unique data elements and assigning them new names, a Worksheet describing each existing data-name found anywhere in the system should be created. This Worksheet, one page per data-name, contains all the attributes of each element. It also should contain space for users or analysts to enter additional narrative or other formatted fields, that may be entered into the data dictionary. Consider the following illustrative Data Command Model that will be used in Run 5c to actually create the Worksheet page for each data-name.

DATA ELEMENT WORKSHEET

	Group: &2,6
Data name	: &DNAME
Located in Copylib	: &MEMBER
On line number	: &XREF
In record	: &RNAME
Contained in group	: &GNAME
Positional location	: &LOCAT
Logical length	: &LENGTH
Physical length	: &BYTES
Picture	: &PICTURE
Redefines	: &REDEF
Homonym Synonym code	: &NYM
Indexed by	: &IBNAME
Occurs	: &OCCURS TIMES

NEW NAME IS: _____

DESCRIPTION: _____

_____

_____

_____

RANGE OF VALUES: _____

_____

_____

SUBMITTED BY: _____ APPROVED BY: _____

Run 5c: @PM INPUT:

```
@PM.DATA  DCMODEL=WRKMOD
@PM       ATLIST=SYSXATLC
@PM       ETS+ELEMENT,DICT=NO,FIXED
```

ETS=ELEMENT,DICT=NO,FIXED   To suppress the preparation of a dictionary relational structure that is the default assumption when processing an ATLIST. The following is one such example of a Worksheet page. Additional runs similar to Run 5c may be made for the data elements found in the Data Division of the program, etc.

GROUP: 0009

1	DATA NAME	: FUNC-CODE
2	LOCATED IN COPYLIB	: PC34
3	ON LINE MEMBER	: 000484
4	IN RECORD	: FUNCTION-RECORD
5	CONTAINED IN GROUP	: FUNCTION-GROUP
6	POSITIONAL LOCATION	: 1
7	LOGICAL LENGTH	: 40
8	PHYSICAL LENGTH	: 40
9	PICTURE	: X(40)
10	REDEFINES	:
11	HOMONYM SYNONYM CODE	:
12	INDEXED BY	:
13	OCCURS	: 25 TIMES

14
15 NEW NAME IS: _____
16
17 DESCRIPTION: _____
18 _____
19 _____
20 _____
21
22 RANGE OF VALUES: _____
23 _____
24 _____
25
26 SUBMITTED BY: _____ APPROVED BY: _____

It should be emphasized that identifying all unique data element name groups, and giving the appropriate ones a unique new name, is the technical substance of the data-name rationalization project. This is, of course, the most difficult and time consuming part of the project. As will be seen, the mechanics of substitution are quite straightforward. The most difficult steps are establishing the data-name standards and control policies.

As a minimum, most of the policies and procedures described in Application No. 8 (Data Name Validation) must be in place before data-name assignment and substitution can be done. As a part of this overall procedure, data administration must develop their own control procedures to correlate the Worksheets prepared by Run 5c with the special homonym, synonym, and DTRANS reports, etc.

6. SOME SUGGESTIONS ABOUT RENAMING

More and more organizations are developing specific, and in some cases quite sophisticated, naming standards or conventions. The following are some DO's and DON'Ts that have been frequently observed as they apply to data dictionaries.

For dictionizing purposes, potential data-names should be defined without consideration of the requirements of the programming language's requirements for uniqueness. The Cobol language has several methods of allowing the same record layout to be addressed differently in the Procedure Division, e.g., qualified (OF) names, or the COPY REPLACING option.

Similarly, most data dictionaries have record layout "synthesis" techniques to allow a prefix or suffix to be added to each data element's name for purposes of compilation.

Except for such computation uniqueness, data-name construction rules are usually based upon:

1. A simple, honest, meaningful name, or standard syllable abbreviation
2. A (user) responsibility code or Entity Type
3. A data type Classification description

ENTITY TYPE (3 character):

> PCH: purchasing
> EMP: employee
> SAL: sales
> CUS: customer

Another component (syllable) of a complete data-name is its data "class." These are frequently entered as a suffix.

CLASS (3 character):

> AMT: dollar amount
> QTY: quantity
> CNT: counter
> TOT: total accumulation
> SWI: switch

Refer to Application No. 8 for a complete description of various data-name validation runs that can be made by PM/SS.

7. PREPARING THE WAS/IS LIST

We will now assume that all, or a significant volume of the Worksheets have been completed, in preparation for the actual data-name substitution phase. To simplify this initial explanation of the complete data-name rationalization procedure, the special and more difficult cases will be deferred until later in this report. For the moment, let us assume that the procedures used so far have perfectly identified all aliases. However, this complete procedure should be studied before making actual production runs. It will also increase your understanding of these procedures to make a few experimental runs on a small subset of members. Actually seeing examples of the output of these runs based upon your program files will add considerable insight into the entire process. The Attribute List SYSXATL3 output from Run 5b is the source of input to form the WAS/IS list used for the data-name substitution process.

Run 7a: @PM INPUT:

```
---> @PM LIST  ATLIST=SYSXATL3
---> @PM        SORT=(LIBRARY,MEMBER,XREF)
---> @PM        CATAL=(SYSXWIL,WILIST)
```

SORT=(LIBRARY,MEMBER,XREF)   The Attribute List that now contains each element's alias group name (in position 2–6), is now sorted into a sequence that will facilitate the preparation of the WAS/IS substitution lists. Sorting by the fields shown here will cause all of the elements, by copylib, etc., to be grouped together. This is in the same order that renaming and substituting will be done.

CATAL=(SYSXWIL,WILIST)   At this time only the data-name information needs to be retained, and the more extensive attribute data dropped. Using the 2 parameter forms of the CATAL statement, the WILIST option value creates the WAS portion of the WAS/IS list, leaving a blank space for the desired IS name. Manual data entry is now used to place the new name from the Worksheet into the WAS/IS list. This step is usually done via normal interactive member editing procedures.

8. SUBSTITUTION OF DATA-NAMES

Substitution by Subsystem Groups

Depending upon the size of the complete system being rationalized, the actual process of substitution should be done as a series of runs, each dealing with a manageable set of records and their related programs. This description suggests some of the run groupings that seem practical in a typical situation: First, substitution runs must always be done in at least two runs: (1) the Copylib and/or Include library records; and (2) their corresponding programs. If it is desirable to process small groups (subsystems) of programs, rather than the entire system at one time, the programs must still be grouped by their Copylib records. To perform the grouping the following runs should be made.

Run 8a: @PM INPUT:

```
---> @PM.COPY ALL=SYSX,CATAL=SYSXCOP1
```

Separate process vectors may be selected from this list that will insure that all of the programs that use only certain Copylib records will be processed together.

Unique Name Validation

Before the actual substitution runs are made, the new names must first be validated to insure that they are not already in use. This is done by the following two search runs. These two runs insure that all of the IS names that are to be substituted into the current programs are not already in use. The rationale for performing this function in two separate runs is the same as applied to Runs 2a and 2b earlier.

Run 8b: @PM INPUT:

```
---> @PM.DNAME  MLIST=SYSXC,KWIC
---> @PM         DNLIST=SYSXWIL
---> @PM         SOURCE=COPYLIB
```

Run 8c: @PM INPUT:

```
---> @PM.DNAME  MLIST=SYSXP,KWIC
---> @PM         DNLIST=SYSXWIL
---> @PM         COPY=NO,INC-NO
```

DNLIST=SYSXWIL In this case the WILIST is treated as a DNLIST. Thus, the IS names in positions 31–60 will form the second argument to be used by the @PM.DNAMES search function.

KWIC To report on the entire record on which a "hit" occurs.

All names appearing in this report must be examined and the duplicates ("hits") resolved, before the final @PM.REFORMAT substitution run can be made.

Copylib Substitution

The final substitution run uses the @PM.REFORMAT function of WHERE. In addition to performing the data-name substitutions, if the REFORM-NO option is not entered (to suppress the feature), each member will also be reformatted as part of the substitution process. Refer to the PM/SS Reference Manual for a complete description of the reformatting rules.

As with Runs 2a/2b and 3a/3b, this substitution function should be done in two separate runs. Run 8d applies to the copylib records and Run 8e applies to the programs. Before submitting the substitution Run 8d, the following additional steps should be done.

1. Review the @PM.REFORMAT section of the PM/SS Reference manual to see what custom options are preferred for your circumstances. Make any necessary modifications to the PMRUNSTD member in your PMLIB.

2. Perform a sample run on any member of the Cobol source library. Cataloging the results of that sample run is not necessary. The only purpose of this run is to obtain a sample of the reformatted program to make sure it is satisfactory to your standards.

3. Examine the allocation size of the OUTLIB PDS to insure that there will be sufficient space to receive all of the programs that are performed.

Run 8d: @PM INPUT:

```
---> @PM.REFORMAT  MLIST=COPYSET1
---> @PM                SOURCE=COPYLIB
---> @PM                WILIST=SYSXWIL
---> @PM                CATAL=*
```

WILIST=SYSXWIL; CATAL=* All of the Copylib records in the MLIST have their WAS names replaced by their IS names if the Copylib member name in position 61–70 of the WAS/IS list corresponds to the Copylib member being processed. If position 61–70 of any line of the WAS/IS list is blank, such names will be globally substituted wherever they occur. If position 1 of the IS name field (position 31) is blank, no substitution of the WAS name will be done.

Program Substitution

Run 8e: @PM INPUT:

```
---> @PM.REFORMAT  MLIST=PGMSET1
---> @PM                WILIST=SYSXWIL,CATAL-*
```

CATAL=* The updated Copylib members will be cataloged in the DDNAME=OUTLIB library. The CATAL=* form of this option specifies that the name given to the reformatted member in OUTLIB is the same name it is cataloged in SYSLIB (or COPYLIB). If it is desirable to change its name, it may be done by entering each new member name in positions 21–28 of the MLIST input control vector. If position 21 of the MLIST is blank this also specifies that the output name is the same as the input name.

Before submitting this run, the list of program member names that will be cataloged in OUTLIB should be examined to ensure they do not conflict with names already placed there in Run 8d.

MLIST=PGMSET1 This vector should be created from member names selected from the original Copylib vector SYSXCOPY1 created in Run 8a. The members processed here should correspond to the same programs whose Copylib records were used in Run 8d.

WILIST=SYSXWIL Using the member-name field in position 61–70, the data administrator has complete control over the data-names that will be substituted in each program. Those data-names that can be substituted globally will have positions 61–70 set to blanks, while those that are unique to a specific program must have the member name of the program in positions 61–70 of the corresponding line of the WILIST.

9. SUBSTITUTION VALIDATION

If care is exercised in managing the WAS/IS list, with regard to the old name, new name, and the members being modified, a complete system of programs may be retrofitted with complete assurance that the executable code will not have been altered in any way whatsoever.

The accuracy of this procedure can be assured by comparing the complete load module before and after substitution. That is, both before and after substitution is done, each program should be compiled and linked into two different load libraries. Members of these libraries can be easily compared using any compare utility program, such as IEBCOMPR. If differences occur, then the printed address storage map should be examined. In most cases the improper name substitution field can be immediately found and usually obvious corrective action taken. Such reprocessing should be very infrequent, or else a tighter management of the WAS/IS list preparation procedures should be instituted before proceeding with the substitution of other members.

Validation of results, purely on the basis of the load module comparison should be sufficient validation and complete program retesting should not be necessary. As a special note, care must also be taken to assure that both the pre and post compilation runs are done using the exact same version of the COBOL compiler, and the same compiler options.

10. SPECIAL PROBLEMS

The previous discussion described the standard data-name rationalization procedure without any difficult or unusual cases. This section, which will probably be continuously expanded in succeeding versions based upon user contributions, describes some of the more frequently occurring problems.

Common Working Storage Data-Names

Consider the following example:

Program 1:

```
MOVE TR-AMT-PD  TO WORK-8N
MOVE WORK-8N    TO MF-AMOUNT-PD
```

Program 2:

```
MOVE MF-AMOUNT-PD  TO GLA-PD-VALUE
MOVE AMOUNT-DUE    TO WORK-8N
```

In this case, since WORK-8N is related to both AMOUNT-PD and AMOUNT-DUE, both fields will be incorrectly grouped into a single alias group prepared by the @PM.DTRAN (Run 5b). If this is a relatively rare occurrence, the problem can be ignored, since when each data-name of each alias group is studied, it will usually be apparent that those names are related as true aliases and those that are not. If there are many instances of using such common working storage fields (usually done in older systems to save storage space), the problem should be dealt with.

To absolutely minimize the coupling coefficient of a system, no such common data-name elements should be used. Theoretically, and ideally, each "module" of a system, where a module may be defined as either a whole program, ENTRY section, or a paragraph within a program, should have its own set of unique data-names. In most structured programming methodologies, common names would only be used when data is required to cross a program boundary, e.g., a record, or record segment, etc.

Thus, even within a single program it is generally regarded as poorer coding technique (with regard to maintenance difficulty) to share common work areas, simply to save space. If it is determined to actually eliminate this problem as part of the data-name rationalization procedure, some code changes will have to be made.

In this example, all code involving any use of WORK-8N throughout the system should be changed. The change can be as slight as suffixing each use with a unique character. If several different unrelated uses of the same field are located within the same program, a corresponding new data element should be entered in the working storage area of the program. Whenever any changes are made, the program should be recompiled and cataloged for use in the substitution validation step 9 described earlier.

Upon completion of this phase of analysis, Runs 2a and 3a should be redone using the revised set of data transfer groupings. The new alias group report prepared by Run 5b will be a more accurate alias report. This accuracy will have additional payoff in the later manual steps using the Data Transfer Report, and the Worksheets, in making the final determination of alias elements.

Copylib Creation

This is the ideal time to establish better Copylib usage policies. The following are several policies that are commonly used. Naturally, practical variations of these policies should be developed as the programming standards for each organization.

1. Any 01 level record that contains any data element(s) used in more than one compilable load module should be placed in a Copylib.

2. Any 01 level record that contains any data element(s) transferred to or from a system input or output source (or sink), e.g., SYSIN, SYSPRINT, SCREEN, etc., should be placed in a Copylib. These are usually the "external" data elements that are "viewed" by the end user, and hence the data that is most subject to maintenance activity.

3. A more extreme policy that extends the rule stated in 1 above is: Any subordinate level record segment (a non-01 level) that contains any data element(s) used by more than one PERFORMed subroutine within a program, should be rearranged into a separate Copylib record. Thus, paragraph structures, that ideally should also be single function processes, should have separate 01 level records containing only their required data structures. This rule will significantly reduce the coupling coef-

ficient of a program, and in the long run will lead to a much higher ratio of reusable code, which of course, is highly desirable.

11. ENTERING THE DATA ELEMENTS INTO THE DICTIONARY

PM/SS does not write directly into each of the different data dictionary processors. Rather, it provides a general purpose method of creating the actual input file that virtually any data dictionary scheme might require. There are several custom options (in the PMRUNSTD custom record) that accommodate the slight differences in various dictionary processors e.g., DICTIONARY, DCTYPE.

In PM/SS, the dictionary input file is called a Data Command List (DCLIST). It is created simply by bringing together in one SYNTH run; (1) a set of model instructions of the Data Commands required by the specific data dictionary product; and (2) the data to be entered (ATLIST). There are a number of complete run examples at the end of this application report that show the use of this technique.

Naturally, before the run that will actually create the DCLIST is performed, a new Attribute List, using the fully-substituted records has been created. The final attribute list is produced by performing the same 2 runs as was done in Runs 2a, 2b.

Run 11a: @PM INPUT:

```
---> @PM.ATTRIBUTE  MLIST=SYSXC
---> @PM            SOURCE=COPYLIB
---> @PM            CATAL=SYSXATLC
```

Run 11b: @PM INPUT:

```
---> @PM.ATTRIBUTE  MLIST=SYSXP,COPY=NO
---> @PM            CATAL=SYSXATLP
```

The actual Data Command List being processed depends upon the particular dictionary being used. The following is an example of the @PM control statements required for creating a complete relational input file for the DATAMANAGER dictionary in the INSERT format.

Run 11c: @PM INPUT:

```
---> @PM.DATA  ATLIST=SYSXATL,DCMODEL=SYSXDCM
---> @PM       DICTIONARY=DMAN,DCTYPE=INSERT
---> @PM       CATAL=SYSDCL
```

Simply by changing the DICTIONARY = option, the data in the same ATLIST may be prepared for input to any one of the following dictionaries.

```
DICT-DB/DC  IBM, DB/DC
DICT-DDICT  ADR, DATA DICTIONARY
DICT-DMAN   MSP, DATAMANAGER
DICT-IDD    CULLINET, IDD
```

If the PMRUNSTD record in the PMLIB has been customized to the proper dictionary usage standards, and a standard ATLIST model is used, then only the ATLIST and CATAL options are required. The other options will be automatically invoked based upon the PMRUNSTD option values.

Run 11d: @PM INPUT:

```
---> @PM.DATA  ATLIST=SYSXATL
---> @PM        CATAL=SYSXDCL
```

Note also that the PREFIX-NO or PREFIX-IGNORE (or SUFFIX) option may also be used to control the inclusion or exclusion of a prefix or suffix in the DCLIST. PREFIX-NO is the assumed default.

All that remains now is to actually perform the input run(s) required by each data dictionary product using the Data Command List SYSXDCL. This step is not described here, since it is too specific to each installation's standard operating system procedures. There are a number of complete examples at the end of this Application that show the Data Command Lists that can be created using the same ATLIST.

12. ENTERING OTHER DATA INTO THE DICTIONARY

A Word of Caution

It must be pointed out that because of the ease by which PM/SS can allow users to extract and enter information into data dictionaries, this horsepower should not be abused. *That is, not everything that can be entered into the dictionary should be entered.* For example, since PM/SS can so easily prepare a list of "where used" COPY member names, it is questionable as to whether this information should be entered in the dictionary, since it will also require continuing maintenance. Thus, each user should adopt policies that compromise these and other related questions before building a data dictionary that may eventually become an obsolete dinosaur, rather than the workhorse that it was originally envisioned to be.

The following are a set of runs that can be made to catalog various types of source code information, and, thereby, may also be entered into a dictionary.

Function	*Description*
@PM.ATTRIB	Data element attributes
@PM.DNAMES	Data names
@PM.CALL	Call statements
@PM.COPY	Copy statements
@PM.ROUTINES	Paragraph names
@PM.IONAMES	I/O record names
@PM.DSNAMES	Data set names,
@PM.LIST	Correlated I/O and DSN
@PM.NARRATIVES	REMARKS (or other comments).
@PM.PROC	PROC data
@PM.JOB	Job data

Refer to the following example section of this Application Report for a variety of complete examples of batch lists that may be created by PM/SS, and their corresponding dictionary input files.

Transforming Procedure Division Literals to Data-Name Elements

In almost all COBOL code developed prior to the use of data dictionaries, important keywords were entered as literals in the Procedure Division of the programs. By today's standards, many of these should be defined as data elements in the Data Division, with a corresponding value phrase. PM/SS has the ability to extract literals from the Procedure Division and to catalog them in the PMLIB. Since their member names and line numbers are also retained, they can be readily examined and reformatted in preparation for their entry into the data dictionary.

Run 12a: @PM INPUT:

```
---> @PM.LITERALS  MLIST=SYSXP
---> @PM              CATAL=SYSXLIT
```

MEMBER NAME	PROGRAM IDENT	DATA NAME
11 ----------------	21 -----------------	31 ---
PC31	PC31	'DEFINED '
PC31	PC31	'DELETE '
PC31	PC31	'DELETED '
PC31	PC31	'EMP-NO ='
PC31	PC31	'EOB WHEN READY'
PC31	PC31	'FILE CONTROL TOTALS'
PC31	PC31	'HOURS SCHEDULED/NOT WORKED'
PC31	PC31	'INCOMING PROJECTS '
PC31	PC31	0000
PC31	PC31	100.00
PC31	PC31	850101
PC31	PC31	999999

To create the initial version of the WAS/IS list the following run may be made using the output of Run 13a.

Run 12b: @PM INPUT:

```
---> @PM.LIST  DNLIST=SYSXLIT
---> @PM          CATAL=(SYSXLIT1,STLIST)
```

13. ENTERING PROCESS INFORMATION INTO THE DICTIONARY

Until now we have only described the method of screening and entering information pertaining to data elements into the data dictionary. The steps described above, of preparing a Data Command List, apply equally well to entering virtually any other data that can be extracted from the current source libraries. For example, many users desire to place in their data dictionary, the names of each of the COPY member names that each program uses. In order to create this DCLIST, a list of such COPY names must first be created and cataloged in the PMLIB.

Run 13a: @PM INPUT:

```
---> @PM.COPY MLIST=SYSXP=CATALSYSXCOPY
```

```
COPY
```

MEMBER	PROGRAM	DATA
NAME	IDENT	NAME
11 --------------------	21--------------------	31 ---
PC12	PC12	PCLRDWR
PC21	PC21	PCLRDWR
PC12	PC12	PCMSTREC
PC21	PC21	PCMSTREC
PC22	PC22	PCMSTREC
PC62	PC62	PCMSTREC
PC65	PC65	PCPRNTREC
PC69F	PC69F	PCPRNTREC
PCMSDKTP	PCMSDKTP	PCPRNTREC
PCMSDKTP	PCMSDKTP	PCTRREC
PCMSLD	PCMSTLD	PCTRREC
PC61	PC61	PCTRRECA
PC63	PC63	PCTRRECB
PC69F	PC69F	PCTR14
PC12	PC12	PCTR14

It should be obvious, even without an example of the actual DCMODEL (specific to each data dictionary) that performing the SYNTH function similar to Run 14 above will produce an appropriate DCLIST for entering the COPY usage information. Refer to the SYNTH section of the PM/SS Reference Manual for a complete description of the general principals of data dictionary input synthesis.

NOTE

1. PM/SS has been developed by the Adpac Corporation and is its solely owned proprietary product. Article is reprinted by permission of Adpac Corporation.

B

Annotated COBOL Reserved Word List

Any word with a $_{74}$ subscript is an obsolete word in $COBOL_{85}$ and should be eliminated from existing programs. The word will become unreserved in the next revision to COBOL and will be rejected.

Any word with a $_{On}$ subscript is an obsolete word in $COBOL_{85}$ in some usages; $_n$ is the footnote that describes the obsolete usages. These usages should also be eliminated from existing programs since that usage will also become unsupported in the next revision to COBOL.

Any word with a ^{pn} superscript is a $COBOL_{74}$ word that ANSI has identified as potentially executing incorrectly in $COBOL_{85}$; ^{n} is the footnote that describes the potential problem. Existing use of these words in $COBOL_{74}$ programs should be reviewed and corrected if their usage would cause problems in $COBOL_{85}$.

Any word with a ^{cd} superscript is only used in the $COBOL_{85}$ optional COMMUNI-CATION module; a conforming $COBOL_{85}$ compiler does *not* have to support and its function should be transferred to other software for future portability.

Any word with a ^{rw} superscript is only used in the $COBOL_{85}$ optional REPORT WRITER module; a conforming $COBOL_{85}$ compiler does *not* have to support and its function should be transferred to other software for future portability.

Any word with $_{85}$ subscript is a new reserved word for $COBOL_{85}$. Usage of these words in $COBOL_{74}$ programs should be eliminated to prevent $COBOL_{85}$ syntax problems.

ACCEPT	ACCESS	ADD
ADVANCING	AFTER	ALL[01,2][p14]
ALPHABET[85][p21]	ALPHABETIC	ALPHABETIC-LOWER[85]
ALPHABETIC-UPPER[85]	ALPHANUMERIC[85]	ALPHANUMERIC-EDITED[85]
ALSO[85]	ALTER[74]	ALTERNATE
AND[p25]	ANY[85]	ARE[08]
AREA	AREAS	ASCENDING
ASSIGN[p2]	AT	AUTHOR[74]
BEFORE	BINARY[85]	BLANK
BLOCK	BOTTOM	BY
CALL[p13]	CANCEL[p26]	CD[cd]
CF[rw]	CH[rw]	CHARACTER
CHARACTERS[03,10]	CLASS[85]	CLOCK-UNITS[74]
CLOSE	COBOL	CODE[rw]
CODE-SET[p6]	COLLATING[03,10]	COLUMN[rw]
COMMA	COMMON[85]	COMMUNICATION
COMP	COMPUTATIONAL	COMPUTE
CONFIGURATION	CONTAINS	CONTENT[85]
CONTINUE[85]	CONTROL[rw]	CONTROLS[rw]
CONVERTING[85]	COPY	CORR
CORRESPONDING	COUNT	CURRENCY[p22]
DATA[05]	DATE	DATE-COMPILED[74]
DATE-WRITTEN[74]	DAY	DAY-OF-WEEK[85]
DE[rw]	DEBUG-CONTENTS[74]	DEBUG-ITEM[74]
DEBUG-LINE[74]	DEBUG-NAME[74]	DEBUG-SUB-1[74]
DEBUG-SUB-2[74]	DEBUG-SUB-3[74]	DEBUGGING[74]
DECIMAL-POINT	DECLARATIVES[02]	DELETE
DELIMITED	DELIMITER	DEPENDING
DESCENDING	DESTINATION[cd]	DETAIL[rw]
DISABLE[cd]	DISPLAY	DIVIDE
DIVISION	DOWN	DUPLICATES
DYNAMIC		
EGI[cd]	ELSE	EMI[cd]
ENABLE[cd]	END[02]	END-ADD[85]
END-CALL[85]	END-COMPUTE[85]	END-DELETE[85]
END-DIVIDE[85]	END-EVALUATE[85]	END-IF[85]
END-MULTIPLY[85]	END-OF-PAGE[p23]	END-PERFORM[85]
END-READ[85]	END-RECEIVE[85]	END-RETURN[85]
END-REWRITE[85]	END-SEARCH[85]	END-START[85]
END-STRING[85]	END-SUBTRACT[85]	END-UNSTRING[85]
END-WRITE[85]	ENTER[74]	ENVIRONMENT

EOP	EQUAL	ERROR
ESI[cd]	EVALUATE[85]	EVERY[04]
EXCEPTION	EXIT	EXTEND[p16]
EXTERNAL[85]		

FALSE[85]	FD	FILE[09]
FILE-CONTROL	FILLER[02][p8]	FINAL[rw]
FIRST	FOOTING	FOR[02]
FROM		

GENERATE[rw]	GIVING	GLOBAL[85]
GO	GREATER	GROUP[rw]

HEADING[rw]	HIGH-VALUE	HIGH-VALUES

I-O	I-O-CONTROL[p5]	IDENTIFICATION
IF	IN	INDEX
INDEXED	INDICATE	INITIAL
INITIALIZED[85]	INITIATE[rw]	INPUT
INPUT-OUTPUT	INSPECT[p28]	INSTALLATION
INTO[p29]	INVALID	IS[03,6,8,10]

JUST	JUSTIFIED

KEY[07]

LABEL[08]	LAST[rw]	LEADING
LEFT	LENGTH[cd]	LESS
LIMIT[rw]	LIMITS[rw]	LINAGE[p7]
LINAGE-COUNTER	LINE	LINE-COUNTER[rw]
LINES	LINKAGE	LOCK
LOW-VALUE	LOW-VALUES	

MEMORY[03,10]	MERGE[p15]	MESSAGE[cd]
MODE[74]	MODULES[03,10]	MOVE
MULTIPLE[09]	MULTIPLY	

NATIVE	NEGATIVE	NEXT
NO	NOT	NUMBER[rw]
NUMERIC	NUMERIC-EDITED[85]	

OBJECT-COMPUTER[010]	OCCURS[p9]	OF[06]
OFF	OMITTED[08]	ON[02,4]
OPEN	OPTIONAL[p3]	OR[p25]
ORDER[85]	ORGANIZATION[p4]	OTHER[85]
OUTPUT	OVERFLOW	

PACKED-DECIMAL[85]   PADDING[85]   PAGE
PAGE-COUNTER[rw]   PERFORM[p17]   PF[rw]
PH[rw]   PIC   PICTURE
PLUS[rw]   POINTER   POSITION
POSITIVE   PRINTING   PROCEDURE
PROCEDURES[02]   PROCEED   PROGRAM[03,10]
PROGRAM-ID   PURGE[85]

QUEUE[cd]   QUOTE   QUOTES

RANDOM   RD[rw]   READ
RECEIVE[cd]   RECORD[08]   RECORDS[04,5,8]
REDEFINES[p10]   REEL[04]   REFERENCE[85]
REFERENCES[02]   RELATIVE   RELEASE
REMAINDER[p27]   REMOVAL   RENAMES
REPLACE[85]   REPLACING   REPORT[rw]
REPORTING   REPORTS[rw]   RERUN[74]
RESERVE   RESET[rw]   RETURN[p18]
RESERVED[74]   REWIND   REWRITE[p19]
RF[rw]   RH[rw]   RIGHT
ROUNDED   RUN

SAME   SD   SEARCH
SECTION[02,10]   SECURITY   SEGMENT[74]
SEGMENT-LIMIT[74]   SELECT   SEND
SENTENCE   SEPARATE   SEQUENCE[03,10]
SEQUENTIAL   SET   SIGN[p11]
SIZE[03,10]   SORT[p15]   SORT-MERGE
SOURCE[rw]   SOURCE-COMPUTER   SPACE
SPACES   SPECIAL-NAMES   STANDARD[08]
STANDARD-1   STANDARD-2[85]   START
STATUS[cd]   STOP   STRING[p20,30]
SUB-QUEUE-1[cd]   SUB-QUEUE-2[cd]   SUB-QUEUE-3[cd]
SUBTRACT   SUM[rw]   SUPPRESS[rw]
SYMBOLIC   SYNC   SYNCHRONIZED

TABLE   TALLYING   TAPE[09]
TERMINAL[cd]   TERMINATE[cd]   TEST[85]
TEXT   THAN   THEN[85]
THROUGH[85]   THRU   TIME
TIMES   TO   TOP
TRAILING   TRUE[85]   TYPE[rw]

UNIT[04]   UNSTRING[p30]   UNTIL
UP   UPON   USAGE
USE[02]   USING[p24]

VALUE$_{06}$^{p12}	VALUES	VARYING
WHEN$_{07}$	WITH$_{02}$	WORDS$_{03,10}$
WORKING-STORAGE	WRITE	
ZERO^{p1}	ZEROES	ZEROS

+	−	*
/	**	>
<	=	> =$_{85}$
< =$_{85}$		

There are also some new COBOL$_{85}$ rules pertaining to the punctuation marks:

1. colon [:] is used in reference modification
2. COMMA [,] and semicolon [;] and space [ ] are interchangeable
3. period (.) and COMMA (,) can be last CHARACTER in a PIC clause

Other COBOL$_{85}$ language modifications:

1. nonnumeric literal can be up to 160 CHARACTERS in LENGTH
2. there can be fifty [50] levels of qualification
3. a TABLE can have seven [7] dimensions
4. relative subscripting is allowed
5. subscripts and indexes can be intermixed
6. DATA can be referenced by specifying a leftmost CHARACTER and LENGTH
7. sequence field can contain any CHARACTER
8. DATA DIVISION word following level indicator, 01, or 77 can start in A area
9. END PROGRAM can be followed by the IDENTIFICATION DIVISION of another COBOL PROGRAM
10. programs can be nested
11. the ENVIRONMENT, DATA, and PROCEDURE DIVISION are optional
12. a MOVE of NUMERIC-EDITED DATA item to NUMERIC DATA item causes de-editing
13. P in PIC clause has new limitations
14. exponentiation results have been redefined
15. new I-O status values have been added

OBSOLETE FOOTNOTES:

1. when used as a figurative constant liberal associated with a NUMERIC or NUMERIC-EDITED item with a LENGTH > 1
2. when used in DEBUG module

3. when used in MEMORY SIZE clause
4. when used in RERUN clause
5. when used in DATA RECORDS clause
6. when used in VALUE OF clause
7. when used in COMMUNICATION module
8. when used in LABEL RECORD and LABEL RECORDS clauses
9. when used in MULTIPLE FILE TAPE clause
10. when used in SEGMENTATION module

PROBLEM FOOTNOTES:

1. ZERO is allowed in arithmetic expressions
2. nonnumeric literal allowed in ASSIGN clause
3. OPTIONAL can be used with RELATIVE and INDEXED FILE which are OPEN in the INPUT, I-O, or EXTEND MODE
4. ORGANIZATION is optional in the FILE control entry
5. clause order is immaterial
6. CODE-SET can be specified for any SEQUENTIAL FILE ORGANIZATION
7. data-names can be qualified; a FILE cannot be OPEN in the EXTEND MODE
8. FILLER is optional
9. OCCURS can have a ZERO VALUE
10. REDEFINES item may have a smaller size than the redefined item
11. multiple SIGN clauses can be specified; SIGN allowed in REPORT GROUP
12. VALUE allowed in OCCURS clause
13. parameter can be subscripted and/or referenced modified
14. ALL allowed in DISPLAY statement; LENGTH may be defined as the literal LENGTH
15. multiple file-names allowed; FILE can be variable LENGTH and be RELATIVE or INDEXED; explicit transfers of control allowed outside of INPUT-OUTPUT procedures
16. EXTEND can be used with RELATIVE or INDEXED FILE
17. PERFORM can be in-line; six [6] AFTER phrases must be allowed; the order of initialization of multiple VARYING identifiers is specified; the order of execution for evaluating subscripts is specified
18. variable LENGTH RECORDS allowed
19. different LENGTH RECORDS can replace a RECORD within a RELATIVE or INDEXED FILE
20. identifier in INTO phrase can be a group item
21. ALPHABET must precede the alphabet-name clause of the SPECIAL-NAMES paragraph
22. figurative constant cannot be specified in the CURRENCY SIGN clause

23. END-OF-PAGE condition does not exist if a FOOTING phrase is not specified; cannot be specified with ADVANCING PAGE in a single WRITE statement

24. USING DATA item cannot be redefined

25. AND/OR order of execution has been redefined for conditional expressions

26. CANCEL CLOSE all OPEN FILE

27. subscripts for the REMAINDER phrase are evaluated after the quotient is stored

28. INSPECT subscript evaluation has been specified

29. INTO phrase of READ statement has new rules

30. subscripting rules are specified

CAVEAT: THE ANSI X3.23-1985 [ISO 1989-1985] COBOL MANUAL CONTAINS MANY OTHER CHANGES THAT HAVE <u>NOT</u> BEEN SPECIFIED IN THIS ANNOTATION; PLEASE REFER TO THIS MANUAL FOR COMPLETE DESCRIPTION.

C

Glossary

This glossary is a combination of the ANSI-1974 and 1985 manuals. Terms are defined according to their meaning in COBOL and may not have the same meaning in other languages. CAPITALIZED words are reserved words used in their COBOL sense.

Abbreviated combined relation condition   The combined condition that results from the explicit omission of a common subject or a common subject and common relational operator in a consecutive sequence of relation conditions.

Access mode   The manner in which RECORDS are to be operated on within a FILE.

Actual DECIMAL-POINT   The physical representation, using the DECIMAL-POINT CHARACTERS period (.) or COMMA (,), of the DECIMAL-POINT POSITION in a DATA item.

Alphabetic character   A letter or a SPACE CHARACTER.

Alphabet name   A user-defined word, in the SPECIAL-NAMES paragraph of the ENVIRONMENT DIVISION, that assigns a name to a specific CHARACTER SET and/or COLLATING SEQUENCE.

Alphanumeric character   Any CHARACTER in the computer's CHARACTER SET.

Alternate record key   A KEY, other than the prime RECORD KEY, whose contents identify a RECORD in an INDEXED FILE.

Arithmetic expression   An identifier of a NUMERIC elementary item, a NUMERIC literal, such identifiers and literals separated by arithmetic operators, two arithmetic expressions separated by an arithmetic operator, or an arithmetic expression enclosed in parentheses.

Arithmetic operation$_{85}$ The process caused by the execution of an arithmetic statement, or the evaluation of an arithmetic expression, that results in a mathematically correct solution to the arguments presented.

Arithmetic operator   A single CHARACTER or fixed two-character combination that belongs to the following set:

CHARACTER	Meaning
+	Addition
−	Subtraction
*	Multiplication
/	Division
**	Exponentiation

Arithmetic statements$_{85}$ A statement that causes an arithmetic operation to be executed. The arithmetic statements are the ADD, COMPUTE, DIVIDE, MULTIPLY, and SUBTRACT statements.

Ascending key   A KEY upon the values of which DATA is ordered, starting with the lowest value of the KEY up to the highest value of the KEY, in accordance with the rules for comparing DATA items.

Assumed DECIMAL-POINT   A DECIMAL-POINT position that does not involve the existence of an actual CHARACTER in a DATA item. The assumed DECIMAL-POINT has logical meaning but no physical representation.

AT END condition   A condition caused (1) during the execution of a READ statement for a sequentially accessed FILE when no NEXT logical RECORD exists in the FILE, when the number of significant digits in the RELATIVE RECORD NUMBER is larger than the size of the RELATIVE KEY DATA item, or when an OPTIONAL INPUT FILE is not present; (2) during the execution of a RETURN statement when no NEXT logical RECORD exists for the associated SORT or MERGE FILE; or (3) during the execution of a SEARCH statement when the SEARCH operation terminates without satisfying the condition specified in any of the associated WHEN phrases.

Block   A physical unit of DATA that is normally composed of one or more logical RECORDS. For mass storage files, a BLOCK may contain a portion of a logical RECORD. The size of a BLOCK has no direct relationship to the size of the FILE within which the BLOCK is contained or to the size of the logical RECORDS that are either contained within the BLOCK or overlap the BLOCK. The term is synonymous with *physical RECORD*.

Body GROUP   Generic name for a REPORT GROUP of TYPE DETAIL, CONTROL HEADING, or CONTROL FOOTING.

Bottom margin$_{85}$ An empty area that follows the PAGE body.

Called PROGRAM   A PROGRAM that is the object of a CALL statement combined at object time with the calling PROGRAM to produce a run unit.

Calling PROGRAM   A PROGRAM that executes a CALL to another PROGRAM.

Cd-name   A user-defined word that names an mcs interface area described in a COMMUNICATION description entry in the COMMUNICATION SECTION of the DATA DIVISION.

CHARACTER   The basic indivisible unit of the language.

CHARACTER POSITION   The amount of physical storage required to store a single standard DATA format character described by USAGE IS DISPLAY. Further characteristics of the physical storage are defined by the implementor.

Character-string   A sequence of contiguous CHARACTERS that form a COBOL word, a literal, a PICTURE character-string, or a comment-entry.

CLASS condition   The proposition, for which a truth value can be determined, that the content of an item is wholly ALPHABETIC or is wholly NUMERIC or consists exclusively of the CHARACTERS listed in the definition of a class-name.

Class-name$_{85}$ A user-defined word defined in the SPECIAL-NAMES paragraph of the ENVIRONMENT DIVISION that assigns a name to the proposition for which a truth value can be defined, that the content of a DATA item consists exclusively of the CHARACTERS listed in the definition of the class-name.

Clause   An ordered set of consecutive COBOL character-strings whose purpose is to specify an attribute of an entry.

COBOL CHARACTER set   The following characters:

CHARACTER	Meaning
0, 1,..., 9	Digit
A, B,..., Z	Uppercase letter
a, b, ..., z	Lowercase letter
	SPACE
+	PLUS SIGN
−	MINUS SIGN (hyphen)
*	Asterisk
/	Slant (solidus)
=	EQUAL SIGN
$	CURRENCY SIGN (represented as @ in the International Reference Version of International Standard ISO 646-1973)
,	COMMA (decimal point)
;	Semicolon
.	Period (DECIMAL-POINT, full stop)
"	Quotation mark
(	Left parenthesis
)	Right parenthesis
>	GREATER THAN symbol
<	LESS THAN symbol
:	Colon

Note 1: In the cases where an implementation does not provide all of the COBOL character set to be graphically represented, substitute graphics may be specified by the implementor to replace the characters not represented.

The COBOL CHARACTER SET graphics are a subset of American National Standard X3.4-1977, Code for Information Interchange. With the exception of $, they are also a subset of the graphics defined for the International Reference Version of International Standard ISO 646-1973, 7-Bit Coded Character Set for Information Processing Interchange.

Note 2: When the computer CHARACTER SET includes lowercase letters, they may be used in character-strings. Except when used in nonnumeric literals and some PICTURE symbols, each lowercase letter is equivalent to the corresponding uppercase letter.

COBOL word   A character-string of not more then 30 CHARACTERS that forms a user-defined word, a system-name, or a reserved word.

COLLATING SEQUENCE   The SEQUENCE in which the CHARACTERS that are acceptable to a computer are ordered for purposes of sorting, merging, and comparing and for processing an INDEXED FILE sequentially.

COLUMN   A CHARACTER POSITION within a print line. The columns are numbered sequentially, starting at the leftmost CHARACTER POSITION of the print line and extending to the rightmost position of the print line.

Combined condition   A condition that is the result of connecting two or more conditions with the AND or the OR logical operator.

Comment-entry   An entry in the IDENTIFICATION DIVISION that may be any combination of CHARACTERS from the computer's CHARACTER SET.

Comment line   A SOURCE PROGRAM line represented by an asterisk (*) in the indicator area of the line and any CHARACTERS from the computer's CHARACTER SET in area A and area B of that line. The comment line serves only for documentation in a PROGRAM. A special form of comment line represented by a slant (/) in the indicator area of the line and any CHARACTERS from the computer's CHARACTER SET in area A and area B of that line causes PAGE ejection prior to printing the comment.

COMMON PROGRAM$_{85}$ A PROGRAM that, despite being contained within another PROGRAM, may be called from any PROGRAM contained directly or indirectly in that other PROGRAM.

COMMUNICATION description entry   An entry in the COMMUNICATION SECTION of the DATA DIVISION that is composed of the level indicator CD, followed by a cd-name, and then followed by a set of clauses as required. It describes the interface between the message control system and the COBOL PROGRAM.

Communication device   A mechanism (hardware or hardware/software) capable of sending DATA to a QUEUE and/or receiving DATA from a QUEUE. This mechanism may be a computer or a peripheral device. One or more programs containing COMMUNICATION description entries and residing within the same computer define one or more of these mechanisms.

COMMUNICATION SECTION   The SECTION of the DATA DIVISION that describes the interface areas between the message control system and the program, composed of one or more COMMUNICATION description AREAS.

Compiler directing statement   A statement, beginning with a compiler directing verb, that causes the compiler to take a specific action during compilation. The compiler directing statements are the COPY, ENTER, REPLACE, and USE statements.

Compile time   The time at which a COBOL SOURCE PROGRAM is translated, by a COBOL compiler, to a COBOL object PROGRAM.

Complex condition   A condition in which one or more logical operators act on one or more conditions. (See *negated simple condition, combined condition, negated combined condition.*)

Computer-name   A system-name that identifies the computer on which the PROGRAM is to be compiled or run.

Condition   A status of a PROGRAM at execution time for which a truth value can be determined. Where the term *condition* (**condition-1, condition-2,** . . .) appears in these language specifications, it is a conditional expression consisting of either a simple condition optionally parenthesized or a combined condition consisting of the syntactically correct combination of simple conditions, logical operators, and parentheses for which a truth value can be determined.

Conditional expression   A simple condition or a complex condition specified in an EVALUATE, IF, PERFORM, or SEARCH statement. (See *simple condition, complex condition.*)

Conditional phrase$_{85}$ A phrase that specifies the action to be taken upon determination of the truth VALUE of a condition resulting from the execution of a conditional statement.

Conditional statement   A statement that specifies that the truth VALUE of a condition is to be determined and that the subsequent action of the object program is dependent on this truth VALUE.

Conditional variable   A DATA item, one or more VALUES of which has a condition name assigned to it.

Condition-name   A user-defined word that assigns a name to a subset of VALUES that a conditional variable may assume, or a user-defined word assigned to a status of an implementor-defined switch or device. When **condition-name** is used in the general formats, it represents a unique data item reference consisting of a syntactically correct combination of a condition-name, together with qualifiers and subscripts, as required for uniqueness of reference.

Condition-name condition   The proposition, for which a truth VALUE can be determined, that the VALUE of a conditional variable is a member of the set of VALUES attributed to a condition-name associated with the conditional variable.

CONFIGURATION SECTION   A SECTION of the ENVIRONMENT DIVISION that describes overall specifications of source and object programs.

Connective$_{74}$ A reserved word that is used (1) to associate a data-name, paragraph-name, condition-name, or text-name with its qualifier, (2) to link two or more operands written in a series, or (3) to form conditions (logical connectives). (See *logical operator.*)

Contiguous items   Items that are described by consecutive entries in the DATA DIVISION and that bear a definite hierarchical relationship to each other.

CONTROL break   A change in the VALUE of a DATA item that is referenced in the CONTROL clause. More generally, a change in the VALUE of a DATA item that is used to CONTROL the hierarchical structure of a REPORT.

CONTROL break level   The relative position in a CONTROL hierarchy at which the most major CONTROL break occurred.

CONTROL DATA item   A DATA item, a change in whose contents may produce a CONTROL break.

CONTROL data-name   A data-name that appears in a CONTROL clause and refers to a CONTROL DATA item.

CONTROL FOOTING   A REPORT GROUP that is presented at the end of the CONTROL GROUP of which it is a member.

CONTROL GROUP   A set of body groups that is presented for a given VALUE of a CONTROL DATA item or of FINAL. Each CONTROL GROUP may begin with a CONTROL HEADING, end with a CONTROL FOOTING, and contain detail REPORT groups.

CONTROL HEADING   A REPORT GROUP that is presented at the beginning of the CONTROL GROUP of which it is a member.

CONTROL hierarchy   A designated sequence of REPORT subdivisions defined by the positional order of FINAL and the data-names in a CONTROL clause.

Counter   A DATA item used for storing numbers or number representations in a manner that permits these numbers to be increased or decreased by the value of another number or to be changed or reset to ZERO or to an arbitrary POSITIVE or NEGATIVE value.

CURRENCY SIGN   The CHARACTER $ of the COBOL CHARACTER SET.

CURRENCY symbol   The CHARACTER defined by the CURRENCY SIGN clause in the SPECIAL-NAMES paragraph. If no CURRENCY SIGN clause is present in a COBOL SOURCE PROGRAM, the CURRENCY symbol is identical to the CURRENCY SIGN.

Current RECORD   In FILE processing, the RECORD that is available in the RECORD AREA associated with the FILE.

Current RECORD POINTER$_{74}$ A conceptual entity that is used in the selection of the NEXT RECORD.

Current volume POINTER$_{85}$ A conceptual entity that points to the current volume of a SEQUENTIAL FILE.

DATA clause   A clause appearing in a DATA description entry in the DATA DIVISION of a COBOL program that provides information describing a particular attribute of a DATA item.

DATA description entry   An entry in the DATA DIVISION of a COBOL program that is composed of a level-number followed by a data-name, if required, and then by a set of DATA clauses, as required.

DATA item   A unit of DATA (excluding literals) defined by the COBOL PROGRAM.

Data-name   A user-defined word that names a DATA item described in a DATA description entry. When used in the general formats, **data-name** represents a word that must not be reference-modified, subscripted, or qualified unless specifically permitted by the rules of the format.

DEBUGGING line   Any line with D in the indicator area of the line.

DEBUGGING SECTION   A SECTION that contains a USE FOR DEBUGGING statement.

DECLARATIVES   A set of one or more special-purpose sections, written at the beginning of the PROCEDURE DIVISION, the first of which is preceded by the key word DECLARATIVES and the last of which is followed by the key words END DECLARATIVES. A declarative is composed of a SECTION header, followed by a USE compiler directing sentence, followed by a set of zero, one, or more associated paragraphs.

Declarative sentence   A compiler directing sentence consisting of a single USE statement terminated by the separator period.

De-edit$_{85}$ The logical removal of all editing characters from a NUMERIC-EDITED data item in order to determine that item's unedited NUMERIC value.

DELIMITED scope statement$_{85}$ Any statement that includes its explicit scope terminator.

DELIMITER   A CHARACTER or a sequence of contiguous CHARACTERS that identifies the end of a STRING of CHARACTERS and separates that STRING of CHARACTERS from the following STRING of CHARACTERS. A DELIMITER is not part of the STRING of CHARACTERS that it delimits.

DESCENDING KEY   A KEY upon the values of which DATA is ordered, starting with the highest value of KEY down to the lowest value of KEY, in accordance with the rules for comparing DATA items.

DESTINATION   The symbolic identification of the receiver of a transmission from a QUEUE.

Digit POSITION   The amount of physical storage required to store a single digit. This amount may vary depending on the USAGE specified in the DATA description entry that defines the DATA item. If the DATA description entry specifies that USAGE IS DISPLAY, a digit position is synonymous with a CHARACTER POSITION. Further characteristics of the physical storage are defined by the implementor.

DIVISION   A collection of zero, one, or more sections of paragraphs, called the DIVISION body, that are formed and combined in accordance with a specific set of rules. Each DIVISION consists of the DIVISION header and the related DIVISION body. There are four divisions in a COBOL PROGRAM: IDENTIFICATION, ENVIRONMENT, DATA, and PROCEDURE.

DIVISION header   A combination of words, followed by a separator period, that indicates the beginning of a DIVISION. The DIVISION headers in a COBOL PROGRAM are

```
IDENTIFICATION DIVISION.
ENVIRONMENT DIVISION.
DATA DIVISION.
PROCEDURE DIVISION (USING {data-name-1} ... ).
```

DYNAMIC ACCESS   An ACCESS MODE in which specific logical RECORDS can be obtained from or placed into a mass storage file in a nonsequential manner and obtained from a FILE in a SEQUENTIAL manner during the scope of the same OPEN statement.

Editing CHARACTER   A single CHARACTER or a fixed two-character combination belonging to the following set:

Character	Meaning
B	SPACE
0	ZERO
+	PLUS
−	MINUS
CR	Credit
DB	Debit
Z	ZERO suppress
*	Check protect
$	CURRENCY SIGN
,	COMMA (DECIMAL-POINT)
.	Period (DECIMAL-POINT)
/	Slant (solidus)

Elementary item   A DATA item that is described as not being further logically subdivided.

END OF PROCEDURE DIVISION   The physical position in a COBOL SOURCE PROGRAM after which no further procedures appear.

END PROGRAM header$_{85}$ A combination of words, followed by a separator period, that indicates the end of a COBOL SOURCE PROGRAM. The END PROGRAM header is

END PROGRAM program-name.

Entry   Any descriptive set of consecutive clauses terminated by a period and written in the IDENTIFICATION, ENVIRONMENT, or DATA DIVISION of a COBOL program.

ENVIRONMENT clause   A clause that appears as part of an ENVIRONMENT DIVISION entry.

Execution time   The time at which an object PROGRAM is executed. The term is synonymous with *object time*.

Explicit scope terminator$_{85}$ A reserved word that terminates the scope of a particular PROCEDURE DIVISION statement.

Expression$_{85}$ An arithmetic or conditional expression.

EXTEND MODE   The state of a FILE after execution of an OPEN statement, with the EXTEND phrase specified, for that FILE and before the execution of a CLOSE statement without the REEL or UNIT phrase for that FILE.

EXTERNAL DATA$_{85}$ The DATA described in a program as EXTERNAL data items and EXTERNAL FILE connectors.

EXTERNAL data item$_{85}$ A data item that is described as part of an EXTERNAL RECORD in one or more programs of a run unit and may itself be referenced from any PROGRAM in which it is described.

EXTERNAL DATA RECORD$_{85}$ A logical RECORD that is described in one or more programs of a run unit and whose constituent DATA items may be referenced from any PROGRAM in which they are described.

EXTERNAL FILE connector$_{85}$ A FILE connector that is accessible to one or more object programs in the run unit.

EXTERNAL switch$_{85}$ A hardware or software device, defined and named by the implementor, that is used to indicate that one of two alternate states exists.

Figurative constant   A compiler-generated VALUE referenced through the use of certain reserved words.

FILE   A collection of logical RECORDS.

FILE attribute conflict condition$_{85}$ A condition that results when an unsuccessful attempt has been made to execute an INPUT-OUTPUT operation on a FILE and the FILE attributes, as specified for that FILE in the PROGRAM, do not match the fixed attributes for that FILE.

FILE clause   A clause that appears as part of either of the following DATA DIVISION entries: FILE description entry (FD entry), sort-merge FILE description entry (SD entry.)

FILE connector$_{85}$ A storage area that contains information about a FILE and is used as the linkage between a file-name and a physical FILE and between a file-name and its associated RECORD AREA.

FILE-CONTROL   An ENVIRONMENT DIVISION paragraph in which the DATA files for a given SOURCE PROGRAM are declared.

FILE CONTROL entry$_{85}$ A SELECT clause and all its subordinate clauses that declare the relevant physical attributes of a FILE.

FILE description entry   An entry in the FILE SECTION of the DATA DIVISION that is composed of the level indicator FD, followed by a file-name and then by a set of FILE clauses as required.

File-name   A user-defined word that names a FILE connector described in a FILE description entry or a sort-merge FILE description entry in the FILE SECTION of the DATA DIVISION.

FILE organization   The permanent logical FILE structure established at the time that a FILE is created.

FILE POSITION indicator$_{85}$ A conceptual entity that contains the VALUE of the current KEY within the KEY of reference for an INDEXED FILE, the RECORD NUMBER of the current RECORD for a SEQUENTIAL FILE, the RELATIVE RECORD NUMBER of the current RECORD for a RELATIVE FILE, or an indication that no NEXT logical RECORD exists, that the number of significant digits in the RELATIVE RECORD NUMBER is larger than the size of the RELATIVE KEY DATA item, that an OPTIONAL INPUT FILE is not present, that the AT-END condition already exists, or that no valid NEXT RECORD has been established.

FILE SECTION   The SECTION of the DATA DIVISION that contains FILE description entries and sort-merge FILE description entries together with their associated RECORD descriptions.

Fixed FILE attributes$_{85}$ Information about a FILE that is established when a FILE is created and cannot subsequently be changed during the existence of the FILE. These attributes include the organization of the FILE (SEQUENTIAL, RELATIVE, or INDEXED), the prime RECORD KEY, the ALTERNATE RECORD KEY, the CODE-SET, the minimum and maximum RECORD size, the RECORD type (fixed or variable), the COLLATING SEQUENCE of the KEY for INDEXED FILES, the blocking factor, the PADDING CHARACTER, and the RECORD DELIMITER.

Fixed-length RECORD$_{85}$ A RECORD associated with a FILE whose FILE description or sort-merge description entry requires that all RECORDS contain the same number of CHARACTER positions.

FOOTING area$_{85}$ The position of the PAGE body adjacent to the BOTTOM margin.

Format   A specific arrangement of a set of DATA.

GLOBAL name$_{85}$ A name that is declared in only one PROGRAM but may be referenced from that PROGRAM and from any PROGRAM contained within that PROGRAM. Condition-names, data-names, file-names, record-names, report-names, and some special registers may be GLOBAL names.

GROUP item   A DATA item that is composed of subordinate DATA items.

High-order end   The leftmost CHARACTER of a string of CHARACTERS.

Identifier   A syntactically correct combination of a data-name, with its qualifiers, subscripts, and reference modifiers, as required for uniqueness of reference, that names a DATA item. The rules for an identifier associated with the general formats may, however, specifically prohibit qualification, subscripting, or reference modification.

Imperative statement   A statement that either begins with an imperative verb and specifies an unconditional action to be taken or is a conditional statement that is DELIMITED by its explicit scope terminator (DELIMITED scope statement). An imperative statement may consist of a sequence of imperative statements.

Implementor-name   A system-name that refers to a particular feature available on that implementor's computing system.

Implicit scope terminator$_{85}$ A separator period that terminates the scope of any preceding unterminated statement, or a phrase of a statement that by its occurrence indicates the end of the scope of any statement contained within the preceding phrase.

INDEX   A computer storage area or register, the contents of which represent the identification of a particular element in a TABLE.

INDEX data item   A data item in which the VALUES associated with an index-name can be stored in a form specified by the implementor.

INDEXED data-name$_{74}$ An identifier that is composed of a data-name, followed by one or more index-names enclosed in parentheses.

INDEXED FILE   A FILE with INDEXED ORGANIZATION.

INDEXED ORGANIZATION   The permanent logical FILE structure in which each RECORD is identified by the value of one or more keys in that RECORD.

Index-name   A user-defined word that names an INDEX associated with a specific TABLE.

INITIAL PROGRAM$_{85}$ A PROGRAM that is placed into an INITIAL state every time the PROGRAM is called in a run unit.

INITIAL state$_{85}$ The state of a PROGRAM when it is first called in a run unit.

INPUT FILE   A FILE that is open in the INPUT MODE.

INPUT MODE   The state of a FILE after execution of an OPEN statement, with the INPUT phrase specified, for that FILE and before the execution of a CLOSE statement without the REEL or UNIT phrase for that FILE

INPUT-OUTPUT FILE   A FILE that is open in the I-O mode.

INPUT-OUTPUT SECTION   The SECTION of the ENVIRONMENT DIVISION that names each FILE and the external media required by an object PROGRAM and provides information required for transmission and handling of DATA during execution of the object PROGRAM.

INPUT-OUTPUT statement$_{85}$ A statement that causes a FILE to be processed by performing operations on individual RECORDS or on the FILE as a unit. The input-output statements are ACCEPT (with the identifier phrase), CLOSE, DELETE, DISABLE, DISPLAY, ENABLE, OPEN, PURGE, READ, RECEIVE, REWRITE, SEND, SET (with the TO ON or TO OFF phrase), START, and WRITE.

INPUT PROCEDURE   A set of statements to which control is given during the execution of a SORT statement for the purpose of controlling the RELEASE of specified RECORDS to sort.

Integer   A NUMERIC literal or NUMERIC DATA item that does not include any digit position to the right of the assumed DECIMAL-POINT. Where the term *integer* appears in general formats, it must not be a NUMERIC DATA item and must not be signed or zero unless explicitly allowed by the rules of that format.

Internal DATA$_{85}$ The DATA described in a PROGRAM excluding all EXTERNAL DATA items and EXTERNAL FILE connectors. Items described in the LINKAGE SECTION of a PROGRAM are treated as internal DATA.

Internal DATA item$_{85}$ A DATA item that is described in one PROGRAM in a run unit. An internal DATA item may have a GLOBAL name.

Internal FILE connector$_{85}$ A FILE connector that is accessible to only one object PROGRAM in the run unit.

Intra-record DATA structure$_{85}$ The entire collection of groups and elementary DATA items from a logical RECORD that is defined by a contiguous subset of the DATA description entries that describe that RECORD. These DATA description entries include all entries whose level-number is greater than the level-number of the first DATA description entry describing the intra-record DATA structure.

INVALID KEY condition   A condition, at object time, caused when a specific value of the KEY associated with an INDEXED or RELATIVE FILE is determined to be INVALID.

I-O-CONTROL   An ENVIRONMENT DIVISION paragraph in which object PROGRAM requirements for rerun points, sharing of same AREAS by several DATA files, and multiple FILE storage on a single input-output device are specified.

I-O-CONTROL entry$_{85}$ An entry in the I-O-CONTROL paragraph of the ENVIRONMENT DIVISION that contains clauses that provide information required for the transmission and handling of DATA on named files during the execution of a PROGRAM.

I-O MODE   The state of a FILE after execution of an OPEN statement, with the I-O phrase specified, for that FILE and before the execution of a CLOSE statement without the REEL or UNIT phrase for that FILE.

I-O STATUS$_{85}$ A conceptual entity that contains the two-character value indicating the resulting status of an input-output operation. This value is made available to the PROGRAM through the use of the FILE-STATUS clause in the FILE-CONTROL entry for the FILE.

KEY   A DATA item that identifies the location of a RECORD or a set of DATA items that serve to identify the ordering of DATA.

KEY of REFERENCE   The KEY, either prime or ALTERNATE, currently being used to access RECORDS in an INDEXED FILE.

KEY word   A reserved word whose presence is required when the format in which the word appears is used in a SOURCE PROGRAM.

Language-name   A system-name that specifies a particular programming language.

Letter$_{85}$ A character belonging to one of the following two sets: 1. uppercase letters: A, B, C, D, E, F, G, H, I, J, K, L, M, N, O, P, Q, R, S, T, U, V, W, X, Y, Z; 2. lowercase letters: a, b, c, d, e, f, g, h, i, j, k, l, m, n, o, p, q, r, s, t, u, v, w, x, y, z.

Level indicator   Two ALPHABETIC CHARACTERS that identify a specific type of FILE or a position in a hierarchy. The level indicators in the DATA DIVISION are CD, FD, RD, and SD.

Level-number   A user-defined word, expressed as a one- or two-digit number, that indicates the hierarchical position of a DATA item or the special properties of a DATA description entry. Level-numbers in the range 1 through 49 indicate the position of a DATA item in the hierarchical structure of a logical RECORD. Level-numbers in the range 1 through 9 may be written either as a single digit or as a zero followed by a significant digit. Level-numbers 66, 77, and 88 identify special properties of a DATA description entry.

Library-name   A user-defined word that names a COBOL library that is to be used by the compiler for a given SOURCE PROGRAM compilation.

Library TEXT   A sequence of TEXT words, comment lines, the separator space, or the separator pseudo-text DELIMITER in a COBOL library.

LINAGE-COUNTER$_{85}$ A special register whose value points to the current POSITION in the PAGE body.

LINE   A division of a PAGE representing one row of horizontal character positions. Each character position of a REPORT LINE is aligned vertically beneath the corresponding character position of the REPORT LINE above it. REPORT lines are numbered sequentially from 1, starting at the TOP of the PAGE. The term is synonymous with *REPORT LINE*.

LINE NUMBER   An integer that denotes the vertical position of a REPORT LINE on a PAGE.

LINKAGE SECTION   The SECTION in the DATA DIVISION of the called PROGRAM that describes DATA items available from the calling PROGRAM. These DATA items may be referred to by both the calling PROGRAM and the called PROGRAM.

Literal   A character-string whose value is implied by the ordered set of CHARACTERS comprising the STRING.

Logical operator   One of the reserved words AND, OR, or NOT. In the formation of a condition, AND, OR, or both can be used as logical connectives. NOT can be used for logical negation.

Logical PAGE$_{85}$ A conceptual entity consisting of the TOP margin, the PAGE body, and the BOTTOM margin.

Logical RECORD   The most inclusive DATA item. The level-number for a RECORD is 01. A RECORD may be either an elementary item or a group item. The term is synonymous with *RECORD*.

Low-order end   The rightmost CHARACTER of a STRING of CHARACTERS.

Mass storage   A storage medium in which DATA may be organized and maintained in both a SEQUENTIAL and nonsequential manner.

Mass storage control system   An input-output control system that directs, or controls, the processing of mass storage files.

Mass storage FILE   A collection of RECORDS that is assigned to a mass storage medium.

MERGE FILE   A collection of RECORDS to be merged by a MERGE statement. The MERGE FILE is created and can be used only by the MERGE function.

MESSAGE   DATA associated with an END of MESSAGE indicator or an END of GROUP indicator.

Message control system   A COMMUNICATION control system that supports the processing of messages.

MESSAGE COUNT   The COUNT of the number of complete messages that exist in the designated QUEUE of messages.

MESSAGE Indicators   EGI (END of GROUP indicator), EMI (END of MESSAGE indicator), and ESI (END of SEGMENT indicator) are conceptual indications that serve to notify the MESSAGE CONTROL system that a specific condition exists (END of GROUP, END of MESSAGE, END of SEGMENT). Within the top-down hierarchy of EGI, EMI, and ESI, each indicator is conceptually equivalent to those below it. Thus a SEGMENT may be terminated by an ESI, EMI, or EGI, and a MESSAGE may be terminated by an EMI or EGI (but not an ESI).

MESSAGE SEGMENT   DATA that forms a logical subdivision of a MESSAGE, normally associated with an END of SEGMENT indicator. (See *MESSAGE indicators*.)

Mnemonic-name   A user-defined word that is associated in the ENVIRONMENT DIVISION with a specific implementor-name.

NATIVE CHARACTER SET   The implementor-defined CHARACTER SET associated with the computer specified in the OBJECT-COMPUTER paragraph.

NATIVE COLLATING SEQUENCE   The implementor-defined COLLATING SEQUENCE associated with the computer specified in the OBJECT-COMPUTER paragraph.

Negated combined condition   The NOT logical operator immediately followed by a parenthesized combined condition.

Negated simple condition   The NOT logical operator immediately followed by a simple condition.

NEXT executable SENTENCE   The NEXT SENTENCE to which control will be transferred after execution of the current statement is complete.

NEXT executable statement   The NEXT statement to which control will be transferred after execution of the current statement is complete.

NEXT RECORD   The RECORD that logically follows the current RECORD of a FILE.

Noncontiguous item   An elementary DATA item, in the WORKING-STORAGE and LINKAGE sections, that bears no hierarchic relationship to other DATA items.

Nonnumeric item   A DATA item whose description permits its contents to be composed of any combination of CHARACTERS taken from the computer's CHARACTER SET. Certain categories of nonnumeric items may be formed from more restricted CHARACTER SETS.

Nonnumeric literal   A literal bounded by quotation marks. The STRING of CHARACTERS may include any CHARACTER in the computer's CHARACTER SET.

NUMERIC CHARACTER   A CHARACTER that belongs to the following set of digits: 0, 1, 2, 3, 4, 5, 6, 7, 8, 9.

NUMERIC item   A DATA item whose description restricts its contents to a VALUE represented by characters chosen from the digits 0 through 9: if signed, the item may also contain +, −, or any other operational SIGN.

NUMERIC literal   A literal composed of one or more NUMERIC CHARACTERS that may contain a DECIMAL-POINT, an algebraic SIGN, or both. The DECIMAL-POINT must not be the rightmost CHARACTER. The algebraic SIGN, if present, must be the leftmost CHARACTER.

OBJECT-COMPUTER   The name of an ENVIRONMENT DIVISION paragraph in which the computer ENVIRONMENT, within which the object PROGRAM is executed, is described.

OBJECT-COMPUTER entry$_{85}$ An entry in the OBJECT-COMPUTER paragraph of the ENVIRONMENT DIVISION that contains clauses that describe the computer ENVIRONMENT in which the object PROGRAM is to be executed.

Object of entry   A set of operands and reserved words, within a DATA DIVISION entry of a COBOL program, that immediately follows the subject of the entry.

Object PROGRAM   A set or group of executable machine language instructions and other material designed to interact with DATA to provide solutions to problems. In this context, an object PROGRAM is generally the machine language result of the operation of a COBOL compiler on a SOURCE PROGRAM. Where there is no danger of ambiguity, the word PROGRAM alone may be used in place of the phrase *object PROGRAM*.

Object time   The time at which an object PROGRAM is executed. The term is synonymous with *execution time*.

Obsolete element$_{85}$ A COBOL-language element in Standard COBOL that is to be deleted from the next revision of Standard COBOL.

OPEN MODE   The state of a FILE after execution of an OPEN statement for that FILE and before the execution of a CLOSE statement without the REEL or UNIT phrase for that FILE. The particular OPEN MODE is specified in the OPEN statement as either INPUT, OUTPUT, I-O, or EXTEND.

Operand   Any lowercase word (or words) that appears in a statement or entry format, an implied reference to the data indicated by the operand.

Operational SIGN   An algebraic SIGN, associated with a NUMERIC DATA item or a NUMERIC literal, to indicate whether its VALUE is POSITIVE or NEGATIVE.

OPTIONAL FILE$_{85}$ A FILE that is declared as being not necessarily present each time the object PROGRAM is executed. The object PROGRAM causes an interrogation for the presence or absence of the FILE.

Optional word   A reserved word that is included in a specific format only to improve the readability of the language and whose presence is optional to the user when the format in which the word appears is used in a SOURCE PROGRAM.

OUTPUT FILE   A file that is OPEN in either OUTPUT MODE or EXTEND MODE.

OUTPUT MODE   The state of a FILE after execution of an OPEN statement, with the OUTPUT or EXTEND phrase specified for that FILE and before the execution of a CLOSE statement without the REEL or UNIT phrase for that FILE.

OUTPUT PROCEDURE   A set of statements to which control is given during execution of a SORT statement after the SORT function is completed or during execution of a MERGE statement after the MERGE function reaches a point at which it can select the NEXT RECORD in merged order when requested.

PADDING CHARACTER$_{85}$ An ALPHANUMERIC CHARACTER used to fill the unused CHARACTER positions in a physical RECORD.

PAGE   A vertical division of a REPORT representing a physical separation of REPORT DATA, the separation being based on internal reporting requirements and/or external characteristics of the reporting medium.

PAGE body   The part of the logical PAGE in which LINES can be written and/or spaced.

PAGE FOOTING   A REPORT GROUP that is presented at the END of a REPORT PAGE as determined by the REPORT writer CONTROL system.

PAGE HEADING   A REPORT GROUP that is presented at the beginning of a REPORT PAGE and determined by the REPORT writer CONTROL system.

Paragraph   In the PROCEDURE DIVISION, a paragraph-name followed by a separator period and by zero, one, or more sentences. In the IDENTIFICATION and ENVIRONMENT divisions, a paragraph header followed by zero, one, or more entries.

Paragraph header   A reserved word, followed by the separator period, that indicates the beginning of a paragraph in the IDENTIFICATION and ENVIRONMENT divisions. The permissible paragraph headers in the IDENTIFICATION DIVISION are

```
PROGRAM-ID.
AUTHOR.
INSTALLATION.
DATE-WRITTEN.
DATE-COMPILED.
SECURITY.
```

The permissible paragraph headers in the ENVIRONMENT DIVISION are

> SOURCE-COMPUTER.
> OBJECT-COMPUTER.
> SPECIAL-NAMES.
> FILE-CONTROL.
> I-O-CONTROL.

Paragraph-name   A user-defined word that identifies and begins a paragraph in the PROCEDURE DIVISION.

Phrase   A phrase is an ordered set of one or more consecutive COBOL character-strings that form a portion of a COBOL procedural statement or clause.

Physical PAGE$_{85}$ A device-dependent concept defined by the implementor.

Physical RECORD   See BLOCK.

Prime RECORD KEY   A KEY whose contents uniquely identify a RECORD in an INDEXED FILE.

Printable GROUP   A REPORT GROUP that contains at least one print LINE.

Printable item.   A DATA item, the extent and contents of which are specified by an elementary REPORT entry. This elementary REPORT entry contains a COLUMN NUMBER clause, a PICTURE clause, and a SOURCE, SUM, or VALUE clause.

Procedure   A paragraph or group of logically successive paragraphs, or a SECTION or group of logically successive sections, in the PROCEDURE DIVISION.

Procedure branching statement$_{85}$ A statement that causes the explicit transfer of control to a statement other than the NEXT executable statement in the sequence in which the statements are written in the source program. The procedure branching statements are ALTER, CALL, EXIT, EXIT PROGRAM, GO TO, MERGE (with the OUTPUT PROCEDURE phrase), PERFORM, and SORT (with the INPUT PROCEDURE or OUTPUT PROCEDURE phrase).

Procedure-name   A user-defined word that is used to name a paragraph or SECTION in the PROCEDURE DIVISION. It consists of a paragraph-name (which may be qualified) or a section-name.

PROGRAM IDENTIFICATION entry$_{85}$ An entry in the PROGRAM-ID paragraph of the IDENTIFICATION DIVISION that contains clauses that specify the program-name and assign selected PROGRAM attributes to the PROGRAM.

Program-name   In the IDENTIFICATION DIVISION and the END PROGRAM header, a user-defined word that identifies a COBOL SOURCE PROGRAM.

Pseudo-text   A sequence of TEXT WORDS, comment lines, or the separator spaces in a source program or COBOL library bounded by, but not including, pseudo-text delimiters.

Pseudo-text DELIMITER   Two contiguous equal sign (=) characters used to delimit pseudo-text.

Punctuation CHARACTER   A CHARACTER that belongs to the following set:

CHARACTER	Meaning
,	COMMA
;	Semicolon
:	Colon
.	Period (full stop)
"	Quotation mark
(	LEFT parenthesis
)	RIGHT parenthesis
	SPACE
=	EQUAL SIGN

Qualified data-name   An identifier that is composed of a data-name followed by one or more sets of either of the connectives OF and IN followed by a data-name qualifier.

Qualifier   (1) A data-name or a name associated with a level indicator that is used in a reference either together with another DATA name that is a name of an item that is subordinate to the qualifier or together with a condition-name. (2) A section-name that is used in a reference together with a paragraph-name specified in that SEC-TION. (3) A library-name that is used in a reference together with a text-name associated with that library.

QUEUE   A logical collection of messages awaiting transmission or processing.

QUEUE name   A symbolic name that indicates to the message control system the logical path by which a MESSAGE or a portion of a completed MESSAGE may be accessible in a QUEUE.

RANDOM ACCESS   An ACCESS MODE in which the program-specified value of a KEY data item identifies the logical RECORD that is obtained from, deleted from, or placed into a RELATIVE or INDEXED FILE.

RECORD   The most inclusive DATA item. The level-number for a RECORD is 01. A RECORD may be either an elementary item or a group item. The term is synonymous with *logical RECORD*.

RECORD AREA   A storage AREA allocated for the purpose of processing the RECORD described in a RECORD description entry in the FILE SECTION of the DATA DIVISION. In the FILE SECTION, the current number of character positions in the RECORD area is determined by the explicit or implicit RECORD clause.

RECORD description   See *RECORD description entry*.

RECORD description entry   The total set of DATA description entries associated with a particular RECORD. The term is synonymous with *RECORD description*.

RECORD KEY   A KEY whose contents identify a RECORD in an INDEXED FILE. In an INDEXED FILE, a RECORD KEY is either the prime RECORD KEY or an ALTERNATE RECORD KEY.

Record-name   A user-defined word that names a RECORD described in a RECORD description entry in the DATA DIVISION of a COBOL program.

RECORD NUMBER$_{85}$ The ordinal NUMBER of a RECORD in the FILE whose ORGANIZATION IS SEQUENTIAL.

REEL₈₅   A discrete portion of a storage medium, the dimensions of which are determined by each implementor, that contains part of a FILE, all of a FILE, or any number of files. The term is synonymous with *UNIT* and *volume*.

Reference format   A format that provides a standard method for describing a COBOL SOURCE PROGRAM.

Reference modifier₈₅   The leftmost-character-position and LENGTH used to establish and reference a DATA item.

Relation   See *relational operator*.

Relational operator   A reserved word, a relation CHARACTER, a group of consecutive reserved words, or a group of consecutive reserved words and relation CHARACTERS used in the construction of a relation condition. The permissible operators and their meanings are as follows:

Relational Operator	Meaning
IS [NOT] GREATER THAN IS [NOT] >	GREATER THAN OR NOT GREATER THAN
IS [NOT] LESS THAN IS [NOT] <	LESS THAN OR NOT LESS THAN
IS [NOT] EQUAL TO IS [NOT] =	EQUAL TO OR NOT EQUAL TO
IS GREATER THAN OR EQUAL TO IS <=	GREATER THAN OR EQUAL TO
IS LESS THAN OR EQUAL TO IS <=	LESS THAN OR EQUAL TO

Relation CHARACTER   A character that belongs to the following set:

CHARACTER	Meaning
>	GREATER THAN
<	LESS THAN
=	EQUAL TO

Relation condition   The proposition, for which a truth VALUE can be determined, that the VALUE of an arithmetic expression, DATA item, nonnumeric literal, or index-name has a specific relationship to the VALUE of another arithmetic expression, DATA item, nonnumeric literal, or index-name.

RELATIVE FILE   A FILE with RELATIVE ORGANIZATION.

RELATIVE KEY   A KEY whose contents identify a logical RECORD in a RELATIVE FILE.

RELATIVE ORGANIZATION   The permanent logical FILE structure in which each RECORD is uniquely identified by an integer value greater than zero that specifies the record's logical ordinal POSITION in the FILE.

RELATIVE RECORD NUMBER₈₅   The ordinal NUMBER of a RECORD in a FILE whose ORGANIZATION IS RELATIVE. This NUMBER is treated as a NUMERIC literal that is an integer.

REPORT clause   A clause in the REPORT SECTION of the DATA DIVISION that appears in a REPORT description entry or a REPORT GROUP description entry.

REPORT description entry   An entry in the REPORT SECTION of the DATA DIVISION that is composed of the level indicator RD, followed by the report-name, followed by a set of REPORT clauses as required.

REPORT FILE   An OUTPUT FILE whose FILE description entry contains a REPORT clause. The contents of a REPORT FILE consist of RECORDS that are written under control of the REPORT writer CONTROL system.

REPORT FOOTING   A REPORT GROUP that is presented only at the END of a REPORT.

REPORT GROUP   In the REPORT SECTION of the DATA DIVISION, an 01-level entry and its subordinate entries.

REPORT GROUP description entry   An entry in the REPORT SECTION of the DATA DIVISION that is composed of the level-number 01, an optional data-name, a TYPE clause, and an optional set of REPORT clauses.

REPORT HEADING.   A REPORT GROUP that is presented only at the beginning of a REPORT.

REPORT LINE   A division of a PAGE representing one row of horizontal character positions. Each character position of a REPORT LINE is aligned vertically beneath the corresponding character position of the REPORT LINE above it. REPORT LINES are numbered sequentially from 1, starting at the TOP of the PAGE.

Report-name   A user-defined word that names a REPORT described in a REPORT description entry in the REPORT SECTION of the DATA DIVISION.

REPORT SECTION   The SECTION of the DATA DIVISION that contains zero, one, or more REPORT description entries and their associated REPORT GROUP description entries.

REPORT writer CONTROL system   An object time CONTROL system, provided by the implementor, that accomplishes the construction of reports.

REPORT writer logical RECORD   A RECORD that consists of the REPORT writer print LINE and associated control information necessary for its selection and vertical positioning.

Reserved word   A COBOL word specified in the list of words that may be used in a COBOL SOURCE PROGRAM but must not appear in the PROGRAM as user-defined words or system-names.

Resource₈₅   A facility or service, controlled by the operating system, that can be used by an executing PROGRAM.

Resultant identifier₈₅   A user-defined DATA item that is to contain the result of an arithmetic operation.

Routine-name   A user-defined word that identifies a procedure written in a language other than COBOL.

Run unit   One or more object programs that interact with one another and function at object time as an entity to provide problem solutions.

SECTION   A set of zero, one, or more paragraphs or entries, called a SECTION body, the first of which is preceded by a SECTION header. Each SECTION consists of the SECTION header and the related SECTION body.

SECTION header   A combination of words followed by a separator period that indicates the beginning of a SECTION in the ENVIRONMENT, DATA, and PROCEDURE divisions. In the ENVIRONMENT and DATA divisions, a SECTION header is composed of reserved words followed by a separator period. The permissible SECTION headers in the ENVIRONMENT DIVISION are

> CONFIGURATION SECTION.
> INPUT-OUTPUT SECTION.

The permissible SECTION headers in the DATA DIVISION are

> FILE SECTION.
> WORKING-STORAGE SECTION.
> LINKAGE SECTION.
> COMMUNICATION SECTION.
> REPORT SECTION.

In the PROCEDURE DIVISION, a SECTION header is composed of a section-name, followed by the reserved word SECTION, followed by a segment-number (optional), followed by a separator period.

Section-name   A user-defined word that names a SECTION in the PROCEDURE DIVISION.

Segment-number   A user-defined word that classifies each SECTION in the PROCEDURE DIVISION for purposes of segmentation. Segment-numbers may contain only the characters 0 through 9. A segment-number may be expressed as a one- or two-digit number.

Sentence   A sequence of one or more statements, the last of which is terminated by a separator period.

Separately compiled PROGRAM₈₅   A PROGRAM that together with its contained programs is compiled separately from all other programs.

Separator   A CHARACTER or two contiguous CHARACTERS used to delimit character strings.

SEQUENTIAL ACCESS   An ACCESS MODE in which logical RECORDS are obtained from or placed into a FILE in a consecutive predecessor-to-successor logical RECORD SEQUENCE determined by the order of RECORDS in the FILE.

SEQUENTIAL FILE   A FILE with SEQUENTIAL ORGANIZATION.

SEQUENTIAL ORGANIZATION   The permanent logical FILE structure in which a RECORD is identified by a predecessor-successor relationship established when the RECORD is placed into the FILE.

SIGN condition   The proposition, for which a truth VALUE can be determined, that the algebraic VALUE of a DATA item or an arithmetic expression is either LESS THAN, GREATER THAN, OR EQUAL TO ZERO.

Simple condition   Any single condition chosen from the set

> Relation condition
>
> CLASS condition
>
> Condition-name condition
>
> Switch-status condition
>
> SIGN condition
>
> (Simple-condition)

SORT FILE   A collection of RECORDS to be sorted by a SORT statement. The SORT FILE is created and can be used by the SORT function only.

SORT-MERGE FILE description entry   An entry in the FILE SECTION of the DATA DIVISION that is composed of the level indicator SD, followed by a file-name and then a set of FILE clauses as required.

SOURCE   The symbolic identification of the originator of a transmission to a QUEUE.

SOURCE-COMPUTER   An ENVIRONMENT DIVISION paragraph in which the computer ENVIRONMENT within which the SOURCE PROGRAM is compiled is described.

SOURCE computer entry$_{85}$ An entry in the SOURCE-COMPUTER paragraph of the ENVIRONMENT DIVISION that contains clauses that describe the computer ENVIRONMENT in which the SOURCE PROGRAM is to be compiled.

SOURCE item   An identifier designated by a SOURCE clause that provides the VALUE of a printable item.

SOURCE PROGRAM   A syntactically correct set of COBOL statements. A COBOL SOURCE PROGRAM commences with the IDENTIFICATION DIVISION, a COPY statement, or a REPLACE statement. A COBOL source program is terminated by the END PROGRAM header, if specified, or by the absence of additional SOURCE PROGRAM lines.

Special CHARACTER   A CHARACTER that belongs to the following set:

CHARACTER	Meaning
+	PLUS SIGN
–	MINUS SIGN
*	Asterisk
/	Slant (solidus)
=	EQUAL to symbol
$	CURRENCY SIGN
,	Comma (decimal point)
;	Semicolon

CHARACTER	Meaning
.	Period (DECIMAL POINT, full stop)
"	Quotation mark
(	LEFT parenthesis
)	RIGHT parenthesis
>	GREATER THAN symbol
<	LESS THAN symbol
:	Colon

Special-character word   A reserved word that is an arithmetic operator or a relation CHARACTER.

SPECIAL NAMES   An ENVIRONMENT DIVISION paragraph in which implementor-names are related to user-specified mnemonic-names.

SPECIAL-NAMES entry$_{85}$ An entry in the SPECIAL-NAMES paragraph of the ENVIRONMENT DIVISION that provides a means for specifying the CURRENCY SIGN, choosing the DECIMAL-POINT, specifying SYMBOLIC CHARACTERS, relating implementor-names to user-specified mnemonic-names, relating alphabet-names to CHARACTER sets or COLLATING SEQUENCES, and relating class-names to sets of CHARACTERS.

Special registers   Compiler-generated storage areas whose primary use is to store information produced in conjunction with the use of specific COBOL features.

Standard DATA format   The concept used in describing DATA in a COBOL DATA DIVISION under which the characteristics or properties of the DATA are expressed in a form oriented to the appearance of the DATA on a printed PAGE of infinite length and breadth, rather than a form oriented to the manner in which the DATA is stored internally in the computer or on a particular medium.

Statement   A syntactically valid combination of words, literals, and separators, beginning with a verb, written in a COBOL SOURCE PROGRAM.

Sub-queue   A logical hierarchical division of a QUEUE.

Subject of entry   An operand or reserved word that appears immediately following the level indicator or the level-number in a DATA DIVISION entry.

Subprogram   A PROGRAM that is the object of a CALL statement combined at object time with the calling PROGRAM to produce a run unit. The term is synonymous with *called PROGRAM*.

Subscript   An occurrence NUMBER, represented by either an integer, a data-name optionally followed by an integer with the operator $+$ or $-$, or an index-name optionally followed by an integer with the operator $+$ or $-$, that identifies a particular element in a TABLE.

Subscripted data-name   An identifier that is composed of a data-name followed by one or more subscripts enclosed in parentheses.

SUM counter   A signed NUMERIC DATA item established by a SUM clause in the REPORT SECTION of the DATA DIVISION. The SUM counter is used by the REPORT writer CONTROL system to contain the result of designated summing operations that take place during production of a REPORT.

Switch-status condition   The proposition, for which a truth VALUE can be determined, that an implementor-defined switch, capable of being set to ON or OFF status, has been set to a specific STATUS.

Symbolic-character$_{85}$ A user-defined word that specifies a user-defined figurative constant.

System-name   A COBOL word that is used to communicate with the operating ENVIRONMENT.

TABLE   A set of logically consecutive items of DATA that are defined in the DATA DIVISION of a COBOL program by means of the OCCURS clause.

TABLE element   A DATA item that belongs to the set of repeated items comprising a TABLE.

TERMINAL   The originator of a transmission to a QUEUE or the receiver of a transmission from a QUEUE.

Text-name   A user-defined word that identifies library TEXT.

Text-word   Any CHARACTER or a sequence of contiguous CHARACTERS between margin A and margin R in a COBOL library, SOURCE PROGRAM, or in pseudo-text that is (1) a separator, except for space; a pseudo-text DELIMITER; and the opening and closing delimiters for nonnumeric literals. The RIGHT parenthesis and LEFT parenthesis CHARACTERS, regardless of context in the library, SOURCE PROGRAM, or pseudo-text, are always considered TEXT WORDS. (2) A literal including, in the case of nonnumeric literals, the opening quotation mark and the closing quotation mark that bound the literal. (3) Any other sequence of contiguous COBOL CHARACTERS except comment lines and the word COPY, bounded by separators, that is neither a separator nor a literal.

TOP margin$_{85}$ An empty AREA that precedes the PAGE body.

Truth VALUE   The representation of the result of the evaluation of a condition in terms of one of two VALUES: TRUE OR FALSE.

Unary operator   A PLUS ($+$) or a MINUS ($-$) sign, that precedes a variable or a LEFT parenthesis in an arithmetic expression and has the effect of multiplying the expression by $+1$ or -1, respectively.

UNIT   A discrete portion of a storage medium, the dimensions of which are determined by each implementor, that contains part of a FILE, all of a FILE, or any number of files. The term is synonymous with *REEL* and *volume*.

Unsuccessful execution$_{85}$ The attempted execution of a statement that does not result in the execution of all the operations specified by that statement. The unsuccessful execution of a statement does not affect any DATA referenced by that statement but may affect STATUS indicators.

User-defined word   A COBOL word that must be supplied by the user to satisfy the format of a clause or statement.

Variable   A DATA item whose VALUE may be changed by execution of the object PROGRAM. A variable used in an arithmetic-expression must be a NUMERIC elementary item.

Variable-LENGTH RECORD$_{85}$ A RECORD associated with a FILE whose FILE description or sort-merge description entry permits RECORDS to contain a VARYING number of character positions.

Variable-occurrence DATA item₈₅   A TABLE element that is repeated a variable number of TIMES. Such an item must contain an OCCURS DEPENDING ON clause in its DATA description entry or be subordinate to such an item.

Verb   A word that expresses an action to be taken by a COBOL compiler or object PROGRAM.

Volume₈₅   A discrete portion of a storage medium, the dimensions of which are determined by each implementor, that contains part of a FILE, all of a FILE, or any number of files. The term is synonymous with *REEL* and *UNIT*.

Word   A character-string of not more than 30 characters that forms a user-defined word, a system-name, or a reserved word.

WORKING-STORAGE SECTION   The SECTION of the DATA DIVISION that describes working storage DATA items, composed of noncontiguous items, working storage RECORDS, or both.

D

Vendor List

ADPAC Computing Languages Corporation
340 Brannan Street, Suite 501
San Francisco, CA 94119
(415) 974-6699

The Analyst Workbench
302/27 Waruda Street
Kirribilli, NSW 2061
Australia
#-61-2-922-6313

Arthur Andersen & Company
33 West Monroe Street
Chicago, IL 60603
(312) 580-0033
(or your local Arthur Andersen office)

D. Appleton Company, Inc.
1334 Park View Avenue, Suite 220
Manhattan Beach, CA 90266
(213) 546-7575

Ashisuto
3-1-1 Toranomon Minato-Ku
Tokyo 105 Japan
#-81-3-437-0654

ASYST Technologies, Inc.
50 Staniford Street, Suite 800
Boston, MA 02114
(617) 523-2636

M. Bryce & Associates
777 Alderman Road
Palm Harbor, FL 33563
(813) 786-4567

Cadre Technologies, Inc.
222 Richmond Street
Providence, RI 02903
(401) 351-5950

The CADWARE Group, Ltd.
869 Whalley Avenue
New Haven, CT 06515
(203) 397-2908

Cap Gemini Software Products, Inc.
2350 Valley View Lane, Suite 420
Dallas, TX 75234
(214) 247-5454

CGI Systems Inc.
One Blue Hill Plaza
Pearl Hill, NY 10965
(914) 735-5030

Chen & Associates
4884 Constitution Avenue, Suite 1E
Baton Rouge, LA 70808
(504) 928-5765

Composer Technology Corporation
3062 Miller Street
Santa Clara, CA 95051

Computer Command and Control Company
2401 Walnut Street, Suite 402
Philadelphia, PA 19103
(215) 854-0555

Cortex Corporation
138 Technology Drive
Waltham, MA 02154
(617) 894-7000

Cullinet Software, Inc.
400 Blue Hill Drive
Westwood, MA 02090
(617) 329-7700

Data Design Inc. (DDI)
2020 Hogback Road
Ann Arbor, MI 48104

Dialogic Systems Corporation
175 East Tasman Drive
San Jose, CA 95134
(408) 745-1300

Digital Equipment Corporation
146 Main Street
Maynard, MA 01754
(617) 897-5111

Group Operations
1110 Vermont Avenue, N.W.
Washington, DC 20005

GUIDE International
111 East Wacker Drive
Chicago, IL 60601

Hewlett-Packard Company
8020 Foothills
Roseville, CA 95678
(800) FOR-HPPC

Holland Systems Corporation
3131 South State Street
Ann Arbor, MI 48104

IBM
your local marketing representative or local
branch office

Index Technology Corporation
101 Main Street
Cambridge, MA 02142
(617) 491-2100

InfoModel, Inc.
137 West 25th Street, Room 508
New York, NY 10001
(212) 877-8912

Michael Jackson Systems Limited
23 Little Portland Street
London, England W1N 5AF

KnowledgeWare, Inc.
23340 Peachtree Road, N.E., Suite 2900
Atlanta, GA 30326
(404) 231-8575

Language Technology Corporation
27 Congress Street
Salem, MA 01970

Leading Software Technologies Corporation
26250 Euclid Avenue, Suite 307
Cleveland, OH 44132
(216) 261-0187

Manager Software Products, Inc.
131 Hartwell Avenue
Lexington, MA 02173
(617) 863-5800

McDonnell Douglas Automation Company
P.O. Box 516
St. Louis, MO 63166
(800) 325-1087

Meta Software Corporation
55 Wheeler Street
Cambridge, MA 02138
(617) 576-6920

Meta Systems
315 East Eisenhower Parkway, Suite 200
Ann Arbor, MI 48108
(313) 663-6027

Nastec Corporation
24861 Northwestern Highway
Southfield, MI 48075
(313) 353-3300

Netron, Inc.
99 St. Regis Crescent North
Downsview, Ontario M3J 1Y9
(416) 636-8333

Ken Orr & Associates, Inc.
1725 Gage Boulevard
Topeka, KS 66604
(800) 255-2459

Peat Marwick
The Catalyst Group
303 East Wacker Drive
Chicago, IL 60601

POLYTRON Corporation
1815 N.W. 169th Place, Suite 2110
Beaverton, OR 97006
(503) 645-1150

Promod, Inc.
22981 Alcalde Drive
Laguna Hills, CA 92653
(714) 855-3046

Sage Software, Inc.
3200 Monroe Street
Rockville, MD 20852
(301) 230-3200

Softlab Systems, Inc.
188 The Embarcadero, 7th Floor
San Francisco, CA 94105
(415) 957-9175

SYSCORP International
12710 Research Boulevard, Suite 301
Austin, TX 78759
(512) 331-0077

Technology Information Products Corporation
12 New England Executive Park
Burlington, MA 01803
(617) 273-5818

Tektronix, Inc.
P.O. Box 14752
Portland, OR 97214
(800) 342-5548

Texas Instruments Inc.
P.O. Box 869305
Plano, TX 75086
(214) 575-4404

Transform Logic Corporation
8502 East Via de Ventura
Scottsdale, AZ 85258
(602) 948-2600

TSI International
50 Washington Street
Norwalk, CT 06854

The Waterfield Company
270 Pacific Highway
Crows Nest, NSW 2065
Australia
#-61-2-436-3244

Yourdon, Inc.
1501 Broadway Avenue
New York, NY 10036
(212) 391-2828

—————— *E* ——————

Source Driven Documentation for Master Update Program

¹The structure chart was only printed for the program invocation and the mainline. A complete set of documentation is available from either ADPAC or The Analyst Workbench. (See Vendor List.)

T A B L E   O F   C O N T E N T S

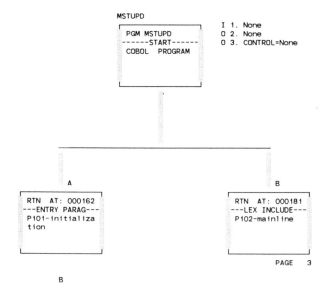

MSTUPD

```
┌─────────────────────┐        I  1. None
│  PGM MSTUPD         │        O  2. None
│ ------START------   │        O  3. CONTROL=None
│  COBOL    PROGRAM   │
│                     │
└─────────────────────┘
```

```
A                                              B
┌─────────────────────┐          ┌─────────────────────┐
│ RTN  AT: 000162     │          │ RTN  AT: 000181     │
│ ---ENTRY PARAG---   │          │ ---LEX INCLUDE---   │
│ P101-initializa     │          │ P102-mainline       │
│ tion                │          │                     │
│                     │          │                     │
└─────────────────────┘          └─────────────────────┘
```

PAGE   3

```
A
--------------------
I  1. None
O  2. None
O  3. CONTROL=None
```

```
B
--------------------
I  1. Master-record-key-field
I  2. Transaction-record-key-field
O  3. None
O  4. CONTROL=None
```

```
***********************************************************
*               MSTUPD    COBOL   PROGRAM                 *
***********************************************************
```

                                Generalized shell to match a
                                RECORD KEY in the
                                transaction-record to the RECORD
                                KEY in the master record.

                                IF master-record-key low then
                                    read new mater record;
                                IF master-record-key equal then
                                    update master-record or
                                    delete master-record if delete
                                    read new master-record
                                    read new
                                    transaction-record;
                                IF master-record-key high then
                                    write new master-record
                                    from transaction record
                                    read new
                                    transaction-record.

A   P101-initialization
                perform initialization

B   P102-mainline
                compares master-record-key-filed (M) to transaction-
                record-key-field (T) to control processing.
                        IF M < T then READ M;
                        IF M = T then update M
                                    READ T;
                        IF M > T then WRITE M from T
                                    READ T.

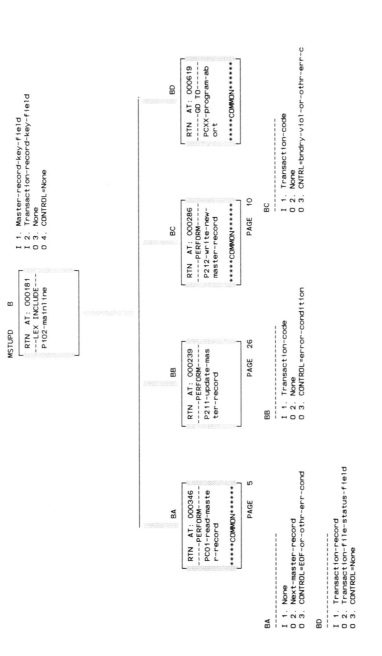

MSTUPD   B

RTN AT: 000181
----LEX INCLUDE----
P102-mainline

I 1. Master-record-key-field
I 2. Transaction-record-key-field
O 3. None
O 4. CONTROL=None

BA

RTN AT: 000346
----PERFORM----
PC01-read-maste
r-record
*****COMMON******

PAGE   5

BB

RTN AT: 000239
----PERFORM----
P211-update-mas
ter-record

PAGE 26

BC

RTN AT: 000286
----PERFORM----
P212-write-new-
master-record
*****COMMON******

PAGE 10

BD

RTN AT: 000619
----GO TO----
PCXX-program-ab
ort
*****COMMON******

BA

I 1. None
O 2. Next-master-record
O 3. CONTROL=EOF-or-othr-err-cond

BD

I 1. Transaction-record
O 2. Transaction-file-status-field
O 3. CONTROL=None

BB

I 1. Transaction-code
O 2. None
O 3. CONTROL=error-condition

BC

I 1. Transaction-code
O 2. None
O 3. CNTRL=bndry-viol-or-othr-err-c

387

```
****************************************************************
*   B                        P102-mainline                   *
****************************************************************
```

compares master-record-key-filed (M) to transaction-
record-key-field (T) to control processing.
```
        IF M < T then READ M;
        IF M = T then update M
                     READ T;
        IF M > T then WRITE M from T
                     READ T.
```

BA   PC01-read-master-record
                  read next master-record
                  check for AT END and FILE STATUS error conditions
                  add one to master-record-read
                  move master-record-actual-key to master-record-key-field

BB   P211-update-master-record
                  validate that transaction code is update or delete
                  if update then validate transaction-record
                                  read next master-record
                                  read next transaction-record
                  if delete then delete current master-record
                                  read next master-record
                                  read next transaction-record

BC   P212-write-new-master-record
                  validate that transaction code is add
                  if add then   validate transaction-record
                                  write master-record from transaction-record
                                  read next transaction-record

BD   PCXX-program-abort
                  Paragraph only invoked if mainline <=> comparison fails.
                  Each installation should have standard program abort routine
                  which is copied into the program.

CROSS REFERENCE OF PROGRAM TITLE

TITLE	IDENT	STRUCTURE CHART PAGE NUMBER				
COBOL PROGRAM	MSTUPD	1				
PCXX-program-abort		3	12	23		
PC01-read-master-record		3	5	7	25	
PC01a-master-file-eof		5	12			
PC01b-master-filestatus-inv		5	6	14	16	17 21
PC02-rewrite-master-record		7	17	25		
PC03-delete-master-record		7	21	25		
PC05-read-transaction-record		7	10	19	25	
PC05a-transaction-file-eof		19	23			
PC05b-trans-filestatus-invalid		19				
PC07-validate-transaction-rec		7	10	25		
PRUN-runaway-abort		14	23	26		
P101-initialization		1				
P102-mainline		3	1			
P103-termination		23				
P211-update-master-record		3	7	24	25	
P212-write-new-master-record		3	10	12		
P321-invalid-update-transcode		7	25			
P332-invalid-add-transaction		10				

CROSS REFERENCE OF I/O PARM NAME

I/O PARM NAME	STRUCTURE CHART PAGE NUMBER
CNTRL=bndry-viol-or-othr-err-c	3 10 12 19
CONTROL=error-condition	3 7
CONTROL=error-conditions	7 17 25
CONTROL=EOF-and-othr-err-cond	7 10 19 25
CONTROL=EOF-or-othr-err-cond	3 5 5 5 7 23
CONTROL=None	3 3 5 5 5 5 7 7 7 23 7 23 10 25 10 25 12 25 12 26 14 1 16 1 17 1 19
Incorrect-master-file-status	5 16 19 21
Installation-error-report	5 17 16 17
Invalid-add-transaction-code	10 25
Invalid-transaction-file-statu	19 21
Invalid-update-transaction-cod	7 25
Master-record-key-field	3 1
Master-records-read	5 12
New-master-record	7 17 25
Next-master-record	3 5 5 7 7 19
Next-transaction-record	7 10 19
None	12 17 19 1 3 3 3 19 5 21 7 23 7 23 7 23 7 25 10 25 10 25 12 1
Total-transaction-records	1 1 19 23
Transaction-code	3 3 7 10 12 12 23 14
Transaction-file-status-field	3 7 10 12 14 23 17 25 26
Transaction-record	3 7 7 10 12 12 25 25 26
Transaction-record-key-field	3 1

```
                                                    PFM: PERFORM   PFMT: TIMES   PFMJ: UNTIL
                                                    COM: COMMON       LEX: FALLTHRU
                                                                                  PFMV: VARYING

RPT HOW  NO.  --LINE NO--   COM LVL
LINE INVK USE INVOKE LOCATE USE NO.  MODULE IDENT AND TITLE
---- ---- --- ------ ------ -------  --------------------------------------------------

  1  @PM                      00     MSTUPD   COBOL   PROGRAM

                                              Generalized shell to match a
                                              RECORD KEY in the
                                              transaction-record to the RECORD
                                              KEY in the master record.

                                              IF master-record-key low then
                                                 read new mater record;
                                              IF master-record-key equal then
                                                 update master-record or
                                                 delete master-record if delete
                                                 read new master-record
                                                 read new
                                                 transaction-record;
                                              IF master-record-key high then
                                                 write new master-record
                                                 from transaction record
                                                 read new
                                                 transaction-record.

 22  PFM        000162        01     P101-initialization
                                              perform initialization

                                                 initialization statements
                                              CONTINUE

 28  LEX        000181        01     P102-mainline
                                              compares master-record-key-filed (M) to transaction-
                                              record-key-field (T) to control processing.
                                                 IF M < T then READ M;
                                                 IF M = T then update M
                                                             READ T;
                                                 IF M > T then WRITE M from T
                                                             READ T.

 39  PFM    000200 000346  COM 02    PC01-read-master-record
                                              read next master-record
                                              check for AT END and FILE STATUS error conditions
                                              add one to master-record-read
                                              move master-record-actual-key to master-record-key-field

 46  GOTO   000361 000383      03    PC01a-master-file-eof
                                              check for legitimate master-file EOF
                                              writes any remaining transaction-file-records with add
                                              transaction code to master-file
```

PROFILE   MSTUPD   COBOL   PROGRAM

PFM: PERFORM   PFMT: TIMES   PFMJ: UNTIL   PFMV: VARYING
COM: COMMON   LEX: FALLTHRU

RPT HOW NO.	--LINE NO---	COM LVL	
LINE INVK USE	INVOKE LOCATE	USE NO.	MODULE IDENT AND TITLE

```
50
51                                          transaction-eof is a "dummy": loop is terminated by the
52                                          AT END clause of the transaction-file read.
53

54 GOTO   000396 000619   COM 04   PCXX-program-abort
55                                          Paragraph only invoked if mainline <=> comparison fails.
56                                          Each installation should have standard program abort routine
57                                          which is copied into the program.
58
59

60 PFMJ   000398 000286   COM 04   P212-write-new-master-record
61                                          validate that transaction code is add
62                                          if add then    validate transaction-record
63                                                         write master-record from transaction-record
64                                                         read next transaction-record
65

66 LEX           000403   COM 03   PC01b-master-filestatus-inv

67 GOTO   000421 000637   COM 04   PRUN-runaway-abort
68                                          Paragraph only invoked if runaway happens.
69                                          Each installation should have standard program abort routine
70                                          which is copied into the program.
71
72

73 PFM    000367 000405   COM 03   PC01b-master-filestatus-inv   /SEE LINE 66
74                                          ****************************************************************
75                                          Paragraph only invoked if master file status is invalid
76                                          each installation should have standard error routines
77                                          which are copied into programs
78
79

80 PFM    000205 000239   02       P211-update-master-record
81                                          validate that transaction code is update or delete
82                                          if update then validate transaction-record
83                                                         read next master-record
84                                                         read next transaction-record
85                                          if delete then delete current master-record
86                                                         read next master-record
87                                                         read next transaction-record
88
89                                          transaction-code is initialized to null. After
90                                          initialization, M = T and P212 is invoked. The
91                                          null "primes the pump".
92

93 PFM    000256 000600   COM 03   PC07-validate-transaction-rec
94                                          Each installation should have standard validation routine
95                                          which is copied into the program.
96
```

PFM: PERFORM   PFMT: TIMES   PFMU: UNTIL   PFMV: VARYING
COM: COMMON   LEX: FALLTHRU

RPT LINE	HOW INVK USE	NO. USE	--LINE NO-- INVOKE LOCATE	COM LVL USE NO.	MODULE IDENT AND TITLE
97					
98	PFM		000257 000424	03	PCO2-rewrite-master-record
99					rewrite a master-record from the transaction-record
100					check for FILE STATUS error conditions
101					add one to master-records-modified
102					
103					
104	PFM		000444 000405	COM 04	PCO1b-master-filestatus-inv /SEE LINE 66
105					***
106					Paragraph only invoked if master file status is invalid
107					each installation should have standard error routines
108					which are copied into programs
109					
110					
111	PFM	3	000258 000522	COM 03	PCO5-read-transaction-record
112					***
113					read next transaction-record
114					check for EOF and FILE STATUS error conditions
115					add one to total-transaction-records
116					move transaction-record-actual-key to
117					TRANSACTION-RECORD-KEY-FIELD
118					
119					
120	GOTO		000538 000557	04	PCO5a-transaction-file-eof
121					read legitimate transaction-file-EOF
122					terminate run by going to P103-termination.
123					
124					
125	GOTO		000569 000619	COM 05	PCXX-program-abort
126					Paragraph only invoked if mainline <=> comparison fails.
127					Each installation should have standard program abort routine
128					which is copied into the program.
129					
130					
131	GOTO		000571 000219	05	P103-termination
132					perform termination
133					
134					
135					Installation standard routine which includes balancing
136					control fields
137					
138	LEX		000571	05	P211-update-master-record
139					transaction-code is initialized to null. After
140					initialization, M = T and P212 is invoked. The
141					null "primes the pump".
142	PFM		000256 000600	COM 06	PCO7-validate-transaction-rec

393

```
                                    PFM: PERFORM   PFMT: TIMES    PFMJ: UNTIL
                                    COM: COMMON    LEX: FALLTHRU  PFMV: VARYING
```

RPT LINE	HOW INVK	NO. USE	INVOKE	LOCATE	COM USE	LVL NO.	MODULE IDENT AND TITLE
143	PFM						Each installation should have standard validation routine
144							which is copied into the program.
145							
146	PFM		000257	000424	COM	06	PCO2-rewrite-master-record
147							rewrite a master-record from the transaction-record
148							check for FILE STATUS error conditions
149							add one to master-records-modified
150							
151	PFM	3	000258	000522	COM	06	PCO5-read-transaction-record /SEE LINE 111
152							**
153							read next transaction-record
154							check for EOF and FILE STATUS error conditions
155							add one to total-transaction-records
156							move transaction-record-actual-key to
157							TRANSACTION-RECORD-KEY-FIELD
158							
159	PFM		000261	000456	COM	06	PCO3-delete-master-record
160							delete current master-record
161							check for FILE STATUS error conditions
162							add one to master-records-deleted
163							
164	PFM	2	000262	000346	COM	06	PCO1-read-master-record /SEE LINE 39
165							read next master-record
166							check for AT END and FILE STATUS error conditions
167							add one to master-record-read
168							move master-record-actual-key to master-record-key-field
169							
170	PFM		000274	000312	COM	06	P321-invalid-update-transcode
171							installations should have standard error routine
172							which is copied into the program.
173							
174	GOTO		000280	000637	COM	06	PRUN-runaway-abort
175							Paragraph only invoked if runaway happens.
176							Each installation should have standard program abort routine
177							which is copied into the program.
178							
179	GOTO		000576	000637	COM	05	PRUN-runaway-abort
180							Paragraph only invoked if runaway happens.
181							Each installation should have standard program abort routine
182							which is copied into the program.
183							
184							
185	PFM		000544	000580		04	PCO5b-trans-filestatus-invalid
186							Paragraph only invoked if transaction file status invalid.
187							Each installation should have standard error routine
188							which is copied into the program.

PFM: PERFORM   PFMT: TIMES   PFMJ: UNTIL   PFMV: VARYING
COM: COMMON   LEX: FALLTHRU

RPT LINE	HOW INVK	NO. USE	INVOKE	LINE NO LOCATE	COM USE	LVL NO.	MODULE IDENT AND TITLE
189							
190							
191	PFM		000261	000456	COM	03	PC03-delete-master-record
192							delete current master-record
193							check for FILE STATUS error conditions
194							add one to master-records-deleted
195							
196							
197	PFM		000474	000405	COM	04	PC01b-master-filestatus-inv /SEE LINE 66
198							**
199							Paragraph only invoked if master file status is invalid
200							each installation should have standard error routines
201							which are copied into programs
202							
203							
204	PFM	2	000262	000346	COM	03	PC01-read-master-record /SEE LINE 39
205							read next master-record
206							check for AT END and FILE STATUS error conditions
207							add one to master-record-read
208							move master-record-actual-key to master-record-key-field
209							
210							
211	PFM		000274	000312	COM	03	P321-invalid-update-transcode
212							installations should have standard error routine
213							which is copied into the program.
214							
215	PFM		000210	000286	COM	02	P212-write-new-master-record
216							validate that transaction code is add
217							if add then validate transaction-record
218							write master-record from transaction-record
219							read next transaction-record
220							
221	PFM		000299	000600	COM	03	PC07-validate-transaction-rec
222							Each installation should have standard validation routine
223							which is copied into the program.
224							
225							
226	PFM		000301	000522	COM	03	PC05-read-transaction-record /SEE LINE 111
227							**
228							read next transaction-record
229							check for EOF and FILE STATUS error conditions
231							add one to total-transaction-records
232							move transaction-record-actual-key to
233							TRANSACTION-RECORD-KEY-FIELD
234							

PROFILE   MSTUPD   COBOL   PROGRAM

PFM: PERFORM   PFMT: TIMES   PFMJ: UNTIL   PFMV: VARYING
COM: COMMON   LEX: FALLTHRU

RPT	HOW	NO.	--LINE	NO--	COM	LVL.	
LINE	INVK	USE	INVOKE	LOCATE	USE	NO.	MODULE IDENT AND TITLE
----	----	---	------	------	---	---	
235	PFM		000303	000329		03	P332-invalid-add-transaction
236							installations should have standard error routine
237							which is copied into the program.
238							
239	GOTO		000213	000619	COM	02	PCXX-program-abort
240							Paragraph only invoked if mainline <=> comparison fails.
241							Each installation should have standard program abort routine
242							which is copied into the program.
243							
244							

PROFILE

CROSS REFERENCE OF PROGRAM TITLE

TITLE	IDENT	PROFILE LINE NUMER		
COBOL PROGRAM	MSTUPD	1		
PCXX-program-abort		54	125	239
PC01-read-master-record		39	164	204
PC01a-master-file-eof		46		
PC01b-master-filestatus-inv		66	73	104	197
PC02-rewrite-master-record		98	146	
PC03-delete-master-record		159	191	
PC05-read-transaction-record		111	151	226
PC05a-transaction-file-eof		120		
PC05b-trans-filestatus-invalid		185		
PC07-validate-transaction-rec		93	142	221
PRUN-runaway-abort		67	174	179
P101-initialization		22		
P102-mainline		28		
P103-termination		131		
P211-update-master-record		80	138	
P212-write-new-master-record		60	215	
P321-invalid-update-transcode		170	211	
P332-invalid-add-transaction		235		

DIAGRAM   MSTUPD   COBOL   PROGRAM

```
MSTUPD ---P101-ini
          P102-mai---PC01-rea---PC01a-ma---PCXX-pro
                                           P212-wr1
                                PC01b-ma---PRUN-run
                                PC01b-ma
                     P211-upd---PC07-va1
                                PC02-rew---PC01b-ma
                                PC05-rea---PC05a-tr---PCXX-pro
                                                      P103-ter---PC07-va1
                                                                 PC02-rew
                                                                 PC05-rea
                                                                 PC03-de1
                                                                 PC01-rea
                                                                 P321-inv
                                                                 PRUN-run
                                           PC05b-tr---PC01b-ma
                                                      P211-upd
                                                      PRUN-run
                     P212-wr1---PC03-de1---PC07-va1
                                PC01-rea   PC05-rea
                                P321-inv   P332-inv
                     PCXX-pro
```

DIAGRAM   MSTUPD   COBOL PROGRAM

```
---P101-initializat
   -P102-mainline  ---PC01-read-master---PC01a-master-fil-----PCXX-program-abo
                                                            --P212-write-new-m
                                        --PC01b-master-fil----PRUN-runaway-abo
                                        --PC01b-master-fil

                      -P211-update-mast---PC07-validate-tr
                                        --PC02-rewrite-mas---PC01b-master-fil
                                        --PC05-read-transa---PC05a-transactio---PCXX-program-abo
                                                                              --P103-termination---PC07-validate-tr
                                                                                                 --PC02-rewrite-mas
                                                                                                 --PC05-read-transa
                                                                                                 --PC03-delete-mast
                                                                                                 --PC01-read-master
                                                                                                 --P321-invalid-upd
                                                                                                 --PRUN-runaway-abo
                                                           --P211-update-mast
                                                           --PRUN-runaway-abo
                                        --PC03-delete-mast---PC01b-master-fil
                                        --PC01-read-master
                                        --P321-invalid-upd
                                                           --PC05b-trans-file

                      -P212-write-new-m---PC07-validate-tr
                                        --PC05-read-transa
                                        --P332-invalid-add

                      -PCXX-program-abo
```

399

Index

A

ACCEPT statement, 116
  syntax, 195
ACCESS clause, 26
ADD statement, 128–29
  syntax, 195–96
ADPAC Corporation, 212, 216, 226, 227, 238, 239
  PM/SS, 9
Aliases, 39, 229, 253, 256, 257, 331
  definition of, 334
  alias identification, 334–38
    Data Element Worksheets, 336–38
    data-name rationalization and, DTRANS options, 335–36
ALTER$_{74}$ statement
  definition of, 3
  recommendation against, 95
ALTERNATE RECORD KEY, 135
The Analyst Workbench (AWB), 212, 316, 318, 327
Annotated COBOL reserve word list, 349–55
ANSI, enforcement powers, 206
Architectural quadrant ratings, 245–48
  Quadrant 1, 245–46
  Quadrant 2, 246

Quadrant 3, 246–47
Quadrant 4, 247–48
Area A, 9–13
  division headers, 9–10
  level indicators, 12
  level-numbers, 13
  miscellaneous, 13
  paragraph headers, 10
  paragraph-names, 11
  section headers, 10
Area B, 13
Arithmetic
  defensive programming and, 115, 128–33
    ADD statement, 128–29
    COMPUTE statement, 131–33
    DIVIDE statement, 129–31
    MULTIPLY statement, 131
    SUBTRACT statement, 129
ASCENDING/DESCENDING optional clause, 57
Attribute clustering, 265–66
AUTHOR$_{74}$, 16, 18
Automated superprogrammers, 298
Automated tools, 46